Revisiting Ecumenical Theological Education in India

Christian Heritage Rediscovered

The Series, as the name suggests, is meant to focus on Christian Faith & Living vis-à-vis topics like Literature & Poetry, Indigenous Philosophizing, Ethical response towards Agriculture, Health & Healing, Science & Technology, Ecofeminist Theology, Sociological approach towards Human Rights, Law & Politics, Arts, History of Ideas, Ancient Civilizations, Cultural Contiguity, Religious Cosmologies & Mysticism, Footsteps of famous Theologians, World Peace & Harmony, Global Capitalism, Network Marketing, Cybertheology, Population & Demographics, Epigraphic Studies, Contextualized Education, and many others. We welcome a Mss. on any topic/s mentioned, whether they are original works, scholarly monographs, collections of conference papers, revised dissertations, or translations of historical documents. Through the Series we, the Publishers, are striving to put forward published works that may help Institutions, Academic Bodies, Researchers, Scholars and the World at large in furthering their respective knowledge and understanding on the concerned subject. We welcome your comments on our efforts and further suggestions on how we can foster the upcoming thoughtful theologically grounded books.

Christian Heritage Rediscovered - 34

Revisiting Ecumenical Theological Education in India

With a Special Reference to the Senate of Serampore College

Rev. Dr. Woba James

CWI
Christian World Imprints™

First Published in 2016 by

Christian World Imprints™
Christian Publishing & Books from India
H-12 Bali Nagar, **New Delhi-110015**
info@christianworldimprints.com
www.ChristianWorldImprints.com
Phone: +91 11 25465925

ISBN: 978-93-5148-115-7 (HB) ISBN: 978-93-5148-116-4 (PB)

Cataloging in Publication Data--DK
Courtesy: D.K. Agencies (P) Ltd. <docinfo@dkagencies.com>

James, Woba, author.
Revisiting ecumenical theological education in India : with a special reference to the Senate of Serampore College / Rev. Dr. Woba James.
pages cm. -- (Christian heritage rediscovered ; 34)
Includes bibliographical references.
ISBN 9789351481157 (HB)
ISBN 9789351481164 (PB)

1. Theology--Study and teaching--India. 2. Serampore College. Senate. I. Title. II. Series: Christian heritage rediscovered ; 34.

BV4140.I5J36 2016 DDC 230.071154 23

Printed at D. K. Fine Art Press Pvt. Ltd.

Dedicated to the

Undying Souls of the Senate of
Serampore College (SSC) Founders,

The Serampore Trio:

WILLIAM CAREY, JOSHUA MARSHMAN,
WILLIAM WARD
and to the
Successive Leaders of the SSC till date.

The Book

This book seriously researches the significance of theological education in the pluralistic context of Asia and particularly India. It vividly recalls the historical development of theological education under different denominations and different periods. In particular detail, it analyses the history of the Senate of Serampore College/University (SSC), its curriculum and its role in fostering ecumenism in India through theological education. It critically exposes the indispensable need of interdependent and networking relationship between theological education and the ministry of the church in order to make our theological education relevant, contextual, transforming and thus meaningful for the people and the context that we are to serve. In connection to that, the book strongly emphasized the need for designing the entire system and structure of our theological education along embracing and ecumenical lines so that it fittingly relates and responds to India's pluralistic context and the many challenging facets that form India's uniqueness as well as its complex nature.

The Author

Rev. Dr. Woba James is an ordained minister of the Baptist Church. He is an Associate Professor in the Department of History of Christianity at Eastern Theological College, Jorhat, Assam. He received his Bachelor of Theology, Bachelor of Divinity, Master of Theology and Doctor of Theology degrees from Serampore College/University. He is also an active person in peace initiative activities in the region. He teaches peace concerns for Master of Arts in Peace Studies at Eastern Theological College under the department of Institute of Leadership Enhancement and Ministry Augmentation (ILEMA). He also involves in Peace programs in the region with the department of Peace and Justice of the Council of Baptist Churches in North East India. Before joining in the teaching field he has worked as a missionary in North India (Delhi, U.P, and Punjab) for three years under the **Pocket Testament League of India**, and has also served as the Traveling Mission Secretary for **Evangelical Medical Fellowship of India** in the Calcutta and Orissa region for a year.

He has been involved in the teaching field for many years. He is married to Dr. Lovely Awomi who is also an Associate Professor in the Department of Christian Theology at Eastern Theological College, Jorhat, Assam, and they have three children. His other works are: *Major Issues in the History of Christianity in India: A Post Colonial Reading* (2013); He has also co-edited *Peacemaking in North East India: Social and Theological Exploration* (Yangkahao Vashum & Woba James); *Towards Advancement: Voices from Diverse Theological Disciplines* (Woba James & Lovely Awomi James); *Nurturing Children in the Tribal Society of North East India: A Search for Values* (Razouselie Lasetso, I. Toshi Jamir & Woba James). In addition, he has published good number of articles in various theological journals and he travels for seminars as resource person and speaker for several programs of different churches.

Foreword

It gives me immense pleasure to go through this book written by Dr. Woba James, a young, dynamic and up-coming bright scholar in the field of History of Christianity. In this well-documented research book, the author has made a strong attempt to make a historical analysis on the role of the SSC in fostering ecumenism in its theological education in India. Having thoroughly surveyed the whole history of SSC, he comes up with some concrete constructive suggestions for strengthening and deepening wider ecumenism through theological education. Reading this book will lead any reader to understand the whole history of the Senate of Serampore College/University (SSC) and its effort in fostering, imparting and promoting ecumenism through theological education in South Asia, mainly in India.

John Pobee, an African Theologian rightly pointed out the importance of ecumenical dimensions and theological education. I quote:

There is a need to keep before the churches and the younger generation a concern for the visible unity which links sharing in God's mission and the pursuit together of justice and peace with their need to heal divisions between the churches through mutual dialogue, mutual recognition and reconciliation. Those involved in theological education and ministerial formation have a vital part to play, not only through the sharing of resources, the establishment of ecumenical colleges, institutions, courses and federations, and the interchange of faculty and students of different traditions. A genuine ecumenical institution will not only acknowledge the differences between churches, but will work towards their reconciliation. Faced by the challenges of the world, the prophetic voice calls out to the churches to respond to them together across cultural and geographical boundaries and not to reinforce divisions and hostilities between people. Those engaged in ecumenical theological education and ministerial formation can respond to that call as they can digest and reflect on significant ecumenical documents and live out new possibilities for common actions.

The contextual reality at the local and global arenas calls for an ecumenical theological education. It calls for re-shaping of curriculum, methodology, and the whole approach to theological education that is contextual, ecumenical and biblical.

Realising the contextual challenges and ecumenical learning in theological education especially in the Indian context, the author offers a clear perspective on the historical and theological undertakings of the past and the current theological education stance of the Senate of Serampore College (University). To prove his research valid and authentic, the author critically looks into the overall theological educational structure and ecumenical initiatives undertaken by the SSC. Beginning with the initial vision and aim of its founders like William Carey to the present SSC's role in fostering ecumenism in its theological education, the author argues that, although the ecumenical character of the SSC in its theological education in India is obvious and visible, it still needs to adequately respond to the present context of India, particularly in structuring its curriculum along ecumenical lines - ecumenical realities, gender issues, scholarship fund and so on and so forth. The author wishes to see the SCC "re-energizing itself and hastening to keep-up with the present day India's realities if it wishes to commit itself realistically and effectively to the context of the Indian Church and Indian society."

This book is a 'must-have' for all theological teachers, institutions, students, church leaders and laity as well, for wider understanding of the ecumenical theological education in India in general and the SSC system of theological education in particular.

Prof. Akheto Sema
Principal
Eastern Theological College, Jorhat (Assam)

Acknowledgment

I am deeply indebted to many people and institutions for their help and support throughout the duration and process of my research work.

The book in its original form was my dissertation submitted towards the Doctor of Theology (D.Th.) degree course under the Senate of Serampore College (University). Therefore, I am is responsible for the title, contents and opinions expressed in it. The title of the dissertation is reconstructed to the present form for the purpose of publication.

First and foremost, I would like to express my profound gratitude along with my respect to *Rev. Dr. Fr. T. I. Varghese, Professor of History of Christianity, FFRRC and Orthodox Theological Seminary, Kottayam (Kerala);* who was also my guide and supervisor. I thank him particularly for taking the pain of reading my scripts thoroughly, and contributing constructive criticisms and creative suggestions, without which, this research work would not have been complete. I am also grateful to him for his unwavering interest in the subject of my choice and his amazing scholarship in the field of History Christianity in India when combined, served as a powerful source of great inspiration.

Indeed, I consider myself blessed to be able to express my heartfelt gratitude to *Rt. Rev. Dr. J. W. Gladstone, Bishop and former Moderator of Church of South India* for his invaluable guidance rendered to me especially in the initial stage of my research work.

I am deeply indebted to *Rev. Dr. Fr. Bishop. K. J. Gabriel former Registrar of FFRRC,* for all the assistance and support I received at the beginning of my doctoral program.

I take this wonderful opportunity to extend my indebtedness to *Rev. Dr. P. L. Panicker also former Registrar of FFRRC,* for his help and support given to me and my family especially during the residential period of my study.

I extend my deepest gratitude to *the library authorities of the Mar Thoma Theological Seminary, Kottayam; Orthodox Theological Seminary, Kottayam; Kerala United Theological Seminary, Thiruvananthapuram; Serampore College, Hooghly, Serampore; Carey Library, Serampore; The United Theological College, Bangalore; Ecumenical Christian Centre, Whitefield, Bangalore; St. Thomas Apostolic Seminary,*

Vadavathoor, Kottayam; Manganam Ecumenical Counseling Centre, Kottayam; for allowing me to have access to the library resources and facilities by availing every possibility.

I also would like to extend my sincere gratitude to *Dr. Tiwari, the former Registrar of thè Senate of Serampore,* for making it possible for me to have access to the needed original and old documents such as minutes, reports, etc., that are preserved in the Senate office.

I regret for not being able to mention their names but I am indeed grateful to *my friends and colleagues who are working in both the Senate affiliated and non-Senate affiliated Seminaries* for extending valuable informations and ideas regarding their colleges, which were needed for my work.

I am truly thankful to my wife *Lovely;* our three children*, Ashi, Avi and Ane;* for their support, understanding, prayers and sacrifices throughout my research period.

I am deeply indebted to *my mother, sisters and their families, my brothers and families* for their moral and financial support, throughout my theological journey for without which, my theological studies would not have been possible.

I also extend my gratitude to *all my friends and well-wishers* for their encouragements and assistance rendered to me any time that I needed them.

Last, but not the least, I am grateful to the Christian World Imprints for coming forward to take this great responsibility of publishing my work.

Above all, I am thankful to God Almighty for calling me, guiding me and enabling me to complete all my theological studies till D.Th. so that I would be well-equipped for His/Her ministry in His/Her **OIKOUMENE**.

Rev. Dr. Woba James

Abbreviations

ACTC	:	Andhra Christian Theological College
AETEI	:	Association of Evangelical Theological Education in India
AIDS	:	Acquired Immunodeficiency Syndrome
ATA	:	Asia Theological Association
B.D.	:	Bachelor of Divinity
B.Miss.	:	Bachelor of Missiology
B.Th.	:	Bachelor of Theology
BAC	:	Bengal and Assam Christian Council
BRE	:	Bachelor of Religious Education
BTE	:	Board of Theological Education
BTESSC	:	Board of Theological Education of the Senate of Serampore College
CCA	:	Christian Conference of Asia
CNI	:	Church of North India
CSI	:	Church of South India
CTE	:	Christian Theological Education
D.Min.	:	Doctor of Ministry
D.Miss.	:	Doctor of Missiology
D.Th.	:	Doctor of Theology
DCPC	:	Diploma in Clinical Pastoral Counseling
DEIC	:	Danish East India Company
EEIC	:	English East Indian Company
EMW	:	Evangelical Movement of Wales
ETC	:	Ecumenical Theological Education
FFRRC	:	Federated Faculty for Research in Religion and Culture
HIV	:	Human Immunodeficiency Virus
IMC	:	International Missionary Council

ITRI	:	Indian Theological Research Institute
JPIC	:	Justice, Peace and Integrity of Creation
KTC	:	Karnataka Theological College
L.Th.	:	Licentiate in Theology
LCR	:	Lindsay Commission Report
M.Min.	:	Masters in Ministry
M.Miss.	:	Master of Missiology
M.Th.	:	Master of Theology
NACO	:	National AIDS Control Organization
NCC	:	National Christian Council
NCCI	:	National Council of Churches in India
NIIPGTS	:	North India Institute of Post Graduate Studies
NMC	:	National Missionary Council
RSS	:	Rasthriya Swayamsevak Sangh
SATHRI	:	South Asia Theological Research Institute
SSC	:	Senate of Serampore College
TEE	:	Theological Education by Extension
UBS	:	Union Biblical Seminary
UGC	:	University Grants Commission
US	:	Union Society
WCC	:	World Council of Churches
YMCA	:	Young Men Christian Association
YWCA	:	Young Women Christian Association

Introduction

1. Statement of the Problem

The Senate of Serampore College (Hereafter cited as SSC) has been serving for decades as a center of Theological Education in India. It has become the main locus for training people, for Church and Christian ministry in India. The ministry of the Church in India is rooted in the midst of pluralities and diversities of cultures, religions, and traditions of India's population and hence it calls for a contextually relevant theological education. The SSC Act of 1918 incorporates the ecumenical dimension within its umbrella by stating that the Council of the SSC be based on interdenominational character and nature.[1] As a result, over the years, the SSC also has known to grow as an ecumenical agency in the country taking into consideration the Indian pluralistic situation.[2] Moreover, very often it is affirmed that the theological education under the SSC is contextual and ecumenical.[3] The present research therefore seeks to analyze the role of the SSC in fostering ecumenism in the context of theological education in India.

2. Elaboration of the Problem

The SSC has a special place as a pioneer institution in India. It was established on July 15, 1818, in the Danish Settlement of Serampore, Calcutta, by the Serampore missionaries William Carey, Joshua Marshman and William Ward, basically for instructing Indian youth on Christianity and European Science. In 1827, after

---

[1]*Bengal Act No. IV of 1918, The Serampore College Act, 1918* (Published in the "Calcutta Gazette" of the 1st May, 1918), 1. Section IX(a) of the Act stated that the members of the Senate be at least one and not more than three from each denomination like, Anglican, Baptist, Congregational, Lutheran, Methodist, Presbyterian and Syrian, etc. (Hereafter *Serampore College Act, 1918*).

[2]J. W. Gladstone, "Ministerial Formation in a Context of Pluralities," in *Together with People: Essays in Honor of Rev. D. S. Satyaranjan*, edited by Samson Prabhakar (Bangalore: SATHRI/ BTESSC, 2004), 2. (Hereafter Gladstone, *Ministerial Formation*).

[3]J. W. Gladstone, *Report of the President of the Senate for the Year 2004-2005*, during the Serampore College Convocation held at Eastern Theological College, Jorhat, on February 12, 2005, 18. It calls for further strengthening of Serampore's ecumenical endeavors. (Hereafter Gladstone, *Report of the President 2004-2005*).

being incorporated by the Royal Charter by the Danish King Frederick VI with University powers under the control of an independent council, it was opened to all castes and creeds of the Christian population of India.[4]

On February 22, 1845, Denmark sold all of its Indian assets to Great Britain and thus the ownership of Serampore College was transferred to the British Government. In 1856, the Baptist Missionary Society in England took over the management of the College, and in the following year, i.e., 1857, the College got affiliated to Calcutta University for Arts and Science degrees although the affiliation was revoked in 1883 and restarted only in 1911 under the principalship of George Howells, the person who was instrumental in enabling the passage of 1918 West Bengal Act; providing a council of up to 16 members and a Senate of up to 18 members to determine eligible candidates for the award of degrees.[5] By 1949, the location of the Council of SSC was transferred from London to Serampore, India.[6]

At the initial period, the College though it functioned as a Christian Training Institute, it always reserves a special place for the Baptist denomination.[7] However, we see a gradual change in the course of time that it began to embark on its ecumenical theological vision and mission. To start with, its faculty was interdenominational. Its interdenominational character became evident with Anglicans, Baptists, Congregationalists, Disciples, Lutherans, Methodists, Presbyterians, Syrian Orthodox, and Welsh Calvinists, who were either enrolled as students or served on the faculty.[8] By 1960, twenty other Indian Colleges and Seminaries were affiliated to Serampore with United Theological College, Bangalore as early as 1919, and Bishop's College, Calcutta in 1920.[9] Serampore College thus began to function as a center for theological education covering within its umbrella a good number of theological colleges and seminaries in India.[10]

---

[4]*Senate of Serampore College, Regulations for Internal and External Candidates: Relating to the Bachelor of Divinity Degree* (December, 1962), 2.

[5]*SSC, Regulations for Internal and External Candidates: Relating to the Bachelor of Divinity (B.D.)* Degree (December, 1962), 3. Cf. D. K. Sahu, "Reorganizing the Structure: A Possibility for Mission Today," in *Church's Participation in Theological Education*, edited by Samson Prabhakar and M. J. Joseph (Bangalore: BTESSC/SATHRI, 2003), 12, 13. (Hereafter Sahu, *Reorganizing the Structure*).

[6]*SSC, Regulations for Internal and External Candidates: Relating to the Bachelor of Divinity (B.D.)* Degree (December, 1962), 4. Cf. *Serampore Convocation 2002, 10th February at Aizawl Theological College*, 2002, 20.

[7]For instance, Section 2(2) of the Serampore Act states that at least one third of the members of the Council shall be members of the Baptist denomination. *Serampore College Act, 1918…*, 2.

[8]Serampore College, Est. 1818, *Friends of Serampore*, July 21, 2003.

[9]Sahu, *Reorganizing the Structure…*, 12, 13.

[10]It is to be noted here that the present researcher is also aware of the fact that Serampore also serves as a Center of Theological Training not only for the Indian nation but also for neighbouring

2.1. The Board of Theological Education of Senate of Serampore College (BTESSC)

Earlier, there were two major organizations at the national level functioning in the interests of theological education, the SSC and the Board of Theological Education (hereafter cited as BTE), formerly under the National Christian Council (NCC). These organizations have made significant contributions to the cause of theological education in India. The former has largely exercised academic functions while the latter has mainly been a co-coordinating and consultative body. Despite their significances, there has been overlapping of their functions. Moreover, the aspect of advanced theological research on a national level has not received sufficient attention, for which reason, the above two organizations jointly mooted the idea of an Indian Theological Research Institute (ITRI) commission to explore possibilities.

The BTE and the SSC when met at successive joint consultations first at Bangalore in 1968 and then at Yeotmal in 1972, and at various separate meetings; the point they arrived repeatedly is that there is a need of one national organization for theological education in the country, undertaking all the above three functions, i.e., academic administration, consultation and research organization. After series of joint consultations, the BTE of NCCI decided that the SSC, which already serves theological institutions and interests all over the country, might be best suited to become this one national organization.[11]

The forms and constitution of the Senate closely defined by the Serampore College Act, lays down among other things an upper limit of 19 members, which makes it impossible for all institutions to be directly represented in the membership of the Senate, which is appointed by the Council of Serampore College. Hence, at the annual meeting of the Senate held at Serampore in 1974, an Implementation Committee consisting of three members each from the Senate, the BTE and the ITRI was appointed with a mandate to bring proposals to the Senate for the total improvement of the standard of theological education in India.

The concerned committee then brought the proposals that emphasized mainly on the necessity to re-organize the college in order to meet the challenges of the new trends and demands of the ministry. It proposed that the College should be an instrument of change, transformation and be able to relate the gospel and its teachings to the real life of the people or that theological education

---

nations namely, Sri Lanka and Bangladesh, however due to the limited scope of the research it does not go beyond India. Cf. *SSC Proceedings of the Theological Senate and its Committees* (January 28th- October 1st 1975), 352.

[11] *Minutes of the Meeting of the Executive of the Senate of Serampore College, held at Serampore January 28th 1975*, 232. *Senate of Serampore College Proceedings of the Theological Senate and its Committees January 28th 1975-October 1st 1975. (Minutes of the Meeting of the Implementation Committee Appointed to Consider Reorganization of the Functioning of the Serampore Senate held at Lee Memorial Mission House, Wellington Square, Calcutta on March 22nd and 23rd, 1974*, 352.

in India especially, should aim to have concrete relevance to the world where it is situated. Besides, the committee also stated very strongly the necessity of re-organizing the functions of the Senate wherein it stresses the inclusion of the three aspects namely, the academic administration (at present the SSC's responsibility); co-ordination and ecumenical relations (the BTE concern); and, research (ITRI Committee). The committee then concluded that the three concerns must interact and contribute to the total theological task in India.[12]

As a result, when SSC accepted the proposal, a joint structure was formed in July 1975 as the Board of Theological Education of the Senate of Serampore College (hereafter cited as BTESSC). It thus brought together not only theological colleges affiliated to SSC but also a large number of organizations that were experimenting and articulating relevant modes of theologizing in Indian context.[13]

Till 1978, SSC was the only means of validating theological training in India. Though SSC was open to affiliate evangelical colleges, the evangelical leaders were not willing but rather they decided to form the Association of Evangelical Theological Education in India (AETEI) in 1979 to provide a forum for fellowship and reflection and soon linked it with Asia Theological Association (ATA), which was founded as an alternative validating agency for evangelical theological education in Asia.[14]

The BTESSC today is one of the major representative bodies of Churches legally constituted and responsible for administering theological education in South Asia. It stands as a unique model of ecumenical participation of the Churches and theological institutions in curriculum planning and evaluation towards common degrees and in their quest for holistic training for ministry. The SSC carries out its theological function through the BTESSC – the arm of theological education under the SSC.[15] The functions of the Board as given in the Constitution of the BTESSC (Revised and adopted on February 3-4, 1994) are:

i) Reflection and pioneering on new methods and style in theological education in relation to the need of the country and of the Churches.

---

[12]Section XII of the Act states that the Senate shall make rules and regulations for the convening of its meetings and for the proper conduct of its business. *Serampore College Act…, 1918*, 3.

[13]*Report on Implementation of the Scheme of the One Structure for Theological Education Under SSC* (January 28th 1976), 507. Cf. Sahu, *Reorganizing the Structure*, 13.

[14]*Report on Implementation of the Scheme of the One Structure for Theological Education Under* SSC (January 28th 1976), 507. Cf. Sahu, *Reorganizing the Structure…*, 13.

[15]M. J. Joseph and J. S. Sadananda, "The Board of Theological Education – The Senate of Serampore College (BTESSC) – An Evaluation," in *Church's Participation in Theological Education*, edited by Samson Prabhakar and M. J. Joseph (Bangalore: BTESSC/SATHRI, 2003), 1. (Hereafter Joseph, *BTESSC*).

ii) Production of theological literature in general especially in regional languages.
iii) Promotion of the welfare of theological teachers and students.
iv) Development of ecumenical co-operation among theological institutions and their libraries.
v) Promotion of relationship between Churches, Theological Institutions and Study Centres.
vi) Any other issues related to theological education.
vii) The Board shall recommend names of persons to be considered by the Senate for nomination to be appointed as Senators.[16]

We observe that the BTESSC continues to carry the ecumenical character of the SSC particularly as listed in the above (iv) and (v). Moreover, it has been through the efforts of the BTESSC's Research wing alongside South Asia Theological Research Institute (SATHRI) that continues to provide contextually relevant theological literature for theological education in India.[17] The Senate of Serampore therefore is known to be continuing its ecumenical pursuit.

The SSC had been earnestly incorporating the need for widening and enlarging its horizons depending on the need of the hour and context within which its theological education is situated. Ecumenism thus, becomes one of its pertinent priorities in its theological education process and context. The word 'ecumenical' originate from the Greek word 'Oikoumene' meaning the whole inhabited world of the universe, and therefore ecumenism in theological education or ecumenical theological education suggests that it transcends ethnic, cultural, and linguistic, gender, denominational[18] and human-nonhuman barriers. Therefore, ecumenical theological education is committed to life in its totality and fullness.[19]

2.2. The Context of Theological Education in India

Theological education as a process does not occur in a vacuum rather it occurs in the context of the Church and Society. Theological education is part of the Churches' ministry and hence the period that students spent in the seminaries becomes the ministerial formation period for them. This calls for a closer interaction between the theological institutions and the Churches. Listening to each other's views, critical negotiation between their faith experience and meanings, respecting each other's traditions, and striving towards an understanding of a holistic ministry are the inevitable characteristics of an enriching interactive relationship between

---

[16]Joseph, *BTESSC ...*, 4-5.

[17]Gladstone, *Report of the President, 2004-2005...*, 15.

[18]Samson Prabhakar, "Church's Participation in Theological Education," in *Church's Participation in Theological Education*, edited by Samson Prabhakar and M. J. Joseph (Bangalore:BTESSC/SATHRI, 2003), 28. (Hereafter Prabhakar, *Church's Participation in Theological Education*).

[19]*Ibid.*

them.[20] This can be developed only on the basis of mutual responsibility, respect and accountability between the Church and theological institutions. As J. G. Muthuraj states in his response to 'Priorities in Theological Education in India' the Churches and theological colleges should be friends, partners and critics.[21] Such a relationship calls for mutual recognition of both identities and autonomy. How far is the gap between theological education and the Church? How united are they or should they be? These questions need to be at the core of theological education concerns as well as at the core of the Church's ministerial concern. The SSC and its diverse Church-affiliated seminaries and colleges need to take this dimension of mutual enhancing relationship into serious consideration.

Churches in India need to recognize and enhance the theological education's ecumenical commitment and academic autonomy as part of the Churches' wider ministry. Despite the zeal and contributions of the Churches toward sending missionaries across the countries as part of the Churches' extended ministry, theological institutions in India face huge hurdles to raise funds from these many missionary-oriented Indian Churches. As theological training is part of the Church's ministerial formation agency, the Churches' support becomes necessary.

The task of theological education is to make it relevant and effective in the present Indian context. Theological education takes the context of the people of India as a framework for interpreting the biblical texts, their Churches' traditions and their faith experiences. Theological education requires interaction between the reflective analysis on the global and ecumenical perspective and of local issues and problems, together with the active existential discernment of the presence of the divine, through active involvement in the local situations.[22]

India's context of plurality is becoming more emphatic today with its socio-economic, religio-cultural and political pluralism coupled with multiplicity of issues related to them. Within this context of pluralism, there is also the growing awareness and feeling of inter-dependency and inter-relatedness of all. Theological education is thus challenged as well as shaped by such realities within which it is situated. Inter-faith reality occupies an important place in the Indian society either for positive or for negative impacts. Caste and communalism are taken to be the two most destructive evils manifested in the Indian society in the context of Hinduism. Theological education unlike the past, today in its ecumenical vision and perspective is challenged to consider its attitude and role in ministering within

---

[20]John Joshva Raja, "Relevant and Effective Theological Education in the Twenty First Century India," in http/:www.wcc.coe.org/wcc/what/education/mf100.pdf. (11.01.05), 9. (Hereafter Raja, *Relevant and Effective Theological Education*).

[21]J. G. Muthuraj, "A Response to Priorities in Theological Education in India." A paper presented at the Regional Consultation, Bangalore: UTC, 2001.

[22]Raja, *Relevant and Effective Theological Education* ..., 12.

such context. K. P. Aleaz proposes *Pluralistic Inclusivism*[23] as a potential alternative to the defective Exclusivism, Inclusivism, and Pluralism, in India's religious pluralistic context. This perspective is considered to be essential for ecumenical theological education in India's pluralistic context. The SSC is thus challenged to evolve a more comprehensive role for other religions in its theological and Christian experience.

Theological education is not only essential for the formation of Church leaders, though it is necessary, but it is equally necessary for the society as well. K. C. Abraham observes,

> theology is not a systematic explication of timeless truths nor is it a matter of laying a pre-fabricated system of ideas to a situation. It is a reflection on the articulation of the faith experience of people in a given context. Theology is not a detached academic exercise; it is a critical reflective process.[24]

Theological education being contextual thus becomes essential. It should be rooted and carried out within the context of the people and the community in their diverse situations and thus should go beyond purely academic elements, without ignoring their importance.[25] Theological education therefore should be contextual, an agent of liberation by raising critical consciousness, empowerment and giving hope to the people. It should play an integral part in people's ongoing search for their identity and human dignity. Hence, our theological education should be an interactive, dialogical, liberative and community related endeavour.[26] It would then be able to transcend religious, social and cultural bias by becoming ecumenical, with its principal preoccupation being the *oikos*, the universal home of all.

Contextual theological education inevitably leads to ecumenism because it is within this context that diversity and the specificities that mark our differences manifest themselves. From this perspective, ecumenism constitutes the harmonious with the contrasting and distinct. It acquires a complementary character while

---

[23]Pluralistic Inclusivism inspires each religious to be pluralistically inclusive in that on the one hand each living faith is to become truly pluralistic by other faiths contributing to its conceptual content and on the other hand, Inclusivism is to transform its meaning to witness the fulfillment of the theological and spiritual contents of one's own faith in and through the contributions of other living faiths. K. P. Aleaz, "Inter-Faith Reality and Ecumenical Theological Education," *http://www.wcc.coe.org/wcc/what/education/mf100.pdf.* (11.01.05), 82.

[24]K. C. Abraham, "A Broken God for Broken People: A Theology in Solidarity with the Suffering", *Reformed World*, ed., Odair Pedroso Mateus Vol. 56/3 (Geneva: World Alliance of Reformed Churches, 2006), 296.

[25]Romer Portillo, "The Contextual and Ecumenical in Venezuelan Theological Education," in *http://www.coe.org/wcc/what/education/mf100.pdf.* (11.01.05), 40. (Herafter Portillo, *The Contextual and Ecumenical Theological Education*).

[26]John Mohan Razu, "Contextual Theologies and Methodologies: An Outline," A paper presented during the D.Th. Methodology Course at UTC, Bangalore, May 2003.

emphasizing the specifities and the particularities of each context in connection with a greater reality, without ignoring the plurality and autonomy of each context. Hence, ecumenism can be defined as *unity in diversity*.[27] Ecumenism therefore reminds us that we are all one, and that history is the result of everyone's participation.

Ecumenism has manifested the different faces of the people: dalit, tribal, women, children and the old. Today, the face of ecumenism in India contains many shades, and it is diverse as well as abundant. These faces are not only becoming visible but are also being heard. They have begun to transform the human knowledge and sciences like theology, sociology, philosophy and hermeneutics. They are proposing alternative models in contrast to those imposed upon them by western culture and Indian elite culture. Hence, ecumenical theological education becomes one of those alternative models, which are constructed from within the particularities of distinct histories, cultures, peoples and individuals in India.

The SSC has a unique place in the field of theological education in India, though we cannot discount other significant organizations beside the SSC. It has come a long way not only in terms of its age but also in terms of its achievements. There has been a growth in the number of programs relevant to India's context, an increase in the number of colleges affiliated to it, a good number of denominations, which have accepted its credibility in relation to its ecumenical openness etc.[28] However, that does not imply that the SSC has no further need for change or improvements. In the words of Bishop J. W. Gladstone in his Presidential Report during the recent convocation of Serampore College held at Eastern Theological College, on 12th of February, 2005:

> We face several challenges today. Ecumenical endeavours needs further strengthening. We experience the impact of globalization. The world around us, the creation of God, has been facing threat of its extinction. The development of Dalit and Tribal Communities yet to form the major agenda of different decision making bodies. Identities within religious communities are gaining strength. HIV+/AIDS raises serious threat. Poverty is still growing. Emancipation of women needs to be affirmed. These and several other factors make theological education in our country to take up key role in enabling the Church and equipping the people of God in a contextually relevant way. In this endeavour ecumenical partnership needs to be strengthened. Various programmes of the Senate of Serampore are intended to address these issues.[29]

Hence, despite the fact that the SSC has been incorporating the ecumenical dimension in its theological endeavour, it still has enough space to strengthen

---

[27]Portillo, *The Contextual and Ecumenical Theological Education* ..., 41.

[28]Gladstone, *Ministerial Formation*..., 2.

[29]Gladstone, *Report of the President, 2004-2005*..., 18.

that dimension in its attempt for a contextually relevant theological education in India.

3. Working Definitions

3.1. Theological Education

"Theological Education" is defined here as "an ongoing process in which participants (theological teachers and students) are engaged in creating, sharing, interpreting, mediating and analyzing each one's faith experiences and religious meanings in relation to one's contexts, traditions and communities."[30] In this, both the participants are enriched through dialogical and interactive education method of learning. It offers sufficient space for the students to voice their understandings, opinions, concerns that arises out of their pre-seminaries contexts and also helps them to prepare well for their future ministries during their ministerial formation period by taking into consideration their present socio-religious and cultural contexts within which their calling and vocation is headed for.

3.2. Ecumenism

The term "ecumenism" is derived from the Greek word *Oikoumene*, meaning "the inhabited world". The word is usually used in regard to movements toward religious unity. In its broader sense, ecumenism means the religious initiative toward, worldwide unity. In its narrower sense, ecumenism refers to the promotion of unity, cooperation or improved understanding between distinct religious groups or denominations within the same religion. Two general types of ecumenism are discernible. One, ecumenism within a faith-group, and two, ecumenism between diverse world's religions which strives for greater mutual respect, toleration and cooperation for peaceful co-existence.

However, keeping these classical understandings and definitions of ecumenism at the background, the present research employs the term "ecumenism" to mean the promotion of unity, respect, transformation, liberation and mutual enriching relationships that comes out of the recognition and experience of living and interacting together in the midst of much diversity amongst peoples, contexts, faiths, Churches, denominations, institutions, issues, concerns, etc., within the purview of theological education in India under the SSC.

3.3. Pluralistic Context

Pluralistic Context in this study is taken to mean the reality of India's multi-religious, ideologies, social, communal and cultural context, where people belonging to these diverse facets of life live, work and interact with one another every day. It is a context with multi structures and dimensions of life – the diverse stratified groups of people like the so-called upper castes, the lower castes, outcastes/outclass – dalits, tribals, women, nature etc.

---

[30]Raja, *Relevant and Effective Theological Education ...*, 6.

4. Importance of the Research

The importance of the research lies in its assessment to see whether the SSC has been sufficiently responding to the ecumenical concerns of India's pluralistic context, or, whether what has been so far achieved is merely a "skin-deep" contribution. Most importantly, it would focus on the ecumenical formation of the SSC in its theological education, without which there could not be any viable and enriching ecumenism in the wider society in which Christian ministry is rooted. Eventually, this research hopes to expose the still-unreached ecumenical dimensions of the SSC, for its further involvement and participation. The research work is also important in that it may contribute to the ongoing pursuit for an ecumenical theological education in India. Students, teachers, and theological institutions may benefit from it. It may also further strengthen the relationship between the Churches and theological education in India for united efforts in ministry. Lastly but not the least, it may enable the SSC to critically yet constructively reflect upon its own self for further improvement.

5. Hypothesis

1. That the SSC has been playing an important role in fostering ecumenism in India's pluralistic context.
2. That right from the time of the Serampore College Act (1918), theological education under the SSC was not limited to the Baptists alone though William Carey was a Baptist, and not limited to India alone but to South Asia.
3. That it was able to bring together different Churches, Seminaries and Colleges through its ecumenical theological education program.
4. That it still need to further the ecumenical nature and character of its theological education for more effective and meaningful relevance in India's multi-faceted context.

6. Methodology Adopted

Basically it would be a historical analysis of the SSC giving particular focus on the impetus given to ecumenism and encouragement given to contextually relevant theological education in India. The stated assumption (the hypothesis given above) will be tested by the available documents. The attempt will be based on an indepth analysis of the context and verification of sources from the perspective of the present interpretation and a search for relevance.

7. Sources of the Research

Sources for the research include: accessible primary sources (original books, writings, documents, minutes preserved on the SSC and its history) collected from the SSC, Serampore Hooghly; other primary and secondary sources or writings collected and accessed from different Senate affiliated colleges, seminaries and their libraries in India; also including other accessible informations and sources related to the subject matter of the present research.

8. Scope and Limitations

The present research will focus on theological education in India under the SSC. This research will mainly concentrate on the role of the SSC in fostering "ecumenism" in India's pluralistic context, particularly in the context of theological education in India. The aspect of wider ecumenism outside the umbrella of theological education of the SSC does not come under the concern of the present research.

9. Previous Research

Several researches have been done on Theological Education in India, carried out under the Social Scientists on such important topics like,

a) "Content Analysis of Theological Curricula and Syllabi," in *Religion and Society* Vol. XXXII, No. 3, Sep. 1985. It examines what is happening in existing instructional programs, whether it sufficiently meets the major needs for Christian ministry. It exposes the need for contextually relevant Syllabi; and suggests the urgent need for the use and production of local theological literature, and to avoid the almost total dependency on foreign theological literature.

b) Oommen, T. K. and Hunter P. Mabry, *The Christian Clergy in India Vol. I: Social Structure and Social Roles*. Delhi: Sage Publications with CISRS, 2001. This is an extensive study on the social background of India's non-Catholic clergy over two decades which spelt out for the first time "some of the most difficult and pressing problems of Churches in India," as the authors described. It exposes the inequalities in Church leadership mainly owing to the caste/class factor that accommodates the upper castes who forms the minority among the Christian community to occupy the influential and higher positions in the ministry of the Church, which causes frustration and discontent among the Christian community in India. The book also exposes serious issues like the rural-urban gap in the ratio of clergy to congregations, the hostility to women's ordination, etc. The authors warn that if adequate measures were not taken to reverse this trend, Christian clergy would endanger rural India. Despite the significant research work done by these authors in exposing the various factors that threatens the Indian clergy, it fails to identify the ecumenical dimension factor in Indian theological education, that is very much necessary for a relevant ministry in India's pluralistic context.

c) Amalorpavadass, D. S. (Ed). *Ministries in the Church in India: Research Seminar and Pastoral Consultation*. New Delhi: C.B.C.I. Centre, 1976.

It emphasizes the importance of the Indian Church reality, the need for openness to other churches and traditions. It most importantly deals with the reality of the diversified Church ministries in India and the need for the renewal and creation of new ministries that would bring further meaning and enrichment for the Church, Christians and the wider world in general, in keeping with the teaching of the Holy Scriptures.

d) Wilfred, Felix (Ed). *Theological Education in India Today*. Bangalore: ATC, 1985. It stresses the importance of theologizing in the cultural, philosophical and religious context of India. It calls for shifting of our system of theological education from the abstract tradition-based model to the active people-oriented model of theology, which is the need of the hour in India. However, the various writers sadly failed to incorporate the urgent need for an ecumenical theological education in India.

Without discounting the incomparable significances of these stated earlier researches done by these renowned scholars and writers, the present research differs from them by limiting the study mainly to the role of the SSC in fostering "ecumenism" in the context of theological education in India, which all of the above work failed to touch upon it.

10. Structure of the Research

The structure of this research comprises of Introduction, six main chapters and Conclusion. In the Introduction the researcher presents the Statement of the Problem; Elaboration of the Problem; Working Definitions; Importance of the Research; Hypothesis; Methodology Adopted; Sources of the Research; Scope and Limitations; and, Previous Research.

The First Chapter analyzes the *Development of Theological Education in India, from a Historical Perspective*, i.e., the historical backgrounds of the different trends of theological education in the history of Christianity in India. It follows a systematic analysis beginning with the Syrian Christian Training; the Roman Catholic Training; the Protestant Christian Training, etc., from the early century to the present day Christianity in India.

Chapter Two examines the *Historical Background of the Senate of Serampore College*. It notes the conditions of India during the 18th and the 19th centuries, the early Western missionary enterprise that emerged with the burning desire to evangelize the different corners of the world, leading on to the coming of the Baptist Mission to India in the person of William Carey in 1793, followed by his companions successively. It examines the important events and factors that surround the formation of the College; its growing years and its related aspects of struggles and how the untiring efforts and determination of the missionaries and its leaders has helped the College to wade through the centuries for which, today the Senate of Serampore College thus stands as a living legacy of the undying vision and mission of its founders William Carey, Joshua Marshman and William Ward.

Chapter Three markedly focuses its attention upon the *Theological Education in the Multi-Faceted Context of India.* It analyzes the importance of structuring our theological education toward the line of being critically self-evaluative and reflective in relating itself against its complexly-rooted and diversified context.

Chapter Four is completely committed to the study of *Theological Education under the Senate of Serampore College.* It scrutinizes the aims and objectives of the College; the nature, content and functions of the College; its courses offered; its affiliating member colleges, seminaries, institutions and the traditions of the churches that these represent etc.

Chapter Five works out the main concern under the subject of this dissertation and that is, *The Role of the Senate of Serampore College in Fostering Ecumenism in the Context of Theological Education in India.*

Chapter Six presents the findings and some prospective suggestions.

Finally, the research ends with a conclusion, providing a retrospection on the present research work.

Contents

Chapter 1

The Development of Theological Education in India A Historical Analysis

Introduction

Theological education in India has come quite far today. It has had its fair share of achievements alongside its many challenging trysts and hurdles along its historic journey. Before we venture headlong into our subject area of research, it is necessary for us to go back to our historic past to re-discover and understand the 'beginnings' of our theological education. This will perhaps give us meaningful wisdom and insights about our great Indian theological heritage and that will serve as a positive guide to our learning and engagement in the present theological journey of ours. As such, this first chapter of our research is committed to study the historical development of theological education in India.

1. The Indian Background

The rich religious heritage of India offers many patterns and vehicles of expression of which the Christians in India must consider its effort to communicate the revelation of God in Christ in an idiom and a setting, which render it intelligible to the people of the country. The gurukula system, closely associated with the development of the ashrama, represents a tradition closely akin, in method at least, to the task of Christian theological education.[1] The ashramas were the earliest theological institutions of Hinduism. The gurukula system of education was at its inception a necessity of the times when there were no printed books or professional teachers. However, with the passage of time, it began to wane as

[1]C. W. Ranson, *The Christian Minister in India* (Madras: CLS, 1945), 12. (Hereafter, Ranson, *The Christian Minister...*).

students increased in number and teachers shifted to town in search of teaching profession to support their livelihood. It was in the ashramas and as a result of the nature of religious education imparted therein that the gurukula system was transformed into an educational ideal, above the vicissitudes of the times and circumstances.[2] The ashramas were selective schools and hence received a limited number of pupils.

The ancient ashrama was an outcome of naturalist religion, which sought self-realization and deliverance from the world, in a sense quite foreign to the historic Christian faith. But, the gurukula system of the intimate association of the teacher with the pupil represents a method, which bears a resemblance to the example of our Lord in training of His disciples and represents an indigenous parallel to the catechetical schools of the Christian church. It sets a precedence, which should make the pursuit of Christian theological training appear natural and proper to Indian eyes.

2. Theological Education in the St. Thomas Christian Church

2.1. Theological Education of the St. Thomas Christian Church before the Arrival of the European Power in India

The St. Thomas Christian Church in India is one of the most ancient churches of Christendom.[3] From the first century itself it appears that India had a native clergy of her own on the Malabar Coast.[4] This clergy belong to the St. Thomas Christians. The history of the formation of theological education therefore starts with the St. Thomas Christians although their training may have been just the basics. For many years, the theological education in India remained almost unchanged in the same early state. It was only after the arrival of the Portuguese and Protestant Christianity that the systematic and organized efforts were made in the field of theological education in India. The theological training among the St. Thomas clergy in the early centuries did not maintain a high standard,[5] which would anyhow have been impossible under the given circumstances.[6] Simple

[2]Cf. Ranson, *The Christian Minister…*, 13. "The ashramas" writes P. Chenchiah, "were the earliest theological institutions of Hinduism."

[3]Stephen, Neill, *The Story of the Christian Church in India and Pakistan*. Grand Rapids: William B. Eerdmans, 1970, 19.

[4]George M. Anithil, *The Theological Formation of the Clergy in India* (Poona: Pontifical Athenaeus, 1966), 1. (Hereafter, Anithil, *The Theological Formation of the Clergy…*).

[5]Tisserant and Hambye, E. R. *Eastern Christianity in India* (Calcutta: 1957), 42. (Hereafter, Tisserant and Hambye, *Eastern Christianity …*). Moreover, the theological education in the pre-Portuguese and pre-Protestant should not be judged according to the modern standards of theological training, which are fairly recent even in Europe. The general theological education of Malabar priests before the arrival of the Portuguese and Protestant was probably as good as in many countries in the World.

[6]It is argued that the general formation of the St. Thomas Christian clergy before the coming of other European Christianity was probably good as in other parts of the Christian world of that day.

priests may have learned just enough to perform the different functions attached to their office. These functions do not appear to have gone beyond Holy Eucharist and attending to the office on certain days and assisting at marriages, funerals and family functions. All that a priest had to learn was the liturgical functions and an elementary knowledge of Syriac and the Holy Scriptures from elderly priest.[7]

The circumstances for such an elementary training were quite adequate for that particular time. Also as higher castes, Christians had an easy access to education. It is said that they were the most cultured among the people of Malabar and were mentally alert, talented and reasonable.[8] The prayers used in the home for morning and night prayers were also taught to the children in the village schools. They were written on palm leaves and the children had to learn them by heart. The pupil entered a special relationship with his teacher similar to that of the Guru-Chela relation of the early Indian educational system.[9] Christians in Malabar enjoyed a good and high reputation in agricultural trade and military service. They were very useful helpers to the Rajahs in their administrations and often held high posts, e.g., like that of collecting revenues. A traveler of the 14th century tells that there were Christians in charge of public weighing office of the Quilon customs.[10] Whether education in professions, which Christians shared with other castes, was common to all, or whether the Christian community developed a professional education of its own, we do not know.[11]

The growth and development of this early Christianity of Malabar was impeded by adverse circumstances.[12] With the rise of Islam in the East, the Malabar Church suffered an irretrievable setback. Persecuted at home and divided within itself, the East Syrian Church neglected its distant mission, sending prelates

---

[7]Cf. Anithil, *The Theological Formation of the Clergy...*, 7.

[8]M. V. La Croze, *Histoire du Christianisme des Indesl*, 1758, 1, cited by Anithil, *The Theological Formation of the Clergy...*, 7.

[9]Cf. L.W. Brown, *The Indian Christian of St. Thomas* (Cambridge: 1956), 186.

[10]Cf. F. E. Keay, *A History of Education in India and Pakistan* (London: Oxford University Press, 1939), 180-181. For additional source on this cf. also M. K. Kuriakose, *History of Christianity in India: Source Materials* (Madras: CLS, 1961), 19.

[11]Anithil, *The Theological Formation of the Clergy...*, 8.

[12]The East Syrian Church upon which the Church of Malabar was depending succumbed to Nestorian heresy towards the end of the 5th century and the Church in South India soon came under Nestorian influence. The important question in this connection is: were the early Syrian Christians of Malabar formal heretics since they were depending entirely on the East Syrian Church? There is no agreement among the scholars on this point, on the contrary a long-standing controversy. It cannot be denied that the liturgy of this early Christian community may have the influences of the Nestorian. This is evident from the fact that names of Nestorius Theodore of Mopsuestia and Diodorus of Tarsus, were found in the canon. See Tisserant and Hambye, *Eastern Christianity...*, 45. As for the doctrinal aspect, the Christians took the Nestorian teaching however, it is also evident that they cannot be called formal heretics since the Christians of Malabar had little knowledge about the Christological controversies. Hence, Malabar Christians never were heretics.

to Malabar at irregular intervals.[13] Also the economic position and political influence of the Malabar Christian community declined from the moment when the sea-borne trade passed from them to the Muslims.[14] The Malabar Christians had no hierarchy of their own but depended for all essential religious needs on Mesopotamia. Each Patriarch selected his candidates from among his own monks and sent them into distant territories of his jurisdiction, instead of creating an indigenous hierarchy there.[15] Thus the Catholicos of the Chaldean Church at irregular intervals sent such prelates down to Malabar and even to the Far East, partly on his own initiative and partly due to the request of the communities in need of bishops.[16] At times several bishops appeared in Malabar, simultaneously exercising their office. They ordained priests and consecrated altars.[17]

The system followed by St. Thomas Church in Malabar was the Malpanate system, which corresponds rather closely to the Hindu Gurukulavasam. The general procedure was that an elderly and experienced priest gathers around himself some young candidates for priesthood and tried to train them in all those things, which he considered necessary or useful for their office.[18] For example, there was a cathanar in Angamali who was like a father among them and in him they had great confidence on account of his old age and learning. It is for 50 years he was teaching the sacred scripture and has many disciples from all parts of Malabar.[19] The subjects taught in such learning were Syriac, Scripture and Liturgy.[20] The method of instruction was that, the beginners were exercised in writing and learning the alphabets. The others had to write the lessons the master

---

[13]Cf. G. Schurhammer, *The Malabar Church and Rome during the Early Portuguese Period and Before* (Trichinapaly: 1934), 25-30.

[14]P. Thomas, *Christian and Christianity in India and Pakistan* (London: 1945), 38.

[15]Tisserant and Hambye, *Eastern Christianity…*, 25.

[16]Joseph the Indian, a sixteenth century witness, testifies that the Catholicos nominated the prelates for India and Cathay (China). Cf. Paesi, *Vespucii Reprint, Text and Studies*, Vol. VI (London: 1916), 165. See also Anithil, *The Theological Formation of the Clergy…*, 4.

[17]Tisserant and Hambye, *Eastern Christianity…*, 25. It is not clear how far these bishops were assisted by the native priests they had ordained or what powers these native priests actually had. In some cases their priestly power was severely restricted e.g., it seems that at times they were not even allowed to baptize children without previous authorization from the Syrian prelates. See M. Mathias, *The St. Thomas Christians of Malabar under Mar Jacob* (Rome: 1960), 314-317. (Hereafter, Mathias, *The St. Thomas Christians* ...).The Intermediary between the foreign prelates and the native priests was the Archdeacon who acted at the same time as the national representative of the native community.

[18]Such a Malpanate might have had only few students and pupils for long periods none at all. But it is quite natural that some outstanding priests may have gathered a greater number of candidates among themselves and thus, one or the other old church may have become a kind of theological training center e.g., Angamali. J. Wicki, *Documenta Indica*, Vol. III, 804, cited by Anithil, *The Theological Formation of the Clergy…*, 9.

[19]Cf. Anithil, *The Theological Formation of the Clergy…*, 9.

[20]*Ibid.* However, whether there was any formal speculative theology is doubtful.

gave them and to exercise themselves at length in them.[21] The main aim of their studies was to be able to read and interpret the sacred scriptures, although some were also given to study of the Fathers and theologians. Some copied the books of the Fathers and theologians and kept them as treasures.[22]

The priests ordained by these Syrian prelates looked after the needs of the community and gathered around them candidates for priesthood.[23] They instructed and prepared them, that one day they might be ordained by the next bishop from Syrian. The clergy were customarily all men belonging to the parishes themselves, elected by the parishioners when they were boys and ordained and commissioned by the bishops for the work of the parish at the appeal of the parishioners. Then they undertake a course of theological training in one of the theological institutions attached to the bishop or elderly priest.[24] After preliminary training as a deacon, the person is ordained as a priest. This custom continued for many centuries among the Malabar Christian community.[25]

Dogmatic thought, which had such an important place in the contemporary world of theological education, seems to have been almost absent in the early St. Thomas Christian training system in Malabar. Their theological training remained closer to the original form of Christianity being based on liturgy and scripture.[26] Their main source of spirituality was liturgy and scripture. However, with the arrival of Portuguese in India during the 15th century the picture in Malabar and the system of theological education of the St. Thomas Christian came into contact with different situations.

---

[21]Cf. Anithil, *The Theological Formation of the Clergy...*, 9. However, whether there was any formal speculative theology is doubtful.

[22]Mathias, *The St. Thomas Christians...*, 327. But, it is not clear of which Fathers and Theologians they studied.

[23]Cf. J. C. Houpert, *Christianity in India, Burma and Ceylon: 52-1952 A.D.* (Tiruchirapally: 1957), 7-8.

[24]This does not offer a systematic course in theology, church history, the Bible and pastoralia. The instruction is mostly confined to the study of the Syrian liturgy, the proper performance of which is regarded as a very important part of the priest's training. A. M. Varki, *The Growing Church* (n.p. n.d.) 226.

[25]There were views that there was the continual fear for long periods no bishop might be able to come and that consequently there might not be enough priests to care for the growing community. To solve this problem, rather strange means were used at times. Young boys, even children, were ordained priests. Cf. Tisserant and Hambye, *Eastern Christianity...*, 99.

[26]For long period we do not know of a single theological attempt made in India, which would have tried to penetrate deeper, the Christian doctrine, or relate it to Indian philosophy and present it in India. Cf. Anithil, *The Theological Formation of Clergy...*, 9.

2.2. Theological Education of St. Thomas Christians during Portuguese Period and After

Pope Alexander VI, acting on his Papal authority, had granted to Portuguese king and Spanish king the exclusive right of evangelizing all the countries already discovered and in future still to be discovered. These two nations began to set out to discover and conquer the West and the East for evangelization; however, both political and religious concerns were mixed in their exploration. With this authorization on May 20th 1498 Vasco da Gama landed at the port of Calicut, India. Good relations prevailed in the beginning. The Portuguese and Malabar Christians discovered each other as brothers among a vast majority of Hindus and Mohammedans. But, with closer contacts they realized more and more the deep differences that separate them from each other and they developed quite an unchristian contempt for each other.[27]

Roman Catholic in this situation began their efforts to bring the St. Thomas Christians of Malabar under their jurisdiction. The presence of new advanced Latin form of training that spread more and more constituted a serious challenge to the form in which so far the Syrian priests had been trained. St. Thomas Christians in Malabar had never had any established Seminary of its own. "The first sporadic attempts to establish seminaries for the training of the Syrian clergy were made by the Latin missionaries".[28] Such a training center for native priests in India was started in 1540 in Goa, the capital of Portuguese empire in the East. Another was also started in Malabar with a more limited scope namely to give an adequate and up-to-date seminary training to Indian clergy. Frey Vicente, a Franciscan, founded the Seminary-College at Cranganore in 1540/41.[29] The College was intended mainly, if not exclusively, for the children of St. Thomas Christians. The training given in the Cranganore Seminary to the Indian clergy was evidently Latinized training.[30] No regard was given in Cranganore seminary to the age-old St. Thomas Christians rites from which almost all of the students

---

[27]These differences were first of all of social nature. The Syrian Christians who from time immemorial had maintained the status of a high caste in the Hindu social structure feared their status would be impaired by contact with the Pharangees and their Western way of life and also by their affiliation to large numbers of new converts from low castes and outcastes. Another thing, much resented by the Syrian Christians, was Latinization of the Syrian Church by the Portuguese. The growing tension and the final explosion had its roots in a complex variety of causes most of which are anything but religious. See also A. M. Mundadan, *History of Christianity in India*, Vol. I (Bangalore: TPI, 1984), 17ff. A. M. Mundadan, *Tradition of St. Thomas Christians* (Bangalore: Dharmaram College Publication, 1970), 20-36.

[28]Anithil, *The Theological Formation of Clergy*…,14.

[29]Cf. T. K. Oommen and Hunter P. Mabry, *The Christian Clergy in India*, Vol. I (New Delhi: Sage Publications, 2000), 59-60. (Hereafter, Oommen and Hunter P. Mabry, *The Christian Clergy in India*…).

[30]Ferroli, *The Jesuits in Malabar*, Vol. I (Bangalore: Dharmaram Publications, 1939), 151. (Hereafter, Ferroli, *The Jesuits in Malabar*…).

came. The study was instructed only in Latin theology and only Latin liturgy was taught and practiced. The liturgy and worship is centered on the Latin Mass and the Latin office.

The policy of Latinization was so successful for the priests working among the Latin, but that proved a failure and danger among the St. Thomas Christians.[31] The Indian Christians (St. Thomas Christians) who were at the beginning very enthusiastic about the education which their children received in the college began to resent it when they saw that their children were fully formed in the Latin ways and customs and had little regard for the St. Thomas Christians' customs and traditions.[32] In the course of time it had become the common opinion among the St. Thomas Christians that the Cranganore seminary served only one purpose, namely, to Latinize the students and through them to Latinize the whole Malabar Christians community in mentality, jurisdiction and rite.[33] The St. Thomas Christians on the other hand felt the strong necessity for a better theological education of their priests, but on the other hand they did not want a Latinize theological training. They preferred rather to return to their own Malpanate system of training the clergy.[34]

Another training center was started at Vaipincotta to give training to Syrian clergy by Jesuits.[35] The first thing that the students had to learn was Latin. However, the growing tensions between Syrian Christians of Malabar and Latinos, especially after the Synod of Diamper, led at the end to the Coonen Cross revolt and this swept away also the Seminary at Vaipincotta. Thus, in 1652 the seminary was closed down.[36] The Jesuits also established at Ambazhakad and at Angamali seminaries. In the course of time the Seminary at Ambazhakad became a famous

---

[31]Cf. Tisserant and Hambye, *Eastern Christianity...*, 70.

[32]Cf. Anithil, *The Theological Formation of Clergy...*, 17-18.

[33]Cf. Mathia, *St. Thomas Christians of Malabar...*, 425. See also Thomas Puthiakunnel *Syro-Malabar Clergy* (Ernakkulam: Vincentian Publishing, 1964), 15-16.

[34]Cf. Anithil, *The Theological Formation of Clergy...*, 17-18. The Malpanate taught them to read Syriac, gave them practical notions about liturgy, together with the elements of dogmatic and moral theology. The Malpanate system being the original form of the training among the Syrian Christians of Malabar was deeply rooted in the consciousness of the community. It also closes affinity to the Guru system of the surrounding Hindu majority. Therefore, even after so many efforts made by the Roman Catholic priests to eradicate this system but the Malpanate system did not disappear. This system developed from the catechetical schools of the early Christian era as that of Alexandria (180 A.D.), Antioch (290 A.D.), and Edessa (363 A.D.), which later on spread rapidly in the East as well as in the West. Such catechetical schools were at the first centers for training candidates for the priesthood.

[35]Cf. Ferroli, *The Jesuits in Malabar...*, 166. See also Tisserant and Hambye, *Eastern Christianity...*, 45-46.

[36]Cf. Andrew Lopez, *A Short Account of the Mission under the Charge of the Father of the Society of Jesus of the Malabar Province in the East Indies* (Trichy: 1644), 7. See also Ferroli, *The Jesuits in Malabar...*, 33. After the Dutch conquest the seminary was turned into lepers' asylum.

center for linguistic studies.[37] However, the seminary was destroyed toward the end of 18th century, probably in 1790 during the raid of Tipu Sultan.[38] The Common feature of all these seminaries usually attached to or established in religious houses is that they were governed by foreign religious superiors of the Latin rite and not by the Syrian clergy. They tried to Latinize the whole St. Thomas Christians of Malabar through these seminaries, which was a success to some extent.

2.3. A Brief History of the 19th and 20th Century Syrian Christian Church in India

The Church Missionary Society (CMS) which entered the Syrian community in the early part of the 19th century had a great impact upon the succeeding course of the history of the Syrian Christian Church. The missionaries were very strong in their conviction that there are sufficient opportunities all awaiting their transformatory works both socially as well as religiously. Despite some commendable contributions toward the Syrian community, the mission could not make a lasting impression of relationship with the Syrian Christian church. This strained relationship between the two might have been the result of their differences of opinion especially in relation to the matters that surround the question of whether it is morally right to reform or affect new changes upon their age-old or time-honored religious traditions both of the faith and its practices. Eventually, the Mission had had to dissociate itself from the Syrian Church and go its own way toward the directions where its goodwill mission was needed and hence welcomed.[39] Hence, in the year 1836 the work of the Mission of help sent by the Church Missionary Society among the Syrian Christians, was terminated and the missionaries of the Mission took their evangelism and educational works toward the non-Christian Indians.[40]

---

[37]Tisserant and Hambye, *Eastern Christianity...*, 89. It was noted that the seminary taught Sanskrit, Tamil, Malayalam, and Syriac with great success. A good printing press for all languages was also established there.

[38]Cf. Ferroli, *The Jesuits in Malabar...*, 550.

[39]It is worthy of note here that before entering the Syrian Community the missionaries were given strong warning by their mission's main head against any attempt to pull down the ancient Church for raising another but were given permission only to remove the garbage and to repair the decaying areas. In the light of such clear demarcated boundaries and also considering the sour outcome of their relationship, one could therefore presume that the missionaries must have applied too much liberty upon their 'sweeping' and 'mending' work that the Syrian Christians were pushed to feel invaded and even threatened of everything that they hold dear about their faith and traditions. Cf. C. P. Mathew and M. M. Thomas, *The Indian Churches of St. Thomas*, Revised Edition (Delhi: ISPCK, 2005), 56. (Hereafter Mathew, *Churches of St. Thomas...*).

[40]Cf. Juhanon Mar Thoma, Metropolitan, Mar Thoma Syrian Church, *Christianity in India and a Brief History of the Mar Thoma Syrian Church* (Madras: K. M. Cherian, 1968), 22. (Hereafter Juhanon, *History of the Mar Thoma Syrian Church...*).

Nevertheless, the impact of the Mission upon the Syrian Church[41] did not have its pre-mature end then and there but instead continued to take its effects which led to several significant events in the history of the Syrian Christian Church. Earlier, the Syrian Church was one united church with its congregations held under one common vision and well-being but very gradually, there emerged a distinguishing line between the members in thoughts and understanding especially with the coming of the Mission. Although, it might seem an extravagant assumption to some, a critical reflection could lead one to conclude that there appeared 3 different groups within the then original members of the Church. The first group is constituted by those that personally felt that what the Mission preached and proposed regarding the necessity for change in the various aspects of their traditional faith and life is true, finally left their Mother Church to join the Anglican Church; the second group consists of those who also saw the importance of reform actions in their traditional Syrian Church but who nevertheless did not consider desertion as the correct direction and therefore decided to stay put where they are and to attempt to work out their reform ideas within itself; and finally there was that third group (although they were not that audible or visible during that particular event), who refused to budge an inch and therefore continued to hold the entire package of their traditional faith as satisfactory and perfect thereby saw no reason whatsoever why they should be in any need for reform or correction.

It was during this significant period in the history of the Syrian Christian Church that the seminary at Kottayam namely the Old Seminary (today it is under the name Orthodox Theological Seminary) was established in 1815. This seminary served (and still continue to) the purpose of training their clergy for parish ministry. Although, in the beginning it was exclusively meant for the training of their own tradition candidates, it gradually opened up itself to enroll other affiliations' candidates as it began to actively respond to the challenging mission of ecumenism. Besides, it is furthermore ecumenized by becoming a federated member with two other seminaries of different traditions namely the Mar Thoma Theological Seminary at Kottayam and the Kerala United Theological Seminary (CSI) at Thiruvananthapuram, all under the name the Federated Faculty for Research in Religion and Culture (FFRRC).[42]

---

[41]It is important to note also beside the ensuing discussion coming up above, some of the remarkable or commendable contributions of the Mission toward the Syrian Christians in the early part of that short-lived relationship of the two. The missionaries have to their credit the historical records of the Syrian Christian community, the translation of the Bible into Malayalam, 2 Malayalam dictionaries, compilation of a Malayalam grammar for English students and several other educational schools opened in about 70-72 different villages. The missionaries also supervised the running of the Syrian Church's seminary at Kottayam where besides theology; Latin, Greek and Syriac were taught. Cf. Mathew, *Churches of St. Thomas...*, 56.

[42]It serves as a study center for theological education in Post-Graduate degree levels/courses – Masters in Theology (M.Th.) and Doctoral in Theology (D.Th.) in almost all the disciplines

Retracing a little bit back, we will find that with the departure of the first group from the Mother Church and then with the dissociation of the Mission from it, there remained only the two groups – one that is ready to reform their church from within, and then the other that is sworn to remain loyal till the end to their original tradition. The former of the two remnants began to carry out its reforming work with such an effect that the latter loyal group broke its silence and opposed the reformists. Consequently, the differences between the two began to give birth to unpleasant events, confrontations, suspicions and ugly accusations that the reformed party moved itself away from the adamant original party and thus brought in a great schism between the 'once-united' Syrian Christian Church.

The long years of battle between the reform group and the anti-reform group within the Syrian Christian Church (which also indirectly represent the long-lasting effects of the Mission's remarkable imprint upon the history of the Syrian Church) culminated with the final disposal in the Royal Court of Appeal in Trivandrum in the year 1889. It was under the leadership of Thomas Mar Athanasius, nephew of Mathews Mar Athanasius (and son of Abraham Malpan while Mathews Mar Athanasius was the nephew of Abraham Malpan) that the reform party left the Old Seminary to the anti-reform party and received by the court's sanction, the Maramon and Kozencherry Churches and the Kottarakara Church. This departed group assumed a new name called the 'Mar Thoma Syrian Church'[43] and the traditionalist group left behind also assumed a new and more emphatic name called the 'Syrian Orthodox Church.'

2.4. Theological Education of the St. Thomas Christians at Present

The political power of the Dutch in India yielded to that of the British. This change had a far-reaching consequence for the Syrian Church. From the year 1806 missionaries of the Church of England began to make contacts with it, and encouraged by the sympathy which they expressed, the Syrian Church welcomed the offer of a *Good Will Mission* to be sent by the Anglican Church. The Mission started its work, but in less than two decades it proved a failure. So, in 1836 those Syrian Christians who had accepted the Protestant teaching of the missionaries had embraced the Anglican Church.[44]

Another group endeavored to reform the entire Church in the light of ideas imbibed from the missionaries. The work of this latter group is of some importance for an understanding of the nineteenth century history of the Syrian Church. Supported by the Anglican mission, they sent their nominee,

---

of theology which include Old Testament; New Testament; History of Christianity; Christian Theology; Religion; Christian Ministry etc., under the Senate of Serampore University.

[43]Cf. Juhanon, *History of the Mar Thoma Syrian Church…*, 26-27.

[44]Cf. F. E. Keay, *A History of the Syrian Church in India* 3rd edition (Delhi: ISPCK, 1960), 85. (Hereafter, Keay, *A History of the Syrian Church in India…*).

Deacon Mathews. The Syrian Patriarch of Antioch had a hope of having him consecrated as Metropolitan of the Indian Church, so that through him their reform activity might be carried out successfully. Thinking in all probability that he was helping the ancient Church of India, the Patriarch consecrated Deacon Mathews as Metropolitan Mathews Mar Athanasius, without a proper enquiry into the question at issue. He was in fact the first Indian bishop to be consecrated directly by the Syrian Patriarch of Antioch. On his return to India, Mathews Mar Athanasius had to face strong opposition from the Church, which had now come to split into two groups - one supporting the new Metropolitan and the other refusing him.[45]

The party opposed to Mar Athanasius made representations to the Patriarch and even sent their candidate Father Joseph, for consecration as Metropolitan. He came back as Metropolitan Joseph Mar Dionysius and began to work in opposition to Mar Athanasius, who had now lost his confidence with the Patriarch. Mar Athanasius died in 1877 but before his death he and his party appointed a successor without reference to the Patriarch. The struggle between the two parties lasted several decades with litigation in court, which was decided finally against the reform party. Now, they organized themselves as an independent Church and in course of time assumed the name 'Mar Thoma Syrian Church'. This Mar Thoma Syrian Church claims to be the reformed branch of the ancient Syrian Church. Now, it is an independent Episcopal Church. For the purpose of training its priesthood they maintained a theological seminary at Kottayam namely Mar Thoma Theological Seminary, which is developed in line with the contemporary trends of theological education.[46]

In 1875 Patriarch Peter IV visited the Syrian Church in India and consecrated six Metropolitans in addition to Joseph Mar Dionysius. In spite of the fact that during the three centuries following the sixteenth century the ancient Syrian Church in India came to suffer a considerable loss in its membership, it emerged in the twentieth century as quite a strong Christian community in Kerala, South India. But, soon it fell into evil days involving internal feuds and litigations in court, which lasted about half a century. However, this was also a period of many developments and great achievements. Thus, the Catholicate was established in 1912. The Syrian Patriarchs in the See of Antioch opposed this as well as about a third of the Church's own membership and it resulted in a split in the Church for half a century. However, the problem has been solved by the Patriarch Ignatius Yacub III who recognized the Catholicate unconditionally. By this action of Patriarch Ignatius Yacub III unity has been restored in the Orthodox Syrian Church of India. During this period the Church organized the Sunday

---

[45]Cf. Keay, *A History of the Syrian Church in India...*, 87-89. See also Xavier, Koodapuzha, *Christianity in India* (Kottayam: OIRSI, 1998), 134-137. (Hereafter, Koodapuzha, *Christianity in India...*).

[46]Keay, *A History of the Syrian Church in India...*, 90-92.

School Association, Youth Movements, and Evangelistic Associations etc.[47] The Church has also reconstituted its Theological Seminary along modern lines and organized churches and congregations in almost all important cities in India as well as in a few places outside.

It was in the year 1815 the Orthodox Syrian Christians started the Orthodox Theological Seminary in Kottayam, Kerala, to train their clergy.[48] The indigenous ministry of the Syrian Churches and the methods it uses in its ministerial training programmes until recently has affinities with the ***guru-chela*** ideal of Hindu tradition.[49]

Although, the Syrian Churches in general have also come to some extent in relation to their attempts in improvising their theological education structures and methods toward modern lines, several aspects of its ecclesiastical forms still cling on to the traditional patterns. For instance, parochial autonomy, a cherished tradition among the Syrian Christians, still continues to grow strong. The clergy of the Syrian Orthodox Church are elected by the parishioners when they were boys. After the completion of their theological training at the seminaries, they are commissioned by the bishops for the work of the parish. It is after the completion of their theological training at the Institutions, which are attached to the Seats of bishops that they are ordained deacons, priests and so on.[50]

In those early days, the institutions and seminaries of the Syrian Orthodox Church does not offer as today, systematic course in theology, church history, the Bible and pastoralia. Their theological instruction was mainly confined to the study of the Syrian liturgy, the proper performance of which is regarded as an important part of the priest's training.

The Orthodox Theological Seminary at Kottayam, Kerala represents a modern form of theological education under the Syrian Orthodox Christians. Here, a systematic course in divinity is combined with their traditional liturgical teaching. Although there is a growing desire among the Syrian Orthodox Christians to ordain only those men who have completed their theological training to priesthood, the old heritage of parochial autonomy serve to hinder its progress, so also the traditional practice of ordaining young boys to the deaconate continue to exist.[51] Nevertheless, despite some hindrances toward its attempts for changes,

---

[47]Cf. Koodapuzha, *Christianity in India...*, 152.

[48]Cf. Oommen-Mabry, *The Christian Clergy in India...*, 60.

[49]Cf. Ranson, *The Christian Minister...*, 18. Its method of training the clergy was characterized by their custom of ordaining young boys to the deaconate and then sends them to live with some experienced priests for a period of years. Usually, a group of two or three young deacons would live together with mentor as members of his family. It is from the mentor that they acquire knowledge of the liturgy and the Bible besides which, they also gain some practical experiences of parish ministry. Even today, some traces of this old method remains.

[50]Cf. Oommen-Mabry, *The Christian Clergy in India...*, 62. However, practice of this tradition has now become uncommon.

[51]Cf. Ranson, *The Christian Minister...*, 19.

the Syrian Orthodox Church continues to grow in its ministry especially in its training of the clergy in its various theological seminaries and institutions.

From 1914 onward the significant development within the Syrian Churches is that good numbers of Syrian Christian students, both from the Orthodox as well as the Mar Thoma Churches have received theological training in different seminaries outside their own seminaries. Moreover, they have joined in furthering theological education in India in the form of ecumenism by coming together with the Church of South India by forming FFRRC[52] in which they give training for both Masters Level and Doctoral Level for all the candidates drawn from various denominations today.

3. Theological Education under the Roman Catholic Church in India

In 1493 Pope Alexander VI divided the Eastern Western worlds between the kings of Portugal and Spain. The king of Spain was given the West and the king of Portugal, the East[53], as their respective spheres of influence.[54] In 1514 Pope Leo X granted the king of Portugal patronage over churches which they established in the East[55] and thus, under the aegis of the Portuguese imperial dominion, the Western church was established in India. Goa became the principal pivot of the Portuguese India. The first attempts to train Indian priests were made by the architect of the Portuguese empire in the East, Albuquerque himself. In 1514 he sent an Indian, Antonio de Costa to Portugal in order to be trained there as a preacher, "to learn what belongs to the Faith and how to preach the Faith".[56] In 1521 the first four Indian Franciscans received Holy Orders in Goa.[57] In 1532, after ecclesiastical affairs were more consolidated, some more were ordained.[58] However, throughout the first four decades there was no organized attempt to

[52]It stands for 'Federated Faculty for Religion and Culture in Kerala.' However, at present, owing to its sensitivity toward the reality and need for ecumenism, the addition 'in Kerala' is not in use. Another important factor behind its change is because under the FFRRC program, enrolment of student candidates is open to all regions, states and denominations in India.

[53]When on May 20th 1498 Vasco da Gama steered his flagship St. Gabriel with European soldiers and missionaries on board into the port of Calicut, a new epoch began for the whole of the East. A chain of trading stations was opened along the West coast of India and in each commercial center a resident chaplain was appointed.

[54]Cf. Ranson, *The Christian Minister...*, 20.

[55]In 1518 Pope Leo X also granted an important privilege to the king of Portugal, the permission to ordain colored candidates who had come to Portugal, giving at the same time generous dispensations from the ecclesiastical impediments resulting from their former pagan background.

[56]Anithil, *The Theological Formation of Clergy...*, 33.

[57]*Ibid.*

[58]In 1537 the Sacred Penitentiary granted the bishop of Goa the faculty of conferring Holy Orders on any baptized candidate, whether newly converted to the faith or Christian descent, of his own diocese or of another diocese, secular or religious, provided he was fit, and in the case of a secular, provided he had the necessary title.

train native candidates for priesthood. Most of them, in order to reach their goal had to undergo the long and dangerous journey to Portugal and back to India.[59]

3.1. The First Organized Attempts to Train Clergy under the Roman Catholicism

The first attempt to establish a seminary in the East was made by Fr. Diego da Borba, a former Franciscan, and Miguel Vaz, the Vicar General of Goa. This effort of giving theological education to the native clergy was followed by Franciscans and the Jesuits missionaries. Later on, the Dominicans and Augustinians followed suit. All of them started their own training centers and colleges, catering for the education of the native youth with the ultimate intention of fostering also indigenous vocations.[60]

3.1.1. *The Seminary of Santa Fe' (St. Paul's College) Goa*

In 1541 Fr. Diego da Borba and Miguel Vaz founded a pious association called 'Confraria de Sante Fe' with the general aim of promoting the propagation of Catholic faith and of assisting the new converts in their manifold needs.[61] It was in this confraternity that the first seminary of the East took shape,[62] in fact a central seminary for the whole of the Portuguese empire in the East.[63] The seminary remained in the control of the Confraternity till 1548. It was offered first to the Franciscans who declined the offer, and then to the Jesuits who finally took over.[64] In 1548 the seminary received its first rector in the person of Fr. Antonio Gomes, S. J. who was specially sent from Portugal for this post.[65] The new rector started immediately to make the college a model seminary for the East. He took the University of Paris as his ideal for the intellectual formation and the ascetical formation according to the Jesuits seminary of Coimbra. The result of these

---

[59]In India there was hardly any chance for the native to be ordained as priests, mainly due to the low standard of education and the lack of appropriate schools.

[60]Cf. Anithil, *The Theological Formation of Clergy*..., 33. Indian boys were taken in large numbers into such colleges and some of them were eventually selected and trained for the priesthood.

[61]Cf. C. Merces De Melo, *The Recruitment and Formation of the Native Clergy in India* (Lisbon: 1955), 70. (Hereafter, De Melo, *The Recruitment and Formation of the Native Clergy*...).

[62]It was first conceived only as a kind of catechetical school to train suitable helpers for the missionaries.

[63]The new seminary was called the 'Seminary of Santa Fe' but later on it came to be known as the 'College of St. Paul.' It was to recruit its candidates from all races of the eastern world, from the Negroes to the Chinese. They were to be taken only at an age when they would not forget their mother tongue anymore, that is, when they were at least thirteen years old.

[64]Cf. Anithil, *The Theological Formation of Clergy*..., 71. The number of the alumni grew fast and in the first five years it reached sixty native candidates, which were accepted for the training. Twice a day they conversed in their mother tongue according to the different languages groups.

[65]Cf. *Ibid.*, 34. Besides Francis Xavier there were no able Jesuits in India at that time.

changes had an adverse affect on the seminary, as most of the students ran away and the rests were dismissed.[66] In 1515 the seminary was formally entrusted to the Society of Jesus and henceforth the whole intellectual and spiritual formation as well as administration was taken over by the Jesuits. The rector was removed and replaced by Fr. Barzaeus a Jesuits.[67] In the course of time the college became an ecclesiastical multipurpose institute, destined for the training of catechists, of secular priests and of candidates for the Society of Jesus and Jesuits scholastics. The daily order followed the general Jesuit pattern: daily meditations, examination of conscience, rosary and litanies. The students had to sing, in the morning and evening, for half an hour St. Francis Xavier's catechism called 'Doutrina' a very original form of the monastic hours.[68] The College continued more or less in this way till the suppression of the Society in Portuguese territories by Pombal in 1759.[69]

3.1.2. *The Regional Seminaries of the Different Religious Orders*

3.1.2.1. *The Jesuits*

By 1600 the Jesuits had established the following colleges: St. Paul's College in Goa; the Colleges of Margao; Chaul; Cochin and Damao. These were added with those of Quilon, Mannar, Basein, Vaipincotta and Tuticorin, which developed into full-fledged seminaries.[70] Fr. Lancilotto founded the college of Quilon in 1549 as a small catechetical school where at the beginning only reading and Latin grammer was taught. The seminary of Tuticorin was founded in 1587 under General Aquaviva. In 1596 the first 3 priests of this seminary were ordained. The seminary of Basein was originally founded by the Franciscan Fr. Antonio de Porta and handed over to the Jesuits in 1551. The seminary of Vaipincotta as mentioned earlier was intended for the St. Thomas Christians.[71]

3.1.2.2. *The Franciscans*

The Franciscans, prior to the Jesuits, had started schools and colleges and finally some seminaries. Their main seminary was in Reis Magos on the Peninsula of Bardez, and in the North, in the region of Bombay, they had the houses of Caranja, Nagasaim and Sasette; in the South the College of Cranganore and in Ceylon the College of Colombo and Jaffna.[72] In studies as well as in the whole training the

[66]In their place some two dozens Portuguese boys were taken in, though this was explicitly against the original status of both the ecclesiastical and state authorities.

[67]Cf. Anithil, *The Theological Formation of Clergy…*, 35.

[68]Ibid., 36.

[69]Cf. De Melo, *The Recruitment and Formation of the Native Clergy…*, 73-74.

[70]Cf. Anithil, Anithil, *The Theological Formation of Clergy…*, 39-40.

[71]Cf. De Melo, *The Recruitment and Formation of the Native Clergy…*, 136-139.

[72]Cf. Anithil, *The Theological Formation of Clergy…*, 40.

Franciscans followed their own old tradition. In the system of teaching they did not confine themselves to any particular schools. There was no compulsion in this matter and good deal of freedom was left to the individual teacher.[73]

3.1.2.3. *The Dominicans*

The Dominicans came to India entirely dedicated to their specific task of teaching the sacred sciences. In 1548 they established themselves in Goa. In 1596 at Panelim they opened the academic college of St. Thomas Aquinas. The teaching was public and was attended both by the religious of the convent as well as by outsiders, clerics and lay people. The principal subject taught was, according to Dominican tradition, the Holy Scripture in connection with the different theological questions were treated. Also the usual art course was taught, which constituted the basis for theological studies.[74]

3.1.2.4. *The Augustinians*

They too established their own seminary on the outskirts of Goa, in Neura-o-Grande in 1622. Though they came to India in 1572, it was only after many years that they received natives into their orders of trainings.[75]

3.2. The Ecclesiastical Legislation on Seminary Training

The norms which the Council of Trent gave for the priestly training in general and for theological studies in particular, were a new approach to the age old problem: how to train priests in the best way for their future ministry?[76] The Tridentine decrees mark a decisive point in the history of theological training for the Roman Catholic Church in India.[77] The 3rd Council of Goa in 1585 took up the decrees of Trent that had been published before 20 years back concerning seminary training and applied them to India.[78] Ecclesiastical legislation on seminary training was mainly concerned with the Latin clergy. Here, three important modifications of the general directions given by the Council of Trent were made effective for the seminary training in India. They were:

---

[73]Cf. *Ibid.*, 41. They had four classes a day. Great stress was laid on singing. Strong emphasis was also laid on liturgy.

[74]Cf. *Ibid.*, 41. They had four classes a day. Great stress was laid on singing. Strong emphasis was also laid on liturgy.

[75]Cf. Anithil, *The Theological Formation of Clergy...*, 42.

[76]Cf. S. J. Kane, *A History of Education* (Chicago: 1935), 149-156. See also, Anithil, *The Theological Formation of Clergy...*, 43-45.

[77]Cf. A. P. Farrel, *The Jesuit Code of Liberal Education* (Milwaukee: 1938), 342.

[78]Two subsequent councils of Goa confirmed the same policy, stressing or the other point.

i) The age for ordination was raised from 25 as given by Trent, to 30.[79] The 5th Council of Goa, 21 years later, when the number of the native clergy had already increased, took even stricter measures in these points.[80]
ii) The caste restrictions, which in practice were officially extended to the clerics. Henceforth only sons of noble castes could be admitted to the priesthood.[81] The 5th Council of Goa gave further specifications in this regard. Only Brahmins and Prabus could be ordained.
iii) The standards of clerical studies, required for a priest with the Indian situation were: first of all, a candidate must have a good knowledge of the vernacular of the country for which they were destined. They should have also sufficient knowledge of Latin and enough training in dealing with moral problems of the ordinary life. Finally, they would be given such a general pastoral formation that would enable them to help in the conversation work and in the care of the newly converted Christians.[82]

The seventeenth and the eighteenth centuries are considered as the dark period for the mission of the Roman Catholic Church in India. Internal conflicts intensify external upheaval in the virtual extinction of the Church in many parts of India.[83] It was only in the nineteenth century that the restoration of the Roman Catholic missions in India took place, under the inspiration of Pope Gregory XVI. His policy of extension of vicariates apostolic and his significant contributions, all helped to consolidate and revive the mission work of the Roman Catholic Church in India. The most outstanding feature of this rehabilitation period was the expansion of seminaries for training of Indian clergy. For the purpose of serving the whole of India, the Papal seminary at Kandy was established in 1896. The Jesuit scholasticates of Kurseong in Bengal and Shembaganur in South India, were established in 1889 and 1895 respectively.

With the influx of foreign missionaries and the expansion of the indigenous priesthood, the Roman Catholic Church and its mission grew in number as well as in its religious influence. Its increasing growth continued in the twentieth century and reached up to 4,061,451 in its number of baptized membership. Between

---

[79]Those candidates who were converted as adults were to be ordained only 15 years after their conversion, and only after 30 years they could be entrusted with the regular care of souls. No sons of pagan parents could be ordained.

[80]Cf. Anithil, *The Theological Formation of Clergy...*, 46-47.

[81]The lower castes and the vast majority of outcastes were to be excluded. In any case, only those castes that were considered respectable in the countries for which the candidates were to be ordained would be admitted. Two reasons were given for these restrictions (i) A better selection and, (ii).A higher esteem for the priesthood as a whole which otherwise would have been exposed to the contempt of the higher classes, if access to it would have been open to the lower or outcastes.

[82]Cf. Anithil, *The Theological Formation of Clergy...*, 47.

[83]Cf. Ranson, *The Christian Minister...*, 23.

1851 and 1941, the priesthood of the Roman Catholic Church has expanded from 1092 to 4578.[84] Beside its general expansion, there is also the expansion of its theological seminaries in India. Diocesan seminaries, scholasticates of the religious orders, junior seminaries, apostolic schools and novitiates have all been gradually increased. Thus, the indigenous ministry under the Roman Catholic Church grew and expanded mostly due to their increasing establishments of their seminaries where they train their clergy in theological education for the mission of the Church in India.

3.3. Individual Churches-centered and deep indigenized-oriented theological education in the 20th century within the various rites of the Indian Roman Catholics: A departure from the earlier Tridentine form of Theological Education

3.3.1. *The Tridentine form of Theological Education of the Roman Catholic Church*

The ecclesiastical legislation on Seminary Training made in the council of Trent through its popular decrees concerning the establishment of seminaries eventually achieved the decisive reforms that were promulgated in 1553 and made obligatory in the following year in 1554. This became the fundamental law of the Latin Church and served as the norm for the training of her priests.[85] This Tridentine decrees revolve around the following aspects of reforms:

1. To establish separate seminaries for theological training of the secular priests.
2. These ecclesiastical training centers to be diocesan institutions and under the direct jurisdiction of the bishops. Every diocese is to have its own seminaries (with the provision for joint-ventures for those dioceses that are too small in structure to establish own seminaries).
3. Selection of fitting candidates (with special emphasis on those coming from poor backgrounds), good moral testimony and other necessary qualifications. Age for enrolment is not to be below 12.
4. Ecclesiastical resources to be the basic source of support for these seminaries.
5. The main aim of the seminaries being a life of separation from the worldly pleasures, being marked for the priestly future, the seminarians were required to don their tonsure and habit throughout their ministerial life.

[84]Of which, 2,795 are secular or diocesan priests and 1,783 are members of religious orders or societies. Cf. Ranson, *The Christian Minister...*, 24.

[85]Cf. Anithil, *The Theological Formation of the Clergy...*, 43-44.

A remarkable aspect about this Tridentine form was its emphasis on solid intellectual training after the principles of a sound scholastic philosophy which mean that formation of priesthood is constituted by 3 main parts namely, humanistic studies; philosophy; and, theology. The underlying principle of this form is the conviction that the whole theological formation must be on organic unity, and that the supernatural must be built upon the solid ground of nature as per the theological axiom "gratia supponit naturam."[86]

Theological Formation of the Roman Catholics in the Post-Tridentine Especially the 20th Century.

While the Latin Church in general and the Indian Roman Catholic Church in particular held in great respect the Tridentine decrees, the Churches also had to experience a great deal of struggles with the ever-increasing winds and aspects of changing times. Hence, as time and atmosphere progresses, the Church faces the serious challenges that confront its theological training form and contents especially with regard to meaning and relevancy.

India's cultural realities serve as a Herculean task for both the parent church at Rome and the native churches here in India. There were several attempts invested in responding meaningfully to the issues faced by the churches theological formation program. Amidst various efforts of the church to make theological training in India realistically relevant for India's context, the emphasis on learning vernacular language was commendable. Seminaries in India therefore stress upon this vernacular aspect so that their candidates could easily communicate and work among the given non-Christian population. Besides, seminaries in India were not required to be strictly along Western line in their theological program as their goal is to train and produce missionaries for the conversion of India.[87]

In accordance with the Tridentine decrees, a number of minor seminaries were established in India especially during the period between the latter part of the 19th and the early part of the 20th centuries. On the 18th of May 1893, a central seminary for the whole of India was established at Kandy (Ceylon), which was a stepping-stone in the history of the formation of the Indian clergy. Nevertheless, in the historic period of transition, the goal of the formation of the Indian clergy was not left undisturbed by several threatening obstacles. Major among the obstacles was the lack of financial resources that were needed for the survival and maintenance of the seminaries including also the lack of enough teaching personnel.[88]

Another serious obstacle was the caste factor of the Indian society and its inextricable imprint upon the total structure of its population. In fact, this obstacle could have easily given a hair-splitting dilemma to those early mission personnel

---

[86]Cf. Anithil, *The Theological Formation of the Clergy...*, 44.

[87]*Ibid.*, 106.

[88]*Ibid.*, 116.

taking charge of the seminaries and their training programs.[89] Eventually, after weighing every alternate possibilities they could come up with only one solution and that was, to bring in Western/European form of education that would not have anything to do with caste issue and by which (the personnel assumed) the Indian candidates could be made to overcome their slavery to casteism. While it served well to unite the hitherto divided members of the Indian church and brought them all under a greater sense and structure of unity and also very importantly brought the standard of India's theological formation at the same level with their European counterparts, yet this western-oriented form of theological education failed miserably in responding to the concrete problems of India's population and the Indian church as a whole.

As such, even in the first decades of the 20th century, theological formation in India especially in the Roman Catholic churches, remained or followed western standards laid down by Rome, the headquarter of the Roman Catholic mission. However, things began to change and there appeared within the general atmosphere of the Roman Church a growing consciousness for the accommodation and adaptation of the local cultures and contextual realities of the mission churches and most especially too in India in its theological formation of the Indian clergy. Eventually, the Indian clergy could qualify themselves for taking up the responsibility to oversee the needs and functions of the native church. Hence, by the third decade of the 20th century (1926 to be exact), the central seminary at Kandy was empowered to confer all degrees in philosophy and theology including the doctoral degrees. In 1931 therefore, this papal seminary in India achieved its momentum by being recognized academically on a par with the Gregorian University in Rome.[90]

A characteristic feature that distinguishes the Papal seminary from the Senate of Serampore College under the Protestant mission is that the Papal seminary unlike the latter, did not become an affiliating center for other Roman Catholic seminaries and instead it then stood as the one and only Catholic Degree faculty in the whole of India, Pakistan, Burma and Ceylon. Following this nature of difference between the Roman Catholic form of theological education and the

---

[89]We are informed that the major part of the church's congregation being made up of people from the lower/outcastes, it is also this section that forms the majority among the candidates who come for theological training. This serve to trouble the decisions of the responsible personnel who discover that almost all of these candidates do not have the potentiality to take up rigorous theological education besides which, even when they are finally sent out to the fields for the ministry, people do not take them seriously or respect them due to their lower caste background. On the other hand, candidates from the higher castes show great potentiality but are very few in number and at the same time, when this successful candidates are sent out for the mission work, they identify themselves as high castes and therefore they refuse to work among the low castes population and vice-versa. Such were the obstacles that the early missionaries confronted in their missionary work among the caste-stratified population of India.

[90]Cf. Anithil, *The Theological Formation of the Clergy*..., 132.

SSC's, several other differences could be discovered. Prominent among them would be like the variety of curriculum between the different Catholic seminaries and institutions, non-uniformity in their structural sizes, their size or number of staff, and also their medium of instructions where the papal seminaries emphasizes more on the learning of the Latin, Portuguese, French, and English with little or no emphasis at all for the vernacular language. In contrast, the colleges and seminaries under the SSC and Protestant mission stresses on the importance of the vernacular or the native tongue as it is seen as a pre-requisite thing for the spread and work of the Gospel among the native population.

3.4. The 20th Century Roman Catholic Training Program in India: A Radical Shift from the Earlier Tridentine Form

The actual change in Indian Roman Catholic theological formation began toward the end of the 1st half of the 20th century. The earlier conformation to the western Catholic theological tradition began to wear off in relation to the church and its mission in India. Hence, despite great significance in the standardizing of Indian theological system, its failure to adapt and respond meaningfully to peoples' practical life situations became more pronounced and more urgent. Modernization and Indianization emerged as catalysts that necessitated a radical upheaval in the total structure of theological formation of the Indian clergy. In other words, what India needed at this juncture was to re-shaping its theological system after the nature of the challenging demands of India's changing context so that it could adequately and meaningfully respond to the needs of the then Indian society.

Thus, Indian theological system gradually welcomed the structure of modernization into its system and introduced some important secular subjects such as the natural sciences, mathematics, physics and chemistry. Besides, it also introduced into the training of its ministerial candidates, a great measure of experimental psychology, pedagogy, and sociology. It is also with equal fervor that Indian theological system welcomed the growing movement of Indianization within its structure of clergy formation. Although, there were some sporadic concerns and efforts of the Indian seminaries toward emphasizing the necessity of indianization, it was not until the post-independent era that indianization took concrete form.[91] The study of the vernaculars, Sanskrit, Indian Religions, Indian Philosophy and India's Historic Cultural Reality thus became the core components of seminary training curriculum in India.

The Charter of 27th July 1926, issued by the Holy See, upgraded the Papal Seminary at Kandi to the status of a Pontifical College with the right and privilege of conferring the academic degrees of Baccalaureate, Licentiate and Doctorate in Philosophy and Theology. Then again, in the Statutes of 1940 that was approved by the Congregation for Catholic Education, the Pontifical Athenaeum with its

---

[91]Cf. Anithil, *The Theological Formation of the Clergy...*, 138.

Faculties of Philosophy and Theology was given an independent status with its own academic and administrative set up.[92]

In 1955, the Papal Seminary along with the Pontifical Athenaeum was transferred from Kandi, Sri Lanka to Pune and very close to De Nobili College – the Jesuit Formation.

House, which was already there at Ramwadi, Pune. The entire process of transfer and relocation to Pune was done under the supervision of the then Jesuit Superior of Pune. It was after this event that the Pontifical Athenaeum stretched itself beyond its limited scope (i.e., catering to the needs of the Papal seminarians) and opened itself up to the students of the Society of Jesus as well as to students of other religious congregations. Eventually in the revised Statutes of 1972, the Pontifical Athenaeum adopted an Indian name for itself as 'Jnana-Deepa Vidyapeeth.' At present, JDV is open to all students who fullfil its admission requirement irrespective of creed or gender and the degrees it confer in Philosophy and Theology are Bachelors, Masters and Doctoral degrees.

4. Theological Education under the Protestant Church

Protestant Christianity in India[93] was direct results of the European and American.

---

[92] *jdvindia.googlepages.com/historyofjdv-23k*, 1.06.09.

[93] The first Protestant Christianity came to India in the early part of the 18th century. During this century the European nations that settled in India were the Dutch at Pulicat (1609), Sadras (1647) and Negapatam (1660), the British at Masulipatam (1622), Madras (1639), Cuddalore (1683) and Calcutta (1669), the French at Pondicherry (1674), the Danes at Tranquebar (1620), and Serampore (1676). The French were Roman Catholics and the rests were Protestants. However, they had no intention to spread the gospel in India, but their sole aim and concern was for trade and profit. Cf. C. B. Firth, *An Introduction to Indian Church History* (New Delhi: ISPCK, 2001), 131. (Hereafter, Firth, *An Introduction to Indian Church History*...). Though, the Protestant Christianity goes side by side with the colonial flag, it was not the colonial expansion, which spread Protestant Christianity. It was the 18th century spiritual awakenings that gave Protestant Christians the biblical motive to share the gospel of Jesus Christ to others. In England, the Society for Promoting Christian Knowledge (SPCK) was formed in 1698, and Society for the Propagation of the Gospel (SPG) in 1701 for the purpose of carrying the gospel to foreign land. In 1705 King Fredrick IV of Denmark founded the Danish Halle Mission (Tranquebar Mission), and it had sent the first Protestant missionaries to India in 1706. In 1792 the British Missionary Society was founded; in 1795 the London Missionary Society; the Church Missionary Society in 1799; the Religious Tract Society in 1799; the British and Foreign Bible Society in 1804. In Europe, the Netherlands Missionary Society was founded in 1796; Basel Mission in 1815; the Gossner Society in 1836. In USA, the American Board of Commission for Foreign Mission was founded in 1810; the American Baptist Mission in 1814; the Methodist Mission and Bible Society in 1819; the Presbyterian Foreign Mission Society in 1837. These Protestant missionary societies sent numerous missionaries to Asian countries, which resulted in the spread of Protestant Christianity in India also. Cf. F. Hrangkhuma, *An Introduction to Church History* (Bangalore: Theological Book Trust, 1999), 351-357. Van Den Berg, Johannes, *Constrained by Jesus' Love* (Rotterdam: J.H. Kok and N.V. Kampen, 1956), 45-56.

Colonial, commercial and missionary expansion during the post reformation period, particularly the eighteenth and the nineteenth centuries. [94] In India till 1813 mission work was forbidden by the charter of the East India Company, the then ruling British India. During this period the first organized protestant missionary efforts were limited to Tranquebar[95] and Serampore under Danish settlement.[96] With the removal of the clause in 1813, the protestant mission in India started large scale of theological training. Each denomination maintained their position and propagated its own method of teaching and its own pattern of organizing discipline; as a result, the Christian denominations came into existence in India, [97] such as Methodist, Baptist, Anglican, Presbyterian and so on. This

[94]Cf. R.W. Scott, *Evangelism in India* (Geneva: WCC Publications, 1952), 15-16. See also Siga Arles, *Theological Education for the Mission of the Church in India, 1947-1987* (New York: Peter Lang, 1991), 160. What was developed in India was a perfect imitation of the Western Patterns, with minor altercations either proposed by few bearers of Western Christianity or more often demanded by the Indian converts. Both the denominational disunity of Christians and the development of polarization within Indian Protestantism had their precedents in Western Christianity.

[95]It was King Fredrick of Denmark who first took the initiative to sent Protestant missionaries to India. In 1706 Bartholomew Ziegenbalg and Henry Pluetschau were sent to India. In spite of unwelcoming attitude, they began their work by learning Portuguese and Tamil. A printing press was set up at Tranquebar in 1712. In 1711 Ziegenbalg completed a translation of New Testament into Tamil. The first baptism took place on the 12th May 1707. In 1707 on 15th August the native Church named 'the Jerusalem Church' was established. Hence, a strong Protestant Christian congregation was established in South India at Tranquebar. Cf. V. Titus Varghese and P. P. Philip, *Glimpses of the History of the Christian Churches in India* (Madras: CLS, 1983), 53-55.

[96]Cf. Firth, *An Introduction to Indian Church History...*, 233. William Carey an English Baptist arrived in Bengal on the 11th of November 1793 settled at Mudnabalty, 150 miles north of Calcutta for six years and worked as superintendent of indigo factory. In 1799 Joshua Marshman, a schoolmaster and William Ward, a printer, joined him and they went and settled at Serampore under the Danish authority. Thus, began the Serampore mission in 1800.

[97]Moreover, when the East India Company's charter was renewed in 1813, the restrictions against missionaries were removed and consequently the Protestant Missions and missionaries came to the country in rapid succession. Thus, nearly every large Protestant Mission now laboring in India laid its foundations in the 19th century. In 1806 LMS at Travancore; in 1812 the American Board of Commissioners for Foreign Missions at Bombay' and 1834 at Madras,; in 1814 CMS at Madras, 1816 at Travancore, 1820 at Tirunnelvelly, in 1854 at Peshawar; in 1814 Welsh Calvinistic Mission at Bengal; in 1816 Wesleyan Missionary Society in South India; in 1816 the English Baptist Mission at Benares, 1818 at New Delhi; in 1822 the General Baptist in Orissa; 1825 SPG takes over SPCK mission in South India, 1833 at Kanpur, in 1842 at Secunderabad, in 1854 at Delhi; in 1836 Alexander Duff at Calcutta, from Church of Scotland; in 1834 American Presbyterian Mission at Ludhiana; in 1834 Basel German Mission in Malabar; in 1835 American Baptist Mission in Andhra Pradesh, in 1836 at Assam; 1841 Irish Presbyterian Mission in Gujarat; in 1842 American Evangelical Lutheran Mission at Guntur, in 1844 the Free Church of Scotland at Nagpur, in 1846 Gossner's Germen Mission at Ranchi; in 1855 American United Presbyterian Mission at Sialkot; and in 1856 Methodist Episcopal Mission at Bareilly; in 1860 the United Free Church Mission at Rajputana; in 1874 the Canadian Baptist Mission and English Friends Mission on the Andhra coastal area; in 1877 the Cambridge Mission at Delhi; in 1889 the Christian Alliance Mission at Bombay, and large number of smaller organizations and several interdenominational organizations

vast array of different denominations with divergent views on non-essentials and different practices rendered great difficulties among the Christians in India.[98] As such they could present only a divided and disunited front to the people of other faiths. However, in the midst of these diversified denominations, their efforts in theological education were a remarkable one. The pioneer in this field was the Lutheran, the Baptist and the Anglican.[99]

4.1. The Lutheran Training

With the arrival of Ziegenbalg and Pluetschau in Tranquebar on July 9th 1706 Protestant mission began in India. They never lost sight of the great object of forming a native class of ministries. They devoted their time for preaching, translation of Bible into Tamil and establishment of schools. They appointed catechists from the first converts for ministry.[100] After 27 years of their work, the first candidate Mr. Aaron was ordained in 1733 and thus became the first Protestant Indian minister. From 1733-1827 there were only 16 Indians who were ordained in the Tamil Lutheran Church. Almost all of them were trained as catechists before they were ordained.[101] No specifically ministerial Bible Colleges existed for the Lutheran Tamil Church till the 20th century. The Tranquebar Catechist School provided the only theological training on a catechetical level.[102] From the mission boarding schools boys were sent, who after a course of biblical and theological instructions were made catechists in the villages. It was only in the early 20th century that a special Protestant Seminary at Tranquebar was opened for

---

have also come in to the aid of the mission. This record is taken from V. S. Azariah, *India and Christian Movement* (Delhi: CLS, 1936), 67-68.

[98]Cf. Rajaiah D. Paul, *Ecumenism in Action: Church of the South India and Assessment* (Madras: CLS, 1972), 3.

[99]Cf. Anithil, *The Theological Formation of Clergy...*, 182-184. Protestant theological training developed in the West before they were exported to India. The first preachers of the Reformation had been a motley collection of stray scholars, converted priests and monks, pious artisans and the like. These reformers and their successors, and soon the religious bodies organized as Protestant Churches that sprung up everywhere, did not think to establish divinity schools for a formal theological training of their ministers but trained them in an informal way. Later however, under the influence of others they concentrated on the formation of a disciplined and well-trained leadership, taken out of available human materials. Some of the Protestant Churches according to their different structures, required ordained priests, others only laymen who were often chosen mainly for their academic qualifications. The growing churches in the history of Protestant denominations were not to establish formal theological training centers to create educational conditions that could provide suitable men for the ministry. It was with this intention that Protestantism started a large-scale educational movement in all the countries, which it penetrated. The establishment of formal theological training centers, divinity schools and colleges belong to a later period.

[100]The Protestant's first emphasis was laid on catechetical schools rather than on theological colleges.

[101]M. Ward, *Our Theological Task* (Mysore: 1946), 27.

[102]Cf. Anithil, *The Theological Formation of Clergy...*, 184.

classes of ordinands and finally in 1927, the Gurukul Theological Seminary was started in Madras for the training of candidates for the ministry in the Lutheran Church.[103]

The Triennial Conference of the Federation of Evangelical Lutheran Churches in India (later renamed as the United Evangelical Lutheran Church in India – UELCI), which met at Guntur in 1926, felt the need for a theological college for the Lutheran Churches in India. On July 6, 1927 when the college started, only students from TELC were enrolled for the first divinity class. A summer palace bought in 1859 by the Leipzig Evangelical Lutheran Mission from an Indian Raja, became the Centre firstly. Bishop Johannes Sandegren, the first Principal of the college, named it Gurukul, meaning a Guru (teacher) living together with his Sishyas (disciples). Though, it was planned at an All India level it was only in July 1931 that the United Lutheran Theological College (Gurukul) was established with students and staff from United Lutheran Mission (ULM), Andhra Evangelical Lutheran Church (AELC), Church of Sweden Mission (CSWM), Leipzig Evangelical Lutheran Mission (LELM), Danish Missionary Society (DMS) and the Tamil Evangelical Lutheran Church.

In 1953, Gurukul received a new life with a wider participation of the Lutheran Churches and so named as Gurukul Lutheran Theological College & Research Institute. The college was then affiliated to the Senate of Serampore College for Graduate and Post Graduate Studies. Dr. Sigfrid Estborn became its Principal. Then Gurukul merged with the United Theological College, Bangalore and Serampore College, West Bengal in 1971. From then on, Gurukul became a Centre for continuing and extension of education for the churches in India under the stewardship of Dr. K. Rajaratnam.

The reopening of **Bachelor of Divinity (B.D.)** studies at Gurukul by the 20th Triennial Conference held at Madras in 1984 enabled the reviving of the regular B.D. studies at Gurukul from June 1985. A Bold Theological Vision, as envisioned by Dr. K. Rajaratnam, became the cornerstone of academic activities of the college. In 1987, **Master of Theology (M.Th.)** studies was introduced in two branches - Christian Theology and Religions. In fifteen years, new branches - Old Testament, New Testament, History of Christianity, Communication, Women's Studies and Missiology were added. By 1999, with the approval of the SSC, **Doctor of Theology (D.Th.)** program in Christian Theology commenced. Old Testament, Religions, Communication, History of Christianity and others were added later.

Ecumenicity in character and practice is the special feature of the new resurrected Gurukul. It is reflected in the composition of Governing Board, Staff and Students of the College. It is quite obvious as the Gurukul community now is composed of staff and students representing the United Evangelical Lutheran Churches (UELCI), Church of South India (CSI), Church of North India (CNI),

[103]Cf. Anithil, *The Theological Formation of Clergy*..., 184.

Mar Thoma Syrian Church of Malabar (MTC), Orthodox Church, Assembly of God, Mara Evangelical Church, Methodist Church in India (MCI), Baptists, Independent and Charismatic Churches. There are two representatives from the Church of South India and the Church of North India in the College Council.

4.2. The Baptist Theological Education

With the founding of the first Baptist Mission in India in the Danish settlement of Serampore in 1799, the English Baptist Missionaries - William Carey, Joshua Marshman and William Ward, established Serampore College in 1818.[104] According to the charter, the SSC was founded for "the instruction of Asiatic Christians and other youth in Eastern literature and European science".[105] The object of the SSC was "to promote piety and learning particularly among the native Christian population in India".[106] One of the primary concerns of the SSC was the formation of highly qualified Protestant ministers.[107] Though, the college was not exclusively a theological institution but this reflected the aims of the founders (Carey, Ward and Marshman): "that India will never be turned from her grossness of idolatry to serve the true and living God unless the grace of God rest abundantly on converted natives to qualify them for mission work".[108]

In 1827, the Serampore College was granted a charter by the King Fredrick VI of Denmark authorizing it to confer degree in theology and other faculties.[109] The medium of instruction was originally Bengali since the founders were convinced "that the hope of imparting a sound education to the people of the country through the medium of a language not their own was altogether fallacious".[110] Sanskrit had a prominent place in the curriculum and English was to be studied as a learned language. Six years after its foundation, the college had fifty-four students and was reported to receive support from all parties in India irrespective of class or creed. By 1836, the number had risen to one hundred, and the course of study included Greek, Latin, Hebrew, Mathematics, Logic, Natural Philosophy and Divinity.[111]

The Baptist Missionary Society began to support the College actively and in 1856 assumed full responsibility. The SSC got affiliated to the newly founded Calcutta University in 1857. However, in 1884 the Baptist Missionary Society

---

[104]Allen, York, *A Seminary Survey* (New York: 1960), 97. (Hereafter, York, *A Seminary Survey*...).

[105]*Charter of Incorporation of the Serampore College*, 169.

[106]*Ibid.*

[107]Anithil, *The Theological Formation of Clergy*..., l.

[108]Ranson, *The Christian Minister*..., 45.

[109]*Charter of Incorporation of the Serampore College*, 169.

[110]Ranson, *The Christian Minister*..., 46. The vernacular that was gradually given up as the medium of instruction was now finally replaced officially with the English language.

[111]Cf. Ranson, *The Christian Minister*..., 29.

in London decided to stop the university classes at Serampore and henceforth to use the College only for the purpose for which it was originally founded, namely "that of training young men for Christian ministry".[112] Since then, for more than 20 years Serampore College confined its activities exclusively to the theological training.[113] The SSC was again affiliated to the Calcutta University running both Arts and Science section, and the Danish charter was revived for the theological degrees. The first degrees were conferred in 1915.[114] It is now run on Interdenominational level and in 1918 the Serampore Senate was established.[115]

Thus, the SSC occupies a unique place in the history of theological education in India. Besides, its function as a teaching institution, SSC has been fostering ecumenism as the center of the whole collegiate theological education of Protestant Churches in India. It is serving as an ecumenical center by both as an affiliating and examining university and as a theological college providing direct training and preparation for the ministry to students from different denominations and areas. A large portion has come also from South India and especially from the Syrian non-catholic Churches of Malabar, and in this way Serampore has wielded a considerable influence also on the whole of the Churches in India.[116]

4.3. The Anglican Theological Education

The new charter of the East India Company in 1813 allowing the missionaries to work freely in British Indian soil resulted in the establishment of the Anglican mission in India under Bishop Middleton in 1815. His main plan was to work among the Europeans and the policy of converting the native was a slow pace. Though, with much hesitation to ordain the natives, he started mission College Calcutta. The purposes of the institution were to be:

1. It aimed to go as a parallel institution with the Serampore College, by imparting a sound Christian Education to the Christian youth and at the same time at the conversion of the non-Christian students in a cautious way through Western education.
2. It also aimed to instruct the natives and other Christians in the doctrines and discipline of the Church in order to qualify them to become preachers, catechists, and school-masters.

---

[112] Cf. Ranson, *The Christian Minister...*, 47.

[113] Cf. Anithil, *The Theological Formation of Clergy...*, 186.

[114] York, *A Seminary Survey...*, 98.

[115] Cf. Ranson, *The Christian Minister...*, 45-48. See also K. R. Chatterjee, "The Arts-Science Department, 1929-1960" *The Story of Serampore and Its College* (Serampore: The Council of Serampore College, 2005), 57-86.

[116] Cf. Anithil, *The Theological Formation of Clergy...*, 186.

3. For teaching the elements of useful knowledge and the English Language to Mussalmans and Hindus, having no object in such attainments beyond secular advantage.
4. For translating the Scriptures, the Liturgy and moral and religious tracts.
5. For the reception of English missionaries who were to be sent out by the Society, on their first arrival in India.[117]

Hence, the college included for many years both the art and a theological department. However, it did not flourish and for some time ceased to exist. But, with the reorganization of the college in 1918, the college became an exclusively theological institution for training of the Anglican clergy.[118] The College has since served the need of the whole ecclesiastical province in India. Until 1936 the College was very closely associated with Serampore College. However, now the College trains not only the Anglican clergy but also clergies from different denominations who joins the program.

4.4. The Protestant Theological Education at Present

With the removal of the clause forbidding mission work, from the charter of East India Company in 1813, different Protestant denominations came to India. This resulted in extensive conversion campaign, which soon extended all over India. Subsequently mass conversion proved that the need of the hour was not a highly specialized theological trained persons but a numerous village ministry for the rural areas. Thus for instance, "in 1818 there were only 23 ordained Protestant pastors for all the Protestant Societies working in India as against 493 catechists and preachers".[119] The growing need for rural ministers and an increasing number of lay workers caused a shift of theological education policy in India. Without English degrees and even without any knowledge of English, Christian mission native workers were ordained. Thus, most of these ordained Indian ministers between 1830 an1850 had only a rudimentary catechetical training, which was imparted by mission board.[120]

To meet the need of the situation, different Protestant denominations started numbers of seminaries in India. Thus, the C.M.S. started a divinity college at Madras in 1838. The S. P. G. opened a seminary at Sawyerpuram in 1844 and another one at Madras in 1848. The American Mission Societies established seminaries at Ahmednagar and Madurai. The Methodist Episcopal Church opened a seminary at Bareilly. The American Presbyterians Mission and the American United Presbyterian Mission had their training centers at Saharanpur

---

[117]Ranson, *The Christian Minister...*, 32.

[118]Cf. Anithil, *The Theological Formation of Clergy...*, 187.

[119]Ranson, *The Christian Minister...*, 52.

[120]Cf. Anithil, *The Theological Formation of Clergy...*, 187.

and Rawalpindi. The American Baptist opened seminaries in Andhra Pradesh and in Burma. The Dutch Reformed Church of America started their seminary at Vellore. Some of the North Indian seminaries were remarkable for the fact that they insisted on the vernacular as the medium of instruction, and made serious efforts, though with little success, to Indianize their theological education.[121]

In July 1910, the United Theological College, Bangalore was started on interdenominational lines. The aim of the College was to give training of a higher grade of Indian evangelists, pastors and teachers who shall take their place in the growing Indian Church as able and worthy guides and leaders and developers of a rich Christian life and a strenuous propaganda in this land.[122] It was founded by the co-operation of the London Missionary Society, the United Free Church of Scotland (now the Church of Scotland) Mission, and the Arcot Mission of the Reformed Church in America and the Madurai Mission of the American Board of Commissioners for Foreign Missions. Both staff and governing council were composed of representatives of several evangelical Churches. In October 1910 the Serampore College was also organized on the basis of interdenominational line, and in 1918, received its Senate as an examining and affiliating university. In the same year the United Theological College got affiliation to Serampore for the B.D. degree followed by Bishop's College in 1920. In 1922, the Methodist Episcopal Church on Southern Asia established the Indian Methodist Theological College at Bareilly, which was moved to Jabalpur in 1923 and was affiliated with Serampore in 1928. In 1948 it became a union institution and is known today as the Leonard Theological College.[123] BTESSC being the most important theological centre of all Protestant denominations in the region, a growing number of theological schools/colleges/seminaries both in India and abroad are affiliated with the Senate of Serampore College for the recognition of their several theological degrees. At the present day there are around 50 colleges affiliated with the Senate of Serampore College.[124]

However, today the mushrooming of protestant denominational training Bible Seminaries, Colleges, independent institutions and charismatic groups of Bible institutions makes it difficult to bring them under one particular body. Thus, there is a great variety in Protestant theological education both regarding theological input in general, as well as in the practical instruction given. The main group of Seminaries, Colleges affiliated to SSC follows in broad outlines the curriculum prescribed by the Serampore Senate and at the same time, it has given certain space for individual Seminaries and Colleges to choose according to the

---

[121]Cf. Ranson, *The Christian Minister...*, 36-37.

[122]Ibid., 88.

[123]Cf. York, *A Seminary Survey...*, 96-101. See also Ranson, *The Christian Minister...*, 103-113.

[124]For detail information on the affiliated Colleges see appendix I.

given context and relevancy.[125] Those institutions not affiliated to the Senate of Serampore offer their own curricula and courses or just copy some of the western curriculum without seriously considering the relevancy of the context.

Summary

It has been noted that from the first century itself, India had her own native clergy among the St. Thomas Christians on the Malabar Coast. However, the Malabar Christians did not have their own ecclesiastical hierarchy whereby they could ordain their own clergy for priesthood. They had to depend on the ecclesiastical hierarchy of Mesopotamia and therefore, it is the Catholicos of the Chaldean Church who sends his prelates to Malabar at intervals for looking after the needs of the Malabar Christians especially in ordaining the native clergy for the office of priesthood.

The common system for the training of the clergy among the Malabar St. Thomas Christians was established upon the system of *guru-chela* or *gurukulavasam* of the ancient Hindu religious tradition. The *young men* who are elected by the community, are sent to an experienced and elderly priest called Malpan (Syriac Teacher) to be trained under the latter's guidance. It is only after such training is completed were they ordained as deacons and priests by the bishop arriving from South West Asia (or East Syrian Church). Syria. In this system of learning, the young candidates are given basic teaching in Syriac, Scripture and Liturgy. The main purpose of their training as seen was in order that they would be able to read and interpret the sacred Scriptures and at the same time, some of them are given to the study of the Fathers of the Church and theologians. This system of theological training was maintained for several centuries till the 16th century when the first ever attempt for establishing an organized form of theological training surfaced with the Roman Catholic mission under the Portuguese power in India.

It was in the year 1540 that the first seminary for the training of the Syrian clergy was established in Goa, the capital of Portugal Empire in India. However, with the then Roman Catholicism at the wheel of theological education among the Syrian Christians, Latin became the main medium of learning as well as of the Church's life. Not only was the Syrian Christians' fraternal relation with the Churches in the Middle East weakened but also the Syriac language was replaced with Latin. The Portuguese or the Roman Catholic influence thus went beyond trade and military control to that of ecclesiastical control. Thus, half a century later, Syrian Christians rose against the Roman Catholicism marking it in history with the event of the *coonen cross* in 1653, severing their connection with the Roman Catholicism and eventually re-emerged with their own Syrian identity.

Seventeenth and eighteenth centuries saw the Syrian Christians persevering in their reclaimed identity. They did their best in maintaining their own Syrian

[125]In relation to this matter, at the present, the Senate of Serampore's Academic Committee is going through a phase of serious revision of the whole curriculum of the BTESSC.

Christian tradition both in their Church's life as well as in their training system. On the other hand, Roman Catholicism underwent trail period in their mission life and work during these two centuries. It was only in the nineteenth century that Roman Catholicism restored its identity and thenceforth began to steadily expand both in its religious influence as well as in its formation of numerous theological seminaries and institutions in India.

Then the nineteenth and twentieth centuries ushered in the Protestant mission and its influence to India mainly through the Anglican mission (1806) and the Baptist Missionary Society (1800), especially through the missionary efforts of the Serampore Trio. The Syrian Christians in India were once again a subject of the foreign mission's concerns whereby the Anglicans assisted the Syrian Christians of the Malankara Church to start an organized form of theological seminary at Kottayam in 1815. However, despite several positive impacts wrought by the Anglicans toward the Church in India, the Malankara Syrian Christians were not comfortable with the former's impositions of Protestant doctrines upon them, and therefore had to severe their connection with the Anglicans.

With the advent of the English missionaries in the 19th century, new interest in the teaching, liturgy and practices of the local Church took its formation among the Malankara Syrian Church members. They began to critically evaluate certain aspects of the Church's liturgy and practices by weighing them with biblical truths. Yet, such reform spirit was not shared by everyone equally among the Church members. Hence, it resulted in dividing its members between two opposing parties: reformists and non-reformists. Abraham Malpan, a professor of Syriac at the Seminary, and Kaithayail Geevarghese Malpan, led the former group. While still in the Church, they began to implement some of their reforming principles and ideas, which at the end resulted in their excommunication from the Malankar Syrian Church. Those that followed the reformers formed a new Church called *the Syrian Mar Thoma Church* and those that stayed within their old tradition called themselves *the Syrian Orthodox Church.*

For many years, the Church in India has been understood mainly in terms of Western missionary expansion. Today Church historians recognize the fact that while foreign mission has played an important role in its life and growth, the history of the Indian Church is best understood as an independent history.[126] The Protestant mission entered the Indian soil in the 18th century and established itself firmly despite various problems it had to face.[127] The general condition of India during the time the Protestant mission entered was a dilapidated one. Politically, India was under the British rule. Socially, the society was riddled with various social evils. Economically, the people were very poor. Culturally, they were

---

[126]Cf. J. W. Gladstone, *Protestant Christianity and People's Movements in Kerala: A Study of Christian Mass Movements in Relation to Neo-Hindu, Socio-Religious Movements in Kerala, 1850-1936* (Trivandrum: KUTS Publications, 1984), 337-340.

[127]Firth, *An Introduction to Indian Church History...*, 238.

corrupted, and finally religiously, their religion played the source of breeding all kinds of disruptions in the society.[128]

Colonialism and Christian missions went hand-in-hand since the arrival of the Portuguese in India.[129] The Protestant Christianity that came to India during the 18th, 19th centuries followed this colonial expansion[130] alongside their mission of propagating the message of the gospel. During the early period of its inception, the mission and its missionaries could not freely exercise their missionary activities due to various restrictions put up by the British East India Company and its charter. However, with the renewal of its charter in 1813, various Protestant missions and its missionaries thronged to India in rapid succession and thus could establish themselves in almost all the corners of India.

Protestant mission in India had contributed a lot in the area of social activities for the reformation of the Indian society. It established schools and colleges for the education of the illiterate Indian mass for both men and women, which was unheard of in those days; established hospitals and medical institutions that helped care for the sick; organized relief agencies for the needs of the poor and the needy etc. As a result, it came under suspicion by the staunch Hindus and non-Christians that these reforming works of mission were aimed at luring or coercing the poor Indian mass to conversion to Christianity. Although we could not totally refute these accusations, still there is evidence that its mission has indeed immensely improved the condition of the people and has enabled them to restore their total human dignity, which the Hindu religion did not.

We now close our present chapter which focused itself on the historical aspects of the origin, development, nature and structure of the various schools or traditions of theology, and head toward our upcoming second chapter namely, *Historical Background of the Senate of Serampore College* – to see how this historic body of theological education of the Senate of Serampore College came into being and how it developed and began to grow in this great soil of India.

---

[128]Cf. Aleyamma, Zachariah, *Modern Religious and Secular Movements in India* (Bangalore: Theological Book Trust, 1998), 2-4.

[129]Jacob S. Dharmaraj, *Colonialism and Christian Mission: Postcolonial Reflections* (Delhi: ISPCK, 1993), 14.

[130]*Ibid.*, 138.

Chapter 2

Historical Background of the Senate of Serampore College

Introduction

This second chapter will discuss the historical background of the SSC. It will begin with an analysis of the then Political, Socio-Cultural and Religious Conditions of India during the 18th and 19th Centuries, the conditions into which the Serampore Mission entered, encountered and worked for the transformation of the then Indian society in general and particularly for the population of Bengal. Secondly, it will make an attempt to recount the historical background of the Serampore Mission and the College from its inception (1800), till date.

1. Conditions of India during the 18th and 19th Centuries

1.1. Political Condition

India's political history begins not with independence in 1947, but more than 4500 years earlier, when the name *India* referred to the entire subcontinent, including present-day Pakistan and Bangladesh. The earliest of India's known civilizations, the Indus Valley Civilization (about 2500 to 1700 BC)[1], was known for its highly specialized artifacts and stretched throughout northern India. Another early culture, the Vedic culture - dates from approximately 1500 BC

---

[1]The people of India have had a continuous civilization since 2500 B.C., when the inhabitants of the Indus River Valley developed an urban culture based on commerce and sustained by agricultural trade. This civilization declined around 1500 B.C., probably due to ecological changes. The political map of ancient and medieval India was made up of myriad kingdoms with fluctuating boundaries. In the 4th and 5th centuries A.D., northern India was unified under the Gupta Dynasty. During this period, known as India's Golden Age, Hindu culture and political administration reached new heights.

and is considered one of the sources for India's predominantly Hindu culture and for the foundation of several important philosophical traditions. India has been subject to influxes of peoples throughout its history, some coming under arms to loot and conquer, others moving in to trade and settle. India was able to absorb the impact of these intrusions because it was able to assimilate or tolerate foreign ideas and people. Outsiders who came to India during the course of its history include the Greeks under Alexander the Great, the Kushânas from central Asia, the Mongols under Genghis Khan[2], Muslim traders and invaders from the Middle East and Central Asia, and finally the British and other Europeans[3]. Central to Indian history are the people of India who established complex political systems, whether local kingdoms or mighty empires, in which learning and religion flourished. Europeans visited the country to trade for the finest cotton textiles as well as spices. Eventually, the British colonized the region. Their exploitation of India's economic wealth and the subsequent destruction of its indigenous industry provoked and then fueled a nationalist movement, eventually forcing the British to grant India its independence in 1947. Since that time India has developed into a vibrant democracy, making slow but steady progress in development.[4]

The Mughal rule was dying in strength. The Mughal subahdars were struggling to be free within the empire. For example in Bengal, an independent Nawab began to fight to be free. A similar effort was witnessed in Oudh.[5] In the

---

[2]Cf. Valerie, Berinstain, *Discoveries: India and the Mughal Dynasty* (New York: HNA Books, 2005), 234-237. Islam spread across the subcontinent over a period of 500 years. In the 10th and 11th centuries, Turks and Afghans invaded India and established sultanates in Delhi. In the early 16th century, descendants of Genghis Khan swept across the Khyber Pass and established the Mughal (Mogul) Dynasty, which lasted for 200 years.

[3]The first British outpost in South Asia was established in 1619 at Surat on the northwestern coast. Later in the century, the East India Company opened permanent trading stations at Madras, Bombay, and Calcutta, each under the protection of native rulers. The British expanded their influence from these footholds until, by the 1850s, they controlled most of present-day India, Pakistan, and Bangladesh. In 1857, a rebellion in north India led by mutinous Indian soldiers caused the British parliament to transfer all political power from the East India Company to the Crown. Great Britain began administering most of India directly while controlling the rest through treaties with local rulers. Cf. A. M. Mundadan, *History of Christianity in India,* Vol. I (Bangalore: CHAI, 1982), 21-23.

[4]Cf. H. G. Rawlinson, *A Concise History of the Indian People* (Madras: Asia Publication House, 1965), 29-31. See also K. A. Nilakanta Sastri, *A History of South India* (Madras: Asia Publication House, 1976), 44-48. (Hereafter Sastri, *A History of South* India….). Brown, M. Judith, *Modern India, The Origins of an Asian Democracy* (London: Oxford University Press, 1994), 480-483.

[5]The people of India have had a continuous civilization since 2500 B.C., when the inhabitants of the Indus River Valley developed an urban culture based on commerce and sustained by agricultural trade. This civilization declined around 1500 B.C., probably due to ecological changes. The political map of ancient and medieval India was made up of myriad kingdoms with fluctuating boundaries. In the 4th and 5th centuries A.D., northern India was unified under the Gupta Dynasty. During this period, known as India's Golden Age, Hindu culture and political administration reached new heights.

South, the Nizam and his subordinate, the Nawab of Arcot were raising their heads.[6] The Sikhs, the Jats, the Bundelas and the Marathas had established their own independent states and Mysore was emerging as strong power in the South. It was at this situation that the Europeans came to India for trade, but stayed to conquer.[7]

As early as the 15th century, Europeans were interested in developing trade opportunities with India and a new trade route to East Asia. The Portuguese were devoted to this task, and in 1497 Vasco da Gama, a Portuguese royal navigator and explorer, led an expedition around the Cape of Good Hope and across the Indian Ocean. In May 1498 he sailed into the harbor of Calicut on the Malabar Coast, opening a new era of Indian history. Establishing friendly relations with the dominant kingdom of the Deccan, the Portuguese secured lucrative trade routes on the coast of India in the early 16th century.[8]

For about the first two centuries after Europeans arrived in India, their activities were restricted to trade and evangelism, and their presence protected by naval forces. For the entire period of the Mughal Empire, European traders were confined to trading posts along the coast.[9] In the 16th century the Portuguese navy controlled the sea-lanes of the Indian Ocean, protecting the traders settled in Goa, Damân, and Diu on the western coast. Christianity swiftly followed trade. Saint Francis Xavier, a Spanish Jesuit missionary, came to Goa in 1542, converting tens of thousands of Indians along the peninsular coast and in southern India and Ceylon before leaving for Southeast Asia in 1545. In fact, the area of India he and other missionaries traversed was already home to communities of Christians, some converted by Saint Thomas in the 1st century AD and some who fled to India many centuries later to escape persecutions in their own lands.[10]

The Dutch displaced the Portuguese as masters of the seas around India in the 17th century. The Dutch East India Company was founded in 1602, two years after its main rival, the English East India Company. Both companies began by trading in spices, gradually shifting to textiles, particularly India's characteristic light, patterned cottons. The economic effects of purchases made at the coastal

---

[6]Islam spread across the subcontinent over a period of Cf. H.V. Sreenevas, Murthy and S. U. Kamath, *Studies in India Culture* (Madras: Asia Publication House, 1973), 101. (Hereafter Murthy & Kamath, *Studies in Indian Culture*....).

[7]*Ibid.* The Europeans had superior firearms. They had disciplined armies. Their military techniques too were superior. They were, therefore, tempted to turn this strange situation, and created by the petty jealousies and quarrels of the Indian rulers, to their advantage.

[8]Cf. Sastri, *A History of South India*..., 115-120. See also Elamkulam, Kunjan Pillai, *Studies in Kerala History* (Kottayam: 1970), 127-131.

[9]Yusuf, A. Ali, *A Cultural History of India during the British Period* (Bombay: 1969), 147-150. (Hereafter Ali, *A Cultural History of India*....,).

[10]Ferroli, *The Jesuits in Malabar* (Bangalore: Dharmaram, 1939), 234-237.

depots were felt far inland in the cotton-growing areas, but the Europeans did not at that time attempt to extend their political sway.[11]

By the 18th century British sea power matched that of the Dutch, and the European rivalry in India began to take on a military dimension. During the first half of the 18th century the French, who had begun to operate in India in about 1675, emerged as a serious threat to the growing power and prosperity of the English East India Company. By the mid-18th century the British and French were at war with each other throughout the world. This rivalry manifested itself in India in a series of conflicts, called the Carnatic Wars, which stretched over 20 years and established the British as the primary European power in India.[12]

As the French and British skirmished over control of India's foreign trade, the Mughal Empire was experiencing its rapid decline and regional kingdoms were emerging. The continuously warring rulers of these kingdoms used well-trained and disciplined French and British forces to support their military activities. The foreigners, however, had their own agenda, frequently expanding their own political or territorial power under the guise of championing a local ruler.[13] Led by innovative and effective Joseph François Dupleix, the French by 1750 managed to place themselves in a powerful position in southern India, especially in Hyderabad. In 1751, however, British troops under Robert Clive captured the French southeastern stronghold of Arcot in a pivotal battle. With this encounter the balance of power in the south swung to favor the British, although the struggle for control of India's trade continued.[14]

1.1.1. *The East India Company (EIC)*

The political scenario of the country during 18th and 19th centuries in India was marked by incessant warfare. This can be seen in the words of A.B. Purkait, "after the downfall of the Mughal Empire there was no centralized political authority in the country."[15] This gave the opportunity to the British East India Company to exploit the situation and take the advantage upon the internal fighting among the native rulers and began their supremacy in the country.[16] On behalf of the

[11]Cf. Ramakrishna, Mukherjee, *The Rise and Fall of the East India Company: A Sociological Appraisal* (Bombay: Popular Prokashan, 1955), 155-158. (Hereafter Mukherjee, *The Rise and Fall of The East India Company….,*).

[12]*Ibid.*, 177-180.

[13]Ali, *A Cultural History of India…*, 189.

[14]Cf. A. B. Purkait, *Indian Renaissance and Education: From Ram Mohan to Vivekananda* (Calcutta: Firma K.L.M. Ltd, 1992), 15, 16. (Hereafter, Purkait, *Indian Renaissance and Education…*).

[15]*Ibid.*, 39.

[16]Pratap Chandra Gine, *The System of Elementary Education of the Serampore Mission* (Jorhat: ETC, 2001), 11. (Herafter, Gine, *The System of Elementary Education…*). See also Bandyopadhyay, Sekhara, *From Plassey to Partition: A History of Modern India* (New Delhi: Orient Longman, 2004), 525, 526. (Hereafter, Sekhara, *From Plassey to Partition…*).

British East India Company, the resourceful British Governor-General Robert Clive grabbed Bengal in 1757 from its governor Siraj-ud-doulah. Oudh fell from the hands of Wajid Ali Shah and the titular Mughal Emperor Bahadur Shah Zafar was himself packed off in 1857 after the abortive Sepoy Mutiny.[17]

Among the Marathas also this tendency towards disintegration due to rebellious governors like the Bhosales of Nagpur - who never accepted the authority of the Peshwa, the Holkars of Indore, the Gaikwads of Baroda and the Scindias of Gwalior distancing themselves from the authority of the Peshwa at Poona, ultimately caused the downfall of the Maratha empire.[18]

The general increase in defense expenditure, which started with Aurangzeb's Deccan campaign against Shivaji, the firebrand Maratha leader, was kept up later by the numerous battles of Indian monarchs against each other and later against the East India Company. This was an important reason for commercial stagnation.[19] This commercial stagnation of trade within the country was partly responsible for the absence of the rise of a significant merchant capital and its transformation into industrial capital in the 17th and 18th centuries when Indian merchants had established contacts with their European counterparts at Surat, Mumbai (Bombay), Chandranagore, Chennai (Madras), etc. As Indian chieftains and kings badly needed resources to finance their campaigns they levied arbitrary taxes and declared state monopolies over the trade in profitable commodities. Provincial governors often abused their positions to participate in trade either by directly starting trading ventures or by thrusting themselves as partners upon one or more of the prospering merchants, and grabbing fat shares of their profits.[20] These resources were used for financing military campaigns and also for the unproductive squander by the feudal princelings.[21]

Exclusive monopolies for the resale of superior foreign goods were declared much to the detriment of the Indian trading community and the profits were siphoned off to finance a lavish court and feudal lifestyle. In the early days of British rule, the British Viceroys and other colonial administrators collaborated

---

[17]Cf. Alavi, Seema, *The Sepoys and the Company: Tradition and Transition, 1770-1830* (London: Oxford University Press, 1996), 340. (Hereafter, Seema, *The Sepoys and the Company…*). See also Anderson, Clare, *Indian Uprising of 1857-1858: Prisoners, Prisoners and Rebellion* (New York: Anthem Press, 2007), 210-215.

[18]H. S. Bhatia, *Marathas Sikhs and Southern Sultans of India: Their Fight against Foreign Power* (Delhi: Deep and Deep, 2002), 143-150. (Hereafter, Bhatia, *Marathas Sikhs and Southern Sultans of India….*). See also Abraham Eraly, *The Mughal World: India's Tainted Paradise* (New York: HNA Books, 2008), 230-235. (Hereafter, Eraly, *The Mughal World…*).

[19]Bhatia, *Marathas Sikhs and Southern Sultans of India…*, 230.

[20]Sudheer, Birodkar, "Hindu History: A Search for our Present in History," *http://www.hindubooks.org/sudheer_birodkar/hindu_history/index.html* (02-02-2008).

[21]Cf. H. S. Bhatia, *Rival Hindu Kingdoms and Sultans: Fusion of the Hindu Muslim Civilizations* (New Delhi: Deep and Deep Publishers, 2006), 126.

with the Indian feudal nobility to usurp this country.[22] Unlike the fierce struggle between the Muslim monarchy and the Hindu landed nobility in the initial days of Muslim Occupation, the coming of the British power saw a smooth adjustment between the pre-British landed aristocracy and the colonial power. The Jagirdars and Inamdars generally became the Zamindars[23] in the new set-up.

In Bengal, the English East India Company (EEIC) had begun fortifying Calcutta's Fort William to defend against possible attacks by the French. Nominally a part of the Mughal Empire, Bengal was at this time virtually independent under the emperor's nawab (governor). In response to reports of unauthorized activities of the British, the nawab Siraj-ud-Dawhah attacked Calcutta in 1756.[24] Some British survivors of the attack were imprisoned in a small dungeon known as the Black Hole of Calcutta where a number of them died. After the incident, Robert Clive, the then British governor of Fort Saint David, moved north from Madras and, conniving with the commander of his enemy's army, defeated the nawab in the Battle of Plassey in 1757. The battle marked the first stage in the British conquest of India. The French attempted to regain their position in India but were beaten back by the British in 1761. In 1764, the British again defeated local rulers at the Battle of Buxar. This victory firmly established British control over the Bengal region. Treaties made with Indian princes provided for the stationing of British troops within these princely states. To pay for the troops the British were often given revenue-collecting rights in certain parts of the states; this gave them indirect control over these areas. Many of these states were annexed when succession to the throne was in doubt or when the ruler acted in ways that seemed contrary to British interests.[25]

The British made even more significant gains by military means. In the late 1700s they were drawn into a three-way conflict when the Nizam of Hyderâbâd asked for British assistance against his rivals: the Marathas, and Tipu Sahib, the

---

[22]James Tallboys Whether, *India under British Rule from the Foundation of the East India Company* (London: Kessinger Publishing, 2007), 137-140. (Hereafter, Whether, *India Under British Rule*...).

[23]When British rule was established in Bengal and Oudh in the latter part of the 18th century, the colonial administration formed a class of intermediary revenue collectors who were drawn from the native landed nobility itself. These revenue collectors called Zamindars were basically different from the Jaqirdars and Subahdars of the Mughal period in that they did not have the administrative powers of the feudal lords of the Mughal period. True, the Zamindars had many arbitrary powers but this was never formally recognized and the British administration did not interfere with the zamindars till as long as their arbitrary powers did not create a rival centre of power. To begin with no Zamindar had a private army, he could not dispense justice and he could levy no tax, which was not sanctioned by the colonial administration. This prevented a Zamindar from becoming mini or a semi-independent ruler, which the Jagirdars and Mansabdars could easily become under the Mughals. See also Eraly, *The Mughal World*..., 234-236.

[24]Cf. Mukherjee, *The Rise and Fall of East India Company*..., 234-235.

[25]Cf. Whether, *India Under British Rule*..., 240, 241. See also Mukherjee, *The Rise and Fall of East India Company*..., 251.

sultan of Mysore. In 1799 the British marched on Sree Rangapattanam, Tipu's capital, and defeated his troops. Tipu was killed defending the city. The British annexed much of Mysore outright; they controlled the remainder through a new sultan they installed. After a series of battles (1775-1782, 1803-1805, and 1817-1818) with the Marathas, the British also succeeded in bringing Maratha lands under their control.[26]

In 1773, the British Parliament passed the Regulating Act, the first of a series of acts that gave British governors greater control over the English East India Company. Under the Regulating Act the company was still permitted to continue handling all trading matters and to have its own troops, but its activity was now supervised by parliament. The act also established the post of governor-general of India and made the holder of the office directly responsible to the British government. Warren Hastings became the first governor-general of India in 1774.[27]

The British proceeded to make major changes in the administration of their realm. The three presidencies (administrative districts)—Bengal, Bombay, and Madras—adopted different systems of fixing responsibility for the payment of land taxes. In Bengal, the local landed gentry accepted responsibility for a fixed amount of taxes in return for ownership of large estates. Under this arrangement the British did not share in the gains of any potential improvements in agricultural productivity. By contrast, in Madras and Bombay, peasant cultivators paid annual taxes directly to the government. The tax rate could be adjusted at fixed intervals, so in this case the British could reap the benefits of agricultural expansion. A civil service system was developed that admitted British officers through a merit examination, trained them in an administrative college, and paid them handsomely to reduce corruption. Meanwhile, the development of the textile industry in Britain forced a transformation of India's economy: India had to produce raw cotton for export and buy manufactured goods—including cloth—from England, while the cottage industries that produced textiles in India were ruined.[28]

At the same time British attitudes about Indian culture changed. Until about 1800 the East India Company traders adapted themselves to the country, donning Indian dress, learning Sanskrit, and sometimes taking Indian mistresses. As British rule strengthened, and as an influential evangelical Christian movement emerged in the early 19th century, India's customs were judged more harshly. Missionaries, who had been kept out by the company for fear they would upset Indians and thus disrupt commerce, were now brought in. Laws were passed to abolish Indian customs such as suttee (the immolation of a widow on her husband's funeral pyre). The 18th-century company officers, such as Sir William Jones, a scholar of Sanskrit who discovered the relationship of Indo-European languages, were

---

[26]Cf. Whether, *India Under British Rule…*, 178-180.

[27]Cf. Mukherjee, *The Rise and Fall of East India Company…*, 259.

[28]Whether, *India Under British Rule…*, 278-280.

replaced by British subjects who felt Indian thought and literature was of virtually no value. In 1835, English was enforced as the language of government.[29]

Under the leadership of Governor-General James Andrew Broun Ramsay, 10th Earl of Dalhousie, the empire continued to expand. After two wars with the Sikhs, the Sikh state of Punjab was added in 1849. Governor-General Dalhousie also annexed Satara, Jaipur, Sambalpur, Jhansi, and Nagpur on the death of their native rulers, taking advantage of a British doctrine that declared Britain's right to govern any Indian state where there was no natural heir to the throne. The absorption of Oudh, long under Britain's indirect control, was the last major piece added to the company's possessions; it was annexed in 1856. Dalhousie's tenure was also marked by various improvements and reforms: the construction of railroads, bridges, roads, and irrigation systems, the establishment of telegraph and postal services, and restrictions on slave trading and other ancient practices. These innovations and reforms, however, aroused little enthusiasm among Indian people, many of whom regarded the modernization of their country with both fear and mistrust.[30]

1.1.2. *Mutiny and Revolt of 1857*

The annexation of Indian Territory and the rigorous taxation on Indian land contributed to a revolt against British rule in 1857. The revolt began among Indian soldiers (sepoys) in the service of the English East India Company in Meerut, a town northeast of Delhi. The revolt erupted when some sepoys refused to use new Lee-Enfield rifles. To load the rifles, the soldiers had to bite off the ends of greased cartridges. Rumors that the cartridges were greased with the fat of cows and pigs outraged both Hindus, who regard cows as sacred, and Muslims, who regard pigs as unclean. After taking Meerut, the mutineers marched to Delhi and persuaded the nominal sovereign of India, the Mughal emperor Bahadur Shah II, to resume his rule.[31] The revolt spread rapidly, with local rulers playing an active part in expelling or killing the British and putting their garrisons under siege, especially at Lucknow. The revolt extended through Oudh (present-day Uttar Pradesh) and northern Madhya Pradesh. The British were able to crush it, making particular use of Sikh soldiers recruited in the Punjab. The mutiny ended by 1859, with both sides guilty of atrocities.[32]

---

[29]Cf. Whether, *India Under British Rule…*, 300. See also Purkait, *Indian Renaissance and Education…*, 20.

[30]Cf.Whether, *India under British Rule…*, 311. See also Bhatia, *Marathas Sikhs and Southern Sultans of India…*, 167.

[31]Cf. Sekhara, *From Plassey to Partition…*, 12.

[32]J. C. Marshman, *The Life and Times of Carey, Marshman and Ward: Embracing the History of the Serampore Mission*, Vol. I (London: Longmann & Roberts, 1859), 39. (Hereafter, Marshman, *The Life and Times of Carey, Marshman and Ward…*).

The Sepoy Rebellion, with its unanticipated fury and extent, left the British feeling insecure. In August 1858, the British Parliament abolished the English East India Company and transferred the company's responsibilities to the British crown. This launched a period of direct rule in India, ending the fiction of company rule as an agent of the Mughal emperor (who was tried for treason and exiled to Burma). In November 1858, in her proclamation to the "Princes, Chiefs, and Peoples of India," Queen Victoria pledged to preserve the rule of Indian princes in return for loyalty to the crown. More than 560 such enclaves, taking in one-fourth of India's area and one-fifth of its people, were preserved until Indian independence in 1947. In 1876, at the urging of British Prime Minister Benjamin Disraeli, Queen Victoria took the title of Empress of India.[33]

Among the reforms introduced after the adoption of direct rule was a reorganization of the administrative system. A secretary of state, aided by a council, began to control Indian affairs from London. A viceroy (a governor who acts in the name of the British crown) implemented London's policies from Calcutta. An executive and a legislative council provided advice and assistance. Provincial governors made up the next level of authority, and below them were district officials.[34]

The army was also reorganized after the imposition of direct rule. The ratio of British to Indian soldiers was reduced, and recruitment policies were reshaped to favor Sikhs and other 'martial races' that had been loyal during the Sepoy Rebellion. Castes and groups that had been disloyal were carefully screened out.[35]

Although, the system of revenue collection remained largely unchanged, landowners who remained loyal during the mutiny were rewarded with titles and grants of large amounts of land, much of it confiscated from those who rebelled. Later, during agitations for Indian independence, the British were able to rely on many landowners for support.[36]

The British Government vehemently opposed the entry of Christian missions. Accordingly they adopted three policies: (a) They took under their management and patronage a large number of Hindu temples. They granted large sums of money for rebuilding important shrines, for sacrifices, festivals and for feeding of Brahmans. Even cruel and immoral rites, such as hook-swinging, practiced in the worship of gods, and the burning of widows, were carried out under British supervision.[37] (b) They strongly refused to allow any missionaries to settle in their territory. Hence, William Carey got a footing in Bengal by

---

[33]Cf. Whether, *India Under British Rule…*, 380. See also Ali, *A Cultural History of India…*, 127.

[34]Cf. Mukherjee, *The Rise and Fall of East India Company…*, 159.

[35]Cf. Seema, *The Sepoys and the Company…*, 79.

[36]Cf. Ali, *A Cultural History of India…*, 124.

[37]See Julius Richter, *A History of Mission in India* transl. by Sidney Moore (London: Oliphant Anderson and Ferrier, 1908), 185.

becoming an indigo-planter, and he was not able to devote his full time for his mission, until he settled at Serampore under the Danish flag.[38] (c) They refused to employ native Christians in any capacity, and they enforced all the rigors of Hindu law against them. Thence, in the army, if any native soldier wished to become a Christian, he was forcibly prevented by the authorities, or, was expelled from the service.[39] The policy of religious neutrality was reached in 1857, when in the throes of the Mutiny the East India Company came to an end, and the home Government became directly responsible for India.

1.1.3. *The Danes in Serampore*

In 1620, the Danish merchants settled in Ceylon and South India and established the trading center of Tranquebar.[40] In 1755, the Danish East India Company (DEIC) secured a parwana (legal permission) from the Nawab of Bengal for the erection of a factory on sixty bighas of land in Serampore.[41] They selected fifty-seven bighas of land in mawza Akna and three bighas in Serampore for river frontage.[42] Previous to the establishment of this settlement, the Danish factors had landed and shipped their cargoes at the French town of Chanderragore, eight miles higher up the river, but this was founded to be inconvenient, and after a tedious negotiation, and an expenditure of 16,000/- among the favorites and officials at Moorshedabad, they succeeded in obtaining a firman from the Nabob, Aly Verdy Khan, to purchase about land at Serampore, and established a factory. On 8th October 1755, Mr. Soetman, and his assistant, Ziegeuebar, the Danish officers deputed from Tranquebar, hoisted the Danish colors on the spot where they continued to fly for ninety years.[43] The primary purpose of Danish East India Company in setting up factory in Serampore (Bengal) was tapping of cotton yarn and cotton textile for home market.[44] In 1759, the DEIC took pattani of the remainder of the Mawzas of Serampore and Akna and the new mawza of Piarapur to extend their settlement.[45] "The settlement grew and flourished under the predominance of European influence in Bengal and participated in the security for property which the establishment of the English Government had

---

[38]J. N. Farquhar, *Modern Religious Movements in India* (Delhi: Munshiram Manoharlal, 1967), 10. (Hereafter, Farquhar, *Modern Religious Movements in India…*).

[39]Cf. *Ibid.*

[40]Murthy and S. U. Kamath, *Studies in Indian Culture…*, 104.

[41]Pranabranjan, Ray, "Urbanization in Colonial Situation: Serampore," *Carey Day Souvenir 2004*, edited by Swati, Datta et al., Serampore: Serampore College, 2004, 7. (Hereafter, Ray, *Urbanization in Colonial Situation…*).

[42]Cf. George Toynbee, *A Sketch of the Administration of the Hooghly District from 1795-1845*, Calcutta: 1888, 524. (Hereafter, Toynbee, *A Sketch of the Administration of the Hooghly District…*).

[43]Marshman, *The Life and Times of Carey, Marshman and Ward…*, 112.

[44]Ray, *Urbanization in Colonial Situation…*, 8.

[45]Ray, *Urbanization in Colonial Situation…*, 8.

introduced."[46] In 1776, no fewer than 22 ships, amounting in aggregate to more than ten thousand tones cleared out of the port with full cargo in the space of nine months.[47]

Improvement of Serampore under the leadership of Col. Ole Bie started to grow apace and a number of ships under the Danish colors began to leave the port annually. In 1773, the settlement of Serampore was brought under direct administration of the Crown of Denmark. And Bie became the Crown regent. However, he was dismissed in 1785 due to certain controversies[48] but he was reappointed as the chief of Serampore in 1787, when his successor Mr. Berg died on the voyage out.[49] Under him administration in Serampore continued to flourish in trade and commerce at the dawn of 19th century. Col Bie died on the 8th May 1805.[50]

With the changes of political relation between England and Denmark in Europe, the English Government hastened to take possession of the Danish Colonies in India. Thus, on the 8th May 1801, the Serampore town was surrendered without bloodshed to the English rule. But in 1802 the Danish took again from the English. The trade in Serampore was revived, and for the next five years it crossed beyond all previous records. However, Serampore town again fell to the control of the English in 1808, which stayed till 1815.[51] Though, Serampore town was restored after 1815 but by then, the Danes found that its glory had gone. Hence, in 1845 the Danish Colonies in India was completely transferred to the rule of the English. The Danes ruled for 90 years in Serampore.[52]

1.2. Economic Condition

With the imposition of direct rule, the economy of India became even more closely linked than before with that of Britain. The opening of the Suez Canal in 1869 reduced the sailing time between Britain and India from about three months to only three weeks, enabling London to exercise tight control over all aspects of Indian trade. Railroads, roads, and communications were developed to bring raw materials, especially cotton, to ports for shipment to England, and

---

[46]Toynbee, *A Sketch of the Administration of the Hooghly District...*, 25.

[47]Cf. *Ibid.*, 26-27.

[48]The controversies: The custom duty which till then used to be collected by Nawab's collector of Hooghly was licensed to him by the English East India Company for Rs. 7000 annually. This license, though very promising for Danish trade, lasted for one year only, because some adverse criticism compelled Bie to give it up. The two factions of Danish Asiatic Company sent sharp protest to the Directors in Copenhagen and that resulted in a Royal re-script appointing a committee of investigation.

[49]Cf. Sunil Kumar, Chatterjee, *William Carey and Serampore* (Serampore: Laserplus, 2004), 23-25. (Hereafter Chatterjee, *William Carey and Serampore...*).

[50]Chatterjee, *William Carey and Serampore....*, 27.

[51]Cf. *Ibid.*, 29.

[52]Cf. Toynbee, *A Sketch of the Administration of the Hooghly District...*, 525.

manufactured goods from England for sale in an expanding Indian market. Development schemes, such as massive irrigation projects in the Punjab, were also intended to serve the purpose of enriching England. Indian entrepreneurs were not encouraged to develop their own industries.[53]

Although, some industrialization took place during this period, its benefits did not reach the majority of the Indian population. During the 1850s, mechanized jute industries were developed in Bengal and cotton textiles in western India, mainly by British firms. Although, these industries expanded rapidly from 1880 to 1914 and though an Indian iron-and-steel industry was developed in the early 20th century, India remained essentially an agrarian economy. By 1914, industry accounted for less than 5 percent of national income, and less than 1 percent of India's workforce was employed in factories. A succession of severe famines occurred at this time despite the general improvement of agricultural production, the expansion of the railways, and the development of administrative procedures designed to tackle such crises. With only small advances in public health, death rates remained high and life expectancy low.[54]

The assumption of direct British rule in 1858 made Indians British subjects and promised in principle that Indians could participate in their own governance. Few reforms addressed this issue, however. Although, local government councils had been elected even before 1857, it wasn't until the Indian Councils Act of 1861 that Indians were permitted, by appointment, to participate in the Executive Council, the highest council of the land. Indian representation on local and provincial bodies gradually expanded under British rule, though never to the point of complete control. The higher civil service had theoretically been opened to Indians in 1833, and the Queen's Proclamation of 1858 confirmed this point again. Nevertheless, candidates for the service had to go to England to compete in the examination, which emphasized classical European subjects. Those few who managed to overcome these initial obstacles and join the service encountered discrimination that prevented them from advancing.[55]

1.3. Socio-Religious Conditions

By 1800, Hinduism, which was the religion of at least three-fourth of the population of India, consisted, in the main, of two great groups of sects and a mass of wandering celibate ascetics, who were held to be outside society. The two

[53] Cf. Ray, *Urbanization in Colonial Situation…*, 17.

[54]Robert, Eric Frykenberg, ed., *Land Control and Social Structure in Indian History* (London: University of Wisconsin Press, 1969), 257-58. (Hereafter, Frykenberg, ed., *Land Control and Social Structure …*). See also R. Sutharalingam, *Politics and National Awakening in South India, 1852-1891* (Arizona: The University of Arizona Press, 1974), 111. (Hereafter, Sutharalingam, *Politics and National Awakening…*).

[55]Cf. Toynbee, *A Sketch of the Administration of the Hooghly District…*, 425.

great groups of sects are the Vishnuite[56] and the Sivaite.[57] Both sects worship their gurus and teachers, as gods.[58] However, around the Hindu community in every part of the country there lived multitudes of degraded Outcastes, held down in the dirt by Hindu law. Learning had almost ceased; ordinary education scarcely existed; spiritual religion was to be met only in the quietest places; and a coarse idolatry with cruel and immoral rites held all the great centers of population.

1.3.1. *Caste System*[59]

According to the Hindu structure of society the rigid casteism was a must to maintain for the well being of the community. It was the norm of the society.[60] There were several castes and sub-castes. Some are regarded as high castes and other low castes, which is the dividing factor of the Indian society.[61] According to Brahminism, the Brahmins were created from the head of Purusha, Kshatriyas from the shoulders, Vaishyas from the hip and Sudras from the feet.[62] Such an

---

[56]Cf. Farquhar, *Modern Religious Movements in India...*, 1-13. The Vishnuite sects were very numerous, both in the North and in the South, and they were perhaps, on the whole, more homogeneous than the worshippers of Siva. The leading Vishnuite sects declare Vishnu to be the one god, and yet they recognized the existence of all the other divinities of the Hindu pantheon. They also hold that Vishnu has been incarnate among men a great many times, the latest and chief incarnations being Rama and Krishna.

[57]Worshippers of Siva considered that Siva is the one god, but recognized also all other gods. A special group of Sivaite sects has to be noticed, namely, those who pay honor to the wife of Siva as Kali or Durga.

[58]Cf. Farquhar, *Modern Religious Movements in India...*, 3.

[59]It has been argued that the origin of the caste system has nothing to do with the human civil institution. Rather it has a divine appointment, and therefore it is a sacred institution. The birth of an individual in a particular family of a certain caste is not an accident, but it is the result of divine will. It is a reflection of the divine decrees and the need of nature. Whatever may be the practice of caste system, it has created divisions among the people of India. Cf. Batacharya, Nath, Jogedra, *Castes and Sects* (Delhi: Munshiram Manoharlal, 1996), 17-20. (Hereafter, Jogedra, *Castes and Sects...*).

[60]Gine, *The System of Elementary Education...*, 3. See also Bayly, Susan, *Caste, Society and Politics in India from the Eighteenth Century to the Modern Age* (London: Cambridge University Press, 1999), 34-39. (Hereafter, Susan, *Caste, Society and Politics in India...*).

[61]The Brahmins, those belonging to the high caste, were considered as gods, Sudras the low caste were even denied the basic rights of learning and even listening to the Vedas. Manu, the greatest lawgiver of Hinduism, said that molten lead be poured into the ears of Sudras should they listen to the reading of the Vedas. Besides the low castes, there are large numbers of outcastes who were considered as untouchables. The high castes considered that they would be defiled if the shadows of the untouchables fell on them. Highways were not open to the latter. Cf. G. S. Ghuye, *Caste and Race in India* (Bombay: Popular Book Depot, 1969), 79-80. (Hereafter, huye, *Caste and Race in India...*).

[62]Cf. Aleyamma Zachariah, *Modern Religious and Secular Movements in India* (Bangalore: Theological Book Trust, 1998), 2. (Hereafter, Zachariah, *Modern Religious and Secular Movements...*).

understanding of creation justified the hierarchical society and the die-hard casteism. There was neither inter-dining nor inter-marriages between the high and low castes.[63] Hence, the social structures and control of knowledge within a privilege circle kept a vast majority of the Indian populace as slaves. People lived in much ignorance. Only the three upper castes learned the scriptures, mostly at home. The lower castes were even debarred from taking spiritual counsel from high castes.[64] Thus, every aspects of the society were governed by caste system.

1.3.2. *Condition of Women*

Hinduism has a very low opinion of women.[65] The higher castes believed and forced the women that after the death of husband the wife's chastity and faithfulness is proved only by committing *Sati.*[66] Hindu religion hold a very rigid understanding that it was a curse to live as a widow at the same time it was also prohibited for remarriage whereas the widowers (men) were allowed to remarry as many times as they desired, such was the discrimination between the sexes. This practice left many child widows and youthful widows who have to live the rest of their lives in sorrow.[67] This practice was not always a self-devised plan. It was often imposed on the women by the relatives, or sometimes by the parents. It is

---

[63]Cf. G. S. Ghuye, *Caste, Class and Occupation (*Bombay: Popular Book Depot, 1961), 34, 35. (Hereafter, Ghuye, *Caste, Class and Occupation*...). Dubious birth was not the only indicator for outcaste. There was more than one reason or offense that could lead to the loss of one's caste, and thus to be considered as outcaste. Eating prohibited food stuffs, like flesh and drinking spirits; eating food prepared by the cook or any individual from a low caste background, staying with or marrying somebody from the low caste, community, indulging in trades forbidden by the Hindu Scriptures, visiting foreign countries, and so on.

[64]Gine, *The System of Elementary Education*..., 3.

[65]Manu prescribed that a woman should be under the control of her father before marriage, under her husband in marriage and under the control of her son in old age. Cf. Jogedra, *Castes and Sects*..., 77.

[66]Sati is an act of widow entering the pyre of her dead husband voluntarily or involuntarily, most often involuntarily. Some Hindu communities encouraged this cruel custom where *sati* altered inheritance patterns. However, it was never practiced among the so-called low castes. The practice of *Sati* was also performed in two different ways - *Sahamaran* and *Unomaran. Sahamaran* was the burning of a widow on the funeral pyre along with the dead body of the deceased husband. Such was the case where husband and wife were found living together. But where the husband and wife living separately, e.g., the husband was living far away from the wife for the purpose of earning livelihood or any other reason, *Unomaran* was practiced to become a *Sati.* In such a case the widow was burnt along with a memento or relic of her husband. However, a widow of a Brahmin was never allowed to become a *Sati.* This was perhaps a crafty plan to maintain the Brahmanic line. Secondly a pregnant widow was disqualified for being *sati.* This was issued perhaps to protect the yet-to-be-born life. The same principle was followed in the case of a widow who had a suckling baby. Cf. Ghuye, *Caste, Class and Occupation*..., 122-125. See also Ghuye, *Caste and Race in India*..., 67.

[67]Young girls, some of who even before attaining puberty were forced to be married to old men who already have other wives. When the husband dies, the child-wife would be declared a widow, and denied any possibility of remarriage.

believed that on becoming *Sati* a widow purified the families of her husband and her parents.[68] Sometimes, a widow preferred to die in the husband pyre in order to avoid the cruel torture by her relatives throughout the rest of her life.[69] Moreover, the practice of *Sati* became the means of ventilating one's cruel and revengeful nature. Those who were envious of the widow's wealth insist that the widow must go to the pyre.[70]

1.3.3. *Devadasi System and Practice of Female Infanticide*

Moreover, the devadasi system was a custom for Hindus. The term devadasi means female servant of God. But, corrupt priests and worshippers used them to satisfy their lust, which led the devadasis as sacred prostitutes. This practice spoiled the atmosphere of the temples.[71]

The practice of female infanticide among the Hindus was very common. This occurred sometimes due to the practice of dowry system, which was the deciding factor in marriage. Many parents considered it a liability to have girl babies, for it was the girl's father who had to pay the dowry to the boy's father. This cruel practice led to the practice of infanticide.[72] There was also a belief among the Hindus that some of the gods and goddesses required human sacrifices and such sacrifices are highly meritorious. For this purpose often children were kidnapped and slaughtered and their blood was offered - especially to the goddess Kali - to please her in order to get benefits from her. This custom also involved throwing female children or first-born babies into the river,[73] if the child was expected, according to the astrological speculation, not to live long; she was destined to be thrown to the river or sacrificed to goddesses. To some Hindus, the birth of a female child was considered to be bad omen as the girls had little regard in the society, thence, most of the situation they became the victims for any religious

---

[68]Cf. Gine, *The System of Elementary Education...*, 5-6. According to Gine there are several factors that led to this practice. They can be divided into two categories- religious impulse and socio-economic factors. From a religious point of view, the widow was thought of as being given a chance to earn righteousness on behalf of her deceased husband as well as on her own behalf. On the other hand, the socio-economic factors also prompted such an inhuman practice. Sometimes they were encouraged to adhere to such a rite by the officiating Brahmins in order that they might get a handsome reward for officiating over it.

[69]*Ibid.* See also Ghuye, *Caste and Race in India...*, 79.

[70]Cf. Gine, *The System of Elementary Education...*, 7.

[71]Cf. Susan, *Caste, Society and Politics in India...*, 68-70.

[72]Cf. Zachariah, *Modern Religious and Secular Movements...*, 4. See also Susan, *Caste, Society and Politics in India...*, 55-58.

[73]Cf. Gine, *The System of Elementary Education...*, 4.

sacrificial rites.[74] All these factors contributed toward the pitiable condition of Indian women during the 18th and 19th centuries.[75]

Thus looking back, India had not known real peace for several centuries at a stretch – beginning with the Hindu rulers, Muslim rulers and then the European rulers, who ruled India successively under different circumstances and motives. It was a dark period of Indian history.[76] The supremacy of the British Government began to assert in India by the battle of Plassey in 1757, but the rulers had no specific policy until the new century.[77] Initially the East India Company[78] had no desire to rule India but as the time passed by the company do realized that it was impossible to be profitable without the exercise of power. So by the end of the 18th century gradually the company came fully into being as the government of India. The British Empire in India continued to expand during 18th and 19th centuries until it covered the whole of India.[79] The British rule put an end to the political warfare and chaos that prevailed through most of the 18th century, but economically and socially, insecurity continued[80] due to the new legislative measures and administrative practice as well as the impact of Western technologies and ideologies.[81] The British conquest of India was neither sudden nor accidental. The East India Company acquired experience and knowledge of the political, social and economic conditions of India for a period of 150 years before they decided to compete for primacy.[82]

2. The Serampore Mission

The history of Serampore Mission begins in the year 1799, with the arrival of Daniel Brunsdon, William Grant, Joshua Marshman and William Ward.[83]

---

[74]Cf. Gine, *The System of Elementary Education…*, 4.

[75]Cf. Susan, *Caste, Society and Politics in India…*, 78.

[76]E. R. Hambye, *History of Christianity in India*, vol. III, (Bangalore: CHAI, 1997), 1-2.

[77]Farquhar, *Modern Religious Movements in India…*, 2.

[78]We must never forget that the East India Company came to India exclusively for commerce, and that the British Empire sprang altogether from the necessity, which was only very gradually realized, of providing a settled and just government in order to make commerce possible.

[79]Farquhar, *Modern Religious Movements in India…*, 16. Lord Wellesley's policy proved very successful in extending the British Empire far and wide. His policy was completed in 1849, when the last remaining portion of India proper was added to the British Empire at the conclusion of the second Sikh war. Moreover, in 1857 Mutiny by the Indian army led the Indians to be brought directly under the British Crown.

[80]Frykenberg, ed., *Land Control and Social Structure …*, 256. See also Sutharalingam, *Politics and National Awakening…*, 396.

[81]Hugald Grafe, *History of Christianity in India* vol. 4, part. 2 (Bangalore: CHAI, 1990), 18.

[82]K. A. Nilakanta Sastri and G. Srinivasachari, *India: A Historical Survey* (Bombay: Allied Publishers, 1970.), 47.

[83]Cf. Chatterjee, *William Carey and Serampore…*, 15. Before leaving England they had been warned of the obstacles that might be put in their way by the British authorities, and following the

Brunsdon and Grant died within the next two years. Meanwhile Ward visited Carey at his residence with the protection of Danish Passport. After long deliberation between them Carey decided to join the new missionaries at Serampore, with his family consisting of four sons, and wife on the 10th of January 1800. [84] Thus, the Serampore Mission was started on 10th January 1800 under the protection of the Danish flag at Serampore.[85] All were men of high intellectual gifts and of complete devotion to the service of God.[86] It was agreed by them to live together as one family, having all things in common. Concerning this settlement John Clark Marshman writes:

> It was determined to form a common stock, to dine at a common table and to give each family a trifling allowance for personal expenses. All the missionaries were to be considered on a footing of equality and to preach and conduct social devotions in turn. The superintendence of domestic arrangements was to be entrusted to each missionary in rotation for a month.... One evening in the week was to be devoted to adjustment of differences and the renewal of their pledge of mutual love; and it was resolved that no one should engage in any private trade, and that whatever might be earn should be credited to the common stock.[87]

---

advice given by Charles Grant, an influential director of the East India Company they went straight to the Danish settlement of Serampore, and put themselves under the protection of its Governor, Colonel Bie. While the new missionaries waited in Serampore, Carey made every possible effort to secure permits for them to join him in his Indigo factory, but was not possible.

[84]At Kidderpore Carey lived only by sufferance, his license might be revoked at any moment, if he gives any disquietude to Government, and it was likely to be summarily withdrawn when his missionary vocation was discovered, neither would his brethren be permitted to join him. At Serampore, under the protection of the Danish flag, they would be free from molestation by the British authority, they might establish a press and receive additional missionaries. Cf. J. S. Banks, *Three Indian Heroes: The Missionary, The Statesman, The Soldier* (London: Charles H. Kelly, 1870), 78. (Hereafter, Banks, *Three Indian Heroes: The Missionary, The Statesman, The Soldier*...).

[85]Cf. E. L. Wenger, "The Serampore Mission and Its Founder," *The Story of Serampore and Its College* (Serampore: The Council of Serampore College, 1961), 1-2. (Hereafter, Wenger, *The Serampore Mission and Its Founder*...). On the other hand, Carey had purchased an indigo factory, and commenced the erection of buildings for his brethren, which could not be abandoned without lost.

[86]Cf. David, Herbert, Croly, *Biographical Notice of the Rev. William Carey of Serampore* (New Castle: T and J. Hodgson, 1893), 17-20. The power that had encouraged the first protestant missionaries, Ziegenbalg and his associates, in the south India, had now the honor of taking under its protection the infant mission in the north, and sheltering it from the storm that menaced its existence. If the settlement of Serampore had not existed, or if it had not been at the time under the Danish flag, Joshua Marshman and William Ward would, in all human probability have been constrained to return forthwith to England, and the mission might have expired in its cradle. William Carey would not have been permitted either to establish a press for the printing of Scripture, or to receive any addition of missionaries, and his labours would probably have become extinct on his death.

[87]Marshman, *The Life and Times of Carey, Marshman and Ward*..., 124-125.

The missionaries had come to India for one great overriding purpose, i.e., to bring to the people of that land the knowledge of the love of God revealed in Christ.[88] They used every means to fulfill this purpose.

2.1. The Founders of Serampore Mission

2.1.1. *William Carey*

William Carey was born, on August 17th, 1761, in the Village of Paulerspury, Northamptonshire. His father was a weaver, but later arose to be Parish clerk and village schoolmaster.[89] At the age of six he worked out sum in arithmetic in his own mind; that after having learned to read, he manifested an interest for books of science, history, and travels and that his scientific taste became prominent at an early age.[90] His room was crowded with the insects he had collected to mark their development, and he endeavored to acquire a knowledge of drawing to assist these researches. At the age of twelve he obtained a copy of 'Dyche's Latin Vocabulary' and committed nearly the whole of it to memory, and carefully studied the brief sketch of a grammar prefixed to it.[91]

The parents could not afford to send him to school, so at the age of 14 he joined, Clarke Nichols, a shoemaker at Hackleton. He found a commentary on the New Testament, which was interspersed with word in shoemaker's shop. He learned Greek from Tom Jones a journeyman who was educated at Kidderminster. He was brought up as a strict churchman, as the son and grandson of the Parish clerk.[92] At the same time Mr. Sutclif a minister in Olney gave a Latin Grammar and advised him to study it assiduously. He improved his acquaintance with languages in Latin, Greek, and Hebrew.[93]

At the age of 18 he started preaching in the pulpits. While attending one of the Associations meeting at Olney, at which he was obliged to fast all day, not having the means of purchasing a meal, some friends from Earl's Barton, a neighbouring village, were lamenting their spiritual destitution to Mr. Charter, the independent minister at Olney. He at once advised them to request Mr. Carey's services. They called on him soon after, and he accepted their request, and in that

---

[88]Wenger, *The Serampore Mission and Its Founder…*, 5.

[89]Arthur, C. Chute, *William Carey A Sketch of Beginning in Modern Missions* (Chicago: Goodman & Dickerson, 1891), 7. (Hereafter, Chute, *William Carey…*).

[90]Joseph, Belcher, *William Carey: A Biography* (Philadelphia: American Baptist Publication Society, 1853), 43. See also Mary, E. Farwell, *The Life of William Carey* (New York: Flaming H. Ravell, Co., 1888), 12-20.

[91]Cf. Marshman, *The Life and Times of Carey, Marshman and Ward…*, 2. See also W. Macintosh, *William Carey; or Sanctified Scholarship* (London: Book Society, 1870), 79.

[92]Cf. Marshman, *The Life and Times of Carey, Marshman and Ward…*, 3, 4. See also Chute, *William Carey…*, 9-10.

[93]Fred, A. McKenzie, *William Carey: The Story of His Life* (London: James B. Knapp, 1821), 9-15.

village he preached from Sabbath to Sabbath for three years and a half, and once a month in his native village of Pury.[94]

Mr. Nichols died and Mr. Carey took over his business and married his sister before he had reached the age of twenty.[95] After his marriage he rented a cottage at Hackleton. However, trade became dull, and he was constrained to sell off his stock at a great sacrifice. At this time he was attacked by fever which troubled him for eighteen months, even in this crisis he had to move from place to place to dispose off his goods to procure family bread. The Barton congregation where he serves couldn't raise enough funds to buy the clothes to wear in their service. At this period he was reduced to the greatest distress.[96]

At the age of 24 he moved to another village called Moulton where he took in-charge of a Baptist Church, from where he developed missionary zeal, and work in a school.[97] At Moulton he preached four times a week, which increased the numbers of congregations as well as his cultivation of his natural gifts.[98] He adopted that systematic distribution and that stern economy of time, which

---

[94]Cf. *Ibid.*, 5, 6. See also Joshua, Marshman, *The Story of Carey, Marshman and Ward: The Serampore Missionaries* (London: Alexander Strahan, 1864), 48-50. (Hereafter, Marshman, *The Story of Carey, Marshman and Ward...*).

[95]Cf. Marshman, *The Life and Times of Carey, Marshman and Ward...*, 57, 58. It is said that this premature marriage was not simply imprudent under existing circumstances, but was highly inauspicious in reference to his future career. His illiterate wife possessed no feelings in unison with his own, and was altogether unsuited to be his companion. Not withstanding the immense disparity in intellect and attainments between them, Mr. Carey always treated her with the utmost affection, while she manifested no interest in his aspirations for a larger sphere of labor and usefulness. The extreme consideration and tenderness, which invariably marked his conduct towards her, place the meekness and magnanimity of his character in the strongest light. See also W. W. Tulloch, *William Carey and Serampore Mission* (Scotland: 1883), 47.

[96]Cf. Marshman, *The Life and Times of Carey, Marshman and Ward...*, 6. See also George, Smith, *Life of William Carey, Shoemaker & Missionary* (London: 1909), 89. (Hereafter, Smith, *Life of William Carey...*).

[97]Cf. *Ibid.*, 11. The idea of establishing a mission to the heathen had taken such a complete possession of his mind as to absorb his thought and his affections. While engaged in making or mending shoes, his eye was often raised from the last to the map and his mind was employed in traversing the different regions of the globe, and musing on the condition of the various heathen tribes, and devising the means of evangelizing them. It was to this circumstance that Mr. Wilberforce alludes in the House of Commons when urging parliament to grant the missionaries free access to India. See also J. B. Middlebrook, *William Carey* (London: The Carey Kingsgate Press Ltd., 1961), 16-17.

[98]Cf. *Ibid.,* 25. See also Joshua, C. Marshman, *Statement Relative to Serampore Supplementary to a Brief Memoir with Introductory Observations by John Foster* (London: Parbery Allen, 1828), 88, 89. (Hereafter, Marshman, *Statement Relative to Serampore Supplementary...*). He was attracted at Moulton with the prospect having good school. However, he was unable to maintain any control over his pupils, who often took personal liberties with him, totally subversive of all discipline. The old master, however, returned and resumed his occupation. Mr. Carey's school at Moulton vanished without any competition.

subsequently enables him to accomplish labor almost incredible.[99] In 1789, he moved to another town called Leicester. He continued to urge his brethren in the ministry about the indispensable duty of sending the Gospel to the heathen. At the Easter meeting of ministers at Clipstone in 1789, Carey urged that something should be done immediately, on that very day, towards the formation of a Society to propagate the Gospel in heathen lands.[100] However, his proposal was not accepted for another eighteen months, but was asked to print the pamphlet, which was written at Moulton titled 'An Enquiry into the Obligation of Christians to Use Means for the Conversion of the Heathens'. He revised it and sent to the press. And this appeal was substantiated in May 1792, where he preached a sermon based on Isaiah 54:2-3, where he explained and enforced two principles: 'Expect Great Things from God; Attempt Great Things for God'.[101] This brought a transformation among his colleagues, thus they recorded a resolution "that a plan be prepared against the next ministers' meeting at Kettering for the establishment of a Society for Propagating the Gospel among the heathen".[102]

This meeting was held at Kettering on the 2nd of October 1792. After the service twelve ministers of the Northamptonshire Association of Baptist Churches met together and founded a society to be called 'The Particular (Calvinistic) Baptist Society for propagating the Gospel among the Heathen' which later developed into the Baptist Missionary Society of the present day.[103] The ministers consulted further on the matter, and to lay a foundation at least for a society, when the following resolutions were proposed, and unanimously agreed to:

1. Desirous of making an effort for the propagation of the gospel among the heathen, agreeably to what is recommended in brother Carey's late publication on that subject, we, whose names appear to the subsequent subscription, do solemnly agree to act in society together for that purpose.[104]
2. As in the present divided state of Christendom, it seems that each denomination, by exerting itself separately, is most likely to accomplish the great ends of a mission, it is agreed that this society be called The

---

[99]Cf. John, Brown, Myers, *William Carey: The Shoe Maker who became the Father and Founder of Modern Mission* (London: S.W. Partridge, 1887), 68-70. See also Marshman, *The Life and Times of Carey, Marshman and Ward...*, 8.

[100]*Ibid.*, 14. See also Marshman, *The Story of Carey, Marshman and Ward...*, 128.

[101]Gine, *The Sytem of Elementary Education...*, 19. See also, Marshman, *The Story of Carey, Marshman and Ward...*, 89. Marshman, *The Life and Times of Carey, Marshman and Ward...*, 15.

[102]*Ibid.*, 15.

[103]Cf. Chute, *William Carey...*, 1. See also Fenwick, John, *Biographical Sketch of Joshua Marshman, D. D., of Serampore New Castle Chronicle* (New Castle: Emerson Charnley, 1838), 17-25. (Hereafter, John, *Biographical Sketch of Joshua Marshman...*).

[104]John, *Biographical Sketch of Joshua Marshman...*, 2.

Particular [Calvinistic] Baptist Society for Propagating the Gospel among the Heathen. [105]

3. As such an undertaking must be attended with expense; we agree immediately to open a subscription for the above purpose, and to recommend it to others.[106]
4. Every person, who shall subscribe ten pounds at once, or ten shillings and sixpence annually shall be considered a member of the society.[107]
5. That the Rev. John Ryland, Reynold Hogg, William Carey, John Sutcliff, and Andrew Fuller, be appointed a committee, three of whom shall be empowered to act in carrying into effect the purposes of this society.[108]
6. That the Rev. Reynold Hogg be appointed treasurer, and the Rev. Andrew Fuller secretary.[109]

The Baptist Missionary Society resolved to send William Carey to Africa, but with the timely intervention of Dr. John Thomas, who once acted as the company's doctor in India for some years, the Society reviewed its resolution and decided to send its first batch of missionaries to India.[110]

Hence, they began their journey to India on the 13th of June 1793, under a Danish vessel called 'Cron Princessa Maria', commanded by captain Christmas, an Englishman. They landed in Calcutta on the 11th of November 1793.[111]

2.1.2. *William Ward*

William Ward was born at Derby on the 20th of October 1769, and was the son of John Ward, carpenter and builder. His father died when he was a child, and his mother who was a very pious woman, an attendant on the ministry of the Methodists, brought him up.[112] He went through tuition under Mr. Congreve, and then of Mr. Breary, of Derby, and became proficient in the ordinary branches of school education. He was distinguished in childhood for sobriety and

---

105Smith, *Life of William Carey…*, 29, 30. See also Noonkester, C. Myron, *William Carey and Serampore* (Serampore: Kartik Dutta Banik, 1980), 51-52.

106Wenger, *The Serampore Mission and Its Founder….*, 5.

107*Ibid.*, 7.

108*Ibid.*, 8.

109Marshman, *The Life and Times of Carey, Marshman and Ward…*, 17. See also Eustace, Carey, *Memoir of William Carey D.D.: Late Missionary to Bengal; Professor of Oriental Languages in the College of Forth William, Calcutta* (London: Jackson and Walford, 1836), 9-16. (Hereafter, *Memoir of William Carey D.D.: Late Missionary to Bengal…*).

110Cf. Gine, *The System of Elementary Education…*, 18-19.

111Cf. Marshman, *The Life and Times of Carey, Marshman and Ward…*, 60-63.

112Cf. *Ibid.*, 92, 93. See also Crockett, R. Bannie, *The Life and Labours of Carey, Marshman and Ward* (New York: U. D. Ward, 1867), 12-20. (Hereafter, Bannie, *The Life and Labours of Carey, Marshman and Ward…*).

thoughtfulness. On leaving school he was placed as an apprentice with Mr. Drury, who was at the head of a large printing establishment in the town. Ward soon rose to the grade of corrector of the press, which gave him ample opportunities of storing his mind with various and useful knowledge. He undertook at the close of his apprenticeship, of editing the 'Derby Mercury' on behalf of his master. With his elegance in writing, Derby Mercury soon raised the circulation and it became one of the most influential papers in the country. He was led to join a political society in Derby, affiliated with the parent society in London. In one occasion Ward, without the consent of the Church, admitted, Thelwal the well-known democratic orator, into the Baptist meeting-house, to deliver a political lecture. The result was disastrous, the windows were broken by a mob, the lecturer and his audiences were expelled with violence, and great odium was brought on the character of the denomination in the town.[113]

After having thus written up the 'Derby Mercury' and secured for it an unexampled share of patronage, he subsequently proceeded to Hull to undertake the editorial management of the 'Hull Advertiser'. The journals he successively edited were distinguished by a high moral tone, and the period of his editorial labor was contemporary with those noble efforts of Clarkson and his associates[114] to organize public opinion against the iniquities of the slave-trade, which have at length resulted in the high honored distinction that slavery can never again exist in conjunction with the British flag.[115]

In August 1796, he was baptized at Hall by Mr. Pendered, and in 1797, he renounced all interest in politics and journalism, and gave his heart and soul to the nobler vocation of communicating divine truth to his fellow-countrymen.[116] Mr. Faweett, a member of the Baptist Missionary Committee, conversed repeatedly with Ward on the subject of mission, which rekindles his heart to be a missionary as he listened to the narrative of Carey's labours and progress in the New Testament in the Bengalee language. And he decided to offer himself as a missionary to the society without delay, in the hope of being employed in printing the scriptures. The next six months were passed being acquainted with the members of the Society, conversing with Mr. Fuller, which contributed so greatly to the success of the Serampore mission.[117]

[113]Cf. Marshman, *The Life and Times of Carey, Marshman and Ward...*, 94. See also Ward, William, *A View of the History, Literature and Mythology of the Hindoos*, Vol. I (Serampore: Mission Press, 1818), 3-5.

[114]In the journey, which Clarkson undertook through England, he called on Mr. Ward at Derby, to enlist his journal in the cause of humanity. After that interview Mr. Ward became one of the most earnest advocates of abolition, and improved every opportunity to hold up the atrocities of trade of public destination.

[115]Cf. Marshman, *The Life and Times of Carey, Marshman and Ward...*, 95.

[116]Cf. Marshman, *The Life and Times of Carey, Marshman and Ward...*, 96.

[117]Cf. *Ibid.*, 98. See also Ward, William, *Farewell Letters to Few Friends in Britain and America on Return to Bengal in 1821* (London: Kingsbury Barbury and Allen, 1821), 2.

2.1.3. *Joshua Marshman*

Joshua Marshman was born at Westbury Leigh, in Wiltshire, on the 20th of April 1768. In 1764, John Marshman married Mary Couzener, a descendant of one of the French refugees who obtained sheltered in England on the revocation of the Edit of Nantes. She was a woman of great piety and exemplary benevolence, who lived with husband in the practice of Christian virtues for more than half century. It was in this atmosphere of religious piety Joshua Marshman was trained up.[118]

At the age of seven he was sent to a little village school, and remained there till he had exhausted its resources, though he left it with a bare knowledge of reading. There was no school in neighborhood in which writing was taught, or even simple elements of arithmetic. However, in these circumstances he developed thirst for reading, and by the time he was twelve, he had read through more than a hundred volumes.[119] The number of works he had thus read before he was eighteen amounted to more than five hundred.

At the age of fifteen, Mr. Cator, a bookseller in Holborn employed Marshman in his bookshop, with the view of providing for him in his own trade. When other retired to rest, he applied to reading and more than once fell asleep with a book in his hand, and the light burning, and thus endangered the building, to the great annoyance of the inmates of the house. As he get little time to read in shop as was daily sent out with books to the residence of customers, he often read them as he walked in the streets. He came back from London to Westbury Leigh and resumed his labours at the loom, continued to engage in reading every work of fiction or poetry, history, geography, or travels, to which he could obtain access.[120]

He continued to labor as a weaver, and lived in humble association with the honest, god-fearing members of the Church. He had been trained up under the eye of pious, and with the strictest attention to the duties of religion and morality. When Marshman sought admission into the Church, farmer Bachelor and the other deacons opposed and kept in probation for seven years saying that he had too much, heart knowledge of Christian truth. Therefore, he eventually left Westbury without having been baptized.[121]

In 1791, he got married to Hannah Shepherd the grand daughter of the Rev. John Clark. In 1794, he joined in a school as a teacher in Bristol and he also joined the Church at Broadmead, and was received into it by baptism in the course of the year. While working as teacher he read the periodical of Account of the Baptist Missionary Society, and his mind was gradually turned to missionary

---

[118]Cf. Marshman, *The Story of Carey, Marshman and* Ward…, *76.* See also Marshman, *The Life and Times of Carey, Marshman and Ward…*, 100.

[119]Cf. *Ibid.*, 102. See also Sunil, Kumar Chatterjee, *Hanah Marshman: The First Woman Missionary in India* (Serampore: Carey Library, 2002), 5. (Hereafter, Chatterjee, *Hanah Marshman…*).

[120]Cf. Marshman, *The Story of Carey, Marshman and Ward…*, 105.

[121]Cf. Marshman, *The Life and Times of Carey, Marshman and Ward…*, 106.

labor in the East. With the encouragement of Dr. Ryland a committee member of the Society and his friend Grant, he offered his willingness to go to India as Missionary.[122]

The Society thus sent Marshman, Ward and their associates to India on 20th of May 1799. They sailed from an American ship called 'Criterion'. Captain Wikes, a Presbyterian of providence in the United States, commanded the ship. The voyage, which lasted four months and a half, was deprived of its usual inconvenience, by the rare kindness and the Christian sympathy of the commander.[123]

3. The Senate of Serampore College (SSC)

With the introduction of elementary schools, which amount up to forty-five in numbers by 1816, the desire of the native people for learning increased so much so that the missionaries began to struggle very hard to open more mission schools with sufficient efficient teachers. Although, the elementary schools were taken care of by the native teachers, the missionaries were aware that their qualifications were not adequate for the task.[124] Hence, there was an urgent need for an institution, which would produce better-qualified men for the teaching job.[125]

As the desire for higher education and a thirst for English knowledge grew among the better classes of the society, it received support and encouragement from the rulers of the land, and with the blessing of Lord Hastings, the then Governor-General, even some wealthy Hindus gave their support and opened a College for the education of the young men of Calcutta in 1816. Subsequently, agencies and associations for the upliftment of the natives began to spring up liberally.[126]

3.1. The Establishment of the College (1818-1837)

Despite the fact that the missionaries had broken off from the Baptist Missionary Society in England and its support in 1816, they decided to wade against the threatening tide to start a College where the natives, especially of Christian parentage, can be given a higher and more complete education, and where native preachers and school teachers could be efficiently trained up.[127] On the 15th of

---

[122]Cf. Marshman, *The Life and Times of Carey, Marshman and Ward...*, 107. See also James, Culross, *William Carey* (London: Hodder and Stoughton, 1818), 10. (Hereafter, Culross, *William Carey...*).

[123]Cf. Chute, *William Carey...*, 15. See also Marshman, *The Life and Times of Carey, Marshman and Ward...*, 200.

[124]D. A. Christadoss, "The Story of Serampore College, 1818-1929," *The Story of Serampore and Its College*, edited by Wilma S. Stewart (Serampore: The Council of Serampore College, 1961), 20. (Hereafter, Christadoss, *The Story of Serampore College...*).

[125]Cf. Gine, *The System of Elementary Education...*, 31-38.

[126]Cf. Gine, *The System of Elementary Education...*, 35-37.

[127]J. C. Marshman, *History of Serampore Mission or Life and Times of Carey, Marshman and Ward*, Vol. II (Calcutta: 1859), 168.

July 1818, the missionaries issued their prospectus in which the institution was meant to be *A College for the Instruction of Asiatic Christian and Other Youth in Eastern Literature and European Science.*[128] It was Dr. Marshman who wrote the lengthy document, making it very clear that the College was to be a handmaid of evangelization and that the instruction would be given in Sanskrit, Arabic, European Science and English.[129] The medium of learning was to be Vernacular, with English as a required subject. A Normal section for the training of teachers was also to be included. There was also the firm hope that the College was to be considered as most importantly a divinity school, where promising Christian youth for evangelistic work should go through a complete course of instruction in Christian theology.[130] Nevertheless, it was made imperative that the College should be open to all without the distinction of caste or creed thereby divesting its instruction of all sectarian character.[131]

During the first year the missionaries occupied themselves with the arrangements for the admission of the students, the ordering of the classes and the purchase of the plot of land on which the College stands. The first year they had thirty-seven students in the College, of which nineteen were Christians, many of whom were scholarship-holders, and eighteen were non-Christians. They also engaged themselves with plans for the building of the grand edifice as well as other buildings necessary for the accommodation of the staff and students.[132] By 1822, the Trio accomplished their task of completing the great structure. Soon after the completion of the main building and the College House, the Rev. John Mack joined the Trio. He proved to be an invaluable asset to the College. It was Mack who took charge of the secular branches of the curriculum and Ward of the

---

[128]Cf. *SSC Regulations for Internal and External Candidates: Relating to the Bachelor of Divinity (B.D.) Degree,* December, 1962, 6-10. See also *Senate of Serampore College Faculty of Theology Regulations Relating to the Degree of Master of Theology* (Serampore: Serampore College, 1998 and 2007), 2-10. *Senate of Serampore College Faculty of Theology Regulations Relating to the Degree of Bachelor of Divinity* (Serampore: Serampore College, 1993), 3-9.

[129]Cf. Beenie, *The Life and Labours of Carey, Marshman and Ward…*, 29.

[130]Cf. Christadoss, *The Story of Serampore College…*, 21. See also *Senate of Serampore College Faculty of Theology Regulations Relating to the Degree of Bachelor of Theology* (Serampore: Serampore College, 2004), 2. *Senate of Serampore College Criteria for Affiliation and Evaluation Procedure* (Serampore: Serampore College, 2007), 4. *Serampore College Carey Day 17th August 2001: 240th Birth Anniversary of Dr. William Carey* (Serampore: Serampore College, 2001), 3. *Senate of Serampore College Faculty of Theology Regulations Relating to the Degree of Master of Theology* (Serampore: Serampore College, 1998 and 2007), 2. *Senate of Serampore College Faculty of Theology Regulations Relating to the Degree of Bachelor of Divinity* (Serampore: Serampore College, 1993), 3. *Senate of Serampore College Faculty of Theology Regulations Relating to the Degree of Bachelor of Theology* (Serampore: Serampore College, 2004), 3-4. *Senate of Serampore College Criteria for Affiliation and Evaluation Procedure* (Serampore: Serampore College, 2007), 2-23.

[131]Marshman, *History of Serampore Mission…*, 170.

[132]Cf. Marshman, *The Life and Times of Carey, Marshman and Ward…*, 125.

Theology department. By 1822, there were fifty students on the rolls of which fifteen were in the first year and the rest in the upper classes.[133]

These four missionaries, Carey, Marshman, Ward and Mack, together underwent extreme tryst of financial breakdown as they tried their utmost to keep the College and the mission running. Besides their precarious financial state, two grave calamities awaited them. The first was the unexpected death of the Rev. William Ward in March. He was the youngest of the Serampore Trio. It was on the 5th of March that Cholera attacked him, and he died on the 7th of March 1823 although, best medical attention was given. His death left his wife and the Serampore Family in irreparable loss and grief as he had worked and lived together with Carey and Marshman for twenty-three years.[134] The next calamity was the huge loss caused by the devastating floods in the Hooghly River. It washed away an embankment 250 feet long and 16 feet high in front of the Mission buildings. Badly affected by these calamities, Carey and Marshman were left to await the inevitable breakdown. Immediately rescue surfaced. The British and Foreign Bible Society offered them a grant of about 6,000 pounds, enabling them to solve their present difficulties.[135]

As the College grew gradually with maturity, it received support from various angles in India, irrespective of class or creed distinctions.[136] Dr. Marshman left for England toward the end of the year (1822) for two important purposes: to bring about reconciliation between Serampore Mission and the Baptist Missionary Society, and to raise funds for the mission over here in Serampore. However, no matter how much he tried, the first purpose for reconciliation was unsuccessful with not even a glimmer of hope of restoring cordiality in the near future. Hence, for the second purpose, he had to make tedious journey throughout the country searching for people's sympathy and support for the Serampore Mission. He returned to India in May 1829 with much discouragement but soon together with his colleagues began to gear up their energies for the work. Although, the College grew in strength and quality, their financial aspect did not improve. Then again in 1830 there was Bank failures, the detention of dividends in America from the investments of the money collected by Ward in 1820 during his visit there, due to the calumnies against the missionaries reaching America, heavily threatened them. All these struggles presented them an uncertain future.[137]

---

[133]Cf. Christadoss, *The Story of Serampore College…*, 23. See also Marshman, *History of Serampore Mission…*, 180.

[134]Cf. Christadoss, *The Story of Serampore College…*, 20.

[135]Cf. *Ibid.*, 24. See also Sunil Kumar, Chatterjee, *John Clark Marshman: A Trustworthy Friend of India* (Sheoraphuli: Mahamaya Sahitya Mandir, 2001), 48. (Hereafter, Chatterjee, *John Clark Marshman…*)

[136]Cf. Christadoss, *The Story of Serampore College…*, 23-25.

[137]Marshman, *Statement Relative to Serampore Supplementary …*, 33.

By 1830s, they were supporting 13 out-stations mission, 17 European and Eurasian laborers, and 15 native preachers, the College and some widows and orphans. Discovering that there was nowhere else to hope for support, they decided to turn to the public for support. Carey thus appealed to the Christian public in England pointing out:

> If unceasing industry or self-denial could by any means furnish us with the supplies we beg of you, we would toil and deny ourselves with cheerful alacrity and leave you unimportuned. But our hopes are small in this respect, and they are precarious in the extreme... But, a few years have passed away since the Protestant world was awakened to missionary effort. Since that time the annual revenues collected for this project have grown to the then unthought-of of sum of 400,000 pounds. And is it unreasonable to expect that some unnoticeable portion of this should be entrusted to him who was among the first to move in this enterprise, and to his colleagues?[138]

Carey's appeal to the generosity of his countrymen proved to be touchingly successful. Moreover, Mr. Leechman who had joined the work of the College in 1831 also appealed to the English public for the Serampore Mission. People's response to these pleas was indeed tremendous, for, Mr. Hope, the friend and caretaker of the missionaries' interests in England, was able to send thousands of pounds by the first ship itself.[139]

The College despite repeated troubles grew with most talented teaching staff such as Dr. Leechman, and Mr. John Clark Marshman, the son of Dr. Marshman, who joined the staff in 1819, so also with the number of students. Dr. Carey himself conducted the Divinity classes. By now, they had gathered all the means and appliances that are prerequisite for the education of missionaries.[140] Nevertheless, at the same time, they were opposed to the idea of a theological seminary for the training of missionary personnel alone in the College. By 1833, Dr. Carey and his friends began to work for the need of Statutory Laws and Regulations, for the government and administration of the College. The Statutes tackled various matters connected with the administration of the College such as nomination to the Council vacancies, its membership, voting, denominational representation, appointment to the staff, conferring of degrees, discipline, foundations, etc.[141]

During the time that the College was making its roots deep, the College and the Mission were compelled to sustain another great loss with the demise of

---

[138]Christadoss, *The Story of Serampore College...*, 25-26.

[139]Cf. Daniel E. Potts, "A Note on the Serampore Trio," *Baptist Quarterly*, 20 (1963-64), 117. (Hereafter, Potts, *A Note on the Serampore Trio...*).

[140]Cf. Daniel E. Potts, "A Note on the Serampore Trio," *Baptist Quarterly*, 20 (1963-64), 115. See also Marshman, *History of Serampore Mission...*, 181. Marshman, *The Life and Times of Carey, Marshman and Ward...*, 463.

[141]Christadoss, *The Story of Serampore College...*, 25.

the founder, Dr. William Carey. He was for some time been not well physically. He passed away on Sunday, the 9th of June 1834, i.e., while he was in his 73rd year. Thus, the whole burden of the College and the Mission fell upon the feeble shoulders of the aged Dr. Marshman, the second of the Serampore Trio. Dr. Marshman had to wade through many more difficulties and trials as he struggled alone for the running of the College and the Mission.[142]

By 1835, there were above 100 students in the College of whom 10 were Eurasians, and about 50 were Indian Christians. English language replaced Sanskrit, as there was a growing demand particularly for official purposes. In addition to Divinity for the Christian students, Greek, Hebrew, Latin, Mathematics, Logic, and Natural Philosophy were some of the other subjects taught. The same year (1835), Mack and Leechman went to England for reasons of the former's health where they availed themselves of the opportunity to appeal for the Mission's support. During their absence Dr. Marshman's health began to decline rapidly besides which Mr. Barclay, one of the coadjutors died of illness, and so also Mr. Hope, a staunch supporter and friend of the Mission passed away in England.[143] Hence, with all these successive gloom, Mack and Leechman at the advice of friends, negotiated with the Baptist Missionary Society to take charge of the Serampore Mission, thereby to relieve the missionaries of half of the burden. After prolonged negotiations the Society agreed to the proposal. The books and translations work were also to be placed at the disposal of the Society, and the missionaries attached to the College were not to be regarded as agents of the Society.[144]

Marshman's health deteriorated increasingly and he died on the 5th of December 1837. He was spared the pain of hearing the most distressing news of the surrender of the Mission to the Society, which arrived some minutes short after he was buried. Just one day after the burial, the two deputations met in London and the Serampore Mission passed over to the Baptist Missionary Society.[145] Dr. Marshman was 70 years old when he passed away. With the passing away of Dr. Marshman, the first era of the history of the College came to an end.[146]

3.2. The College After the Trio (1837-1883)

After the death of the last Trio Dr. Marshman, Mr. John Clark Marshman with Mr. Mack shouldered the heavy burden of keeping the College alive and running. Although in a way the Society's decision to take over the Mission relieved the

[142]Cf. Daniel, E. Potts, "The Baptist Missionaries of Serampore and the Government of India, 1792-1813," *Journal of Ecclesiastical History*, 15 (1964), 229.

[143]Bannie, *The Life and Labours of Carey, Marshman and Ward...*, 17.

[144]Cf. Chatterjee, *John Clark Marshman...*, 54-55.

[145]Marshman, *History of Serampore Mission...*, 181. Potts, *A Note on the Serampore Trio...*, 116. Marshman, *The Life and Times of Carey, Marshman and Ward...*, 463 & 519.

[146]Cf. Chatterjee, *John Clark Marshman...*, 90-100.

missionaries of the double load, yet still the running of the College was found to be a tough job for the missionaries.[147] John Clark Marshman owned a Paper Mill, the first in India, and he published a Periodical called *The Friend of India*, which he had converted into a Weekly. His companion and friend Mr. Mack helped in its editorial work. Junior Marshman thus had contributed immensely toward the College from his private earning. It was estimated that by the time that he left India for good in 1855, he had spent more than 30,000 pounds for the College from his earning.[148]

By 1844, Marshman and Mack realized that they could not maintain the College owing to the fact that they could no longer depend on the insufficient contribution of the English public. As a result, using their better judgment, they approached the Home Committee of the Baptist Missionary Society to take over the College too. However, the Committee, though they were no longer indifferent to the missionaries as hitherto, they were not yet ready to accept the heavy burden. Instead, the Committee decided to support a theological professor on the staff of the College. Hence, the Rev. W. H. Denham entered the staff as a representative of the Society.[149]

The next year (1845), Rev. J. Mack died of cholera. He was a man who totally identified with the aims and ideals of Carey and Marshman thereby in a way he filled the empty place left by Ward's death. He was most of all helpful to Mr. Marshman particularly in the editorial work of the *Friend of India*. The Principalship of the College passed to the Rev. W. H. Denham after Mack's death. The College gradually developed under the two faithful men, Marshman who continued to support the College through his personal income from his Paper Mill, the sale of his books on Law, and even some amount from his salary as a Government Translator, and Denham an able missionary who headed the College.[150]

The year 1845 is furthermore significant in the history of Serampore as it marked the end of the Danish rule of Serampore town. For 90 years Serampore was a Danish colony since 1755. Owing to the fact the financial bankruptcy that the Indian colonies under the Danish rule were attributing to Denmark, the Government of Denmark sold off its Indian assets to the British East India Company for about twelve and a half lakhs of rupees. As a result, the two *cradles of Christianity in India*, with Tranquebar in the South and Serampore in the North, were handed over to the British on the 11th of October 1845.[151]

In 1855, John Clark Marshman decided to leave India for good. Thus, Denham and Marshman made a proposal to the Home Committee once again to

---

[147]Cf. Carey, *Memoir of William Carey D.D. Late Missionary to Bengal…*, 35.

[148]Christadoss, *The Story of Serampore College…*, 28.

[149]Cf. Culross, *William Carey…*, 27.

[150]Cf. Chatterjee, *Hanah Marshman…*, 57.

[151]Cf. Christadoss, *The Story of Serampore College…*, 29.

take complete control of the college by the Society. With the total agreement from the Committee, Marshman before leaving made over the College, concluding all necessary arrangements for the future of the College and also handed over a large sum of money for the College. Serampore thus broke the last link with its founders. In fact, the College owed a great deal to Marshman for his selfless and tireless contributions toward its existence and growth alongside the unquestionable Trio. Even his final act of turning over of the College to the Society should be understood as his unselfish act for the best for the College.[152]

After the departure of Marshman, Denham and John Trafford who joined the staff in 1853 carried on the work of the College with great zeal and commitment. It was during this time that the University of Calcutta was founded. Although, the College was authorized by virtue of the Charter, to award University degrees and diplomas, these were not put into operation probably because of the constant struggle for its existence that had occupied the founders in the early years.[153] Hence, they quickly perceived the advantages of affiliating the College to the University of Calcutta, which could make Serampore to be of greater service than in being an independent institution. Serampore College thus became affiliated with Calcutta University in 1857.[154]

It was in 1856 that the Society officially brought into effect their taking over of the College. From then on it carried out the Society's Missionary Educational operations in Arts and Theological. Moreover, in due course, the officials of the Society became members as well as officials of the Council of Serampore College. Serampore College functioned with the Calcutta University syllabus, which aimed at training men for the Government service, so also it had its own syllabus, aimed at training Christian youth for the service of the Mission and the Church. It taught important courses and subjects such as Greek, Latin, Philosophy, History, Science, Mathematics and English Literature. It emphasized more on the students' understanding of the subjects and their consequent development of capacity for reasoning rather than on the students' ability in remembering certain facts that were taught from the lessons. Affiliating the College to the Calcutta University was beneficial in that it gave the scholars a stimulus to higher education. At the same time, they were aware of the danger of the exam-oriented tendency of the University that does not encourage extracurricular abilities and activities of the students.[155]

The then principal of the College, Rev. W. H. Denham passed away in Galle, Ceylon on the 28th of October1858, while he was on his way back from furlough. His assistant the Rev. John Trafford then succeeded him in the principalship.

---

[152]Cf. Bannie, *The Life and Labours of Carey, Marshman and Ward...*, 35.

[153]Cf. John, *Biographical Sketch of Joshua Marshman...*, 89.

[154]Cf. Christadoss, *The Story of Serampore College...*, 30. See also Smith, *Life of William Carey...*, 90.

[155]Cf. Christadoss, *The Story of Serampore College...*, 31.

Trafford was connected with the College for 26 years both as a teacher and as a principal. He made a lasting impression on the life and work of the College. He was assisted in different ways by John Robinson, William Sampson, Edward Dakin, J. H. Anderson, Thomas Martin, R. Jordan and E. S. Summers. With the best interest for the College at heart, he shifted the Theological section to a building in Alipore, Calcutta, and placed it under the principalship of the Rev. George Pearce.[156] However, some of his colleagues did not consider it a wise decision on his part especially Summers. In 1879, Trafford was compelled to leave the service due to ill health. He was succeeded by the Rev. Albert Williams, sent out by the Society for the purpose. Trafford spent 11 years in retirement and died in London in 1890. Although, the Rev. Albert Williams' tenure was a short one, he made a very lasting impression in that he restored the status of Serampore as a center for Theological education by re-transferring the Vernacular Theological Department back to Serampore from its exile in the year 1882. The next year, 1883, Williams died in England during his furlough and he was succeeded by the Rev. E. S. Summers in the principalship.[157]

3.3. The Closing Down of the Arts Department and the High School: Ending the College's Affiliation with Calcutta University (1883-1906)

The College under the Principalship of Summers entered into a new period of its history. There had been, for quite some time, the spreading of the negative opinion in the Home circles that the Colleges in India were no longer successful as agencies of evangelization for the millions of India. People began to question the wisdom of spending huge amounts of missionary money on such ventures. Furthermore, there was a suspicion that the College had deviated away from the original object with which the founders established – the training of Christian ministers. As a result, the Society decided, in 1883, to close down the Arts Department and the High School and to totally convert the College into a purely Theological Institution. Hence, the College was compelled to end its affiliation with Calcutta University.[158]

---

[156]Cf. Banks, *Three Indian Heroes: The Missionary, The Statesman, The Soldier...*, 57. See also *The Story of Serampore and Its College* (First Edition) (Serampore: The Council of Serampore College, 1918), 24-26. *The Story of Serampore and Its College* (Second Edition) (Serampore: The Council of Serampore College, 1927), 27-30.

[157]*The Story of Serampore and Its College* (Third Edition). (Serampore: The Council of Serampore College, 1961), 32-339. *The Story of Serampore and Its College* (Fourth Edition) (Serampore: The Council of Serampore College, 2005), 32-37.

[158]*The Story of Serampore and Its College* (Third Edition) (Serampore: The Council of Serampore College, 1961), 32-339. *The Story of Serampore and Its College* (Fourth Edition) (.Serampore: The Council of Serampore College, 2005), 32-37. See also Swati, Datta, "Serampore College: A Retrospection", *Serampore College Theology Department Codex 2003* (Serampore: Serampore College Theology Department, 2003), 1. (Hereafter, Datta, *Serampore College: A Retrospection...*).

Contrary to what has been accused against the College from the Home front, it was argued that the College had neither deviated from the original object of the founders, nor had it lost its vision. Thus, so because, the Charter very clearly stated that admission to the college was to be open to all without any discrimination on the basis of caste, creed, or denomination, and the first Prospectus of the College states that the College was founded for the instruction of Asiatic Christian *and* other youth in Eastern Literature and European Science.[159]

Thus, the College with the severing of its secular department became a purely denominational institution, catering to the needs of the Baptist missionary work alone, training the ministers and other workers in the Theological Department and in the Vernacular Normal and School Departments. However, despite the transformation of the College into a purely theological institution, even after nearly 10 years (1883-1892), its financial situation did not improve thus rendering the College barely existing. Mr. A. H. Baynes, the Joint Secretary of the Society came to India in 1890, on a deputation. On his return to his country he submitted proposals to the Society concerning the College. He proposed that the work in Serampore be either transferred to Barisal or to some other location in India; close down the Serampore Mission; put up the buildings for sale, disperse the Library and surrender the Charter. However, the Committee could not accept his proposals but at the same time the idea was not given up for some time although eventually it was abandoned. The College was miraculously rescued from this fatal crisis through the efforts of Dr. E. B. Underhill, the predecessor of Mr. Baynes in designation. His emphatic plea to the Committee for the resuscitation and re-establishment of the College along with the principal's letter on behalf of the College's welfare saved the College from the threat of extinction of 1892.[160]

Despite the status of the College as a denominational institution for the Baptists, nevertheless, diverse races represent its students' body. For instance, as early as 1884, there were students from Bengal, Garo Hills, and Assam etc. Although, many regretted the decision that reduced the College to a mere Theological Institution, still, there were many who appreciated and praised the earnest and tireless work of Principal Summers. Mr. Howells for instance, despite his displeasure concerning the abandonment of the larger ideals of the founders, nevertheless, had to say:

> No man did more than he for the training through the medium of both the vernacular and English, of evangelists and preachers for the mission and Churches in Bengal...one cannot but recognize the highly efficient and serviceable nature of the work done in the interests of the Baptist denomination in Bengal by Principal Summers.[161]

---

[159]Cf. Christadoss, *The Story of Serampore College...*, 32.

[160]"Serampore College" *http:www.absoluteastronomy.com/topics/Serampore College*, (12-02-2008), 7.

[161] *The Story of Serampore College..., op. cit.*, 35.

Many eminent missionaries assisted Principal Summers in the work of the College at different times such as Sutton Page, J. W. Thomas, R. Jordan, Leonard Tucker, T. R. Edwards, W. R. James, A. T. Teichman, Denham, Robinson and T. W. Norledge, C. E. Wilson, J. W. Gilbert, O. J. Millman and J. D. Raw. Summers was compelled to retire in 1906 due to his failing health.

At the retirement of Mr. Summers in 1906, Mr. Howells became the Principal of the College. It was in the year 1895, almost exactly a century after the coming of Carey that Rev. George Howells arrived in India. It was said that he was endowed with the same spirit and vision that animated the great founder of the Serampore College. He was said to be a genius with the same powers of organization and administration. He is remembered in the College's history as the 'second founder of the College.'[162] He was at first sent as a missionary teacher to the Theological College in Cuttack in Orissa, by the Baptist Missionary Society. It was during his work there that he happened to visit Serampore. He was filled with depression as he discovered that Serampore has become a graveyard filled with monuments of the mighty dead. Hence, in the year 1900 Howells, remaining outside the immediate sphere of Serampore, began to work for the resuscitation of the College in accordance with the founders' vision, and the revival of the Charter and the settlement of the College in accordance with its present needs. It was due to his persistent plea and proposals that appeared in articles in the Indian Christian monthlies, that eventually the Council of the College and the Baptist Missionary Society consented with him in regard to the necessity of reorganizing the College.[163]

3.4. Reorganization of the College under Rev. George Howells (1907-1929)

Mr. Howells, the new Principal began to work tirelessly for the revival of the College from its slumber. Successive conferences of missionary bodies in India took place during the following years and many of these pledged their co-operation and support for the College's scheme. Both the Principal and the Vice-Principal, Rev. W. Sutton Page, went to England for consulting the Council as well as to raise funds. They were successful in collecting thousands of pounds in England and Scotland for the reorganization of the College. Moreover, the Council gave them 25,000 pounds from the Arthington Fund and from public appeal. Then Mr. Howells along with the Rev. William Carey, a great grandson of the founder,

---

162 *The Story of Serampore College..., op. cit.*, 36.

163 Cf. Ravi, Tiwari, "Senate of Serampore College (University) at Ninety: Issues and Concerns", *NCCI* Vol. CXXVIII No. 6 (July, 2008), 29-30. (Hereafter, Tiwari, *Senate of Serampore College (University) at Ninety: Issues and Concerns...*). See also Edward, S. Wenger, *The Story of the Lal Bazar Baptist Church Calcutta: Being the History of Carey's Church from 24th April 1800 to the Present Day* (Calcutta: Edinburgh Press, 1908), 69-70.

went to America and appealed before the American Foundations, but they were not very successful over there.[164]

Howells returned to India early in 1910 and with the help of his colleagues, began his work for the College. It was in October 1910 that the Higher Theological Department was opened, and in 1911, Intermediate Arts classes were re-started in affiliation with Calcutta University. The Principal's report for 1912 refers to the application made to the University of Calcutta for affiliation up to B.A. classes in English (Pass and Honors), Philosophy (Pass and Honors), Sanskrit (Pass and Honors), History (Pass) and Political Philosophy (Pass). Concerning the Theology Department, the report states that there were 13 students, of which 6 were internal and 7 external, taking B.D. Course. These 13 students represented a variety of denominations – Anglican, Baptist, Congregational, Methodist, Presbyterian and Syrian from all parts of India, Bengal, Bombay, Central India, Madras, Punjab, United Provinces and Rajputana.[165]

The 1913 report testifies of the affiliation up to B.A. and the co-operation between Serampore and Bishop's College in matter of lectures; the slight alteration in the Statutes adopted at the instance of the Bengal Conference in connection with the Continuation Committee of the World Missionary Conference of Edinburgh, 1910; the visits of John R. Mott and Bishop Azariah; the appointment of Father Geeverghese of the Syrian Church ensuring the co-operation of the Syrian Church, and the enrolling of the Malayalee students. In the Arts Department the number of students rose to 165, which necessitated the opening of new hostels, and other necessary quarters for the staffs and workers. By 1914, the interest and support of the American Board of Commissioners for Foreign Missions and the Church of Scotland Mission, as well as of the National Missionary Council of India in and toward the work of the College, was secured. The National Missionary Council of India took charge of the efforts for making Serampore more interdenominational.[166]

The next year 1915 became a very significant year for the College in that on the 4th of December; Serampore conferred the Degree of Bachelor of Divinity on the first three Theological graduates of the College in full exercise of the rights under the Charter of 1827. In 1916, the Council instituted the Diploma of Licentiate in Theology Course, and the Theology Department's organ *The Codex* was also founded the same year. There was also the improvement in the area

[164]Cf. *Serampore College Prospectus 2008 Arts, Science and Commerce Department*, (Serampore: Serampore College Computer Bi-Centenary Block, 2008), 2-5. (Hereafter, *Serampore College Prospectus 2008 Arts, Science and Commerce Department…*).

[165]Cf. *The Story of Serampore College…*, 37. It was reported that the then University Inspector, Professor Stephen, recommending the application remarked that there was no reason why Serampore should not be the Oxford College of Bengal.

[166]Cf. Daniel, E. Potts, "William Carey's Arrival in India 1793-1993, Serampore College 1818-1993", *Bicentenary Volume:* (Serampore,: Serampore College, 1993), 15.

of accommodation. The Ganguli plot (the present Mack House) was purchased and it was fitted up as a Hindu Hostel, for the Arts students, with a resident warden.[167]

Just when the College was rapidly progressing, an unprecedented proportion financial crisis occurred in 1922, which threatened the closing down of the College. The Council, the Society and the Faculty were compelled to save the College at a very great sacrifice. The sacrifice was in closing down of the Collegiate School in Serampore, and it was opened in Bishnupur in 1923 under the name 'William Carey High School.' Later, the London Missionary Society and the Church Missionary Society joined in the running of it and changed its name to 'Union Mission High School.' Today it is known as the 'Siksha Sangha High School.'[168]

Despite such great sacrifice, the financial position of the College was still not erased. Although, there was a suggestion that the College be shifted away from Serampore to some other potential place of the country, fortunately it did not find favour within the Society. The National Missionary Council (NMC) proposed for the appointment of a Committee on Theological Education, which would explore all possibilities of co-operation by the missions and Churches in India. It then set up a Committee, which included the Church of England, the Methodist Episcopal Church of Southern Asia, the Lutheran Missions, Baptists, Congregationalists, Disciples, Presbyterians, Wesleyans, and the Young Men Christian Association (YMCA). Then the Principal was sent to England in order to discuss the possibilities of co-operation at the headquarters of the missionary societies in England.[169]

The Theological Education Committee of the Bengal and Assam Christian Council (BAC) proposed for the amalgamation of Bishop's College, Calcutta, and Serampore College, at Serampore. Although, it served as a first step in the matter of the much talked of co-operation in Theological Education, the whole plan dissolved, as the Bishops of the Anglican Church in India rejected the proposal for the amalgamation of the two Colleges, while it sympathizes with the state of Serampore College and offering to assist it in any other possible way than what had been suggested.

The Council thus left alone had to decide its future course. Just when the College was struggling for its existence, the Master died. The Rev. J. H. Oldham of Ecumenical fame became the Master of the College. His acceptance to become the Master relieved the Faculty of much tension. The Faculty recorded on 6th of September 1924:

> In view of the difficulties with which the College is faced and the work in which Mr. Oldham is already engaged, they appreciate the willingness with

---

[167]Cf. Datta, *Serampore College: A Retrospection…*, 2.

[168]*The Story of Serampore College…*, 38.

[169] Cf. *The Story of Serampore College…*, 38-39.

> which he has shouldered this new responsibility, and they trust that under his wide experience of missionary work and close touch with Missionary Societies, the College may enter upon an era of greater stability and ever-increasing usefulness to the whole of the Church of Christ in India.[170]

The Society and the Council were divided concerning their opinions for the next move. The Society's opinion constitutes of drastic measures, and the Council's opinion constitute of total support to the College. It was the latter's opinion that won at the end. In 1925, the Baptist Missionary Society General Committee decided to run the College and accept responsibility for its financial support recognizing that the challenge of Serampore was a call to a venture of faith in the Master's cause. In view of the new financial relationship of the College with the Society, a Co-ordinating Committee of the College and the Baptist Missionary Society was formed. Although, reluctant to do so, the decision was made to close down the Vernacular Theological Department, which has been a consistent feature of the Serampore enterprise for a hundred years. The Rev. J. H. Oldham, Master, the Rev. J. A. Stuart, the Secretary of the Council, Mr. William Carey of the Carey family, and who was a member of the Council, and Mr. Anderson stood firmly behind the College and enabled it to come out safe and sound.[171]

By 1924, the College was affiliated to Calcutta University in B.Sc. by 1927 the student numbers rose to 300 in the Arts and Science Department of which 122 resided in three hostels – the Main Hostel, Mack House and the King's House, the last being a gift to Carey from the King of Denmark in 1821. In 1932, this house was sold to India Jute Mill.[172]

The year 1927 was the year of the Centenary of the Charter. Its celebrations were held on the 7th of January 1928, under the Presidentship of H. E. Sir F. H. Jackson, Governor of Bengal. The Rev. H. Anderson gave the address at the Commemoration Service. Some of the main features of the celebration included an enlarged edition of the book *The Story of Serampore and Its College*, a Centenary Number of the *Codex* and the Charter Centenary Report. On that auspicious day, 18 B.D. students, 1 B.D. honors received their degrees, and 17 students received their L.Th. Diplomas.[173]

Dr. Howells the then Principal of the College retired towards the end of 1929 after rendering his service to the College for 22 years as its Principal. The Rev. G. H. C. Angus, who was already on the staff, was appointed the succeeding Principal after Dr. Howells. Thus, one of the most eventful eras in the history of

---

[170] *The Story of Serampore College...*, 39.

[171] Cf. Brian, Stanley, *The History of the Baptist Missionary Society 1792-1992* (Edinburgh: T & T Clark, 1992), 296-7. (Hereafter, Stanley, *The History of the Baptist Missionary Society...*).

[172] *Ibid.*, 298.

[173] Cf. *The Story of Serampore and Its College...*, 47-48.

Serampore College – the Howells era – came to an end in 1929. Even today, Dr. Howells is remembered as 'the second founder' of Serampore College.[174]

3.5. History of Serampore Continues (1929-1942)

With the appointment of the Rev. G. H. C. Angus as the Principal of the College in 1929 after the retirement of Dr. Howells, the only other original member of the reorganized College staff remaining was the Rev. J. N. Rawson who continued as Vice-Principal. In 1934, the Carey Centenary Year, at the request of the Senate, and under its auspices, Mr. Rawson, who was a Sanskrit scholar, edited the *Katha Upanishad* containing text and commentary. It became a valuable work among the wide circle of readers interested in Philosophy and Religion. He was also very much connected with the local Church and with the Baptist Churches in Bengal as he was one of the architects of the Bengal Baptist Union and also its first President in 1934. When his time for retirement came, neither he nor his friends were happy but their unhappiness was somewhat lightened when he passed away before he could leave, and his body was laid to rest in Indian soil in the Mission Cemetery in Serampore in April 1940.[175]

During these growing years of the College, it was not only the Theology Department but also the Arts and Science Department that constitute the overall function of the College. An important feature of the Arts and Science Department that needs to be mentioned here is the formation of the various student bodies under the auspices of the College. Those student bodies include the Historical Society, Bengali Literary Society, Economics Society, Poor Fund and the Union Society.[176] The last one, although it was not purely a students' body, was managed mainly by students, and for the first time in 1930, a student was appointed its president, which later on became an officially accepted practice in the constitution of the Union Society (US). This Society served as the principal students' body in the College with its great responsibility of looking after all the extra-curricular academic activities of the students' viz., debates, and talks by eminent men, students' dramas, Poor Fund and other host of activities. In 1934, after a gap of twelve years, the Old Students' Association was revived mainly through the efforts of its Secretary, Sri A. L. Mullick. This Society was formed with the main object of keeping the old students in close contact with their alma mater through varied functions and programs, periodical meetings and an annual reunion. It

---

[174]Cf. *Friends of Serampore* (July 21, 2003), 1.

[175]It should also be noted that Mrs. Rawson beside her husband's immense contributions, had also been remembered for her distinctive contribution as a perfect hostess through whom many were drawn toward the causes associated with the College. Cf. W. Stewart, "The Theology Department, 1929-1960," *The Story of Serampore and Its College* (Serampore: The Council of Serampore College, 1961), 60. (Hereafter, Stewart, *The Theology Department, 1929-1960…*).

[176]K. R. Chatterjee, "The Arts-Science Department, 1929-1960," *The Story of Serampore and Its College* (Serampore: The Council of Serampore College, 1961), 50. (Hereafter, Chatterjee, *The Arts-Science Department, 1929-1960…*)

thus succeeded in achieving its aim of creating everlasting interests and ties among the old students for the welfare of the College.[177]

It was during this period that the country was experiencing the full force of the freedom movement. As a result, it was natural that the College was also not left unaffected. There was great excitement among the students and these interrupted the learning atmosphere on few occasions. However, the College was able to maintain a spirit of harmony and accord thereby assuaging the students' excited spirits all due to the sympathy of the College authorities for India's emancipation. Thus, at a time when it was considered a crime for them to publicly express sympathy for the freedom movement, the authorities of the College boldly sympathized and envisaged a new emancipated India.[178] Moreover, it was also a period in which the College was affected by the wind of the Second World War, of which we shall be enlightened in the succeeding point.[179]

3.6. Serampore College and Its Period of Exile (1942-1946)

India's general history recollects how the entry of Japan into the Second World War in 1941 greatly affected India, who had so far remained almost unaffected by it. Serampore College also comes under one of its first victims. It was in relation to this world issue that Serampore College had to undergo its exilic experience. In 1942, the College received notice from the Government that the College premises were to be handed over to the Government for use as a military hospital. This was a great blow to the College with its huge responsibilities and functions for both the Theology Department as well as its Arts-Science Department. There was no other way out than to move the Theology Department to Chandernagore, where classes were reopened in October 1942 in a rented house with Mr. Abraham[180] as the in charge of 14 students. The work of the Department went on with four to five staff members traveling four to five days a week between Serampore (where they were remaining) and Chandernagore and between Calcutta (where one was residing) and Chandernagore. In addition to their difficulties, after about eighteen months, the remaining part of the College property was again requisitioned by the Government and compelled the transfer of the Library of more than 19,000

[177]Chatterjee, *The Arts-Science Department, 1929-1960...*, 53. See also *Serampore College Prospectus 2008 Arts, Science and Commerce Department...*, 5.

[178]It was reported in the 1938 Annual Report of the College thus: 'Working for a new and emancipated India our highest hopes will be fulfilled when we see India taking her destined place in the world's life, in the parliament of man, that federation of the world, to which through the overruling providence of God, the nations of mankind are at last surely and swiftly moving.' Cf. *Ibid.*, 50-51.

[179]*The Story of Serampore College...*, 57.

[180]C. E. Abraham was on the staff for thirty-five years serving the College in several capacities, as Theology Secretary, Librarian, Registrar, Vice-Principal and Principal and also as a Professor of Church History. Cf. Stewart, *The Theology Department, 1929-1960...*, 61.

books.[181] This resulted in their added struggle for the search for places and quarters for the office and families residences. Eventually they were able to get hold of a large rented house in Chandernagore, which had previously been the Hotel de Paris, for the purpose.[182]

Even during the exilic period, the Department carried out its ministry and functions without ceasing. As a result, a wider circle of people learned of the College both its past and its present. Again early in 1945 a further move became inevitable as the French authorities requisitioned the Hotel de Paris, which was renamed as 'Carey House.' Once again the College authorities were put to the brainstorming exercise of wondering how to, and where to move the old Library with its huge volumes. Finally, they moved the theological books section to Somerset House, the main college house in Chandernagore, and the rest of the old Library was taken back to Serampore, where, by the kind permission of the Metropolitan of India, it was housed in the old Danish Church of St. Olave. Other small houses were rented for accommodating the staff and for the office purposes. Still, undaunted, the work of the Theology Department went on at Chandernagore.[183]

It was in May 1946 that the College's period of exile came to an end and all returned to their original home Serampore. It was in that year that a theological student named Mr. A. K. Mukherjee, was for the first time elected as President of the Union Society. This step helped the two departments, who have been separated for quite a long period, to get back to their old relationship of belongingness in one college – Serampore College. The year 1947 was the first full working year back in the College compound although they had to do extra manual work for the clearing away of the extra buildings and rubble, which the military had left behind.[184]

With regard to the Arts-Science Department, when the Government notice arrived in 1942 for the requisitioned of the College premises, it seemed as though the Department had to be closed down for the duration of war. Fortunately, a local high school, the Serampore Union Institution, came and rescued the Department. By transferring the school classes to the morning hours, the Managing Committee of the school offered the College authorities the use of their buildings for College classes from 12-30 to 5-30 p.m. Thus, from September 1942, College classes

---

[181] *Ibid.*, 64. It was said that most of the Library heavy shelves and much of the furniture were sent by riverboats, and the books were transferred on road by army Lorries. Although it was toward the end of the College session, the students volunteered to stay an extra week to help in the shifting.

[182] *The Story of Serampore College*…, 60.

[183] Cf. Chatterjee, *The Arts-Science Department, 1929-1960*…, 51-52. See also Datta, *Serampore College: A Retrospection*…, 2.

[184] Cf. Tapan, Banerjee, "Serampore College towards Glorious Second Century", *Serampore College Carey Day 17th August, 2001* (Serampore: Serampore College, 2001), 8. (Hereafter, Banerjee, *Serampore College towards Glorious Second Century*…).

for the Arts-Science Department were held in the Serampore Union Institution building. In the meantime, the College office remained in College House, but the next year (1943) it was shifted to a rented house as that building also was requisitioned by the Government. Moreover, with the exception of about 1,000 essential books, the Library was transferred to Chandernagore along with the Theology Department. Although, the College was scattered in several places, it was able to successfully carry on all its important extra-curricular activities. All these were made possible mainly due to the tireless efforts of Mr. M. N. Biswas, who was in charge of the College establishment at Serampore.[185]

The College was successful not only in maintaining its normal activities but also was able to make a new progress during this exilic period. It introduced Co-education system in the Arts-Science Department. In the beginning, two women students studied in the College and they were accommodated at Mack House, the home of Mr. and Mrs. Wenger. However in 1943, eight regular women students were admitted to the first Inter. Arts class. Another unique experiment of the College during this time was the use of oral tests instead of written examinations owing to the scarcity of papers. This experiment proved to be interestingly successful.[186]

An important and noteworthy event of this period, as well as in the history of the College, was the visit to the besieged China by the Vice-Principal of the College, the Rev. C. E. Abraham. He went to China in a military plane as visiting lecturer to Nanking University, which was then in exile at Chungking. This event signifies India's genuine interest and participation in her neighbours' struggle and welfare. In January 1946, after three and a half years' stay in the Serampore Union Institution, the Department was shifted to a fairly big house in Lower Circular Road in Serampore. It was toward the middle of the same year 1946 that the College was released by the military authorities and handed back to the College authorities. Restoring the College to its old condition and resettling down to it required an unprecedented strength and efforts from all members. By June, the Hostel was reopened with two messes instead of four as previously. By July, regular classes began in the same old rooms made possible only after putting a great deal of labour.[187]

3.7. The Return of Serampore College and the Challenge of a New India (1946-1960)

In 1946, the College as a whole with its two departments returned to its beloved old Home Serampore after years of difficulties in exile. On its return it finds itself in a very uniquely difficult situation. To revive its pre-1939 conditions with its old traditions and customs, in its entirety became impossible, so also

[185]Chatterjee, *The Arts-Science Department, 1929-1960...*, 51.

[186]Cf. Chatterjee, *The Arts-Science Department, 1929-1960...*, 53.

[187]Cf. Banerjee, *Serampore College towards Glorious Second Century...*, 8.

to create immediately new conditions to meet the needs and opportunities of a 'New India' was equally difficult. In fact, the atmosphere had started as early as 1942 with the invasion in the eastern frontier by Netaji Bose and his Indian National Army, the uprising of 1942, the Cabinet Mission in 1946, and the great communal riots in the same year 1946. All of these effects culminated in August 1947, the birth of the 'New India' in which she received her dignity and status of an independent sovereign state.[188] The overall change in the status of the country brought in its wake immediate affects in every aspects of life, particularly in the field of education. Education became one of the most sought-after aspects. The Arts-Science Department of the Serampore College experienced a great change. In the first year of independence itself (1947), the roll strength of the College rose to 436 in comparison with the pre-war years average of 280. Subsequently, it continued to increase each year and by 1957, ten years after the independence, it rose to 1,052.[189] It could have been much more than that but due to the lack of sufficient accommodations many had to be turned away.[190]

In 1948, the B.Sc. classes, which had been suspended for nearly twenty years were reopened. In 1950, commercial subjects were introduced in Intermediate Arts, and in 1955, Biology in Intermediate Science. They had to convert an army hut into a laboratory at a total cost of Rs. 20,000 of which the West Bengal Government contributed Rs. 13,000. In 1956, the College became affiliated in Honours in History and Physics. In 1960, Chemistry Honours and Biological subjects such as Botany, Zoology and Physiology in B.Sc. Pass, were put up for affiliation.[191]

It was during this period that important changes also took place in the College administration. Rev. G. H. C. Angus, who succeeded Dr. Howells in Principalship in 1929, retired in 1949, and the Rev. C. E. Abraham, the Vice-Principal, was appointed the Principal. It was the year (1949) the location of the Council of Serampore College was transferred from London, England, to Serampore, India.[192] Rev. Abraham thus incidentally became the first Indian Principal of the College in 1949[193] till his retirement in 1959, in which the Rev. William Stewart replaced him. The Degree of Master of Theology was also instituted in 1949, and was conferred for the first time at the Convocation held in January 1950.[194] The transfer of the Council of the College from England to India in 1949, brought about some more significant changes in the administration. For

[188]Chatterjee, *The Arts-Science Department, 1929-1960...*, 53.

[189]*Ibid.*, 54. See also Steward, *Theology Department...*, 79.

[190]Cf. Datta, *Serampore College: A Retrospection...*, 1.

[191]Cf. Datta, *Serampore College: A Retrospection...*, 2.

[192]*Serampore College (University): Handbook for the Year 1957-59*, 1.

[193]Chatterjee, *The Arts-Science Department, 1929-1960...*, 55. Cf. Stewart, Theology *Department...*, 66.

[194]*Handbook for the Year 1957-59...*, 1.

the first time in the history of the College, two non-Christian members of the Arts-Science teaching staff namely, Professors N. N. Mukherjee and H. N. Gupta were appointed members of the College Faculty. The post of Vice-Principal was removed and instead two Deans, one for the Arts-Science Department and the other for Theology Department, were created. Mr. M. N. Biswas, Professor of English and a senior member of the Faculty, was appointed Dean for the Arts-Science Department,[195] and Dr. V. E. Devadutt became the Dean of Theology Department.[196] However, this arrangement was found to be unsatisfactory and therefore, the post of Vice-Principal was revived and Professor Biswas became the Vice-Principal, upon whom the work of the Department rests heavily. Two Boards, one for each department were also formed; however, these Boards were abolished in 1958, and had been replaced by the two Committees of the Faculty, one for each department.[197]

The establishment of the University Grants Commission became a new and welcome feature in the educational life of the country. In India for the first time, a systematic attempt was being made to organize University education on sound lines. Subsidies were introduced to upgrade College teachers' salaries and capital grants were given for the improvement of libraries and laboratories. Another important improvement in the nation's educational field is the introduction of the Three Year Degree Course. It replaced the Two Year Intermediate Degree Course for students passing the Higher Secondary School Examination. A pre-University or Entrance Examination Course was created to prepare students who have passed the ordinary level School Final for the Three Year Degree Course.[198]

In 1960, a new University in Bengal came into existence namely, the University of Burdwan. Under its jurisdiction come most of the districts of the Burwan division of West Bengal. As a result, the Arts-Science-Commerce Department of Serampore College, connected with the University of Calcutta for more than hundred years, was compelled to sever that connection, and come under the new University of Burdwan.[199] The College thus went through a period of transition both internally as well as externally.

Besides the important changes that took place in the Arts-Science Department of Serampore College, its Theology Department was also simultaneously experiencing changes, in the transition period of the College as a whole. One important area of change especially in terms of improvement was the added strength of the Staff by the addition of new members representing varied traditions like the Irish Presbyterian Church, the British Methodist Church, representatives from the Church of South India, the Mar Thoma Church and the Orthodox

[195]Chatterjee, *The Arts-Science Department, 1929-1960 ...*, 56.

[196]Stewart, Theology *Department...*, 66. See also Datta, *Serampore College: A Retrospection...*, 2.

[197]Cf. Banerjee, *Serampore College Towards Glorious Second Century...*, 9.

[198]Cf. Chaterjee, *The Arts-Science Department, 1929-1960...*, 56.

[199]Chaterjee, *The Arts-Science Department, 1929-1960...*, 57.

Syrian Church. For the first time the numbers of the Theology Staff became more adequate thereby the responsibilities given to all in addition to their teaching duties could be shared more widely as well as lighter. Moreover, beside the added regular staff, there were many visiting lecturers from other parts of India and from many different countries. These opportunities gave the students and the College to come in contact with many eminent and learned men through which they were enriched and enabled to develop a wider understanding of peoples and cultures and of the Universal Church of which they are a part.[200]

Another development of the Theology Department was the increase in diversity of races, cultures and languages. It was noted that in 17th August 1960, the birth anniversary celebration of the founder William Carey, during the event of the 'Chain of Verses,' a text recitation in many languages, beside the five classical languages, there were 22 languages as spoken by the resident students. Moreover, it is interesting to know that during this time there were some among them in whose language the Bible was not yet translated fully and therefore many of the Serampore old graduates could play an important part in the work of translation.[201]

3.8. The Senate of Serampore College from 1961 to the Present

The College celebrated the Bicentenary of Carey's birth in 1961.[202] It was during this time that the Carey Library and Carey Museum were brought under the direct control of the College Council. The Art-Science-Commerce Department, which transferred its affiliation with Calcutta University to the University of Burdwan in 1960, was re-affiliated to Calcutta University in 1966.[203] In 1966, William Stewart retired and S. J. Samartha succeeded him as the Principal of the College. Since then, there had been rapid changes of Principals – S. J. Samartha (1966-68), A. K. Mundle (1968-69), M. N. Biswas (1969-72), S. K. Chatterjee (1972-76), R. L. Rodrigues (1976-77), S. Mukhopadhyay (1977-87), G. D. Bhattacharyya (Acting Principal 1987-88), T. K. Swarnakar (1988-89), J. T. K. Daniel (1990-98),[204] Dr. Lalchungnunga (1999-2011) and Dr. Laltluangliana Khiangte (2012 till date). It is also pertinent for us to mention here the list of the names of the Registrars of the SSC - John Drake (1919-20, 1922-26), Dr. G. H. C. Angus (1921, 1926-29), C. E. Abraham (1929-49), W. Winfield (1949-54), William Stewart (1954-59), C. Devasahayam (1960-75), J. T. Krogh (1975-78), D. S. Satyaranjan (1978-2004), Dr. Ravi Tiwari (2004-2013) and Dr. Santanu K. Patro (2013-Till Date).

---

[200]Cf. Stewart, *The Theology Department...*, 89.

[201]Cf. Stewart, *The Theology Department...*, 89.

[202]Cf. Datta, *Serampore College: A Retrospection...*, 2.

[203]*The Story of Serampore College...*, 38.

[204]*The Story of Serampore College...*, 38-39. See also Banerjee, *Serampore College towards Glorious Second Century...*, 9.

In 1968, on the occasion of Ter-Jubilee Celebration of the College, the Government of India issued the Commemorative Stamp of the College. During 1971-72, when the College was faced with serious financial crisis, it received a substantial grant from the University Grants Commission (UGC), for the improvement and expansion of the College Library and the Laboratories for the Arts-Science Department. In 1977, the College observed the Ter-Jubilee of the Royal Charter of 1827.[205]

In 1979, the State Government came to the aid of the College's financial difficulties by taking over the responsibility of paying salaries of the Arts-Science-Commerce Teaching and non-teaching staff against the deposit of 50% of the income realized as Tuition Fees with the State Government according to the West Bengal Colleges (Payment and Salaries) Act, 1978. On the occasion of 150th Death Anniversary of William Carey in 1984, the whole College community paid their homage to Carey. In 1990 the College celebrated the completion of 75 years of the Higher Theology Department.[206]

During the decade 1977-87, when the financial condition of the College was improved to a great extent, the then Principal S. Mukhopadhyay initiated the reorganization work for the upliftment of the Theology Department. It could be completed only in the next decade during the tenure of Dr. J. T. K. Daniel, who labored hard to collect endowments for the overall development, particularly, the expansion of the College and introduction of Honors Course to all the remaining subjects, after completing the plans for Consolidation and improvement programs in 1990.[207]

In 1993, the Government of India published another Postal Stamp in commemoration of the auspicious occasions. In October 1999, the College celebrated the Bicentenary of the Arrival of Marshman and Ward. The Bicentenary of the Foundation of Serampore Mission, along with the Foundation of the Library was celebrated on 10th January 2000 with the naming of the Students' New Common Room as "Angus Hall" in remembrance of former Principal Dr. G. H. C. Angus.[208]

In 1999, the College received its 20th Principal in the line since Carey, and after Dr. J. T. K. Daniel and Dr. Lalchungnunga from Mizoram, one of the North Eastern States of India. Since then till date, the College is under the leadership of Dr. Lalchungnunga. Today, there are more than 50 theological colleges and seminaries under the affiliation of the Senate of Serampore College (University) in India. The Senate of Serampore College (University) stands as a distinguished and notable Theological Education body in India through its excellent and efficient standard in relation to its overall system and structures including Excellency in

---

[205]Banerjee, *Serampore College towards Glorious Second Century...*, 9.

[206]Cf. Stewart, *The Theology Department, 1929-2005...*, 89.

[207]Cf. Banerjee, *Serampore College towards Glorious Second Century...*, 9.

[208]Cf. Banerjee, *Serampore College towards Glorious Second Century...*, 10.

its faculty as well as its students who becomes the proofs/witnesses of being its products. However, it should not be taken to mean that the SSC is exempted from any shortcomings or criticisms. In fact, it has its fair share of criticisms that comes its way in the process of its existence and growth, but those aspects will be noted in the forthcoming chapters of the research. The main thrust of this second chapter being on the historical background and development of the SSC, the researcher has to draw a limiting line up to here.

4. The Royal Charter of 1827

It was on the 15th of July 1818 that the Serampore Trio published the prospectus of the Serampore College under the title 'College for Asiatic Christian and other youth in Eastern Literature and European Science.'[209] From the beginning the King of Denmark, King Frederick VI, showed special and liberal interest in this important venture of the Trio. As a result, when the College came in contact with serious difficulties concerning its uncertain future status, the Trio sought the help of Denmark.[210]

With the precarious status of the College here in Serampore, Dr. Joshua Marshman was sent to England in 1826 for its purpose. He first secured an appointment with the Danish Minister in London, Count Molke. Next he went to Denmark to begin his important mission. He obtained access to the records of the University of Copenhagen and made a translation of that portion of the Charter and Statutes of Copenhagen University, which he believed were applicable to Serampore and with these aid he drew up a sketch of a Charter for the College at Serampore, West Bengal, India. Dr. Marshman then obtained a meeting with the King, King Frederick VI and presented before His Majesty his proposal for the incorporation of the SSC. Subsequently, the Chancellor of the University of Copenhagen was called to examine the work prepared by Dr. Marshman, and was given general approval.[211]

The draft prepared by Dr. Marshman gave to Serampore the same power of conferring degrees, which was enjoyed by the University of Copenhagen and Kiel (then a Danish University). These degrees offer the possessor a certain civic rank in the State, and it was thought possible that a Danish gentleman might seek a degree at Serampore, simply for the position it would grant him in his native land. The Charter was issued on the 23rd of February 1827, duly signed by His Majesty, King Frederick VI of Denmark, and an authorized translation

[209]George Howells and A. C. Underwood, *The Story of Serampore and Its College* (Serampore: Council of Serampore College, 1928), 24. (Hereafter, Howells and A. C. Underwood, *The Story of Serampore and Its College…*).

[210]W. Stewart, "The Serampore Charter," *The Story of Serampore and Its College*, edited by Wilma S. Stewart (Serampore: The Council of Serampore College, 1961), 41. (Hereafter, Stewart, *The Serampore Charter…*).

[211]Stewart, *The Serampore Charter…*, 41-42.

(of which the original is still at Serampore), was read in the Royal Council of Fredericksnagore (Serampore) on the 18th of June 1829.[212]

In 1845, six years after the death of King Frederick VI, the Honorable British East India Company became possessor of all the Danish Settlements in India. However, King Christian VIII, respecting the wishes of his predecessor, Frederick VI, gave an indispensable verdict that the Charter granted to the College should be fully acknowledged. The following clause (Article VI, second section) was therefore added in the treaty of session:

> The rights and immunities granted to the Serampore College by Royal Charter of date 23rd February, 1827, shall not be interfered with, but continue in force in the same manner as if they have been obtained by a Charter from the British Government subject to the general law of British India.[213]

The treaty was duly ratified on 16th of October 1845, and therefore, starting from that date SSC came under the possession of the British Government.[214] Although, SSC was passed from the Danish hand into the British's, its Charter was not taken away from it, but rather it was kept intact as before, with the assurance of the British support to it.[215]

Unfortunately, the years that followed happened to be years of commercial depression, hence, the endowments and money safe-kept for the development of the College were lost in the Bank failures in Calcutta. Therefore, although the College continued to carry out its functions, it could not reach the expected standard of efficiency that would justify for the use of the Charter for conferring University degrees. Nevertheless, the Serampore Trio did not abandon the Charter but rather postponed its usage for a later fitting period. In June 1833 (a year before his death), Carey brought out a series of regulations meant to serve the purpose of permanent statutes of SSC. Carey, Dr. Marshman and his son John Clark Marshman, who with Carey, were members of the first Council under the Charter, then signed on these documents. In the Charter itself a term of ten years was permitted for the preparation of such statutes defining in greater depth the general principles concerning the management and government of the College. This document serves as a significant legacy of the Serampore missionaries that stood for freedom from rigid denominational distinctions, rigid theological tests and freedom from racial, cultural, color and creedal differences.[216]

212Cf. *Serampore College Prospectus 2008 Arts, Science and Commerce Department…*, 3.

213Stewart, *The Serampore Charter…*, 42.

214Serampore had been under the Danish rule since October 8, 1755. Cf. Howells and A. C. Underwood, *The Story of Serampore and Its College…*, 28.

215Cf. Tiwari, *Senate of Serampore College (University) at Ninety: Issues and Concerns…*, 29. See also Stewart, *The Serampore Charter…*, 42.

216Stewart, *Serampore Charter…*, 42. Since 1827, the year Serampore College received the Charter until 1857, the year Serampore was affiliated with Calcutta University, although the

It was in 1895 that George Howells, a young Baptist missionary came to India. After paying a visit to Serampore, he was deeply depressed at his discovery of what Serampore had become. Soon after that, he received a copy of a book entitled *The Principles and Methods of Missionary Labor* authored by Dr. E. B. Underhill, Honorary Secretary of the BMS, and who was a veteran missionary. The Rev. Howells was captivated by one of the papers in this book that deals with Serampore College. In it, Dr. Underhill has written against the suggestion that had been placed before the BMS Committee that the College building be sold, the Library dispersed and the Charter surrendered. Dr. Underhill had boldly counter-proposed the following, among other matters:

1. That the Mission and College at Serampore be resuscitated on the lines laid down by its founders.
2. That this object be presented to the Society's supporters as one of the items of the centenary (1892) fund.
3. That if it be thought expedient an application be made to the proper authorities for the revival of the Charter and the settlement of the College on a foundation consonant with present needs.[217]

Although, the Committee had abandoned the earlier suggestion to close the College, Dr. Underhill's proposals were lost in the Committee due to division among them. Dr. Underhill wrote in 1896 (in the book mentioned):

> The Charter which gives the College the right to confer degrees in Arts and Theology was granted by the Danish Government and confirmed by the British Government... I still cherish the hope that better days may be in store...and that the College may yet become the University it was intended to be by its founders...[218]

In 1900, five years after his arrival in India, George Howells read a paper before a gathering of Baptist missionaries from all across the country. It contains his proposal concerning the revival of the Charter for the purpose of helping the cause of higher theological education in India. However, the Conference, making no reference to the use of the Charter, instead decided to test the opinions of the

---

College fared quite well, owing to the economic depression and an inadequate staff that contribute toward its disqualification from attaining University standard; it becomes impossible to make use of the Charter. Then again with the emergence of State Universities, including Calcutta University to which the College was affiliated, the Charter was rendered unimportant. Its insignificance became more so when in 1883 the University department of the College was closed down and Serampore merely became a High School for Christian boys and a Vernacular Training Institution for the Baptist Missions and Churches in Bengal. Thus, the Charter of 1827 was kept lying in a closed cupboard without it ever being used, and then eventually, in 1883, its existence became totally meaningless, rendering it almost an extinct issue.

[217]Stewart, *Serampore Charter...*, 43.

[218]Cf. *Ibid.*, 44.

missionaries concerning the suggestion whether it would be wise to form a Faculty of Theology in one of the existing State Universities. Nevertheless, Howells, without giving up his strong conviction, continued to write a series of pamphlets stressing the necessity to revive the Charter. The data collected revealed that the larger portion of missionary opinion favored the revival and utilization of the Charter on University lines, rather than the formation of a Faculty of Theology in one of the Universities.[219]

An important Universities Commission under Sir Thomas Raleigh as its President came with the purpose of investigating the University system in India. The issue of establishing a Faculty of Theology in one of the State Universities was also one among the agendas that they deliberated upon. Eventually, they came out with a negative answer to that possibility. This decision enabled the missionary bodies to advocate the formation of an interdenominational Senate during the Decennial Missionary Conference in 1902, at which all the main Missions in India were represented. Thus, a representative committee was appointed to confer with the Serampore College Council concerning the possibility of reviving the Charter.[220]

George Howells then began his long but tireless venture for the reorganization of the College in keeping with the vision of the founders. Armed with a copy of the Charter and all other related documents, he called on Dr. (later Sir) Asutosh Mukherji, a distinguished lawyer in handling University affairs. After meticulous examination, Dr. Mukherji declared the Charter totally valid. The next year (1903), Howells went to England but before meeting with the Committee in London, he sought out Sir Thomas Raleigh, who gave him a note on the legality of the Charter to take to the Committee. Thus, after taking the highest legal opinion concerning the validity of the Charter and the practicability of a Senate as proposed by the Decennial Conference of 1902, Howells received a favorable response from all corners.[221]

In the meantime, both the Baptist Missionary Society and the College Council (then in England) had so far not given their opinion concerning the proposal for reviving the Charter. Howells then met the Committee with the legal consents that he had secured from both in India as well as in England, and hence the Committee gave their decision in favor of the revival of the Charter. Next, both the Society and the Council opined that if the Charter was to be used for the actual conferring of theological degrees, and if these degrees were to be regarded highly, then the College itself had to be made worth. Thus, reorganization of the

---

[219]Cf. Stanley, *The History of the Baptist Missionary Society ...*, 248-252.

[220]It was said that coming to this final decision in favor of the Charter was not without confronting certain strong opponents. In some influential quarters doubt was sowed concerning the validity of the old Danish Charter, as well as there were some who regarded the resurrection of the Charter an impossibility. Stewart, *Serampore Charter...*, 43-46.

[221]Cf. Stewart, *Serampore Charter...*, 45.

College became a foremost concern. At this time the post of Principal was vacant and hence, George Howells was appointed the next Principal. He returned to India in 1907 well prepared to begin the work of reorganization of the College.[222]

With a view of making the College and the Charter available to students of all denominations and Churches, a higher theological department was opened in October 1910. Then in the following year 1911, the College, for Arts purposes, was re-affiliated to the University of Calcutta. It was on the 14th of December 1915 that the College for the first time used the Charter to confer degree on its students. As Dr. Howells writes in the earlier edition of *The Story of Serampore and Its College*, 1928:

> On 14th December, 1915, the powers conferred by the Charter were utilized for the first time and at an assembly presided over by His Excellency Lord Carmichael, Governor of Bengal, I had the pleasure on behalf of the Council in England (of which in the meantime I had become a member) of conferring the degree of Bachelor of Divinity upon three students of the College, members of the Congregational, Presbyterian and Syrian Orthodox Churches.[223]

Then again in 1929, at the time of Dr. Howells' retirement as Principal of the College, the Council for the first time used their right of conferring an Honorary Degree and gave the degree of Doctor of Divinity to the Rev. George Howells. Since then, at the time of Convocation, the College has been conferring degrees on students of Serampore College and all other affiliated Colleges under it. Moreover, it has also been giving Honorary Degrees to those men who have given outstanding services to the Indian Church.[224] In 1960 at the time of transference of the College's affiliation from the University of Calcutta to that of Burdwan, the distinctive rights of Serampore College and its Charter were written into the Constitution of the new University of Burdwan.[225]

5. The Serampore College Act 1918

It is the revival of the Charter under the Bengal Act of 1918. It stands as *an Act to Supplement, and in certain matters to supersede, the Royal Charter of Incorporation and the Statutes and Regulations of the Serampore College*.[226] It was during the time when Serampore College was undergoing extreme struggle for the reorganization of itself that the Council of the College invited the co-operation of the missionary bodies represented during the Decennial Conference of 1902 in reorganization

[222]Cf. Stewart, *Serampore Charter…*, 45.

[223]Cf. Christadoss, *The Story of Serampore College…*, 38.

[224]Cf. Stewart, *Serampore Charter…*, 47.

[225]Cf. Banerjee, *Serampore College towards Glorious Second Century…*, 5.

[226]*Bengal Act No. IV of 1918: The Serampore College Act, 1918* (As has been modified up to the 1st of July, 1951). This has been taken from "Appendix I" *The Story of Serampore and Its College*, edited by Wilma S. Stewart (Serampore: The Council of Serampore College, 1961), 113.

of the College. As a result, it received varying replies in the form of appreciations as well as criticisms. While most of them conveyed their appreciation concerning the efforts being made by the Council for the reorganization of the College, one major criticism that they boldly pointed out was concerning the fourth Statute of the College which requires a Council predominantly Baptist. According to their criticism, this particular Statute of the College clearly made it impossible for other denominations to have any legal guarantee of equality of status and/or privilege in the overall scheme.[227]

After receiving this criticism, the Council seriously considered the whole issue and at a meeting on 11th of March 1909, adopted a proposal to approach the Government of India for powers to enlarge its membership and eliminate the element of Baptist predominance from the Constitution of the College.[228] It involved protracted negotiations with the Secretary of State, the Government of India and the Government of Bengal, and finally the matter was remitted to the Bengal Legislative Council for action on the lines as approved by the Secretary of State. It is noteworthy to know that during the Legislative Council Session of 1918, the then Principal of the College, Dr. George Howells was made an honorable member of that particular body, and therefore he had the privilege of assisting the member in charge, Sir S.P. Sinha (later Lord Sinha), in seeing the bill through the Council.[229]

On 28th of March 1918, the College Bill was passed by the Legislature at its meeting. Subsequently, it received the approval of the Governor-General and was gazetted on 1st May 1918. In place of a Council of not more than five members, one of whom could be a non-Baptist (as was read earlier), it provides for a Council of not less than five and not more than sixteen members, at least one-third of whom shall be members of the Baptist denomination. Moreover, provision is also made for the constitution of a Senate of not less than twelve or more than eighteen members, and which shall include at least one and not more than three of each of the following Christian denominations – Anglican, Baptist, Congregationalist, Lutheran, Methodist, Presbyterian and Syrian.[230] The work of the College thus came to be operational under a Senate and a Council. Beside this enlarged Statute, the rest of the ordinary privileges under the Charter and Statutes remain untouched under this Act.

Summary

SSC stands today as a living legacy of undying vision and mission of its founders William Carey, Joshua Marshman and William Ward, simple men with extraordinary faith and zeal who sowed the timeless seeds of *Learning and Piety*

[227]Christadoss, *The Story of Serampore College...*,, 46.

[228]Cf. *Ibid.*, 36.

[229]Cf. Christadoss, *The Story of Serampore College...*, 37.

[230]Cf. Serampore College, Est. 1818, *Friends of Serampore*, July 21, 2003.

– that was to serve (in the future) as the basic point of reference in our analysis of an ecumenical character of our theological education particularly under the SSC. Now having had a rather detailed analysis on the historical background of the SSC, it calls for the importance of taking the wider historic context of India within which theological education in general had had its genesis historic tradition upon which our present world of theology in general traces its ancestry. As such, with that humble attempt at recounting the historic birth and growth of the SSC in India in the early part of the 19th century, we shall now take up the next essential chapter (third), which will commit itself to the analysis of the living or functioning realities that constitute India's multifaceted context – the very context that theological education seeks to make itself meaningful, coherent and effectively relevant to people's lives and their overall environment.

Chapter 3

Theological Education in a Multi-Faceted Context of India

Introduction

Theological education in this post-modern age is ferment, because all the beliefs and practices of Christians are under fresh and searching scrutiny. Theological education is always confronted with the problem of this multi-facet context. In this complex situation, the problem of theological education becomes a problem of reason and faith. The Multi-faceted context of India makes the scope of theological education more interesting and challenging in that it has to be always vigilant and sensitive to the life and workings of the complicatedly structured environment within which it is integrally situated with its vision and mission. India is one truly pluralistic nation in every sense of the term, be it in religious, cultural, social and political and even in its race and ethnicity of its population and then, resulting from which, there are innumerably unignorable problems and issues constituting one whole reality.

Therefore, the pertinent question undoubtedly is, whether theological education in general and the Board of Theological Education of the Senate of Serampore College in particular, is moving, learning and thereby relevantly contributing to the very real needs of India's context or not? While it may not be possible for us to attain an immediate response, keeping that quest in our minds nevertheless, let us attempt here in this chapter, to make a critical analysis on the subject (as is given in the chapter's title), by first discussing the nature and content of India's multi-faceted context and then move on to the place and role of theological education within that given context.

1. Theological Education and India's Socio-Cultural Context

India's general context during the 18th and 19th century was defined by the depressing aberrations of its political subjugation under the subsequent oppressive powers and authority first under the autocratic Hindu rulers that was followed by the Muslim rulers (for over 600 years or 6 centuries), and finally under the foreign rule (the British). Thus, by 1800 India's socio-cultural life, political and religious conditions were at such a threateningly low standard.[1] India and her population had for quite long not known any peace under the above mentioned successive reigns.[2] Even under the best authority of Mogul rulers, there were frequent instances of wars, injustice, and outbreaks of barbarity. Indian civilization and culture were at their worst. It was a dark period of Indian history.[3]

It is important to note that even with the coming of the British Supremacy India's situation did not improve. When the British came to power, they found that the people were inextricably rooted in their traditional Hindu religion and culture so much so that it bind the people under astonishingly extreme beliefs and practices that indirectly served to enable the foreign power to benefit itself enormously from it.[4] For instance, in the beginning, the factor of caste, a social evil, that rigidly divides and breaks its people into irreconcilable communities as high castes, low castes and sub-castes,[5] were used to its advantage. The supremacy of the British Government began to ascent in India by the battle of Plassey in 1757, but then the rulers had no specific policy until the new century.[6] Initially the East India Company had no desire to rule India but as time passed by, the company did realize that it was impossible to be profitable without the exercise of

---

[1]Cf. Aleyamma Zachariah, *Modern, Religious and Secular Movements in India* (Bangalore: TBT, 1998), 1. (Hereafter, Zachariah, *Modern, Religious and Secular Movements...*). See also J. N. Farquhar, *Modern Religious Movements in India* (Delhi: Munshiram Manoharlal, 1967), 1, 2. (Hereafter, Farquhar, *Modern Religious Movements...*).

[2]Cf. Ibid. See also Eliza F. Kent, *Converting Women: Gender and Protestant Christianity in Colonial South India* (New York Oxford University Press, 2004), 35.

[3]E. R. Hambye, *History of Christianity in India*, Vol. III (Bangalore: CHAI, 1997), 1-2.

[4]The British colonials who took the administrative powers and the later Western European missionaries, albeit their separate missions and objectives in coming to India, both maintained a colonial and imperialist attitude upon the non-Western, non-European and therefore 'uncivilized' and 'uncultured' Indians. While the former politically and economically/commercially oppressed and exploited the natives in the name of India's development, the latter religiously and culturally suppressed and alienated them all in the name of a 'new' and 'true' faith or religion namely Christianity that they generously and charitably offered to the hitherto 'pagan' or 'heathen' nation. For a more detail 'post-colonial' critique on the dual western colonial powers cf. Jacob S. Dharmaraj, *Colonialism and Christian Mission: Post Colonial Reflections* (Delhi: ISPCK, 1993). (Hereafter, Dharmaraj, *Post-Colonial Reflections...*).

[5]Zachariah, *Modern Religious and Secular Movements...*, 2.

[6]Farquhar, *Modern Religious Movements...*, 2.

power.[7] So, by the end of the 18th century, the company gradually came into being as the government of India. The British Empire in India continued to expand during the 18th and 19th centuries until it covered the whole of India.[8] The British rule put an end to the political warfare and chaos that prevailed through most of the 18th century, but economically and socially, insecurity continued[9] due to the new legislative measures and administrative practices as well as due to the impact of Western technologies and ideologies.[10]

It was sin for Hindu society even to cross the seas and live in foreign countries. These structures isolated the people of India from the rest of the world.[11] Moreover, Hinduism has a very low opinion of women.[12] The higher castes believed and therefore practiced sati in which, a woman after the death of her husband is forced[13] to end her life too by ascending the pyre of her husband's body, and thus burnt alive. It is strongly believed that a woman's faithfulness and

---

[7]We should note that the East India Company came to India exclusively for commerce, and that the British Empire sprang altogether mainly due to the necessity, which was only very gradually realized, of providing a settled and just government in order to make commerce possible.

[8]Farquhar, *Modern Religious Movements...*, 16. Lord Wellesley's policy proved very successful in extending the British Empire far and wide. His policy was completed in 1849, when the last remaining portion of India proper was added to the British Empire at the conclusion of the second Sikh war. Moreover, in 1857 Mutiny by the Indian army led the Indians to be brought directly under the British Crown.

[9]An example could be cited here for understanding the socio-economic plight of the native Indians particularly of the poor labourers under the 18th, 19th century British Administrations in India: in the later part of the 18th century, when the Protestant missionary William Carey came to India (1793) when he the following year (1794) joined the Indigo factory as a General Manager (where he was paid rupees 200 per month beside other commissions), the average Indian labourers who worked under him from dawn to dusk, were paid anywhere between 2 or 2.50p to 4 rupees per month. Cf. Dharmaraj, *Post-Colonial Reflections...*, 52-53. Cf. also Robert, Eric Frykenberg, ed., *Land Control and Social Structure in Indian History* (London: University of Wisconsin Press, 1969), 256. See also R. Sutharalingam, *Politics and National Awakening in South India 1852-1891* (Arizona: The University of Arizona Press, 1974), 396.

[10]Hugald Grafe, *History of Christianity in India*, Vol. 4, part 2 (Bangalore: CHAI, 1990), 18.

[11]Parama Roy, *Identities in Question in Colonial and Postcolonial India* (USA: University of California Press, 1998), 28. See also David West Rudner, *Caste and Capitalism in Colonial India* (USA: University of California Press), 1994, 67.

[12]Manu prescribed that a woman should be under the control of her father before marriage, under her husband in marriage and under the control of her son in old age.

[13]Mala Sen, *Death by Fire: Sati, Dowry and Female Infanticide in Modern India* (New Jersey: Rutgers University Press, 2002), 55. (Hereafter, Sen, *Death by Fire: Sati, Dowry and Female Infanticide...*). It is believed that except for those women who blindly accepted any religious-based ideas and practices as divine decrees, in most of the cases, women forced against their will, to follow this horror.

chastity is proved through her obedience and willingness toward this inhuman practice.[14]

Moreover, Hindu religion hold a very rigid belief where it holds that it is a curse for a woman to live as a widow and at the same time prohibited its women for remarriage whereas the widowers (men who had lost their wives) were allowed to remarry. This practice left many child widows and youthful widows who have to live the rest of their life in sorrow.[15] There was also the practice of devadasi system,[16] female infanticide,[17] and human sacrifice[18]all of which were common practices. All these factors contributed toward the dilapidated condition of India's socio-cultural and religious life during the 18th and 19th centuries.

India being a land of variety and differences, it all contributes to the nation's richness and beauty as well as to its divisions and problems. The biggest division is between the rich and the poor. India's most vexed issue is poverty side-by-side with affluence, and great progress accenting backwardness.[19] One group has wealth and power and lives in comfort while the other group lives in deprivation, hunger and squalor, harassed and dishonored in many ways. Contrasts exists between

---

[14]Sati was an act of widow entering the pyre of her dead husband voluntarily or involuntarily, most often involuntarily. Vasudha, Naranayan, *Hinduism: Origins, Beliefs, Practices, Holy Texts, Sacred Places* (NY: Oxford, 2004), 89. With regard to the prohibition of the practice of 'sati', William Carey is remembered as the one who is worthy of being credited with this success. However, some Post-Colonial Indian writers like Dharmaraj, while they consider it commendable for Carey's effort in encouraging the then British-India government to pass laws against such social evils, argue that Carey had miserably failed in raising also his voice against the then European political and economic oppressions in India. He adds that this failure of Carey's was an intentional reality due to the fact that he was not willing to forego the missional and monetary gains without which he (Carey) believed his Christian mission will not be able to run smoothly. For a thought-provoking reading cf. Dharmaraj, *Post-Colonial Reflections*, 51-57.

[15]K. M. Sen, *Hinduism: The World's Oldest Faith* (Harmondsworth: Penguin, 1961), 15-17. Young girls, some of whom even before attaining puberty, were given in marriage to old men, who have other wives. When the husband dies, the child-wife would be declared a widow, and denied any possibility of remarriage.

[16]Nena Talwar Oldenburg, *Dowry Murder the Imperial Origins of a Cultural Crime* (New York: Oxford University Press, 2002), 22. (Hereafter, Oldenburg, *Dowry Murder the Imperial Origins* ...). The term 'devadasi' means female servant of God. But corrupt priests and worshippers used them to satisfy their lusts, which led the devadasis into being sacred prostitutes. This practice spoiled the atmosphere of the temples as it represents temple prostitution.

[17]Sen, *Death by Fire: Sati, Dowry and Female Infanticide...*, 44. Among the high castes, dowry was a deciding factor in marriage.

[18]Oldenburg, *Dowry Murder the Imperial Origins...*, 66. There was a belief that some of the gods and goddesses required human sacrifices and such sacrifices are highly meritorious. For this purpose, often, children were kidnapped and slaughtered and their blood was offered- especially to the goddess Kali - to please her in order to get benefits from her.

[19]Cf. K. R. Ranadiue, "Planning for a Just Society: Illusion and Reality", *Economic and Political Weekly*, XIX/40 (October, 6, 1984), 1747. See also C. J. Fuller, *The Camphor Flame: Popular Hinduism and Society in India*, (Princeton: Princeton UP, 1992), 17.

the privileged classes/castes and the outcastes, the wretched of the earth; between the well-housed and the houseless; the posh residential areas and the foul slums; the costly fashionable eating places and garbage bins where boys and girls, young citizens of India scavenge for something to eat and struggle to prolong the dying process; between the landless and the landlords who own tens of thousand of acres and control the whole clusters of villages and terrorize the entire population with their private police.[20]

India's situation is rife with tensions and contradictions, which erupt naturally or are politically organized into riots, arson and massacres. Violence keeps growing as the compulsions of our economic system weigh heavier on various classes. The contradictions express themselves in the deepening discontent and restlessness of the oppressed, in the politicization and irruption of the poor, the landless and the lumpen proletariats.[21] Despite India being one of the most democratic nations in the world, great progress in industrial development, technology and productivity, the basic human needs of the bulk of India's population have not been satisfied. Hundred million citizens of India are ill-fed, ill-clad, poorly sheltered, ill-treated, despised, exploited and cheated.[22] Such was, and still is, to a very great extent, the condition of India and her population.

1.1. The Problem of Caste-Structured Society

During the 19th and 20th centuries the Hindu structure of society was seriously affected by the rigid caste system.[23] Some are regarded as high castes and other low castes, which are the dividing factors of the Indian society. According to the traditional Hindu Varna system, India's society is divided into five basic categories: a) Brahmin, b) Kshatriya, c) Vaishya, d) Sudra and e) Untouchables. The Brahmins, those belonging to the high caste, were considered as gods, whereas, the Sudras, the low caste were even denied the basic rights of learning and even listening to the Vedas.[24] Manu, the greatest lawgiver of Hinduism, said that molten lead be poured into the ears of Sudras should they listen to the reading of the Vedas. Besides the low castes, there are large numbers of outcastes who were considered as untouchables. The high castes considered that they would be defiled if the shadows of the untouchables fell on them. Highways were not open to the latter. There was neither inter-dining nor inter-marriages between the high castes and

[20]Cf. Samuel, Rayan, "Theological Education in the Social Context of India Today" *Theological Education in India Today*, ed., by Felix Wilfred (Bangalore: ATC, 1985), 18. (Hereafter, Rayan, *Theological Education in the Social Context…*).

[21]Cf. Prem Shankar Jha, "Riots" *Times of India* (December, 22, 1982), 9.

[22]Cf. Rayan, *Theological Education in the Social Context…*, 19.

[23]Taya, Zinkin, *Caste Today* (Bombay: Oxford University Press, 1962), 20.

[24]Brian, K. Smith, *Classifying the Universe: The Ancient Indian Varna System and the Origins of Caste* (New York: Oxford University Press, 1994), 13. (Hereafter, Smith, *Classifying the Universe…*).

the low castes. As mentioned earlier according to Brahmanism, the Brahmins were believed to have been created from the head of the Purusha, Kshatriyas from the shoulders, Vaishyas from the hip and Sudras from the feet.[25] Every aspect of the life structure and functions were governed by the rigid caste system. Thus, for any Hindu to live in foreign countries or even to cross the seas was a great sin.[26] This structure of the Indian Hindu culture has entered even into the life and function of the church today.[27]

From the very first Protestant Mission in India, the problem of caste was a big issue within the Church. When Ziegenbalg died in February 1719, Schultze assumed the leadership in Tranquebar Mission. He tried to stop the castes distinction in the Church, which was strongly opposed by the members, as it had been recognized among the converts a distinction between those who came from various castes.[28] In the New Jerusalem Church, the Sudra men sat on one side of the nave and the others on the other, and likewise the Sudra women in one of the transepts and the other women in the other, at Holy communion all the Sudras, men and women were administered first and the others afterwards.[29] He tried to stop the distinction by order but the result was strong opposition and discontent by the members.[30] When Schultze left Tranquebar, the new missionaries, Walter and Pressier, who arrived in 1725, restored the old practice of caste distinctions.[31]

Even during the early nineteenth century it continued to create difficulties for the Church. In 1833, Bishop Wilson of Calcutta, visited South India and was stupefied at the extent to which he found caste distinctions kept up among the Christians. He issued a strong letter ordering that the distinction of caste must be abandoned, decidedly, immediately and finally, which at once provoked uproar.[32] Great problem aroused among the Sudra Christians of Madras, Tanjore and Trichinopoly. This new policy led many members of the old congregations join the Leipzig Mission after 1846, because the latter was willing to let old caste distinctions be kept.[33] The problem of caste distinctions in the Church was never

---

[25]Zachariah, *Modern Religious and Secular Movements...*, 2.

[26]Ninan, Koshy, *Caste in the Kerala Churches* (Bangalore: CISRS, 1968), 7.

[27]Smith, *Classifying the Universe...*, 79.

[28]C. B. Firth, *An Introduction to Indian Church History* (Delhi: ISPCK, 2000), 137. (Hereafter, Firth, *An Introduction to Indian Church History...*).

[29]J. Richter, *A History of Missions in India* (Oliphant: 1908), 108. (Hereafter, Richter, *A History of Missions...*).

[30]Firth, *An Introduction to Indian Church History...*, 137.

[31]Richter, *A History of Missions...*, 110. See also, Firth, *An Introduction to Indian Church History...*, 139.

[32]*Ibid.*, 162. See also Eliza F. Kent, *Converting Women: Gender and Protestant Christianity in Colonial South India* (New York Oxford University Press, 2004), 16-19. (Hereafter, Kent, *Converting Women: Gender and Protestant Christianity...*).

[33]Richter, *A History of Missions...*, 168.

absent throughout the nineteenth and twentieth centuries. Controversy of castes was a serious problem for the Protestant Church in India. Pickett says that in one area, a group of Sudra converts went back to Hinduism because the Malas caste of several neighboring villages was baptized. In another area, aboriginal converts have refrained from efforts to bring Hindus to Christ for fear that the conversion of the latter would raise the issue of intermarriage.[34] In every area there were found an awareness of this danger and systematic attempts were made to overcome it. On the whole, this problem is more severe in the South than in other parts of India.[35] Within the Church even today, there still exist un-Christian caste division and schism.[36] This is one of the important areas where Christians has to seriously examine the state of the Christian Church.

In the midst of this social contexts of our nation, the structural level of theological education need to be considered with seriousness. Lectures in the classrooms and books alone should not be the main tool and source of theological education. The people are an indispensable source and place of theology.[37] Closeness to the people and participation in their struggles are essential to the theological education in our social situation. The courses will need to remain flexible, subservient to the requirements of the theological education in order to meet the need of the people in their social contexts.

Nineteenth century was also a period of expansion of the social activities of the Church. The social activities in the first half of the 19th century Christian missions were directed towards bringing about a moral reform in Indian society and to emancipate individuals from the age-old superstitious Hindu religion. William Bentinck initiated several measures of social and moral reforms. In the second half of the 19th century, though they increased in number, they were mainly confined to philanthropic activities, such as establishing and maintaining schools, orphanages, hospitals, lepers' asylums and agricultural and industrial training institutions.[38]

---

[34]Richter, *A History of Missions…*, 336. See also Kent, *Converting Women: Gender and Protestant Christianity…*, 25.

[35]This was so because certain sections of the Roman Catholics have permitted such extreme caste distinctions as the segregation of outcastes in Church services and the priority of high-caste converts in receiving the sacrament of the Holy Communion. Cf. Pickett, *Christian Mass Movements in India*, 337.

[36]Edy, Ashirvatham, *Christianity in the Indian Crucible* (Calcutta: YMCA, Publishing House, 1955), 54.

[37]Cf. Rayan, *Theological Education in the Social Context…*, 31.

[38]J. T. Taylor, *The Work of the Canadian Presbyterian Mission* (Canada: Board of Foreign Mission, 1916), 27. (Hereafter, Taylor, *The Work of the Canadian Presbyterian Mission…*). See also M. L. Orchard, *Canadian Baptists at work in India: Missonary Education Department* (Canada: The Foreign Mission Board, 1922), 37. (Hereafter, Orchard, *Canadian Baptists at work in India…*).

1.2. Educational Work of the Protestant Mission: A Responsible Factor in Breaking the Age-Old Hindu Chains around its Low Castes and Women

Education was part of the Protestant missionary activities from the very beginning. The educational endeavors of the Protestant Mission during the 19th and 20th centuries exploded the myth that only the higher castes were destined to learn.[39] It started with elementary schools, followed by secondary schools and colleges, teaching through the medium of English.[40] Thus, some of the outstanding Christian colleges such as the Madras Christian College, at Madras; Noble College at Masulipatnam; Bishop College of Nagpur; and, St. John's College at Agra were founded. These Christian colleges and schools exerted a dominant influence on Indian education and Indian thought.[41]

Protestant Christianity worked for the upliftment of women in India. From the beginning of its mission it felt the urgency for girl's education. It was so because during those days in India, women's education was unheard of. Hence, in the beginning it was mainly the wives of the missionaries along with a handful of single women (either missionaries or individuals) who started the schools for girls.[42] Some organizations were also set up to establish schools and to spread awareness for the importance of women's education. For instance, in 1819, the Calcutta School Society was formed, and in 1834 the Society for Promoting Female Education was formed in London. In 1838, Captain James founded the Scottish Ladies Association for the Advancement of Female Education in India.[43] In 1852, Lady Kinnaired began a school for girls at Dowager, and as a result the Church of England, Zenana Missionary Society and Zenana Bible and Medical Mission were started.[44]

However, establishing of these schools did not function smoothly in the beginning due to the rigid structures and customs of the then Indian society. During those days, practices such as child marriages, female infanticides, the

---

[39]Cf. J. W. Gladstone, *Protestant Christianity and People's Movements in Kerala: A Study of Christian Mass Movements in Relation to Neo-Hindu, Socio-Religious Movements in Kerala, 1850-1936* (Trivandrum: KUTS Publications, 1984), 70-72. It also laid a strong foundation for the cultural renaissance, which had been taking place in the society.

[40]Taylor, *The Work of the Canadian Presbyterian Mission…*, 78.

[41]Orchard, *Canadian Baptists at Work in India…*, 48.In many places, the mission schools provided the people from the depressed classes with the opportunity to educate their children and for which, the Protestant Christians made special efforts to bring them to the schools. Until the government opened schools to the lower castes, mission schools were the only institutions for the lower castes children to learn, though in many places, separate schools were opened for them.

[42]D. Arthur Jeyakumar, *History of Christianity in India: Selected Themes* (Delhi: ISPCK, 2002), 56. (Hereafter, Jeyakumar, *History of Christianity in India…*).

[43]Mar Pongener, *Key Issues in the History of Christianity in India 19th through 20th Centuries* (Jorhat: Barkataki and Co. Ltd., 2000), 90.

[44]Binaya, Bushana Raya, *Zenana Mission: The Role of Christian Missionaries for the Education of Women in the 19th Century Bengal* (Delhi: ISPCK, 1998), 56.

burning of the widows and the pardah system were so prominent that there was little thought for the emancipation of women.[45] Reading and writing was particularly confined to nautch girls and the idea was that education was not for respectable women. As a result, these early schools worked under great difficulties. Even those who attended were rough low castes girls who often had to be paid to attend, and they came so irregularly and left at such an early age that their schooling had little effect.[46]

In Calcutta Drinkwater Bethune, President of the Government Council of Education founded the first school for high caste girls in 1849.[47] Missionaries in 1854 began to send ladies to teach girls in the Zenanas of Hindu families. Mrs. Mullens and Miss. Toogood, were prominent in this work in Calcutta.[48] Thus, began Zenana schools, which was copied in other towns and became a regular feature of the educational-receiving-grants-in-aid from the Government. In 1859, the American Presbyterian Mission started a girls' boarding school at Dehradun, from which in due time came the first female matriculate of Calcutta University.[49] Prominent among the lady missionaries from America was Izabella Thoburn, who came to Lucknow in 1870 and founded a school out of which, the Izabella Thoburn College developed. In 1884, two Christian girls in Bombay namely Miss. Malabai Kukde and Mrs. Shivantibai Nikambe became the first Indian girls to pass the matriculation examination of Bombay University.[50]

Pandita Ramabai (1858-1922) was an Indian woman who played an important role for the emancipation of women in India.[51] She became a Christian in 1883 while she was in England. After finishing her studies, she went to America and stayed there for three more years in Kindergarten training. She wrote a book entitled *The High Caste Hindu Women*, which aroused much interest that sympathizers formed a Ramabai Association to raise money for her work.[52] Back in

---

[45]Firth, *An Introduction to India Church History…*, 192.

[46]Richter, *A History of Missions…*, 329. See also Mary Weitbrecht, *The Women of India and Christian Work in the Zenana* (London: Oxford Univerity Press, 1961), 79. (Hereafter, Weitbrecht, *The Women of India and Christian…*).

[47]Firth, *An Introduction to Indian Church History…*, 192.

[48]Sudha, Kaldate, "Educated Women, Equality and Role Conflict" *Women in India: Equality, Social Justice and Developments*, ed., Leelamma Devasia (New Delhi: India Social Institute, 1990), 57.

[49]M. A. Sherring, The *History of Protestant Missions in India from their Commencement in 1706-1871* (London: Trubner and Co., 1875), 187.

[50]E. G. K. Hewate, *Christ and Western India* (Bombay: J. Kellock, Wilson College, 1950), 286.

[51]Pandita, Ramabai, *A Testimony* (Pune: Ramabai Mukti Mission, 1917), 11. (Hereafter, Ramabai, *A Testimony…*). Her father, a Marathi Brahmin settled in Western Ghats of South Kanara taught his wife and daughter Sanskrit. In 1878 they came to Calcutta. After her brother's death, at the age of 20 she got married but was left a widow by her husband within two years.

[52]Firth, *An Introduction to Indian Church History…*, 194.

India she started *Sarada Saden* (home for Wisdom) in Bombay on March 1st 1889 with the co-operation of Mahadev Govind Ranade and members from Prathna Samaj. In 1890, it was moved to Kedgaon near Pune.[53] She toured the famine area in 1896, rescuing orphan girls more in number than her premises in Pune could accommodate. She sends many to mission boarding homes elsewhere, but she was still left with many. As a result she started the *Mukti Mission* at Kedgoan. Miss Abrams of America joined her.[54] In 1899, buildings were erected and very large Institution was organized containing over a thousand inmates and providing a wonderful variety of occupations such as field work, dairy farming, weaving, sewing, rope-making, etc. Pandita Ramabai's efforts had contributed so much in transforming the position of women in India.[55]

Today girls' education has become the rule rather than an exception. Women graduates are many and they are now taking significant parts in public life. There are now several laws and regulations for the protection of women from discriminations and oppressions, which open the way for Indian women to become visible in both secular as well as in religious set up. Protestant Christianity in India has thus been in the forefront in pioneering women's emancipation movement in India.[56]

BTESSC has taken up very encouraging further steps in providing more possibilities for women in theological education. Now within the SSC affiliated Colleges there are some Seminaries that give serious attention toward the concern for women theological education. We now have Master level studies and even Doctoral studies centre for women study branch.[57] BTESSC have the provision for more scholarship to the women candidates in B.D. level as well as in M.Th. and Doctoral levels. Even the privilege of directly going for continuation of higher theological studies had been made possible for women, i.e., for men, after completion of B.Th. or B.D., they need some ministerial experience (for at least a year) in between before they could qualify for higher studies but for women students that is not required.[58] Thus, for women's education especially theological education, within the social context of India, BTESSC's effort is noteworthy.

---

[53]Jeyakumar, *History of Christianity in India…*, 59.

[54]Firth, *An Introduction to Indian Church History…*, 195.

[55]Ramabal, *A Testimony…*, 16.

[56]Jane, Haggis, *Ironies of Emancipation: Changing Configuration of Women's Work in the Mission of Sisterhood to India* (Bombay: Palgrave Macmillan, 2002), 26. See also Weitbrecht, *The Women of India and Christian…*, 90.

[57]UTC and Gurukul Lutheran Theological College and Research Institute lead in offering Women's studies program. Besides, GLTC&RI has become the main center for Women's Studies.

[58]This has been a significant contribution of the SSC for women students especially because, female graduates often have to be confronted with the common view and practice that society often compel them to oblige and that is, settling down to marriage right after graduating if they happen to take a break before planning for further studies. As such, this opportunity of getting to directly

1.3. Medical Mission: An Important Social Reform Work of Protestant Mission in India

Medical work came to occupy as an outstanding mission work of the Protestant Church. The first mission to adopt a regular policy of sending medical persons as missionaries to India was the American Board.[59] The Protestant Christianity started hospitals and dispensaries both in cities and villages. Christian Medical Colleges and Nurses' Training Institutes were started throughout the country during the 19th and 20th centuries. Some of the important Protestant Medical Colleges are like Vellore Medical College and Hospital, and Ludhiana Medical College, etc. They also started several Tuberculosis Sanatoriums, Leprosy asylums, mental hospitals and more recently psychiatric clinic. In 1926, the Christian Medical Association of India was founded. It sponsors various forms of Medical services and is the central consultative body for Protestant medical work in India.[60] Although the Protestant Christians' involvement in the society in various levels created much disruption in the society, a large number of suppressed people found possibility to break the chains which had bound them for centuries under the traditional culture of the Hindu ideology. Thus, the mission of the Church include beside its emphasis on the spiritual salvation of God's people, the necessity of it being God's instrument in bringing about physical healing or physical salvation of the people from all social physical chains of oppression. Therefore, the focus of our theological education should also be always people-oriented. It should include all sections of society: the rich and the poor; the young and the old; the literate and the illiterate; the healthy and the sick; Christians and people of other living faiths; male and female.[61]

2. Theological Education in the Context of the Poverty-Stricken Population of India

Theological education is to be done in a given context. Implementing theological education in the Indian context has never been easy for the Church in India.[62] India

go for further studies has been enormously helpful for many young women to be qualified in higher theological degrees.

[59]Firth, *An Introduction to Indian Church History...*, 205-207. Attempts of non-professional kind had long been made by missionaries, pastors and catechists to treat sickness; the Tranquebar Mission even sent an occasional doctor to India, and Carey's companion, Thomas, was a medical man, but organized medical missions are a phenomenon of the nineteenth and twentieth centuries.

[60]Kent *Converting Women: Gender and Protestant Christianity...*, 156.

[61]Cf. Samson Prabhakar, "Religious Education in Indian Context: Challenges and Response", *Together with People,* ed., by Samson Prabhakar (Bangalore: SATHRI/BTESSC, 2004), 89. (Hereafter, Prabhakar, *Religious Education in Indian Context...*).

[62]Cf. Yeow Chuo Lak, "Theological Education in Asia Context", *Theological Education and Development,* ed., by Gnana Robinson, Henry Wilson and Christopher Duraising (Bangalore: ATTI, 1984), 23.

is one of the developing countries of the world today, which is very much involved in the matter of the planning of economic development, political development, socio-cultural development, etc. Despite several plans and development projects, the condition of the poor in India remained the same, if not, becoming worse as the population increases every hour of the day.[63] In such situation, the context of the poor becomes an important context for theological education in India today. The context demands a critical self-reflection and evaluation of our theological education as a whole - the structure of our theological institutions, seminaries and life's style of the theologically-trained people as well as its educators. Indian theological education is acknowledging the significance of the context for theological training and the inevitable interaction between the text and the context for the seriousness of bringing the contextually relevant indigenous theological education.[64] The National Take for instance, the Consultation on Theological Education held in Bangalore in 1986 stresses the need for taking the local context seriously. The report says:

> The curriculum in theological colleges should be so oriented that the student should get a basic knowledge of the world around him and of the forces at work in the world. The study of the historic faith and contemporary society are both vital. This would enable him to be sensitive to the hopes, fears and frustrations of the people among whom he is to work. The Christian Gospel, if it is true to its genius, should meet the people at the point of their elemental needs and struggles.[65]

Hence, theological education within India's multi-faceted context needs to critically study its given context and simultaneously, its own theological structure and content in order that its labor becomes meaningful and fulfilling.

2.1. The Context of the Poor in India

The poverty of India is not only the outcome of widespread injustice, but often aggravated by natural calamities such as floods, droughts, famines and earthquakes, some of which may have indirect link with injustice, corruption and greed.[66] Poverty is not an isolated phenomenon. Behind it and behind all the inequalities there is complex economic process and activates. The problem of poverty is a problem of economic and industrial organization. Poverty is not accidental or transitory but structural. Its source lies in the world's and India's uneven

---

[63]Cf. Gnana Robinson, "Challenges to Theological Education in the Context of the Poor and Development", *Theological Education and Development*, ed., Gnana Robinson, Henry Wilson and Christopher Duraising (Bangalore: ATTI, 1984), 1.

[64]Cf. Gnana Robinson, *A Journey through Theological Education* (Madras: CLS, 1989), 74.

[65]*Theological Education in India: Report of the Study Program and Consultation, 1976-1968* (Serampore: BTE and NCCI, 1968), 17.

[66]Cf. Prabhakar, *Religious Education in Indian Context* ..., 3.

development, which has given rise to two unequal humanities: one embarrassingly rich and the other, desperately poor.[67] The gap between the rich and the poor has widened, which mean, the development programs has gone in favor of the rich and the strong. Development, which was supposed to be liberative force for the poor from oppressions, exploitation, marginalization, and discrimination from political and economic, psychological and spiritual, on the contrary, has made the state of poverty to continue.[68] Thus, C.T. Kurien describes:

> In a world where millions of men and women and children worry about their next meal, where human life is reduced to less than the level of animal existence for want of material things of life, we can never underestimate the economic dimensions of development. This is particularly true of our country where even after so many decades of planning for development, life is a bitter struggle day after day for the many millions whom we see and pass by every day. To them, development is not a new name for peace and justice, but the old name for food.[69]

Hence, economic growth without social justice benefits not the poor, but the rich. Consequently our national development and economic growth have failed utterly to eradicate poverty; instead, it increases the gulf between the rich and the poor.[70]

According to Fr. Duartie Barrettp "India is a land of massive poverty and misery and a land of inequalities and injustices".[71] The poor are driven to a state of life where a person is rendered homeless, sick, illiterate and indebted. In India, the poor are reduced to sub-human living. Communicable diseases such as cholera, malaria, smallpox, tuberculosis, HIV/AIDS and trachoma blindness still remain rampant among the poor. No safe water for drinking. Most of these diseases are being communicated through polluted water.[72] The untouchables in India, who constitute nearly 40% of the population, are the most affected among the poor.[73] The untouchables are being murdered, beaten, raped and abused almost every day throughout the country. They undergo atrocities throughout the country every day. In some regions they are not even allowed to draw water from a common well. They cannot walk on the roads through a high castes' street. If one carries

---

[67]Cf. Rayan, *Theological Education in the Social Context of India...*, 20.

[68]Robinson, *A Journey through Theological Education...*, 73.

[69]C. T. Kurien, *Poverty and Development* (Bangalore: CISRS, 1974), 41. (Hereafter, Kurien, *Poverty and Development...*).

[70]Robinson, *A Journey through Theological Education...*, 84.

[71]Duartie, Barreto, *India's Search for Development and Social Justice: Analysis of India Society* (Bangalore: Centre for Social Action, 1977), 16. (Hereafter, Barreto, *India's Search for Development and Social Justice...*).

[72]Cf. Robinson, *Challenges to Theological Education...*, 4-5.

[73]Barbara, Roger, *Racism* (Geneva: WCC, Publication, 1980), 3.

an umbrella open he has to fold it as soon as he sees a high caste man coming opposite to him, if one happens to wear a turban on his head, he has to remove it and tie it around his waist on seeing the high caste man. Wedding or funeral processions have to stop the music while crossing a high caste street. They are denied entrance into teashops; where they are allowed separate glasses are kept outside, which a Harijan has to take and wait outside until the shopkeeper brings the tea outside and pours it into the cup. Raping of Harijan women is a common thing in many parts of India. If one is indebted to a high caste man, then the latter has the women of the indebted as a matter of right.[74] The Harijans, so long as they lack economic power, will continue to struggle for livelihood throughout the country.

The women of the poor are the oppressed of the oppressed. They are oppressed both by their own men who are guided by the sense of male chauvinism, dominant in India, and also by the rich who exploit them in many ways. The children of the poor are also exploited in many parts of our country. Though, the child labor is forbidden by the Indian constitution, poverty forces the parents to send their children to work, for minimal wages.[75] Indebtedness to rich is a common phenomenon among the poor in India. The poor has no means to repay the debt, they bind themselves to serve the rich until the debt is cleared, and the rich, through his exorbitant interests and low wages sees that debt is never cleared.[76] In India, a minority of people live in luxury while the masses subsist below poverty lines. Thus, Barreto notes "luxury in the midst of such poverty is a crying scandal".[77] The affluent countries equate development with comfort and define it in terms of economic and material growth.[78] For the rich in the West, poverty in the third world is not a problem, but a condition that must be endured and this condition might improve if the poor wait for a gradual peaceful, constructive change based on mutually beneficial political security and economic ties with the West.[79]

---

[74]It was reported that in one of the villages in Tamil Nadu, a Hindu, a Harijan teacher, while passing through the street saw a high-caste lad of 5 or 6 years on his way and, in a friendly mood, he addressed the little boy in singular 'nee' means 'you', the boy went and reported this to his parents. In the evening when the teacher was returning from the school, he was caught, tied to a post, stripped naked and beaten. When the matter was presented to the police, the police advised the people to have restraint. Cf. Robinson, *Challenges to Theological Education...*, 4-6.

[75]Cf. Robinson, *A Journey through Theological Education...*, 79-80.

[76]Cf. Kurien, *Poverty and Development...*, 39-40.

[77]Barreto, *India's Search for Development and Social Justice...*, 43.

[78]Nazario, *Learning in Context* (Bromley: TEF, 1973), 21.

[79]B. W. Lefever, *From Amsterdam to Nairobi* (Amsterdam: 1979), 60.

2.2. Theological Education and its Focus on the Poor

Theological education is not just producing some Church functionaries who would fulfill their given duties daily. A proper theological education in the context of the poor is preparing people for God's mission in this world; for training the total people of God, of whom the ordinands stand first. Evangelization or proclamation[80] of the good news to the poor is definitely not enlisting more members to the many denominational Churches in India. Models of theological education and service, which are built on the theology of West, are no more suitable to our context of the poor. They simply condone the existing conditions and they are harmful to the aims and objectives of theological education in the mission of God. According to a Roman Catholic study "evangelism cannot be relevant unless it addresses itself to the unjust and oppressive situations of contemporary India and takes the form of liberation".[81] This is possible through proper theological education.

The context of the poor demands theological education that is oriented in the context of the poor. Imperialism and capitalism did not succeed in bridging the gulf between the rich and the poor. Materialistic ideologies such as communism believed that religion was counter-productive in keeping people under superstition and that once man was enlightened and freed from the influence of religion he would become more ready for an egalitarian communist society. Secular ideologies often forget the spiritual dimension of development and it is here Christian spirituality has a unique contribution to make.[82] In this context of the poor, what we need is a theological education that is oriented from the very context of the poor - a theology, which will sustain the poor in their struggle for liberation. This is possible when theological education is made available to the total people of God, including those at the grass root level of the society. Here, theological education in this context is the poor who should discover for themselves, what good news means in their own context. Struggle with the poor involves suffering and death, having the ultimate goal as the transformation of the life of the poor. In this journey of struggle, the poor need the sustaining power of the Christian faith, the faith in the death and resurrection of Jesus Christ.[83] Thus, theological education in the context of the poor becomes an essential part of the whole theological education in India.

3. Theological Education in the Context of India's Religious Pluralism

The question of other faiths had been one of the main concerns of the modern Ecumenical Movement through the 1950s and 1960s. This concern had led to the serious discussions on the concept of dialogue with other living faiths at an

[80]Cf. Robinson, *A Journey through Theological Education…*, 92-93.

[81]*Report of the Standing Committee of the CBCI: On Evangelization of Modern World* (Bangalore: 1975), 23.

[82]Cf. Robinson, *A Journey through Theological Education…*, 95.

[83]Robinson, *A Journey through Theological Education…*, 96-97.

important meeting in Kandy (1967) and at the WCC assembly in Uppsala in 1968. However, these discussions were among the Christians themselves. One of the landmarks in the WCC's dialogue journey was the first inter-faith dialogue meeting held at Ajaltoun, Lebanon, in March 1970.[84] It was an inter-faith dialogue on dialogue. It brought together three Hindus, four Buddhists, three Muslims and several Christians to explore the meaning and significance of dialogue as a new basis for relationships among religious traditions.[85] The concern was that religion should respect the other faiths and has a full knowledge of their beliefs, enters into a closer relationship with others and should refrain from judgmental attitudes.

3.1. Inter-Religious Dialogue

India is a land of many religions, ideologies and cultures. Religion is a serious affair to every Indian. Indian spirituality is deeply rooted in Indian spiritual heritage. Religion and politics are inseparable in Indian tradition. The politicians have become the spokesperson of every religion here in India. Owing to this meddling of religion and politics, in modern days the religions have become a dividing and destructive force. As a result, Christian faith has to be in constant dialogue with other living faiths.

In India, the Churches, various associations and other groups and organizations have carried out the process of inter-faith dialogue with great importance. Since 1950, under the leadership of P. D. Devanandan and M. M. Thomas, the CISRS, Bangalore, pioneered in the studies about dialogue.[86] Vatican in 1964 opened a secretariat for Non-Christian Religions. In 1975 the WCC, Geneva, established a section for dialogue with other living faiths. In 1975, the National Council of Churches in India started a unit on Unity, Fellowship and Dialogue.[87] Since then it had been playing a significant role in organizing several meetings and seminars on the inter-faith dialogue in connection with other interested bodies. We can briefly look into its several meetings.

i) A Live-in Dialogue with different religious groups was organized by the NCCI on July 9-10, 1991, at Kerala United Theological Seminary campus, Thiruvananthapuram.[88]
ii) Hindu-Christian Dialogue was held in Varanasi on 9-12 February 1992. The theme of the dialogue was **'our heritage and our commitment**

---

[84]Organized by Standly Samartha with approval of the meeting of the WCC Control Committee in August 1969.

[85]S. Wesley Arairajah, "Socio-Political Issues and the Cridibility of Dialogue", *NCCR*, 120/4 (May, 2000), 426.

[86]Paul, Tillich, *Christianity and the Religions of the World* (New York: Columbia University Press, 1963), 22.

[87]Mathai, Zachariah, *Beyond Ecumenism: A Journey in Light* (Thiruvalla: CSS, 2002), 80.

[88]*Minutes of the Meeting of the NCCI 1989-91* (Nagpur: NCCI, 1991), 100.

to harmony'. About 65 Hindus and Christians for four days lived, discussed and prayed together, understanding the two religious traditions and common cultural heritage. The meeting resolved that new methods of inter-religious dialogue should be initiated which will reach the rural masses, students in schools and colleges, and different audiences of children. It stated that inter-religious dialogue must address the problems of poverty and suffering. Religious traditions should be purged of elements of oppression and exploitation, particularly of women and weaker section of the society.[89]

iii) Inter-religious dialogue was conducted by the NCCI in June 1994 at Indian Social Institute, New Delhi. Leaders from different religions participated. The main concern was to bring in communal harmony and development through dialogue.[90]

iv) On 10-11 August 1994, NCCI and Henry Martin Institute of Islamic Studies at Hyderabad organized an inter-faith dialogue and communalism. The main emphasis of the meeting was to bring together both secular and religious leaders of our community.[91]

v) The NCCI, WCC and Madurai Kamraj University organized a program on Hindu-Christian relation from 8-11 October 1995 at Madurai. About 40 participants including 5 women represented both the communities.[92] The aim of the meeting was to draw out a document on Hindu-Christian relations for the use of both the communities for practical living and theological reflection.[93]

vi) NCCI organized an Inter-Faith Dialogue meeting in Padhar Orissa from 17-19 November 1995. The meeting resolved a practical step, i.e., inter-religious group to be organized at the district and village levels in Orissa.[94]

vii) On 13-15 December 1996 a Muslim-Christian Relations was organized by NCCI and Henry Martin Institute of Islamic Studies along with UP Council of Churches at the Bishop Johnson College at Allahabad. The meeting concluded with an agreement that Muslims and Christians living in the pluralistic context of India have to work for deeper

---

[89]*Minutes of the Meetings of the NCCI 1991-92* (Nagpur: NCCI, 1992), 2.

[90]*Minutes of the Meetings of the NCCI 1994* (Nagpur: NCCI, 1994), 82.

[91]*Minutes of the Meetings of the NCCI 1995-96* (Nagpur: NCCI, 1996), 74.

[92]Among the Hindus there were two swamijis- Swami Tattuvamayananda from Sri Ramakrishna Math, Trissur and Swami Sadhashivananda, an organizer for Vishwa Hindu Parishad at Madurai. Among the Christians there were representatives from NCCI, Churches, and the Roman Catholic Church, and Executive Secretary of Dialogue Unit of World Council of Churches.

[93]*NCCI: Nagpur to Ranchi 1996-1999* (Nagpur: NCCI, 1999), 2. (Hereafter, *NCCI: Nagpur to Ranchi 1996-1999 ...*).

[94]*NCCI: Nagpur to Ranchi 1996-1999 ...*, 3.

understanding and better collaboration between each other in order to uphold the values common to all religious people and build up a harmonious, peaceful and just society in our country.[95]

viii) In October 1997 at Varanasi, the NCCI and the UP Council of Churches organized a Hindu-Christian Dialogue meeting. Delegates from various religious groups were present and the main emphasis of the dialogue was a cordial living among religious groups in India.[96]

ix) Inter-religious Consultation on National Issues was conducted by the NCCI on 19 August 2000. Religious leaders from different faiths attended the consultation. They resolved to organize more of such meeting in the near future.[97]

x) The first Inter-religious Dialogue in the North East India was organized by the NCCI and Thomas Jones School of Mission and Evangelism of Cherrapunji from November 28 to December 1, 2000 at Cherrapunji, Meghalaya. 20 leaders of different faiths and about 40 theological students attended the meeting. The participants resolved to extend this inter-faith dialogue throughout the North East region.[98]

xi) The NCCI and YMCA New Delhi organized an Inter-faith Consultation on August 19, 2000 at the YMCA, New Delhi. More than 50 religious leaders and scholars belonging to Hinduism, Islam, Christianity, Buddhism, Jainism, Sikhism, Bahaism and Zoroastrianism participated in the Consultation. It resolved to establish Inter-religious Council of religious leaders of India and an Inter-religious Pilgrimage to be conducted to Mathura so as to soothe the tension and communal violence there.[99]

xii) Inter-Faith Dialogue for Better living was organized by NCCI and Christian Forum on 7 May 2001 at Pune. People from various walks of life such as priests, theologians and leaders of different faiths participated and pledged to see that their regions are kept violent-free and to live with respect and understanding.[100]

xiii) On September 11 2001, the NCCI and the Rashtriya Swayamsevak Sangh (RSS) conducted an Inter-Faith Dialogue in Nagpur. The meeting resolved to continue dialogue between them with mutual respect and understanding for each other's traditions and beliefs.[101]

---

[95] *NCCI: Nagpur to Ranchi 1996-1999 ...*, 11.

[96] *Ibid.*, 17.

[97] *NCCI: Meetings of the Executive Committee and General Body, 3-4 August, 2001*. 15.

[98] *NCCI: Meetings of the Executive Committee and General Body, 3-4 August, 2001*. 17.

[99] *NCCI: Meetings of the Executive Committee and General Body, 3-4 August, 2001*. 32.

[100] *NCCI: Meetings of the Executive Committee and General Body, 3-4 August, 2001*. 18.

[101] *The NCCI Meeting of the Executive Committee and General Body, 6-7 August, 2002*. 10.

xiv) The Madurai Kamaraj University with NCCI conducted a Seminar on Inter-Faith Dialogue on 31 May 2002 at Madurai. The participants from different faiths prayed for the peace and communal harmony in the country.[102]

The dialogue movement shows that people of diverse faiths while disagreeing in beliefs, can agree on the importance of peace and justice, of social action to relieve suffering and on efforts to save the planet. Inter-faith dialogue is particularly essential in a religiously plural context such as India where communal conflict is currently dividing the country.[103] The reality of religious pluralism as well as the validity of different beliefs and way of life needs to be accepted, and dialogue can help create this understanding, for dialogue in its essence is the acceptance irrespective of caste, creed or culture.

3.2. Inter-religious Dialogue and Theological Education

Diversity and plurality are the basic characteristics of one of the largest democracies in the world, namely India. It is a multicultural, multilingual, multiethnic and multireligious nation. In spite of its plurality, India has remained one nation; at the same time, plurality in India has been the reason for many of its conflicts, outburst of violence and atrocities against each other.[104] The pluralities and diversities have become part of the life of the people.[105] But, "national integration remained ever threatened as it faced the problems of linguistic communalism, religious fanaticism and factional politics".[106] In the midst of these realities, the theological education in India is being carried out.

The national integration, nation's unity and sovereignty and people's harmonious existence together solely depend on meaningful and sincere inter-religious dialogue.[107] In India, a pluralistic context, people of different faiths and no faiths have to work together, pull together in the building of our harmonious nation.[108] The Churches should realize that dialogue with other religions and ideologies are inevitable as far as the Christian mission is concerned, and the Church has to make all efforts to enlarge its scope. The Church must stand in solidarity with the rest of the total community in its struggle for greater human

---

[102]*The NCCI Meeting of the Executive Committee and General Body, 6-7 August, 2002.* 12.

[103]Bina Barnabas, "Ecumenism in Action: Living Amongst People of Other Faiths" *Ecumenism: Hope in Action,* edited by Aruna Gnanadason (Nagpur: NCCI, 1990), 139.

[104]Cf. Samson Prabhakar, op. cit., 90.

[105]J. W. Gladstone, "Ministerial Formation in a Context of Pluralities", *Together with People* ed., by Samson Prabhakar (Bangalore: SATHRI/BTESSC, 2004), 2.

[106]Cf. Paul R. Brass, *Factional Politics in an Indian State: The Congress Party in Uttar Pradesh* (Bombay: OUP University of California Press, 1966), 262. Myron Weiner, ed., *State Politics in India* (USA: Princeton University Press, 1968), 25-30.

[107]Thyagorajan, *Inter-religious Dialogue*, n.d. n.p., 500.

[108]M. A. Thomas, *Toward Wider Ecumenism* (Bangalore: ATC, 1993), 106.

dignity and fuller human existence. As shown, dialogue with other living faiths has been an effective tool for ecumenical advance between diverse faiths. They have been able to put centuries old conflicts to some extent into new life and thus have enabled different religions in varying degrees to move beyond these controversies. The dialogue of the future will continue to offer new hopes, for the different religions of the world.

The religious pluralistic context offers a number of challenges to theological education in India today. India is filled with numerous religious communities with innumerable traditions, revivalist movements, militant and terrorist groups with their own exclusively-narrow philosophical and political vision. To add fuel to the fire of religious fanaticism, there are communal, linguistic and regional elements, which flare up emotional factors that break out like volcanoes time to time. Under the shadow of these para-religious spirits, there are human issues completely neglected by interested parties, and a chain of social evils perpetuated which crush the poor class of the society under constant threat, oppression, exploitation, ignorance and irreligion.[109] A radical orientation to the context has become an urgent need within the agenda of theological education in India today. Theological education need to open continuously to other faiths, thoughts and experiences in order to have an authentic approach in the context of religious pluralism.[110]

The task of theological education in this context is to explore and formulate a theology of inter-faith dialogue.[111] Any program of theological education, which fails to perceive or deliberately ignores the reality of religious pluralism in India

[109]Cf. Thomas Manickam, "Theological Education in the Cultural Philosophical Context of India Today", *Theological Education in India Today*, ed., by Felix Wilfred (Bangalore: ATC, 1985), 55.

[110]Cf. Godwin R. Singh, "Theological Education in the Context of Pluralistic Religious Society", *Theological Education and Development*, ed., by Gnana Robinson, Henry Wilson and Christopher Duraising (Bangalore: ATTI, 1984), 4-5. (Hereafter, Singh, *Theological Education in the Context of Pluralistic Religious Society*...).

[111]K. P. Aleaz, "Inter-Faith Reality and Ecumenical Theological Education", *WCC Ministerial Formation* (January, 2003), 86. With regard to the affect of the interfaith dialogue on the theological education, theological institutions are offering courses on Hinduism, Islam, Primal Religions and evangelistic approach to them were taught. In the 1970s the Senate of Serampore makes it a compulsory subject on Modern Religious and Secular Movements in India. Dialogue departments and programmes were opened in some of the theological institutions such as Tamil Nadu Theological Seminary, Madurai; Gurukul Theological College, Madras; United Theological College, Bangalore etc. See the detail B.Th. and B.D. Course Syllabi of the Senate of Serampore College (Serampore: Senate of Serampore College, 1993). In 1980 Arvind Nirmal suggested possible elements of a curriculum revision in the context of Inter-Religious Dialogue. In the study of the Bible to take note of the inter-religious dialogue that shaped the Bible itself and develop a religious criticism of the Bible; in the study of Christian Theology to develop a Christian theology which is in dialogue with other religions, ideologies and other academic disciplines; in the study of Church History to begin to study the history of Christianity as a social history probing into the motivational factors that caused the conversions and developments in a dialogical manner.; and in the study of Christian

is bound to be isolated and irrelevant.[112] Theological education in this location needs to seriously take under its consideration the issues of constant dilemmas, paradoxes, illogicalities and idiosyncrasies.[113]

The Indian historical situation called for a search for a theological education in the context of religious pluralism. In the words of Leslie Newbigin:

> Outstanding (Indian) Christian thinkers... saw both the renaissance of Hinduism and the growth of a concern for nation building... (as) part of the consequences of the impact of Christ upon Indian society. They therefore called their fellow Christians to the work of interfaith dialogue in the context of the quest for national unity with the conviction that this was part of the continuing work of Christ in Indian society. The basis of their call to dialogue was in their Christian faith.[114]

Dialogue is not a secret weapon in the armory of an aggressive Christian militancy.[115] Dialogue must not be misunderstood as a non-committed academic approach to another faith.[116] Basically, interfaith dialogue was understood as an encounter between people who live by different faith traditions, in an atmosphere of mutual trust and acceptance.[117] Dialogue did not require giving up, hiding or seeking to validate one's own religious conviction; in fact, the need for being rooted in one's own tradition to be engaged in a meaningful dialogue was emphasized, as were common humanity and the need to search in a divided world for life in community. Dialogue was seen as a way not only to become informed about the faiths of others but also to rediscover essential dimensions of one's own faith tradition.[118] The benefits of removing historical prejudices and enmities as well as the new possibilities for working together for common good were recognized and affirmed. Some see dialogue primarily as a new and creative relationship

---

Ministry, to take note of the liturgical and worship elements in other religions and the developments in psychology, yoga and meditation for counseling in Indian situation.

[112]Cf. Arvind Nirmal, "Some Theological Issues Connected with Inter-Faith Dialogue and their Implication for Theological Education in India", *BTF*, XII/2 (January-June, 1980), 107-129.

[113]Cf. Singh, *Theological Education in the Context of Pluralistic Religious Society...*, 38.

[114]M. M. Thomas, *Risking Christ for Christ's Sake* (Geneva: WCC Publication, 1987), 111.

[115]Conservative Christians question the purpose of dialogue; they fear that it denies the need for people of other faiths to convert to Christian faith.

[116]The majority of evangelicals take to traditional evangelistic method of preaching, tract distribution and personal evangelism. To them, dialogue takes place at the personal evangelistic setting only, but never at the academic level. Evangelicals disown and distrust the ecumenical dialogue as betraying the gospel of Jesus Christ.

[117]S. W. Ariarajah, "Dialogue, Inter-faith", *The Dictionary of the Ecumenical Movement*, ed., by N. Lossky (Grand Rapids: Wm. B. Eerdmans Publishing Co., 1991), 135. (Hereafter, Ariarajah, *Dialogue, Inter-faith...*).

[118]Cf. Andrew, Wingale, "Interreligious Dialogue, Conflict and Reconciliation", *WCC Current Dialogue*, 14 (July, 2003), 18.

within which one can learn about and respect others but also can give authentic witness to one's own faith. Others see it as an important historical moment in the development of religious traditions, in which each of the faith traditions in dialogue is challenged and transformed by the encounter with others. Still others view dialogue as a common pilgrimage towards the truth, within which each tradition shares with the others the way it has come to perceive and respond to that truth.[119]

Greater awareness of religious plurality has highlighted the need of improved relations and dialogue among people of different faiths. Religion speaks for some of the deepest feeling and sensitive of individuals and communities, it carries profound historical memories and often appeals to uncritical confessional solidarities.[120] Moreover, today, the growing need is not just for dialogue with people of other faiths but for genuine relationships with them. Increased awareness of religious plurality, the potential role of religion in conflict, and the growing place of public life, etc., present urgent challenges that require greater understanding and cooperation among people of diverse faiths.[121] Thus, Stanley J. Samartha called for "a whole new way of understanding the task of the theological education, to speak in inclusive ways so that it recovers the true meaning of the oikoumene and makes senses to the calling of the Church to live in the midst of pluralism".[122] He further elaborates:

> What we need today is a theology that is not less but more true to God by being generous and open, a theology not less but more loving toward the neighbour by being friendly and willing to listen, a theology that does not separate us from our fellow human beings but supports us in our common struggles and hopes. As we live together with our neighbours, what we need today is a theology that refuses to be impregnable, but which, in the spirit of Christ, is both ready and willing to be vulnerable.[123]

Theological education should seek to make dialogue as an indispensable style of living in the pluralistic milieu. Dialogue or inter-religious faith has become a permanent Christian obligation, no longer a triumphalistic understanding of mission in the past. It is an inevitable enterprise in a religious pluralistic context

---

[119]Ariarajah, *Dialogue, Inter-faith…*, 136.

[120]John D'Arcy May, "The Dialogue of Religions; Source of Knowledge Means of Peace", *WCC Current Dialogue*, 43 (July, 2004), 17.

[121]Ariane, Hentsch, "Religious Identities in Pluralistic Societies. How do we Choose them, Manage them, and Live them Fully?" *WCC Current Dialogue*, 46 (December, 2005), 5.

[122]S. J. Samartha, "The Holy Spirit and People of Various Faiths, Cultures and Ideologies", *The Holy Spirit*, edited by Dow Kirpatrick (Tennessee: Tidings Publications, 1974), 37. See also Horst Burkle, "The Debate of the Cosmic Christ as Example of an Ecumenically Oriented Theology" *INDIAN Voices in Today's Theological Debate*, edited by H. Burkle and W. Roth (Delhi: ISPCK, 1972), 199.

[123]*Ibid.*, 38.

in which aspects of Servanthood and Lordship of Christ can be discerned.[124] It should emerge as an authentic process of learning in theological education and develop a contextualized hermeneutics of its own that will lead the learner to a profound encounter between the word of God and its realities in the religious pluralistic context. Theological education in this situation has to be praxis oriented. It must lead those engaged in it to process of involvement in practical context of life and to learn to make decisions and choices. Thus, by participating in the struggles of the communities the authenticities of theological education can be tested. In order to be relevant to the religious pluralistic context, the curricula of the theological program need to be present reality issue oriented.[125]

The thrusts of the theological education in India's context need to be so directed as to allow the students to create an intelligent understanding of the religious and cultural life of the pluralistic context. Theological education should comprehend the totality of the contextual pluralism.[126] Theological education in India's context of religious and cultural pluralism should be able to meaningfully relate and respond to such a context. It is the task of theological education to create in people the motivation to develop an attitude of critical self-realization (replacing self-absolutization); of openness towards others (replacing suspicious reservation and exclusivism); of appreciation of what is good in other religious traditions (replacing condemnation).[127] Our theological education should be theologically sound, pedagogically viable, and practically related to the complex realities of the people's lives within India's context of plurality of faiths.

4. Theological Education in the Context of Ecological Crisis

Ecology is one of the key themes discussed in today's context irrespective of the barriers of religions, nationalities and cultures. Though ecology concerns everyone, (in fact everything on earth), all are not affected by it on an equal scale. For instance, while it is more a question of convenience and healthy growth for the people of the developed nations, for the developing nations it is a matter of one of survival.

The integrity of creation has been one of the urgent concerns for the Ecumenical movement. The ecumenical concern for justice was expressed in different ways since the beginning of the modern ecumenical movement. The World Council of Churches first Assembly, which met at Amsterdam in 1948, defines the concern for justice in terms of responsible society.[128] Following that, in the successive WCC assemblies, attempts were seriously put to redefine the term

[124]Singh, *Theological Education in the Context of Pluralistic Religious Society...*, 41.

[125]Cf. Singh, *Theological Education in the Context of Pluralistic Religious Society...*, 42-43.

[126]Cf. *Ibid.*, 46.

[127]Cf. Prabhakar, *Religious Education in Indian Context...*, 99.

[128]J. Russel Chandran, "Ecology, Peace and Justice," *Challenges and Responses*, edited by Gnana Robinson (Bangalore: UTC, 2000), 194. (Hereafter, Chandran, *Ecology, Peace and Justice...*).

further. The Sixth WCC Assembly in Vancouver (1983), adopted the program on Justice, Peace and Integrity of Creation (JPIC),[129] and also the Seventh WCC Assembly at Canberra (1991), gave more attention to this issue. Since Vancouver the WCC's central executive committees have deepened the understanding of JPIC as a process calling the Churches to a new level of united response to the common threats opposing the wholeness of life.[130] The Canberra Assembly of the WCC suggests that the ecological concern is an integral part of the quest for a just world order. Exploitation of the Earth's resources without any concern to proper stewardship has been seen as responsible for the serious threat at present,[131] to the whole of creation. The earth's resources belong to all sections of life and to all future generations as well without any barriers. This is to be understood as the basis for the proper stewardship over the resources of the whole earth.[132]

Ecological issue as noted poses as an urgent challenge for the ecumenical movement in India. It calls for the Churches to critically evaluate its own contribution in perpetuating in one way or the other, un-ecological spirits, attitudes and actions in the society. It motivates the Churches to take serious and active measures to restore this God-given home of all of God's creatures. As a result, the ecumenical movement in India particularly through the NCCI has begun to work toward this mission and vision, by creating awareness among the individuals and communities about the present deteriorating condition of the planet earth, through various informative and innovative programs at various levels of Churches' life and society.

India's social structure and her economic system are to a great extent responsible for the present increased rate of unemployment, of homelessness, of hunger and thirst, and of the destruction of the natural environment. Majority of India's population depend on the natural resources of the ecosystem for their basic sustenance and survival. However, in the name of development and in the name of economic progress, the natural environment are ransacked and plundered of all life-sustaining resources. Industrialization and capitalism has raided immeasurable areas of India's soil rendering those nature-dependent communities homeless and workless by driving them off from their homeland. Besides, the greatest blow of all to these nature-dependent communities is that of rendering them foodless – it

[129]JPIC is not fundamentally about drafting of documents, or convening of meetings, or supporting of projects – although these may be part of the process. Most fundamentally JPIC is about drawing connections, about weaving together faith responses from the many particular contexts around the world into a diverse but unified whole. JPIC is about enabling and challenging Churches and ecumenical groups working on particular issues to see the connections between their work and the larger struggles for survival and peace on the planet.

[130]Cf. Thomas F. Best, ed., *Vancouver to Canberra 1983-1990, Report of the Central Committee of the WCC to the Seventh Assembly* (Geneva: WCC Publications, 1990), 140.

[131]Cf. Chandran, *Ecology, Peace and Justice…*, 204.

[132]Cf. Calvin B. Dewitt, *The Environment and the Christian- What Can We Learn from the New Testament?* (Michigan: Baker Book House, 1991), 95-96.

includes no water to drink (the second basic need of not just humans but of all creatures and nature itself); no sources of foodstuffs means no meals for the very reason that they are being uprooted completely from their mother (the land) that provides them plots to cultivate, sow, grow, harvest and thus feed on their hard labored yields.[133]

Those downtrodden communities' relationship with the environment is characterized by taking only what is needed for their survival from nature and making sure that they do not exhaust all of nature's resources but continue to protect and preserve the environment, their only home and source of sustenance. Hence, it is basically those communities that sides with nature by understanding the interdependency and interrelatedness of all life and therefore, they become victims along with nature as the developed and affluent communities and agencies do not hesitate to destroy them together for their own selfish accumulation of wealth and power. In India, it has become an everyday issue of conflict in which her citizens are interlocked in a battle between *destruction for profit* and *protection and preservation for survival.*[134]

Theological education in India therefore is situated within such conflicting context. Social transformation of the people or of the society will not be complete without including the ecological care and concerns in our transformatory vision and mission. Our theological education needs to be done in the midst of or taking into account the entire context of the people and their environment. Accumulation of wide range of knowledge on varied important subjects and disciplines no matter how popular they may be in the history of our faith and tradition, unless we rearrange our theological focus and priorities toward our living contexts and realities, our theological education will remain abstract, meaningless and irrelevant. Therefore, to make our theological education potent and meaningful to our immediate context, it is the responsibility of the theological educators, seminaries, curriculum and the entire theological community in engaging ourselves theoretically as well as practically in the transforming mission work not

[133]India is not at all ignorant of the escalating statistics of her poor population's number of suicides, crimes, violence and numerous other related horrors of the poor peoples, individuals, families, innocent children etc., whose deaths and blood weigh heavily upon its minority of those conscienceless filthy rich, their hay-wired greed, their lusts for establishing more structures of accumulating wealth at the very expense of stealing, blackmailing and even murdering those innocent lives. In fact, India's poverty is mostly caused by her own way-ward off springs. It is time therefore, that India begins raiding its own home for those villains instead of blaming non-existent outsiders.

[134]Cf. Kurien Kunnumparam, "Ecology: Issues, Perspectives, Problems" *Ecological Concern: An Indian Christian Response*, edited by Joseph Mattam and Jacob Kavunkal (Bangalore: NBCLC, 1998), 10-12. (Hereafter, Kunnumparam, *Ecology: Issues, Perspective, Problem...*).

only for the human community but also equally for the larger community of the natural environment.[135]

4.1. Ecological Crisis and Response of the Church in India

It is believed that the growing awareness of the ecological crisis in the 1970s and 1980s has seriously challenged on the role of the Indian Ecumenical Movement and one in which there is a need to review and reformulate the understanding and concern of creation as a whole. Ecology has been identified as one of the major challenges for the ecumenical thinking and churches action as well as for the search of new paradigm for human development.[136]

In a country like India, where millions of human beings are deprived of the basic needs of human existence, we have to take effective steps to eradicate poverty and misery as well as to improve the quality of life.[137] Ecological problem in developing countries such as India is a matter of survival. This is so because in India millions of people depend on the natural resources for their basic needs.[138] When we destroy the earth's resources in the name of development of the urban towns and cities, the poorer sections of the society such as Tribals, Dalits, Untouchables, Harijans, Fisher folks, women etc. are immediately deprived of the very resources for their basic sustenance.[139] In the name of development, when the government and the private business groups destroy tress, land and forests; these poor people are even uprooted from their homes and dwelling places.[140] Therefore, ecological crisis has become a very serious survival problem for these millions of people in India. Today, the Indian Churches under the aegis of the ecumenical movement, continue to widen its mission perspective, that include the healing and restoration of the earth through National Council of Churches in India, local Church organizations, Schools and Colleges[141] by organizing seminars, workshops, and awareness programs.

The Utkal Christian Council of Orissa and NCCI conducted an awareness program on *Ecology and Women* at Gopalpur, Orissa in July 1991. This awareness program was organized in order that the Church in Orissa will be more aware of the ecological crisis, which is causing hazardous effects to millions of people in

---

[135]Vandana Shiva, *Staying Alive: Women, Ecology and Survival in India* (New Delhi: Kali For Women, 1998), 36. (Hereafter, Shiva, *Staying Alive: Women, Ecology and Survival...*).

[136]Klaus Schafer, "Healing of Creation: Ecumenical Reflections on the Ecological Mission of the Church" *Ecumenism, Prospects and Challenges,* edited by Vinod Victor, Leslie Nathaniel and P. Surya Prakash (Delhi: ISPCK, 2001), 14.

[137]Kunnumparam, *Ecology: Issues, Perspectives, Problems...*, 12.

[138]Cf. Chandran, *Ecology, Peace and Justice...*, 196.

[139]Shiva, *Staying Alive: Women, Ecology and Survival...*, 38.

[140]*Ibid.*, 45.

[141]*Minutes of the Meetings of the National Council of Churches in India, July 1991* (Nagpur: NCCI, 1992), 89.

India.[142] The Kerala Council of Churches and the National Council of Churches in India organized a seminar on *Ecology and Secular Spirituality* in September 1991 at Adoor, Kerala. The thrust of the meeting was that the Churches must actively involve in educating the society for just and sustainable living.[143]

The NCCI Youth Unit and the Goa Christian Forum organized a workshop on *Church Response to Ecology and Development* from 14-17 November 1996 at Farmagudi Hill Resort, Goa. The main objective of the workshop was to prepare the youth to face the new challenges, which threaten the existence in the name of development.[144] The Kerala Council of Churches and the NCCI again organized *Green Kerala 2000: A Symposium on Ethics and Ecology* from 3-5 June 2000. The meeting brought together people from various environmental groups in Kerala and reflects theologically on ecological concerns and the meeting resolved to motivate Churches to collaborate with environmental movements in common action for eco-justice.[145]

The Ecumenical Christian Centre organized a National seminar on *Sustainable Mobility* from14-16 July 2000 at Bangalore.[146] The participants evaluated the challenges of the rapid increase of mobility and vehicular traffic and its impact on ecology and environment and the social and economic issues surrounding it. The consultation resolved to build a just and participatory community where the integrity of the whole creation will be upheld.[147]

5. Theological Education in the Context of Globalization

Globalization is no longer an alien term or idea. We are living in an era in which we find ourselves impossible to look back or think of those bygone days when we did not have the benefits of what we have today. In fact, we have not just been intimately familiar with globalization but have even surpassed that blissful state to that of somersaulting back to the realization that it (globalization) also have its adverse effect upon our lives to the point that many of us are now struggling with the dilemma of how to or what to do in order to curb its negative effects. This subject of 'globalization' is very much a serious issue of concern that challenges our beliefs, thoughts and praxis as it affects our lives and our world in general. As

---

[142]*Minutes of the Meetings of the National Council of Churches in India, July 1991* (Nagpur: NCCI, 1992), 102.

[143]*Ibid.*

[144]*National Council of Churches in India: Nagpur to Ranchi, 1996-1999* (Nagpur: NCCI, 2001), 84.

[145]*The National Council of Churches in India: Meetings of the Executive Committee and General Body 3-4 August 2001* (Nagpur: NCCI, 2001), 28.

[146]The participants include theological college professors, research scholars and representatives from Orthodox, Mar Thoma, CSI, Presbyterian, Baptist and Pentecostal churches from different states of India

[147]*A Statement from the Workshop of Sustainable Mobility July 14-16 2000* (Bangalore: ECC, 2000), 60.

such, it has also become an urgent concern under the purview of our theological education especially within the context of fostering ecumenical theological education in India.

It is pertinent here to note that the subject of 'globalization' has seriously entered the sphere of Ecumenical discussions in recent times. For instance, within the Christian Conference of Asia (CCA), there have already been numerous references to this issue under the activities of various program units. Globalization is in fact a process that has been going on for centuries, that has involved various levels of human invention, expressing itself mainly in the development of technology and various other fields of human knowledge and endeavor. Globalization has now become irreversible. This is especially true in its technology of communication and instruction.[148] People now communicate and convey information globally, and there is a generation of people (the younger generation in particular), who will soon assume responsibilities in a world that to them has always been global, people, in short, who have known no other world than this new world of global outreach.

Theological education in India's context need to be all the more sensitive to this intimidating figure of globalization mainly because, India as one of the world's most thickly populated nations especially among the third-worlds, majority of its population constitute the struggling poor, for which, the much publicized hype on the 'midas touch' character of globalization in reality steals their very natural plate of rice as globalization turns their very meals into gold for the rich and the affluent. Therefore, theological education should very seriously study this issue in the context of India's population, study (likewise) its own (i.e., theological) structure and content in relation to its meaning and relevance for that very context.

5.1. Globalization and Response of the Church

The adverse effect of globalization particularly on the environment has become one of the major concerns of the Indian Church today. Globalization has wrought severe impact on the entire social fabric of a nation; it questions every aspect of human existence – social, political, economic, cultural, religious, environmental etc. It is depleting the natural resources of our land. An alliance forged by the forces of domination for profit becomes the driving force of much of globalization. The poor and the marginal do not find protection and security under it. Therefore, it is pertinent that the Indian Church becomes aware of the dangers inherent in globalization and participates in the movements and struggles being waged to

---

[148]Cf. Konrad Raiser, *For a Culture of Life: Transforming Globalization and Violence* (Thiruvalla: CSS, 2002), 7-12.

arrest this dangerous, open market and liberalized trend and promote pro-poor, eco-friendly and gender equity development.[149]

One of the main aspects of the ministry of the Church is to identify with the poor and the marginalized in their struggle for justice and liberation from voice bondages. The Indian Church should open all possible doors to the poor for their participation in the decision making process. The church could begin its practical work of transformation through its active participation in the process of providing food for the hungry, health to the sick, dignity to the humiliated and justice to the oppressed.

The Indian Churches through the National Council of Churches in India (NCCI) are believed to have begun to actively involve in the awareness program in relation to the issue of globalization and its impact. The NCCI Youth Unit with Mar Thoma Church Youth organized a workshop on globalization from 18-20 July 1997 at Mar Thoma Youth Centre, Adoor for the Christians in Kerala. Participants came from different denominations in Kerala. The aim of the seminar was to understand the globalization process and how it is affecting the ecumenical youth movement. It was resolved at the end that the Youth wing of different Churches will organize more of such workshop in the near future.[150]

In 1999 from 12-14 January at Bangalore, the NCCI with Indian Social Institute organized an awareness seminar for the Christians in Bangalore on the impact of globalization and Churches' response to this issue. People from different walks of life attended the workshop. The consultation resolved that they would actively organize awareness programs in the congregational levels also.[151]

In 1999 from 24-27 February, Bihar Christian Forum with the National Council of Churches in India organized a seminar on *Globalization and Indigenous People.* The main emphasis of the meeting was the recognition that the indigenous people are the victims of not only the traditional Brahmanical social order in India but also the capitalist forces like globalization. The meeting decided that the Churches in Bihar would fight against the evil forces of globalization in order to uplift the indigenous people of India.[152]

The Young Men Christian Association (YMCA) in Bangalore with the National Council of Churches in India conducted a one-day seminar on *Globalization and Spirituality* on 21st July 2001 at the City YMCA Hall Bangalore. Participants were drawn from different Churches, Organizations, Theological Seminaries, NGOs and also people from other faiths. The meeting resolved to

---

[149]Jetti, A. Oliver, "Recolonization, Globalization and the Role of the Church," *NCCR* 48/5 (May, 1999), 4. (Hereafter, Oliver, *Recolonization, Globalization…*).

[150]*NCCI: Meetings of the Executive Committee and General Body 3-4 August 2001* (Nagpur: NCCI, 1999), 92.

[151]*NCCI: Nagpur to Ranchi, 1996-1999* (Nagpur: NCCI, 2001), 39.

[152]*NCCI: Meetings of the Executive Committee and General Body 3-4 August 2001* (Nagpur: NCCI, 1999), 107.

prepare a small booklet on the various aspects and implications of globalization for wider circulations and distributions, and that leaders of religions should consceintize the members of their own religious traditions about the effects of globalization.[153]

The Presbyterian Church of India and National Council of Churches in India organized an awareness seminar on *Globalization and Christian Response* from 17-18 May 2001 at Shillong, Meghalaya. The meeting decided to organize such seminar at the congregational level especially in the North Eastern Regions of India.[154]

It pertinent therefore, for the Indian Church, to regard global poverty as the supreme challenge to its faith and society. The Indian Church should recognize that men and women are integral, preferred and treasured parts of God's creation, requiring that she treats them with the respect and dignity they deserved. The church should work as an organization free from prejudice and able to work with compassion toward all people.[155] The Indian Church is called to preach the good news to the poor and share the kingdom values of truth, love, equality, prosperity, justice and peace with all living beings, but she is finding it difficult to live up to her calling. On the contrary, in many instances, the Church has tended to side with the rich and the powerful, in order that she protects her privileges and assets and maintain her status quo. The emphasis of Church ministry has been more on institution building than on sharing the life of abundance with the millions of marginalized people living under inhuman conditions in India.

Globalization, on the surface looks alluring and harmless and even beneficial to the developing countries of Asia. The rationale advanced by the champions of globalization is that the revolution that takes place in the communication technologies and transport systems has reduced the world to a global village. So the countries of the world have become close neighbors and hence they should co-operate with one another in transforming the existing national economics into global economy. The developed countries are wielding globalization like a magic wand, which can eliminate poverty from Asia,[156] while in reality it is escalating the graphic scale of poverty.

Therefore, globalization embodies and confronts the churches with benefits, opportunities, challenges, risks, dangers and oppressions. The Church therefore will have to capture a new vision of its mission in the context of globalization and reformulate its ecumenical mission in the present context. The Church as a part of its solidarity with the poor, needs to include in its mission agenda, the struggle

---

[153]*NCCI: Meetings of the Executive Committee and General Body 3-4 August 2001* (Nagpur: NCCI, 1999), 35.

[154]*Ibid.*, 62.

[155]Aloysius Devasayagam, "Globalization: A Continuation of Colonial Legacy" *Globalization: A Challenge to the Church*, 79-81.

[156]Oliver, *Recolonization, Globalization…*, 334.

for a borderless world, free from all trade embargoes and discriminative custom duties. It is therefore an urgent task for the Church in the present situation to eradicate illiteracy and reduce poverty on a war footing, re-launching its mission vocation.[157]

6. Theological Education in the Context of HIV/AIDS

HIV/AIDS was discovered as a medical issue in the early 1980s; however, it has become clear that it is more than just a medical issue. It is observed that it has been expanding globally at an alarming speed. It pervades all areas of our lives: social, economic, political, cultural[158] etc., and it is more than just an individual situation. In other words, it is not just an individual's own problem but that it creates problems for families, communities, nations, the private sector, faith-based and community-based organizations. The global impact of HIV/AIDS demands a multi-sectoral approach to prevention, care and mitigation of its impact. Therefore, it poses as a very serious challenge to theological education in India, necessitating nothing short of the integrating of this issue within its programs – theoretical or knowledge program as well as practical awareness and preventive program. However, before we discuss further, it is necessary to have a brief basic understanding of its definition, meaning and its characteristic components leading to its serious impact upon every section of the people, society, church as well as theological education particularly in relation to the role of theological education within this alarming reality. We shall therefore follow the points below:

6.1. What is HIV/AIDS?

HIV (Human Immunodeficiency Virus) is a virus that causes AIDS[159] (Acquired Immunodeficiency Syndrome), a health condition in which a person is affected by a series of diseases because of poor immunity. HIV by itself is not an illness and does not instantly lead to AIDS.[160] An HIV infected person can lead a healthy life for several years before s/he develops AIDS.[161]

---

[157]Oliver, *Recolonization, Globalization...*, 336.

[158]Musa, W. Dube, *HIV/AIDS and the Curriculum: Methods of Integrating HIV/AIDS in Theological Programs* (Geneva: WCC, 2005), 4. (Hereafter, Dube, *HIV/AIDS and the Curriculum...*).

[159]**AIDS** stands for **A**cquired **I**mmuno**d**eficiency **S**yndrome. Acquired – means that the disease is not hereditary but develops after birth from contact with a disease-causing agent (in this case, HIV). Immunodeficiency – means that the disease is characterized by a weakening of the immune system. Syndrome – refers to a group of symptoms that collectively indicate or characterize a disease. In the case of AIDS this can include the development of certain infections and/or cancers, as well as a decrease in the number of certain cells in a person's immune system. A diagnosis of AIDS is made by a physician using specific clinical or laboratory standards.

[160]The first cases of AIDS were recognized in the United States in 1981.

[161]Anto, Akkara, "Indian Churches Urge Interfaith Response to AIDS Pandemic," *http://www.womenshealth.gov/hiv* (6-08-05). 1.

AIDS is therefore a health condition that results from the deficiency in the body's immunity following HIV infection. HIV attacks the human body by breaking down its immune system that is meant to fight diseases. Over a period of time, the immune system weakens and the body loses its natural ability to fight diseases. At this stage, various diseases affect the infected person.[162]

6.2. Its Transmission

According to the findings of the India's National AIDS Control Organization (NACO), the most common route of HIV transmission in India is by sexual transmission and, transmission through sharing drug injecting equipment (needles); or being accidentally stuck by needles or sharp objects contaminated with infected blood.[163] Other modes of transmission include blood transfusions, i.e., infected blood used in transfusions, and infected blood products used in the treatment of certain diseases and disorders (since 1985, federally mandated screening of the blood supply has reduced the risk of transmission through this route); and from mother to child during the course of pregnancy, birth, or breastfeeding. It is also transmitted through transplanting organs from infected donors (Routine screening of organ donors also began in 1985). Among young children especially, prenatal transmission is the most common source; however, children in India are also acquiring the disease through sexual contact, including sexual abuse; blood transfusions; and unsterilized syringes, including injections in drug use. Girls are more vulnerable especially when they are subjected to sexual abuse, or early marriage, or when denied an education.[164]

However, HIV and AIDS are not transmitted through: sitting on toilet seats; hugging; handshakes; or closed-mouth kissing (there is a small chance of getting HIV from open-mouthed or "French" kissing if there's contact with blood); sharing food or drinks; donating blood; working with or being around someone with HIV; using phones; getting bug bites; tears; or swimming in pools etc.

6.3. HIV/AIDS and India's Present Condition

Since the first cases of AIDS were identified in 1981, more than 20 million people have died. Today, around 38 million people worldwide are living with HIV.[165] The rapid and continuing spread of the epidemic has placed huge demands on

---

[162]Cf. Carlos, Tamez, L, "AIDS: An Ethical and Theological Challenge for Education," *http://www.wcc-coe.org,* (21/08/05). 6.

[163]NACO, "Program Implementation Guidelines for a Phased Scale up of Access to Antiretroviral Therapy for People Living with HIV/AIDS (Draft)"; Country Coordinating Mechanism for the Global Fund to Fight AIDS, Tuberculosis and Malaria—India, *Proposal: Expansion of Effective Public and Private Sector Interventions in HIV, Tuberculosis and Malaria Prevention and Treatment in India,* September 24, 2002, 21.

[164]B. B. Thakur, "Epidemiology of HIV/AIDS in India," *International Symposium on AIDS in India,* held in Pune on 16-19 May 1995, 1.

[165]UNAIDS, Press release, Bangkok, (July 14th 2004), 2.

governments and health and social services, above all in countries with the least resources. With more than 5 million people estimated to be living with HIV/AIDS, India's HIV/AIDS prevalence is second in the world only to South Africa.

The first case of HIV infection in India was diagnosed among commercial sex workers in Chennai, Tamil Nadu in 1986.[166] Soon after, a number of screening centers were established throughout the country. Initially, the focus was on screening foreigners, especially foreign students. Gradually, the focus moved on to screening blood banks. By early 1987, efforts were made to set up a national network of HIV screening centers in major urban areas.[167]

A National AIDS Control Program was launched in 1987 with the program activities covering surveillance, screening blood and blood products and health education. In 1992, the National AIDS Control Organization (NACO) was established.[168] NACO carries out India's National AIDS Program, which includes the formulation of policy, prevention and control programs. The same year that NACO was established, the Government launched a Strategic Plan for HIV/AIDS prevention under the National AIDS Control Project. The Project established the administrative and technical basis for program management and also set up State AIDS bodies in 25 states and 7 union territories. The Project was able to make a number of important improvements in HIV prevention such as improving blood safety.[169]

Various social factors have contributed to the spread of HIV from high-risk groups in India to the general population. Societal pressures lead many men who are gay or bisexual to get married. A survey of 120 male sex workers in Mumbai in November 2001 found, for example, that 43 percent of these men were married. Women married to men who frequent male or female sex workers are also at high risk of HIV infection, which in turn can be passed from mothers to their children *in utero*, in childbirth or during breastfeeding. Government and nongovernmental programs that work effectively and compassionately with persons in marginalized high-risk groups are essential if there is a hope of stemming the country's HIV crisis.

Estimated numbers of adults and children living with HIV/AIDS end of 2003: Adults- 5,000,000; Women- 1,900,000; Children- 120,000= total 5,100,000.[170] It is strongly believed that if this pandemic continues at its present

---

[166]Michael Spencer, "India's Plague," *New Yorker* (December 17, 2001), 7.

[167]D. N. Dakar, and S. N. Dakar, *Combating AIDS in the 21st Century: Issues and Challenges* (Delhi: Sterling Publishers Private Limited, 2001), 33.

[168]M. Bhupesh, *India Disquiet About AIDS Control*, Vol. l 240/8834 (January, 1992), 14.

[169]Cf, *NACO 'National AIDS Control Program Phase I'* (1992-1999), 16. See also *http://www.Naco.ni.c.in/nacp/phase 1.htm.* (Accessed 21/08/05), 8.

[170] *UNAIDS/WHO epidemiological fact sheets on HIV/AIDS and Sexually Transmitted Infections, http://www.who.in (20/08/05). 3.*

pace, it is going to have devastating effects on the entire fabric of our Indian society.

6.4. HIV/AIDS and the Church's Response

Christian Churches have a long tradition of pastoral care, education and healthcare, a concern for social justice and unparalleled local networks. They are therefore well placed to play a crucial role in HIV prevention and care at community level. In many countries, churches are already deeply involved in this work. In the 1980s, some churches responded to HIV with the message that it was a punishment from God for what they understood to be an outcome of their immoral behaviors.[171] This response created a worsening situation whereby people who found themselves infected kept their positive status hidden in order to avoid stigma and rejection by their church and family. As the causes behind the spread of HIV and its links to poverty and injustice became better understood and with the realization that HIV can infect anyone, regardless of their faith, marital status, sexual orientation or social position, churches had to recognize that HIV was and is in their midst. In other words, the Church should realize that her responsibility is not to condemn, but rather to offer comfort and support after the example of the God of hope and love, and to put that recognition into practice.[172] Christian Churches have a responsibility to control the spread of the HIV/AIDS and to care for the infected persons.[173] If covenantal relationships between God and his people, and, by extension, between those people themselves, are to be restored and maintained, the various forms of injustice that underlie the spread of HIV have to be addressed.[174]

It is observed that India at present is experiencing a snowballing increase in the HIV/AIDS pandemic. It is projected that India may become the "AIDS capital of the World" by 2020 if preventive measures are not adapted to curb the pandemic.[175] Church in India is of course involved in the prevention and care of HIV/AIDS to a great extent.[176] But considering the magnitude and urgency of the problem of the HIV/AIDS pandemic, it necessitates the entire Christian

---

[171]Cf. Dube, *HIV/AIDS and the Curriculum…*, 6-7.

[172]Paula Clifford, "Theology and the HIV/AIDS epidemic," *Christian Aid: We Believe in Life Before Death*, (London: 2004), 2.

[173]Ban, Makan, "Response of NGOs to HIV/AIDS in the Region: The Fact about HIV/AIDS in Manipur," *Regional Conference HIV/AIDS for Church Leaders and Theological Educators in NEI*, held at Jorhat on 21st-24th September, 2004, 2.

[174]*http://www.christianaid.org.uk* (09/08/05), 4.

[175]*Report on Special Consultation of Bishops and Major Health Organization* held at St. John's National Academy of Health Sciences, Bangalore, on August 2003, 1.

[176]The Lutheran Church began its work on HIV/AIDS as far as 1989. The Salvation Army, the Church of North India, the Methodists, the Mar Thoma, Orthodox Churches etc., have also responded, some more, some less. The Christian Medical Association of India has conducted several excellent programs. The Catholic Bishops Conference of India's Health wing is very active.

community to be alive, active and to be involved in action, and not just wait or relegate the responsibility to those structural bodies or organizations to carry out the combating work.

The Churches in India need to help those people living with HIV/AIDS to come out of the shadow of despair, gloom and guilt and enter into a joyful hope and acceptance. What we need to acknowledge very importantly is that, people living with HIV/AIDS continue to contribute to their family and society. Christian communities therefore should reach out to those families of HIV/AIDS infected persons. We should create a network of people prepared to assist such families in care, and counseling and support. Hence, HIV/AIDS presents a challenge to the church in its commitment to upholding God's covenantal relationship with his people in every aspect of their daily lives. This challenge relates to the way the church sees herself and understands her mission as a healing, worshipping and prophetic community. Within the church, it is vital that everyone ought to feel welcome and receive pastoral support. Thus, the challenge posed today by the onslaught of HIV/AIDS offers an opportunity to the Church to exercise its creativity and innovativeness.[177] For the church, this involves enabling people to behave responsibly by providing teaching about HIV prevention. It also involves the church itself in acting responsibly, in terms of its theological response to the epidemic and the quality of spiritual care it offers to people infected and affected by HIV. Thence in order to identify the most effective ways of combating the HIV epidemic, churches need to re-examine their relationships with other churches and other faiths. The church must make its voice heard in order to change the structures that are assisting the spread of HIV.

6.5. HIV/AIDS: A Challenge to Theological Education in India

The HIV/AIDS pandemic has prompted some intellectuals in India to pose serious fundamental questions on the role of theological education. As HIV/AIDS continues to cause death, pain and misery to individuals and communities, the role of theological educational and training institutions has come under increasing microscopic scrutiny. Despite India being one of the most affected regions by this pandemic and although the Indian Government, the NGOs, and churches have done some amount of work in awareness program, theological colleges have a long way to go in breaking the silence of this issue.[178] HIV/AIDS needs to be

See detail Philip, Kuruvilla, "HIV/AIDS: The Human Community's Response," *NCCI Review*, Vol. CXXIII/2 (March, 2003), 41-51.

[177]Joseph, George, "HIV/AIDS: Challenges for Creating Innovative Pastoral Care Practices in India," *NCCI Review*, Vol. CXXIII/2 (March, 2003), 58.

[178]Cf. A, Wati, Longchar, "HIV/AIDS: A Challenge to Theological Education in Asia," *NCCI Review*, Vol. CXXIII/2 (March, 2003), 116-17. (Hereafter, Longchar, *HIV/AIDS: A Challenge to Theological Education…*).

integrated into theological curriculum in its entirety.[179] The Training of Trainers initiated by the World Council of Churches has encouraged in many ways in ensuring that theological colleges in India rise to the challenge of HIV/AIDS. A number of training sessions have been held, with academic deans and lecturers participating.[180]

Since HIV/AIDS is a global crisis, which has infected 40 million people, claimed 22 million lives and orphaned 15 million children, worldwide; since it functions through poverty, gender inequalities, racism, human rights violations, child abuse, civil wars, international trade injustice, stigma, sexual and ethnic discrimination – theological reflection and education should be at local, national and global levels.[181] It should be carried out at family, church, community and theological institutional levels.

Theological institutions in India especially Serampore Affiliated Colleges have begun to wrestle with this issue very recently as they seek to become contextually relevant. In addition, some institutions, under the Senate of Serampore Colleges, have started incorporating HIV/AIDS issues in their curriculum.[182] Theological educators have begun to realize that they need to reflect the reality of HIV/AIDS in their teaching of various courses and subjects. The recognition of the fact that HIV/AIDS has a direct bearing on pastoral counseling in India has enabled many institutions to train their ministers in sound ways.

One of the most compelling reasons for the hesitation to integrate HIV/AIDS in the theological curriculum has been lack of expertise. The Indian experience shows that most educators in the different fields of theology/religious studies have the 'willingness' to teach about HIV/AIDS but they feel they lack sufficient knowledge about the subject. Recognizing the fact that the situation on the ground calls for urgent action such as to mobilize various communities of faith to care for the infected and orphans, theological education in India has also begun to acknowledge the necessity of its response to that call. Hence, it realizes that it is not enough that it (theological education) has acquired some theoretical knowledge about the subject of HIV/AIDS or that it has transformed its attitude toward HIV/AIDS infected persons, but that it must get up, pull up its spotless shirt's sleeves and get into the kneading work of prevention and caring of those needy ones amongst us.

---

[179]G. M. Nalunnakkal, "HIV/AIDS: Towards an Ethic of 'Just Care'," *HIV/AIDS: A Challenge to Theological Education*, edited by Samson Prabhakar and G. M. Nalunnakkal, (Bangalore: BTESSC/SATHRI, 2004), 37. (Hereafter, Nalunnakkal, *HIV/AIDS: Towards an Ethic of 'Just Care...*).

[180]Cf. *Report: Ecumenical Church Leaders Conference on HIV/AIDS*, Organized by India Watch Desk, held at Mumbai on February 5-7 2003, 1.

[181]Cf. Bitra, George, "Situational Assessment of HIV/AIDS in India," *NCCI Review*, Vol. CXXIII/2 (March, 2003), 110.

[182]United Theological College, Eastern Theological College, etc., now require their students to take courses that focus on HIV/AIDS.

Theological educators have thus begun to appreciate the fact that HIV/AIDS does not discriminate on the basis of religious affiliation, thereby facilitating co-operation across religious traditions.[183] Theological colleges in India are empowering learners to tap the collective assets of the diverse communities of faith to become a formidable frontier in the struggle against HIV/AIDS. However, theological colleges in India also very importantly need to encourage their students to carry out research projects that have a direct bearing on understanding HIV/AIDS.

Theological colleges in India have gone some way in becoming relevant in the struggle against HIV/AIDS. Having been overwhelmed by the sheer number of people dying every week and the phenomenal rise in orphaned children, these institutions have proffered some creative responses. In this context therefore, it is observed that a theology of hope and love must be accompanied by practical care, which not only aims to improve people's quality of life within their community, but also demands action in the wider world.

Theological Institutions as instruments of the Church (or society) need to seriously acknowledge that it is not just a problem 'out there' but it is a problem that touches every individuals and groups,[184] 'right here' and 'now.' A theological framework that facilitates discussion on the nature of God and his relationship with humankind living with HIV/AIDS needs to accommodate searching questions and changing realities if theology is to be meaningful for the entire people of God.

Therefore, the need of the hour in India's situation is to design a serious theological curriculum in such a way that it will bring transformation in the approaches of theological education with this issue. Here, what G. M. Nalunnakkal argues in his articles about the integration of HIV/AIDS in theological curriculum, is truly important and therefore noteworthy. He proposes that, systematic theology can reflect on such issues as the meaning of suffering in the context of AIDS; Christian ethics can include issues like human sexuality, changing family life; feminist theology, the issue of women's biological, cultural and economic vulnerability to the threat of AIDS; and the contextual theologies[185] can stress how the new form of untouchability, marginalization, discrimination and stigmatization that HIV/AIDS reinforces upon the society.[186] Offering inter-disciplinary courses with particular focus on HIV/AIDS can bring these distinct perspectives and issues together. To create theological education effective and relevant with the situation, the theological community needs to come into contact

---

[183] See *http://www.e-alliance/ch.* (18/08/05), 1-5.

[184] John, S. Sadananda, "HIV/AIDS: A Challenge to Theological Education and some Possible Responses," *NCCI Review*, Vol. CXXIII/2 (March, 2003), 105.

[185] Here it means Dalit theology, Minjung theology, Tribal theology, etc.

[186] Cf. Nalunnakkal, *HIV/AIDS: Towards an Ethic of 'Just Care...*, 118.

with the reality of HIV/AIDS face to face.[187] There is a growing awareness with this concern among the theological educators, but the existing curriculum lacks focus and scope for theological reflection to address such concerns.[188] Therefore, faced with the HIV/AIDS pandemic, theological colleges need to become "AIDS competent" in order to empower ministers to be more effective. Although many challenges remain, theological colleges in India must seek to promote ministries of forgiveness and healing.

Summary

While we do not pretend to maintain that the above treated issues alone constitute what we call 'India's multi-faceted context', still, for purpose of our study, we have limited the area of emphasis. Therefore, this is in no way to be misunderstood as implying any exhaustive idea on the subject. Nevertheless, the researcher holds that, whatever issues of concern that have been discussed in this chapter, they represent the more serious ones amidst several others not mentioned, therefore, it is with what we have discussed thus far, we will have to conclude with a brief analytical summary.

With regard to the context of theological education in India, we have noted that India being a context of multi-faceted context compels our theological education to be critically self-evaluative and reflective in questioning itself against its complexly rooted context. It is the context that prepares the curriculum of our theological education. India's socio-cultural life is characterized by its social stratification of its population, rendering majority of its citizens to be categorized as the poor and the downtrodden; while on the other hand, a minority of its citizens live in the filth of riches and arrogance with self-centered religious and cultural sanctions and authority. The poor in India is comprised of the low caste, the outcastes or the untouchables, the tribals, the women and many children beside which, it also include the nature poor or the exploited environment. Theological education in India's context therefore means theological education in the 'context' of India's multi-layered context.

Religious pluralism is another face of India's reality. Owing to this plurality, besides its beauty of diversity, it also serves as a misused factor through which, India is often laddened with communal tensions, violence and so on. As a result, the question of Interreligious relationship of harmony of mutually-enriching existence, etc., serve as an urgent concern that challenges every individual, society, church and theological education in India's context. It is to that aim of peaceful co-existence in the midst of diversified beauty that people of all faiths, Christians, church and theological education in particular struggles to reach and attain.

Inter-religious Dialogue is an issue of serious concern for the Indian Ecumenical Movement due to the pluralistic realities of the Indian context. India

---

[187]Longchar, *HIV/AIDS: A Challenge to Theological Education*..., 118.

[188]*Ibid.*

is one nation among nations of the world where diverse religions, ideologies and cultures co-exists. As a result, Indian Ecumenical Movement had been taking in its stride this issue of inter-religious dialogue with serious consideration. The National Council of Churches in India (NCCI) being the apex body of the Indian Ecumenical Movement established a separate unit on Unity, Fellowship and Dialogue through which it organizes various inter-faith programs for creating peaceful co-existence between diverse people of diverse religions, ideologies and cultures in India.

Very closely connected to the issue of Interreligious dialogue being an ecumenical vision of the people, church, society and theological education, we have the urgent call toward the issue of ecology as well. Ecology therefore, has also come to be an issue of great concern within the Ecumenical Movement in India. Ecological crisis that we face today calls for a critical examination of our understanding about God and the whole of creation. Ecological crisis in India has become a survival crisis because of its serious effects upon the majority of the Indian population such as the dalits, tribals and women, who depends largely on the natural resources for their basic needs. Hence, the Churches in India through the NCCI as well as through the efforts of the individual organizations and Churches as already noted are actively involved in creating awareness programs to save the environment and its natural resources. This is also a very crucial subject that comes under the consideration of theological education in India. The reality of India's major population dependence on the nature and her resources for survival, theological education is challenged with the responsibility of taking this aspect in its learning, formulations and its liberating and healing messages and praxis of its mission. Thus, the Indian Ecumenical Movement encompasses a wide range of issues within its umbrella.

Globalization, which has been gradually yet very seriously seeping off the natural wealth and resources of the third world countries, is a very serious issue under the Indian Ecumenical Movement in recent times. The Churches in India have now begun to take notice of the adverse effect of globalization upon the Indian mass particularly upon the marginalized section of the Indian society who forms the majority of the total Indian population. The Churches through its ecumenical body the NCCI is trying its best to actively involve in spreading awareness among the people to fight this camouflaged instrument by organizing seminars and meetings at various levels of Church and society on this issue. Besides, globalization is also a heated topic amongst and within the scope of theological education in India. It therefore pose itself as an equally serious issue before the transformatory and liberating task of theological education in India's reality of the doubly-poor context, i.e., the poor majority of India who is the poor within the already poor third world context.

Finally, theological education in the context of HIV/AIDS struggle raises a number of challenges for both the church and theological education structure in

India. We have observed that it is very important for us to first acknowledge the importance of learning- through the creation of awareness at them grassroot level, about HIV/AIDS and then learning to answer in ways that could be effective in counteracting HIV/AIDS. Besides, we should be encouraged and encourage people to speak about human sexuality openly and positively without which, there is no better way to impart, teach and affect positive impacts upon the people in the combined effort of preventing and curbing of this HIV/AIDS pandemic. Finally, but not exhaustively, theological educators are challenged to be ecumenical and contextual in the curriculum in order that it will serve the purpose of the need of the situation.

Therefore, the urgent need of the time is a transformation of our seminary theological education. As the culture of the people passes through winds of change, even our theological education must move along with the changing times, making our theological learning and exercise practically relevant and meaningful to the realities of our given context. The ministry of the Church being rooted with the living context of its people's life, our theological education should be carried out with the life situations of the people setting it at the core of our theological focus if we aspire to make our theological education meaningfully respond and relate to the experiences and needs of the people in their very own context.

Doing theology in India's plurality of context is thus no ordinary feat for any theologian with passion and zeal. It thus remains to be seen that the very pluralistic nature of its overall life confronts theological education with a non-bargainable mandate that there can never be any authentic and meaningful theologizing in India until and unless one very seriously takes under one's consideration the dynamics of the multifaceted aspects and experiences of its nation. Hence, noting that reality of a challenging India's context in our minds, we shall now take up the succeeding important topic of our chosen research subject under chapter four – *Theological Education under the Senate of Serampore College* – with a view to present a detailed description of the form, nature and structure of its system as a super-headed theological education program.

Chapter 4

Theological Education under the Senate of Serampore College (University)

Introduction

In the early part of the centuries theological education was one among the imported goods, having practically no base in the Indian cultural context. The early missionaries were guided by a concept that all other faiths and cultures are the works of evil, heathen or pagan, and they considered it as their mission to condemn and uproot those cultures and plant Christianity. Theological education done in such context was simply the copy of what was offered in the West. Books written in the West alone were available for students and biblical exegesis and theology prepared in Europe and America were taught. Very little concern was given to indigenous heritage in doing theological education and indigenous art, music, drama, etc., were set aside as pagan in favor of whatever the missionaries offered- western art, music, life-style etc.[1] Theological reflections were done on issues which were pertinent to people in the West, and had no immediate relevance to our own situation. However, it was with the dawn of post-colonial era in India, the Indian Church took theological education as their responsibility. The Indian Church realized that a theology, which has its roots in another cultural context, is not adequate enough to meet the needs of an emerging new society in India.[2] Ever since then rethinking is being done on the pattern and content of theological education, in an attempt to make theological education relevant to the context, a process, which has quite rightly been focused by the Serampore.

---

[1]Gnana Robinson, *A Journey Through Theological Education* (Madras: C.L.S., 1989), 29. (Hereafter, Robinson, *A Journey Through Theological Education*...).

[2]*Ibid.*, 12.

The Serampore College occupies a unique place in the history of theological education in India. Besides its function as a teaching institution, Serampore has been till very recently the center of the whole collegiate theological education of Protestant Churches in India. It has served both as an affiliating and examining university and as a theological college providing direct instruction and training for the ministry to students from different denominations and areas. A large portion has come also from South India and especially from the Syrian non-catholic Churches of Malabar, and in this way Serampore has wielded a considerable influence also on the whole Churches in India.[3] Therefore it is a serious challenge for the Senate of Serampore College to see whether or not the theological education under its courses meet the need of the churches in India today.

1. The Vision and Purpose of Theological Education under the Senate of Serampore College

Theological education is at the crossroads. Traditional approaches are under serious review and new schemes are being mooted or introduced. A degree of confusion reigns in the minds of ordinary laypeople, particularly where they find themselves called upon to decide between the alternatives.[4] This is exactly true in our Indian situation. Senate in its regional consultation on curriculum revision of theological education stated that the purpose of theological education is not only to equip students for pastoral ministry and other diversified forms of ministry, but also to equip the whole people of God in meeting new challenges they face in living out their faith and to witness to the gospel in a multi-religious context and in a situation marked by erosion of values.[5] This views resonate with the Vision and Mission of Theological Education in India: "we believe that the Triune God has offered the possibility of renewal of life and hope for the entire creation in and through Jesus Christ, and that as an instrument of God, the Church is called to be involved in God's mission of liberation, reconciliation and community building among all peoples through varied forms of ministry."[6]

Set in the midst of people of other faith and ideologies as well as situations of life-negating forces, we are called upon to equip the whole people of God to respond to the contextual challenges critically and creatively by being faithful to the Gospel of Jesus Christ. In light of this faith and self-understanding, SSC seek

---

[3]Cf. George, Anathil, *The Theological Formation of the Clergy in India* (Pune: Pontifical Athenaeum, 1966), 186.

[4]Cf. Graeme L. Chapman, *Spiritual Development* (London: SCM Press, 1986), 2.

[5]*Senate of Serampore College: Consultations on Curriculum Revision Report of the Bombay Consultation*, 12.

[6]*Senate of Serampore College and the Board of Theological Education of the Senate of Serampore College: Constitution- One National Structure for Theological Education in* India, (February, 2005), 4. Cf. *Senate of Serampore College Proceedings of the Theological Senate and its Committees*, (January 4, 2005 to November 30, 2005), 108.

to equip ministers, leaders, scholars and the whole people of God to be committed to creative discernment of, and active participation in God's liberative mission in the world at large and in South Asia in particular by providing programs of theological study and ministerial formation at various levels through affiliated colleges and institutions.[7]

Theological education is aimed to equip the people of God in ministering to the peoples of God. The purpose of theological education is to evolve a common Christian vision as a sign of Christian commitment to the kingdom of God and its pilgrimage in solidarity with humankind towards its fulfillment.[8] The primary purpose of theological institutions under the SSC is to train students for parish ministry.

The traditional aims of theological education in India have always been the training of candidates for ministry of Word and Sacraments in the Church, and this still remains to be the expectation on the part of the established churches. The churches want the candidates who would faithfully preserve the given traditions, and efficiently carry out their ecclesiastical duties.[9] However, now the situation has changed and the demands on the church are manifold and different. Therefore, a rethinking on theological education is pertinent. It is no more the training of individuals as ecclesiastical functionaries that is in view, but it is more the training of the whole Church that concerns theological education.[10]

Therefore, theological education is an intensive and structured preparation of men and women of the church for participation in the ministry of Christ in the world.[11] Hence, theological education under the SSC undertakes to educate men and women to participate in the ministry that they will be able to lead and serve by their particular calling. This aims to develop a student body that is growing mature both in the academic and spiritual discipline. Also to recognize and develop the different gifts, Christ has given, so that each person may be the person of God complete and equipped for the ministry in any given situation.

---

[7]*Senate of Serampore College and the Board of Theological Education of the Senate of Serampore College: Constitution- One National Structure for Theological Education in* India, (February, 2005), 4. Cf. *also Senate of Serampore College Proceedings of the Theological Senate and its Committees*, (January 4, 2005 to November 30, 2005), 108-109.

[8]Cf. M. J. Joseph and J. L. Sadananda, "The Board of Theological Education - The Senate of Serampore College (BTESSC) - An Evaluation," *Church's Participation in Theological Education*, edited by Samson Prabhakar and M. J. Joseph (Bangalore: BTESSC/SATHRI, 2003), 2. (Hereafter, Joseph and J. L. Sadananda, *The Board of Theological Education...*).

[9]Cf. Robinson, *A Journey through Theological Education....*, 17-18.

[10]Cf. *Ibid.*, 18.

[11]See also *Theological Education in North-East Asia Report of the Seoul Consultation*, 28th November to 2nd December, 1966 (Geneva: WCC, 1967), 15.

2. The Board of Theological Education of the Senate of Serampore College (BTESSC)

2.1. Introduction

SSC through its Senate has for decades served as a centre for theological training for ministry of the church in India and its neighbouring countries in South Asia.[12] The consultations between the Board of Theological Education (hereafter cited as BTE) established by the National Christian Council of India and the SSC decided to work together and jointly sponsored the Indian Theological Research Institute (ITRI), to deal with the advance theological research. The joint consultations in Bangalore (1969), and Yeotmal (1972), also recommended the setting up of a single national structure for theological education in India, to deal with the administration of theological education both formal and non-formal, theological research and consultation on theological education.[13]

In 1975, the BTE and the SSC constituted the Board of Theological Education of the Senate of Serampore College (BTESSC), and its constitution was approved by the SSC Council. The constitution was reviewed in 1979, and the review committee was set up to study the problem of the One National Structure for Theological Education. According to this committee report in 1980 decided that the Senate should continue to be the One National Structure with the BTESSC (Board) acting as an advisory body.[14] In the constitution of 2005, the status and the functions of the Board have been further clarified with the Board's Secretary as its officer and the President of the Senate as its chairperson. The BTESSC was to consist of:

- i) The Principals of all affiliated Colleges.
- ii) The heads of institutions and representatives of Churches recognized by the Senate as having co-operative functions in the theological field and accepted as members of the BTESSC (Board) have fulfilled the criteria for membership. Such membership on the Board shall not exceed 1/3 of the total membership of the BTESSC (Board).

---

[12]*Senate of Serampore College and the Board of Theological Education of the Senate of Serampore College: Constitution- One National Structure for Theological Education in* India, (February, 2005), 1. Cf. *Senate of Serampore College Proceeding of the Theological Senate and its Committees*, (January 4, 2005 to November 30, 2005), 107.

[13]Cf. *Senate of Serampore College Proceeding of the Theological Senate and its Committees*, (January 4, 2005 to November 30, 2005), 107. See also *Senate of Serampore College and the Board of Theological Education of the Senate of Serampore College: Constitution- One National Structure for Theological Education in India*, (February, 2005), 1. (Hereafter, *Constitution - One National Structure for Theological Education in India...*).

[14]Cf. *Senate of Serampore College Proceeding of the Theological Senate and its Committees*, (January 4, 2005 to November 30, 2005), 107.

iii) Three members of different Churches out of which at least one shall be a women nominated by the Concerned Church for a period of three years.
iv) Not more than two educationists nominated by the Board at its annual meeting for the three year period.
v) Three theological teachers who are not otherwise members on the Board selected annually by Rota from affiliated Colleges.
vi) Six student representatives from affiliated Colleges to be selected by Rota each year (1 D.Th; 1 M.Th; 2 B.D.; and 1 B.Th.; 1 B.C.S./ Dip.C.S/D.Min) of which, at least two shall be women.
vii) Two members of the Serampore College Council nominated by the Council for a three year period.
viii) The General Secretary of the NCCI or nominee.
ix) Senators who are not otherwise members of the Board.
x) The Registrar, Director of Research and other Functionaries of the Senate Programs are ex-officio members.
xi) The Board shall have power to co-opt not more than two persons whose expertise is beneficial to its work.
xii) The President of the Senate shall be the Chairperson of the Board
xiii) The Board shall meet at least once every year and normally in conjunction with the annual meeting of the Senate.
xiv) The Secretary of the Board shall be appointed by the Senate on the recommendation of the Board.
xv) The Secretary in consultation with the Chairperson shall convene meetings of the Board.[15]

The following functions were assigned to the Board under the overall supervision of the Senate:

1. Reflection and pioneering on new methods and styles in theological education in relation to the need of the country and of the churches.
2. Production of theological literature in general and theological text books in regional languages through the Board for Theological Text Book program of South Asia (BTTBPSA).
3. Promotion of the welfare of theological teachers and students.
4. Development of ecumenical co-operation among Theological Institutions and their Libraries.
5. Promotion of relationship between churches, Theological Institutions and study centers.

---

[15] *Senate of Serampore College and the Board of Theological Education of the Senate of Serampore College: Constitution - One National Structure for Theological Education in* India, (February, 2005),

6. The Board shall recommend names of persons to be considered by the Senate for nomination to be appointed as Senators, Officers, Chairpersons and members of different committees.[16]

The BTESSC therefore serves as the arm of theological education under the SSC. Since the formation of BTESSC in 1975, there were healthy attempts to make a happy blending of the theological and the pastoral dimension in ministry.[17] During the past three decades number of attempts has been made by the Senate as well as the Board to establish BTESSC identity and status specially to define its role. In 1989 the BTESSC established one advance research centre that is South Asia Theological Research Institute (SATHRI) in Bangalore in order "to develop, co-ordinate and facilitate research at doctoral and non-degree levels emphasizing its indigenous and contextual character".[18]

Writing about the BTESSC and its ministry of ecumenical theological education, Wati Longchar states:

> The BTESSC today is one of the major representative bodies of churches legally constituted and responsible for administering theological education in South Asia. It stands as a unique example of ecumenical participation of the churches and theological institutions in curriculum planning and evaluation towards common degrees for all and in their quest for holistic training for ministry.[19]

Hence, the BTESSC tries to meet the need and demands of the church and society effectively by responding to current challenges in the context and evolving newer curriculum of theological education and research.[20]

2.2. The BTESSC's Major Thrust

2.2.1. *To Promote Relationship between Churches and Theological Education*

The gulf between the Churches and ecumenical theological education has been a serious crisis that our Churches are going through today. This has often interrupted the smooth growth of Christian church in India. To bridge these gaps the BTESSC and the Senate has established a committee for this special concern

---

[16]Cf. *Secretary's Annual Report of the Board of Theological Education of the Senate of Serampore College, 2006-2007* (Serampore: BTESSC, 2007), 1. (Hereafter, *Secretary's Annual Report 2006-2007*).

[17]Joseph and J. L. Sadananda, *The Board of Theological Education...*, 1.

[18]*Secretary's Annual Report, 2006-2007...*, 1.

[19]Wati Longchar, "Challenges for Ecumenical Theological Education: Towards a Common strategy and Mechanism" unpublished article, Jorhat 2002, 2. (Hereafter, Longchar, *Challenges for Ecumenical Theological Education...*).

[20]Cf. Wati Longchar, "The Ecumenical Theological Education in Asia Pacific: Towards a Common Strategy and Mechanism" *Ministerial Formation July, 2003* (Geneva: WCC, 2003), 1.

i.e. "the Committee for ecumenical relations and church ministers."[21] This Committee is represented not only by the Senate officers but also representatives from Churches, the Council, Theological Colleges and related institutions. On 7th June 2005 the first meeting of this Committee was held at New Delhi hosted by the Church of North India (CNI).[22] And secondly, it organized a National Consultation on Church's Ministry and Theological Education in September 1-2, 2005 at CNI Program Centre, Nagpur.[23] This project of BTESSC is opening more and more avenues of interest from the representatives.

The functions of this Committee include:

i) To foster continuing theological conversation between theological colleges, churches, church-related bodies and secular agencies.
ii) To explore the nature and form of the ministries of the church currently needed and the training required in carrying out these ministries, in the socio-political aspects of life.
iii) To organize consultations, seminars and conferences on relevant theological issues in order to stimulate creative theological thinking in the member institutions.
iv) To encourage co-operation and collaboration in theological education in the region, including arrangement for exchange of theological teachers and students.
v) To assist member institutions to strengthen their faculties through staff institutes and any other programs in consultation with the Academic Council.
vi) To promote ecumenical concerns in theological education with a view to strengthening the witness of the church in contemporary society.[24]

BTESSC and NCC sponsored national seminar on "Come Holy Spirit, Renew the whole Creation" on 15-19th, 1990. Altogether 35 people participated representing various regional Christian Councils, Churches and Theological Colleges. The West Bengal Christian Council hosts the conference.[25]

---

[21] *Proceedings of the Theological Senate and Its Committees, January 21, 2006 to November 24,* 2006, Book XIX, Vol. XVIII, 2006, 29. (Hereafter, *Proceedings of the Theological Senate 2006...*).

[22] Cf. *Secretary's Annual Report of the Board of Theological Education of the Senate of Serampore College, 2005-2006* (Serampore: BTESSC, 2067), 1.

[23] Cf. *Proceedings of the Theological Senate 2006...*, 30. The consultation was represented by the CNI, CSI, Mar Thoma Church, Orthodox Church, Lutheran Church, Methodist Church, Presbyterian Church and many other churches. After the Nagpur consultations the Rt. Rev. Dr. Isaac Mar Philoxenos Episcopa of Mar Thoma Church of Malabar invited the BTESSC to conduct the consultation in Kottayam.

[24] *Secretary's Report, 2006-2007 BTESSC...*, 4. See also *Constitution - One National Structure for Theological Education in India...*, 16-17.

[25] Zaihmingthanga, *BTE/SSC, Report of the Associate Director for the Year 1990-1991 on Consultations and Church Relations*, 778. (Hereafter, Zaihmingthanga, *BTE/SSC, Report of the*

On September 13-15, 1990, BTESSC along with GLTC and UELC co-sponsored and hosted a National Seminar on Ecology and development: A theological Perspective was held at Gurukul Lutheran Theological College, Madras. About 70 people from all over the country- scientists, church leaders, theological teachers, social activists and students attended it.[26] The consultation makes an in-depth analysis of various issues relating to the ecology and their challenges to the Church in general and theological colleges in particular.[27]

On January 3-7, 1991, the BTESSC with SCMI co-sponsored the biennial National Theological Students' Conference at the SCM House, Bangalore. The theme was come Holy Spirit, Renew the whole Creation.

The One National Structure of Theological Education in India is now well established. Over the years it has grown in membership with over 50 affiliated theological colleges, federated faculties and research centers, one at Serampore and the other two at Bangalore and Kottayam respectively.[28]

2.3. Degrees Granted by the Senate of Serampore College (University)

As mentioned earlier, 50 institutions and four professional institutions from all over India, Sri Lanka, Bangladesh, and Nepal are affiliated to the Senate of Serampore College (University) and it reaches 15000 students in English and major regional languages. The SSC offers the following degrees through a full-time residential study:

Bachelor of Theology (B.Th.),
Bachelor of Divinity (B.D.),
Master of Theology (M.Th.), and
Doctor of Theology (D.Th.).

2.4. Diplomas and Degrees Granted through Distance Theological Education by the Senate of Serampore College (University)

Diploma in Christian Studies (Dip. C.S.),
Diploma in Clinical Pastoral Counseling (DCPC),
Bachelor of Christian Studies (B.C.S.), and
Doctor of Ministry (D.Min.).[29]

These degrees are designed to train students in various forms of ministry to offer opportunities for theological study and reflection in the light of the challenges faced by the Christians in our own situation.

Associate Director...).

[26] Zaihmingthanga, *BTE/SSC, Report of the Associate Director...*, 779.

[27] *Ibid.*

[28] Cf. *Constitution- One National Structure for Theological Education in India...*, 3.

[29] *Annual Report of the President of the Senate of Serampore College, 2006-07*, 11. (Hereafter, *Annual Report of the President of SSC...*).

3. The Place of Theory and Practice in Theological Education

Local churches and denominational leaders argue today that theological education should be primarily concerned with practical training, for ministry, Churches need effective ministers. The Pietists, particularly Spener and Francke, were responsible for this emphasis. In response to an earlier shift of focus from personal formation to familiarization with scholastic-scientific theology, the Pietists argued for a theological education beyond the educational process which the latter sub-served, i.e., the tasks of ministry. They were concerned to put an end to the notion of the minister as the resident theologian, which was the image the German institutions were developing.[30] Schleiermacher, who argued that theology was a positive science, like law and medicine, rather than a pure science, and that it should be included in State-supported University offerings on the basis of the need to educate the clerical clientele in the theory of their indispensable practice, furthered the emphasis of the Pietists.[31]

Over the recent decades, the mushrooming of educational and pastoral sub-specialties within the curricula of theological trainings, which have drawn heavily of the behavioral sciences, register a response both to the philosophical and practical challenge of the regnant therapeutic and to the urging of the churches who have demonstrated that they increasingly prefer graduates with competency in these areas.

While theological education should concern itself, among other things, with tutoring potential ordinands in ministry skills, to argue that such skillfulness ought to be the principal formational element is to advocate a mechanistic, scheming view of ministry. Furthermore, while it has to be admitted that, in one sense, "every pastor of a congregation is the chief executive officer of an organizational structure"[32] there is something strangely perverse in the image of the minister as a "big operator."[33]

Those arguing that the central purpose of theological education is to prepare students for the practical tasks of ministry naturally enough insist that the curriculum should be integrated around the professional aspects of the vocational task. Theory must inform and direct practice and practice must in turn aid in the critical evaluation and improvement of theory.[34] The student's Christian existence and his/her message are hammered out in encounter with the actual rough world.

---

[30]Cf. F. Farley, *Theologia: The Fragmentation and Unity of Theological Education* (Philadelphia, Fortress, 1983), 41.

[31]Cf. *Ibid.*, 85-88.

[32]Cf. J. D. Anderson, & E. E. Jones, *The Management of Industry; Leadership, Purpose, Structure, Community* (San Francisco, Harper & Row, 1978), 44.

[33]Cf. H. R. Niebuhr, *The Purpose of the Church and Its Ministry: Reflections on the Aims of Theological Education* (N. Y., Harper and Bros., 1956), 27-29. (Hereafter, Niebuhr, *The Purpose of he Church and Its Ministry…*).

[34]Charles R. Feilding, *Education for Ministry* (USA: Thomas W. Klink, 1996), 11.

The theological heritage is not fully recaptured unless it enters in to dialogue with contemporary events and human being. [35] The present system of teaching theory and practice is often haphazard. There is a wide-spread tendency for academic departments to talk about books, doctrines, movements and characters of the past, and for practical departments to talk about books, doctrines, movements and people of today, adding, perhaps, the sciences which help us to understand them.[36] However, these leave a number of awkward impressions towards the theological paternity. Some institutions the academic side dominates, in other institutions the practical. Some institutions are denominational through and through, some welcome members of other denominations. The ignorance and negligence which even neighbouring institutions have of each other is often profound and permits prejudice to abound. In these circumstances it is the ground for encouragement that institutions so various are able to maintain a fellowship in India under the Senate of Serampore College.

The rapidity of social change produces endless new problems such as ambiguous effects of automation; it also exposes old problems like massive rural poverty which churches had barely begun to grasp before being overwhelmed by newer challenges. Yet still there are many seminaries in India who has offered no serious opportunity for either rural or urban training despite long standing need and available services. Therefore, there is growing dissatisfaction with the treatment of theological education which is based on theory alone. There also is been an abhorrence of turning theological institution into a trade institution. Hence, it is time that the Senate of Serampore theological family develops that which is both theoretical as well as practical[37] in order to meet the need of the church in India today.

4. Theological Institutions Affiliated to the Senate of Serampore College

SSC which was started in 1818 had its charter issued by the Danish King Frederick in the year 1827, which was renewed and adopted for higher theological education under the leadership of George Howells. As a result of negotiations with Baptist Missionary Society and Danish Government the higher theological education department preparing candidates for B.D. degree was started in 1910,[38] The first B.D. degrees were conferred in 1915, the Licentiate in Theology Diploma was instituted in 1916 and the reorganization process was completed and an

[35]Cf. Paton, David, *New Forms of Ministry* (London: Edinburgh House, 1965), 45.

[36]Cf. H. Richard Neibuhr, Daniel Day Williams and James M. Gustafson, *The Advancement of Theological Education* (New York: Harper's Publishers, 1957), 4.

[37]Some of the institutions in India have separated the practical and academic. The unfortunate things in this separation is that the so-called practical disciplines theological education have been led to develop pseudo-theologies of their own, while the so-called academic theological education have tended to become semantically isolated and culturally irrelevant.

[38]*Serampore College Theology Department Prospectus 1965*, 2.

(interdenominational) Senate was formed in 1918. With the constitution of the SSC in 1918 the way was opened for other Theological Institutions throughout India to seek affiliation to the College. By such affiliation these institutions become part of the University which has thus been able to help in the maintaining of standards in theological education throughout the country.[39] With this outcome different institutions began to be affiliated with the SSC. For example, the United Theological in 1919, Bishop College, Leonard Theological College and others.[40] The Board of Theological Education developed under the National Christian Council of India in 1955 paved the way for accrediting and assisting small institutions especially the evangelical institutions which were not affiliated with the Serampore family. After much consultation the BTE became a part of the SSC in 1975 and began BTESSC for wider search for the ecumenically relevant theological education in our context. Thus, the SSC today hold a central place of importance in fostering ecumenism in the context of theological Education in India.

At present the Senate has 52 affiliated institutions, they are:

1. Bethel Bible Institution, Salem.
2. Calcutta Bible Seminary, 24 Paragana.
3. Concordia Theological Seminary, Nagarcoil.
4. Dharma Jyoti Vidya Peeth, Faridabad.
5. Gossner Theological College, Ranchi.
6. Gujarat United School of Theology, Ahmedabad.
7. Harding Theological College, Tura.
8. Indian Theological Seminary, Avadi.
9. Madras Theological Seminary & College, Chennai.
10. Mar Thoma Episcopal Jubilee Institute of Evangelism, Thiruvalla.
11. Master's College of Theology, Madhurawada.
12. Methodist Bible Seminary, Vasad.
13. Orissa Christian Theological College, Gopalpur.
14. Santal Theological College, Benagaria.

---

[39]Cf. *Serampore College Handbook for the Year 1954-1955*, 2.

[40]By 1955 the Senate was affiliated with eighteen institutions. Four B.D. Colleges, i.e. 1. The United Theological College of India and Ceylon, Bangalore; 2. Bishop's College, Calcutta; 3. Leonard Theological College, Jabalpur; 4. Gurukul Lutheran Theological College and Research Institute, Madras. L.Th. Colleges, i.e., 1. Mar Thoma Theological Seminary, Kottayam; 2. Theological College, Cherrapunji; 3. Kerala United Theological Seminary, Trivandrum; 4. United Theological College of Western India, Poona; 5. Baptist Theological College, Kakinada; 6. Andhra Union Theological College, Dornakal; 7. Basel Evangelical Mission Theological Seminary, Mangalore; 8. Gujarat United School of theology, Ahmedabad; 9. Lutheran Theological College, Rajahmundry; 10. Lutheran Theological College, Ranchi; 11. Tamilnadu Theological College, Tirumarayur; 12. North India United Theological College, Saharanpur; 13. Union Kanarese Seminary, Tumkur; 14. Union Theological Seminary, Bareilly. However, many of these institutions have changed their name by now and some of them are out of Serampore family.

15. Southern Asia Christian College, Chennai.
16. St. Andrew's Theological College, Dhaka, Bangladesh.
17. United Theological College of Maharashtra, Pune.
18. Academy of Integrated Christian Studies, Aizawl.
19. Aizawl Theological College, Aizawl.
20. Allahabad Bible College, Allahabad.
21. Andhra Christian Theological College, Hyderbad.
22. Baptist Theological College, Pfutsero.
23. Bethel Bible College, Guntur.
24. Bishop's College, Calcutta.
25. Christian Theological Seminary of Sri Lanka, Chunnakam, Sri Lanka.
26. Clark Theological College, Mokokchung.
27. Eastern Theological College, Jorhat.
28. Faith Theological Seminary, Manakala.
29. Gurukul Lutheran Theological College, Chennai.
30. John Robert Theological Seminary, Shillong.
31. Karnataka Theological College, Mangalore.
32. Kerala United Theological Seminary, Trivandrum.
33. Leonard Theological College, Jabalpur.
34. Malankara Syrian Orthodox Theological Seminary, Ernakulam.
35. Manipur Theological College, Kangpokpi.
36. Mar Thoma Theological Seminary, Kottayam.
37. Mennonite Brethren Centenary Bible College, Shamshabad.
38. New Theological College, Dehra Dun.
39. Orthodox Theological Seminary, Kottayam.
40. Serampore College, Serampore.
41. St. Thomas Orthodox Theological Seminary, Nagpur.
42. Tamil Nadu Theological Seminary, Madurai.
43. Theological College of Sri Lanka, Pilimatalawa, Sri Lanka.
44. Trinity Theological College, Dimapur.
45. Trulock Theological Seminary, Imphal.
46. Union Biblical Seminary, Pune
47. United Theological College, Bangalore.
48. Calvin Institute of Theology, Hyderabad.
49. Missionary Training College, Aizawl.
50. Witter Theological College, Wokha.
51. Nav Jyoti Post Graduate and Research Centre, Faridabad.
52. Federated Faculty for Research in Religion & Culture, Kottayam.

Nine institutions are offering the Doctoral Degree.[41] Five other institutions under the recognition of the SSC are offering Diploma in Clinical Pastoral Counseling (DCPC) courses.[42] Alongside these, there are several theological institutions, training schools and lay theological centers, as well as some substantive Para church-based ventures in theological education which are not affiliated to the Senate of Serampore College. In exercising its rights and function as a University in the Faculty of Theology under the Act of Bengal Legislation 1918, the Serampore College confers degrees and diplomas, namely:

Bachelor of Theology (B.Th.),
Bachelor of Divinity (B.D.),
Master of Theology (M.Th.),
Doctor of Theology (D.Th.),
Diploma in Christian Studies (Dip. C.S.),
Diploma in Clinical Pastoral Counseling (DCPC),
Bachelor of Christian Studies (B.C.S.), and
Doctor of Ministry (D.Min.).[43]

According to the latest figures, approximately two-thirds of students are male and one-third are female, though in some theological institutions women make up around 35% percent of the student population.

5. The Nature of Serampore Course (Content Analysis of the Senate of Serampore College's Curricula)

5.1. Introduction

The nature of the SSC has always made it possible through its ecumenical curricula and regulations that its intension is to provide a well rounded course of Biblical and theological study designed for proper equipment of the ministry of the Church and the Society. This is also well supplemented by certain types of practical training depending on local situations. It also provides a systematic of Christian doctrines and the Church, with some understanding of other faith in India. The nature of the SSC gives ample opportunities to regional instructions

[41] 1. Department of Research/SATHRI, Serampore. WB 2. Federated Faculty for Research in Religion and Culture (FFRRC), Kottayam 3. Gurukul Lutheran Theological College and Research Institute, Chennai 4. North India Institute of Post Graduate Theological Studies (NIIPGTS), Serampore 5. United Theological College, Bangalore 6. Tamilnadu Theological Seminary, Arasaradi, Madurai 7. Union Biblical Seminary, Pune 8. Faith Theological Seminary, Manakala , Adur 9. Aizawl Theological College Aizawl.

[42] They are: 1. Life Enrichment Counselling & Training Centre, Thodupuzha, Idukki 2. T.M.A. Institute of Counselling, Kottayam, 3. Christian Medical College & Hospital, Vellore, 4. Marthoma Hospital Guidance, Trivandrum, 5. Christian Medical Association of India, Bangalore.

[43] *Annual Report of the President, 2006-07...*, 11.

and colleges to teach courses in regional languages and freedom to evaluate and examine fifty percent of total number of given courses.[44]

5.2. The Nature of the Diploma of Licentiate in Theology (L.Th.)

A Licentiate in Theology (L.Th.) Diploma course was offered with the intention "to provide a well rounded course of Biblical and theological study designed for the proper equipment of the ministry of the church".[45] Courses were taught in regional languages to equip students to minister to their own people.[46] Senate called attention for the following features of the L.Th. course:

1. It provides for a systematic study of the Bible by each student together with a basic knowledge of Christian doctrine and the history of the church both in India and in other parts of the world, with some understanding of other religions of India;
2. The course is taught in the regional languages in order that students may be prepared by it to minister to their own people in their own languages. At the same time English is taught in order to introduce students to wider theological literature;
3. By providing for certain optional papers, the L.Th. course gives freedom to each regional College to adjust its teaching to the special needs of the people of its area.[47]

The standard of admission to the L.Th. course, was Matriculation, similar to the university degree courses, covers 29 papers and extended over a period of three to four years. The L.Th. first year course was regarded as preliminary. A student who passes with distinction may proceed to the three years B.D. course, students who secure a mere pass will take a further two years course leading to the L.Th. Diploma.[48] During those days the academic year was divided into three sessions:

1. Rain Term- July 1st to September 10th,
2. Winter Term- November 1st to December 22nd,
3. Spring Term- January 2nd to April 30th.

The Senate, following its strict rules, conducted the annual examinations in order to maintain a uniform standard for the Diploma throughout the country

---

[44]Cf. *Senate of Serampore College Proceedings of the Theological Senate and Its Committees*, Book XIX, Vol. XVIII, 14.

[45]*Serampore Senate Minutes Resolution X*, Book No. II, 1956, 816.

[46]Cf. Siga Arles, *Theological Education for the Mission of the Church in India, 1947-1987* (New York: Peter Lang, 1991), 237.

[47]*Serampore Senate Minutes Resolution X*, Book No. II, 1956, 816-818.

[48]*Serampore College Prospectus*, 1920, 4.

in the month of April.[49] In 1916 the Diploma of L.Th was conferred for the first time.[50] 1n 1969 it was upgraded to a new degree, Bachelor of Theology (B.Th) and the course was made up to a four years course. In 1983, it became three year course plus a year of orientation.[51]

5.3. The Nature of Bachelor of Theology (B.Th.)

The SSC, as an outcome of several years of consultations among the L.Th. Colleges under the SSC and the Senate, and on the recommendation of the National Consultation held at Bangalore in 1968 introduced in the year 1969 a new degree course, called the Bachelor of Theology (B.Th), to replace the L.Th. course.[52]

The B.Th. Degree was then extended over to three and half years. It was envisaged that this degree will be adequate for the exercise of pastoral ministry of the church.[53] The course emphasizes study of the Bible, Christian Faith, History of Christianity, and Religions with their missiological implications in the context of a pluralistic world. The practical works provides opportunities for involvement in ministerial practice, exposure to socio-cultural and religious situation with a view to bring integration in the total learning experience.[54]

5.3.1. *The Main Features of the B.Th. Course*

a) The B.Th. degree course is of three and half years duration after registration, requiring the same academic standard and scholarship as is normally expected for the Bachelor Degree Course of secular universities.
b) The course seeks to prepare persons for the pastoral and other essential functions of ministry through:
    (i) foundational and critical study of the Bible to relate/interpret its message to life situations,
    (ii) Personal and spiritual formation and leadership development,
    (iii) Sensitivity to contemporary issues arising out of pluralistic situations and their missiological implications for involvement and witness,

---

[49] *Serampore Senate Minutes Resolution XI,* Book No. II, 1956, 816-818.

[50] *Serampore College Theology Department Prospectus 1952*, 1.

[51] Cf. Ravi Tiwari, "Ecumenical Character of Serampore College Part-II", *The Story of Serampore and Its College*, published by The Council of Serampore College (Serampore: Serampore College, 2005), 117. (Hereafter, Tiwari, *Ecumenical Character of Serampore College...*).

[52] Cf. *Senate of Serampore College Faculty of Theology Regulations Relating to the Bachelor of Theology (B.Th). Degree Course*, 1993, 4.

[53] Cf. *Senate of Serampore College Proceedings of the Theological Senate and Its Committees,* Book XIX, Vol. XVIII, 14.

[54] Cf. *Senate of Serampore College Faculty of Theology Regulations Relating to the Bachelor of Theology (B.Th). Degree Course*, 1993, 5.

(iv) Participation in pastoral, social and developmental activities (Rural & Urban) for meaningful experience.[55]

Primarily, the course is to be taught and examined normally in the regional languages of India in order that the students may be prepared by it to minister to their own language. At the same time, there is provision to teach the course in English medium. The affiliated Colleges are expected to offer courses as prescribed in the B.Th. Regulations and Curriculum of the SSC. The maximum time allowed to complete all the requirements for the B.Th. degree is seven years. However, the extension of time for completion of the degree may be granted by the C.A.A. of the Senate but in exceptional circumstances only.[56]

5.4. The Nature of Bachelor of Divinity (B.D.)

In the year 1910 the SSC instituted the B.D. Course.[57] The aim of the B.D. Course was to prepare students for certain essential functions of the church which require an academic course of this nature.[58] According to B.D. Regulation of 1993 the course is designed to equip persons for essential functions and ministries of the Church in India who could command their faith with relevance in the context of a pluralistic world.[59] It aims at an integrative and interdisciplinary approach among the biblical, theological, historical and religious fields with involvement in practical aspects of the sub-continent. It also ensures adequate grounding in the discipline of linguistic for study of basic texts and provides hermeneutical tools and skills for understanding and interpreting the context of ministry. The B.D. course is available only for internal study through affiliated Colleges at B.D. level.[60] The duration of the B.D. Course was for three years (at present it is four years), in which they had to cover branches from:

I. Old Testament,
II. New Testament,
III. Theology and Ethics,
IV. History of Christianity,

[55]Cf. *Senate of Serampore College Faculty of Theology Regulations Relating to the Bachelor of Theology (B.Th). Degree Course*, 1993, 4-5.

[56]Cf. *Senate of Serampore College Faculty of Theology Regulations Relating to the Bachelor of Theology (B.Th). Degree Course*, 2004, 7-8.

[57]William Stewart, "The Ecumenical Character of Serampore College, Part-I" *The Story of Serampore and Its College*, Published by the Council of Serampore College (Serampore: Serampore College, 2005), 101. (Hereafter, Stewart, *Ecumenical Character of Serampore College…*).

[58]*Serampore Senate Minutes Resolution X,* Book No. II, 1956, 816. See also Stewart, *Ecumenical Character of Serampore College*, 104-105. Cf. M. H. Harrison, *After Ten Years: A Report on Theological Education in India* (Nagpur: NCCI, 1953), 29-30.

[59]Cf. *Senate of Serampore College Bachelor of Divinity Regulations, 1993*, 4.

[60]Cf. *Senate of Serampore College Bachelor of Divinity Regulations, 2005*, 4.

V. Religion and Society,
VI. Christian Ministry,
VII. Communication, and
VIII. Social Analysis.[61]

According to the Senate Regulation No. XII, 1956, on the Nature of the B.D. Degree, it state that the standard for B.D. degree admission is graduation in Arts or Science or Commerce of a recognized university and have passed the entrance examination consisting of papers in Regional language of English, Scripture Knowledge and General Knowledge[62] or qualification accepted by the Senate as its equivalent.[63] Moreover, a candidate who passed 10+2 course or its equivalent with eligibility to enter a University for a Degree course shall qualify for admission to the Five Year Integrated B.D. Degree course. The duration of the Integrated B.D. course is five and half year with a last six months for practical work. A mature person, who is at least 25 years of age and has passed 10th class, was prevented for special reasons from pursuing his/her secular studies and can produce evidence to this effect and has been in a full time vocation/profession/employment for at least two years may apply to sit for Mature Candidates Entrance Examination to be qualified for B.D. Degree study.[64]

In the past the church in India as in other countries, has been served by persons both from India and from overseas of high general education and equipped with a theological training of the graduate type. These forms of service were felt to be required for quite sometime, and the church needed persons who were equipped to teach in Theological College, translate and revise the translations of the scriptures, to write book, articles etc. Moreover, it was for the continued equipment of persons to render these essential services as we required an adequate theological training set in the context of higher education generally. In this context, the B.D. course was meant to provide a necessary foundation for later studies and service.[65]

---

[61]Cf. *Senate of Serampore College Faculty of Theology Regulations Relating to the Bachelor of Divinity (B.D.) Degree Course*, 2005, 10. See also *Serampore College Theology Department Prospectus*, 1920, 2. The Courses offered during 1920s were: I. Old Testament, II. New Testament, III. Christian Theology, IV. The History of Religions, V. Church History, VI. The Philosophy of Religions, VII. Moral Philosophy, VIII Classical Language (Hebrew, Sanskrit or Syriac) and IX. English and Vernacular Essays for B.D. Students.

[62]Cf. *Senate of Serampore College Faculty of Theology Regulations Relating to the Bachelor of Divinity (B.D.) Degree Course*, 2005, 4.

[63]*Serampore Senate Minutes Resolution X,* Book No. II, 1956, 817.

[64]Cf. *Senate of Serampore College Faculty of Theology Regulations Relating to the Bachelor of Divinity (B.D.) Degree Course*, 2005, 4-5.

[65]Cf. *Serampore College Handbook for the Years 1957-1959*, 4-5.

5.5. The Nature of Master of Theology (M.Th.)

The degree of Master of Theology (M.Th.) is a post-graduate degree offered by the SSC.[66] In 1948 the Degree of Master of Theology (M.Th.) was instituted and the Degree was conferred for the first time at the Convocation held in January 1950.[67] At that time the primary purpose of the program was to train teachers for various theological colleges in India. Over the past several years the program has also come to be seen as for the ministry of the Church in its own right and as a program oriented towards equipping men and women at an academic level higher than that of the B.D. program for the various ministries of the Church. Though M.Th. is a degree complete in itself, it also serves as a preparation for advanced study and research at the doctoral level.[68]

Moreover, the contemporary challenges that the Church in India faces in the context of religious awakening and cultural pluralism, the issues of poverty and justice, and the concerns raised by liberation movements call for a contextual and holistic approach to higher theological education paying also attention to our heritage. Therefore, the M.Th. Curriculum was basically designed to include an integrative and interdisciplinary approach to study with due awareness to the need for specialization.[69]

5.5.1. *The Main Purpose of the M.Th. Degrees*

a. to train candidates for teaching in theological colleges,
b. to equip candidates with adequate academic tools and skills for critical and methodological reflection as well as creative participation in the diversified ministries of the Church,
c. to develop such proficiency in the candidates so that they may engage in independent and contextual research which may lead to advanced study at the doctoral level,
d. to promote inter-disciplinary perspectives which will help to achieve the above purpose and lead to an integration of theological knowledge and thinking.[70]

For admission to the M.Th. course, a student must normally have passed the SSC B.D. examination in either the first or the second class[71] and passed at

---

[66] *Senate of Serampore College : Faculty of Theology Regulations Relating to the Degree of Master of Theology* (July, 1998), Revised and Reprint - in 2007, 4.

[67] *Serampore College Theology Department Prospectus, 1952*, 4.

[68] Cf. *Senate of Serampore College Faculty of Theology Regulations Relating to the Degree of Master of Theology (M.Th.),* (July, 1998), 4. (Hereafter, *Regulations Relating to the Degree of Master of Theology.*)

[69] Cf. *Regulations Relating to the Degree of Master of Theology…*, 4.

[70] Cf. *Ibid.*, 4-5.

[71] Candidates write five papers and a thesis in any one of the following branches of study: Old Testament; New Testament; Christian Theology; Church History; History of Religions; Philosophy

least three papers at B.D. level securing at least second class B Grade in the Branch in which he or she plan to do the M.Th. course. A person with B.C.S. degree of SSC in Second Class with B Grade (60%) will be permitted to register for the M.Th. course in the fields of Christian Ministry and Social Analysis provided they undergo a period of exposure/practical work of at least 6 to 8 month prior to admission through the post-graduate college where he/she seeks admission and passes the qualifying papers at the required standard (B Grade) in these branches. A person who holds academic qualification that in the opinion of the Committee on Academic Administration of the SSC is at least equivalent to B.D. in First and Second Class B Grade.[72] A Bachelor of Theology graduate who upgraded to B.D. should have passed at least 2 papers in his/her Branch of Specialization as a part of his/her B.D. course.[73] It is expected of a student to write a Thesis at B.D. level. The Colleges offering M.Th. studies, however, shall take special care to help all candidates qualified to register for M.Th. who have not written thesis at B.D. level.[74] Moreover, before the candidate is registered for the M.Th. course of studies, he should have at least one year of practical experience in some field of Christian service after passing the B.D. or its equivalent theological degree. However, in the case of a candidate who seeks registration to the branch of Christian Ministry, two years of practical experience in ministry shall be required. The women candidates are exempted from this rule for the present.[75] The M.Th. degree course is available for internal (residential) study only through the colleges

---

of Religion; Christian Ethics.

[72]Cf. *Senate of Serampore College Faculty of Theology Regulations Relating to the Degree of Master of Theology (M.Th.),* (July, 1998), 4,5. There is also a provision that a person who has passed the B.D. examination of the Senate of Serampore College securing an over all average and branch average of 50% (C+) separately and retakes four papers at B.D. level in the intended branch of specialization and secures an average of 55% (B-) and not less than 50% (C+) in any course examined by the Senate, in one sitting. (i) Moreover no candidate is allowed more than two attempts to complete the qualifying examination. (ii) Where college papers are not equivalent to the Senate full course, the appropriate committee will decide. (iii) All qualifying examinations shall be conducted by the Senate.

[73]For admission to the M.Th. course in branches of Christian Theology and Christian Ethics, courses taken under B.D. Branches of Theology and Ethics will be taken into account. However, for admission to the M.Th. in Missiology, Social Analysis, Women's Studies and Communication, candidates will be exempted from writing 3 papers in their field of specialization at B.D. level until 2005. Instead, the P.G. Colleges offering these branches shall be required to conduct a minimum of three months intensive coaching in each of these branches prior to the admission of candidates to the M.Th. course in June each year.

[74]Cf *Senate of Serampore College Faculty of Theology Regulations Relating to the Degree of Master of Theology (M.Th.),* (July, 1998), 4-5. 7-8.

[75]The B.Th. degree holders who upgrade to the B.D. degree will be permitted to register for M.Th. course without break of one year provided that they were engage in Christian ministry after receiving the B.Th. degree and produce a certificate from the Church.

affiliated at the M.Th. level.[76] The duration of the course required two full years of study.[77] The maximum time limit for completing all the requirements shall be five years from date of registration.[78]

For qualifying to the study M.Th. degree a person can write qualifying examinations in line with the criteria given below:

i) No candidate shall be allowed more than two attempts to complete the qualifying examination.
ii) Where college papers are not equivalent to the Senate full course, the appropriate committee will decide.
iii) All qualifying examinations shall be conducted by the Senate.[79]

The M.Th. course covers the following branches of study:-

1. Biblical Studies- Old Testament
2. Biblical Studies- New Testament
3. Christian Theology
4. History of Christianity
5. Religion
6. Christian Ethics
7. Christian Ministry
8. Missiology
9. Social Analysis
10. Communication
11. Women's Studies.

5.5.2. *Special Requirements for M.Th. Studies*

The SSC set down the following points as requirements for candidates seeking to enroll for M.Th. studies:

---

[76]The medium of instruction and examination for the M.Th. degree course is English. However, colleges may offer the degree in the Regional Languages subject to approval of the Senate. Cf. *Senate of Serampore College Faculty of Theology Regulations Relating to the Degree of Master of Theology (M.Th.),* (July, 1998), 9-10.

[77]Any exception to this rule should have the prior permission of the Academic Committee failing which the candidate's registration will be terminated. In the case of a candidate holding the M.Th. degree from a recognized college abroad, the Committee on Academic Administration shall determine the number of credits and the duration of study.

[78]However, extension of time to complete the degree beyond the first two years is subject to the approval of the Committee on Academic Administration. Cf. *Senate of Serampore College Faculty of Theology Regulations Relating to the Degree of Master of Theology (M.Th.),* (July, 1998), 10.

[79]*Senate of Serampore College: Faculty of Theology Regulations Relating to the Degree of Master of Theology* (July, 1998), Revised and Reprint - in 2007, 7.

i) Before a candidate is registered for the M.Th. course of studies, he shall have at least a year practical ministry after completing B.D. studies. However, this rule is not applicable for women candidates who are seeking admission to M.Th degree program.[80]
ii) It is expected of a student to write a Thesis at B.D. level.
iii) Old Testament- the person/candidates should have passed in at least two Hebrew courses at B.D. level, securing 2nd class average.
iv) New Testament- the seeking candidate must passed at least three Greek papers at B.D. level with attaining 2nd class percentage.
v) Christian Theology- one paper language(Greek, Hebrew, Latin Syriac or Sanskrit) at the B.D. level is must those who seek for M.Th. admission in this branch.
vi) Religion- a person must passed one advanced paper in the B.D. level of Sanskrit or Pali or Arabic.
vii) History of Christianity-there is no Biblical or Classical language requires being qualified in this branch. However, a candidate needs to have at least a working knowledge of the languages necessary to study the primary resources when writing thesis.
viii) Christian Ethic- same as above
ix) Christian Ministry- same as above
x) Missiology- same as above
xi) Social Analysis- same as above
xii) Communication- same as above
xiii) Women's studies- same as above.[81]

5.6. The Nature of Doctor of Divinity (D.D. Honoris Causa or by Thesis)

The Honorary Degree of Doctor of Divinity (D.D.) was instituted by the Council in 1929, when it was conferred on Dr. Howells, and has been conferred since by the recommendation of the Senate, on a limited number of distinguished servants of the Church. The ecumenical character of the SSC is expressed by the variety of those thus honored, representing such affiliations of the Church as the Lutherans, the Church of South India, Baptists, Methodists, Presbyterians, United Church of North India and others.[82]

Besides the Honorary Degree, provision was made for a doctorate by thesis, which was conferred first to Rev. W. Sweetman.[83] However, in 1959, the Senate Council acceded to a Senate proposal that thereafter the earned degree would

[80]*Senate of Serampore College: Faculty of Theology Regulations Relating to the Degree of Master of Theology* (July, 1998), Revised and Reprint - in 2007, 7.

[81]Cf. *Senate of Serampore College: Faculty of Theology Regulations Relating to the Degree of Master of Theology* (July, 1998), Revised and Reprint - in 2007, 8,9.

[82]Cf. Stewart, *Ecumenical Character of Serampore College…*, 108.

[83]In recognition of Vol. I of his authoritative work: *Islam and Christian Theology.*

be called D.Th. (Doctor of Theology) leaving the D.D. as a purely honorary degree.[84]

5.7. The Nature of the Doctor of Theology (D.Th.)

At the national level, the Senate through the Research Committee took up the task of monitoring the Doctoral program to maintain uniform standards and excellence.[85]

The SSC also offered other degrees than those mentioned the above. Such degrees are: Master of Religious studies,[86] Diploma Course in Religious Knowledge[87] etc.

Thus, SSC tries to impart in its nature of courses by highlighting South-Asian context of the people of God, living among the communities of other faiths and ideologies, facing life-negating forces while remaining faithful to the Gospel of Christ. Hence, SSC continues to equip ministers, leaders, scholars and whole people of God in order to be actively involved in God's mission of liberation, reconciliation and community building among all peoples through varied forms of ministry.[88]

6. Theological Education by Extension (TEE) under the Senate of Serampore College

6.1. Introduction

The word 'extension' itself indicates that our concern in this area is to extend (stretch, expand, spread, adapt) the resources of theological education in order to reach the people who are the natural leaders of our churches. The ***extension*** model educates a person ***where they are*** without requiring any change of environment. Therefore, the person's context remains the same: they stay in the same place, remain with their friends and family, keep on with whatever Christian ministry they are doing, and they keep providing for themselves the way they have been doing it.[89] TEE is co-coordinated from the outside, whether by a church,

[84]Cf. Stewart, *Ecumenical Character of Serampore College…*, 108.

[85]*Report of the President of the Senate for the Year 2000*, 4.

[86]This is a post-graduate course of a high standard which is orientated to the needs of the practical ministry. The admission requirement is the B.D. degree or L.Th. with a qualifying examination and two years of practical experience.

[87]The aim of this course is to equip Christian teachers in Arts and Science Colleges or in High Schools with the essential minimum knowledge of the Bible, Church History and Christian Theology to equip them to conduct classes and lead discussions on religious topics for undergraduates. The requirement for admission was graduation from an Indian University or equivalent and an Entrance Examination.

[88]Cf. *Senate of Serampore College Proceedings of the Theological Senate and Its Committees*, Book XIX, Vol. XVIII, 14.

[89]Cf. David Greeff, *Theological Education By Extension: A Reflection on the Usefulness of theological Extension Work in Namibia-like Contexts, in Comparison to that of Traditional Theological*

or theological institution. Work books were to be obtained from somewhere, or created from scratch. Groups also were to be established, co-coordinated, and facilitators provided, usually by the same organization. Hence, it is an extension of our concept of theological education besides candidates for the ministry; lay workers, elders youth leaders, ordained pastors, i.e., those who carry the primary responsibilities in the churches and congregations especially in those areas where there is scare hope in this generation or the next for an established, fulltime, salaried ministry.[90]

6.2. The Purpose of TEE

The SSC degree programs were directed only towards a section of the people who were committed to the pastoral ministry of the church while excluding majority who were already involved in a career of secular persuasion. Thus, a vast majority of the people was not provided enough theological education to cope with the fast changing realities of the context. The BTESSC felt the need to take this situation seriously. Therefore, in order to meet the needs for these emerging and fast changing realities of our context the Senate Centre for Extension and Pastoral Theological Research (SCEPTRE) project was initiated in 2001.[91] Moreover, this was established in order to promote diversified theological education and practice ministry and continues process of learning in context, which should be made available to both the pastor as well as to the laity. The purpose of this project is trying to provide theological education to the whole people of God by offering BCS and Dip.C.S course through distance learning.[92] The ISPCK, Delhi continues to encourage the extension programme by gifting a set of 15 books from the International Study Guide Series to the first years B.C.S. and Dip.C.S. students.[93]

6.3. Senate Affiliated Institutions and other Bodies Promoting Diploma in Christian Studies (Dip.C.S.), Bachelor of Christian Studies (BCS) and Diploma in Clinical Pastoral Counseling (DCPC) Programmes

The following sixteen SSC affiliated colleges facilitate the extension studies programs in accordance with the regulations and curricula of the Senate. They are:

1. Aizawl Theological College, Aizawl;
2. Allahabad Bible Seminary, Allahabad;

Institutions (USA: St Andrews Hall, 2005), 4.

[90]Cf. F. Ross Kinsler, *The Extension Movement in Theological Education* (California: William Carey Library, 1978), 26.

[91]Cf. Tiwari, *Ecumenical Character of Serampore College...*, 117.

[92]*Ibid.*

[93]*Report of the President of the Senate for the Year 2004-2005*, 16.

3. Andhra Christian Theological College, Hyderabad;
4. Baptist Theological College, Pfutsero;
5. Christian Theological Seminary, Chunnakkam, Sri Lanka;
6. Dharma Jyoti Vidya Peeth, Faridabad;
7. Eastern Theological College, Jorhat;
8. Faith Theological Seminary, Manakala;
9. Gospel for Asia Biblical Seminary, Kuttapuzha;
10. Karnataka Theological College, Mangalore;
11. Mar Thoma Theological Seminary, Kottayam;
12. Mennonite Brethren Centenary Bible College, Shamshabad;
13. St. Thomas Orthodox Theological Seminary, Nagpur;
14. Tamilnadu Theological Seminary, Madurai;
15. Theological College of Lanka, Pilimatawa, Sri Lanka;
16. United Theological Seminary of Maharashtra, Pune.[94]

There are eight other institutions which are not affiliated to the SSC, but have also been involving in promoting the extension programs. They are:

1. A.P. Theological College and Research Institutes, Visakhapatnam;
2. Christian Mission Service School for Deacons, Coonoor;
3. Ebenezer Theological Seminary, Ayur;
4. ECI Theological Seminary, Kaliyakkavila;
5. Grace Ministries, Trivandrum;
6. North India Theological College, Bareilly;
7. National Christian Theological College, Chennai;
8. Satyanniketan Dharmavigyan Mahavidyalaya, Allahabad.[95]

These institutions register candidates, conduct contact seminars, and even provide study materials. The academic year for the extension program run from February to November. According to the CAA's resolution No. XLIV, d, these programs registration should be done by October 15, and by October 31 with payment of late fee, every year.[96] Not only theological institutions but also churches are beginning to register candidates for Dip.C.S, and BCS programs. According to the Director's report of 2006-2007, "the CNI Dioceses of Agra and Maharashtra are registering their candidates for the Dip.C.S and BCS programs by appointing one M.Th. qualified presbyter to serve as a Coordinator for the

[94] *Director's Report of the Theological Education by Extension*, for the year February 2006-January 2007, 1.

[95] Tiwari, *Ecumenical Character of Serampore College...*, 2.

[96] *CAA Resolution No. XLIV*, d, July 2004.

extension programs with full-time evangelists and other laypersons in the diocese are encouraged to go through".[97]

The annual examinations are usually held from November-December. Senate allows candidates to write examinations in regional languages.[98] According to CAA, "institutions which are not affiliated to the Senate can also serve as examination centers for extension programs".[99] The CAA has also resolved that it will be mandatory for BCS candidates to attend three Contact Seminars during their period of study".[100]

To further strengthen the extension programs of the SSC the following matters were brought under serious consideration:

1. *Study Materials*: Effort is to be made to get materials compiled for subjects on which no such literature has as yet been put together. Scholars are to be encouraged to write course materials especially for the extension programs.
2. *Resources in Hindi*: Selected texts from the compiled material for each paper will have to be translated into Hindi so that candidates from North India could have access to helpful literature.
3. *Pedagogical Training*: A special workshop will have to be organized for resource persons engaged in teaching extension program candidates.
4. *Library Development:* The library at SCEPTRE is to be developed so that it could serve as a resource centre for students, teachers and researchers from North and North-East India.
5. *Program for Rural Laity:* Consultation is to be conducted for the proposal to introduce some kind of certificate course in Christian studies, particularly for the rural laity.
6. *Issue-Oriented Programs*: Short term non-formal programs on contemporary issues such as HIV/AIDS, Globalization, Ecology, Human Rights, Dalit and Feminist Concerns, Religious Fundamentalism and Communalism, Missiology, Leadership Training, Ministry to Children, Campus Ministry, etc. under the SCEPTRE could prove to be instrumental in facilitating such non-formal programs.[101]

---

[97] *Director's Report of the Theological Education by Extension*, for the year February 2006-January 2007, 2.

[98] *Proceedings of the Theological Senate and Its Committees*, January 4, 2005 to November 30, 2005, Book XVIII, 2005-2006, 40.

[99] *CAA Resolution No. XLIV*, c, July 2004.

[100] *CAA/100/2004; Resolution No. XLIV, a.*

[101] *Director's Report of the Theological Education by Extension*, for the year February 2006-January 2007, 6.

6.4. The Nature of TEE

6.4.1. *Diploma in Christian Studies (Dip.C.S.) Program*

The SSC also offers Diploma in Christian Studies (Dip.C.S.). This course was introduced for the benefit of people of different religious traditions and ideologies so that they could study Christianity as a religion in its indigenous character in term of its faiths, history and practice.[102] The Dip.C.S is meant for any one who has an eight standard as a minimum educational qualification.[103] The Academic Committee also had approved that the Dip.C.S diploma holder will also be provided the opportunity to seek registration to the B.D. or the B.C.S. degrees from 2000 onward.[104] This course is open for study in regional languages approved by the Senate.

6.4.2. *Diploma in Clinical Pastoral Counseling (DCPC) Program*

In 2000 the Senate decided to introduce a new Diploma in Clinical Pastoral Counseling to train pastors and others with aptitude to learn skills and engage in the ministry of healing among the members of the congregations, hospitals, schools and colleges, industries and other areas of life.[105] According to the decision the Diploma was offered from June 2001 through colleges and professional centers recognized for the purpose. The duration of the program is one year in residence. The syllabi have been prepared by a group of experts in the area of counseling drawn from professional counseling centers, Christian medical hospitals, church related centers, and secular practitioners, colleges and church representatives.

6.4.3. *Bachelor of Christian Studies (B.C.S.) Program*

Besides the residential programs, the SSC, with the help of Colleges, run this B.C.S. degree program for equipping and training of the laity. The program is designed to enable the laity to gain better understanding of Christian faith and to deepen their commitment to service in the context of their vocation.[106] The degree of B.C.S. however, is a replacement of B.D. external which now provides the laity an in-depth understanding of Christian faith, and deepens their commitment to service in the context of their vocation.[107] The Senate Academic Committee meeting in the Neo Theological College, Dehra Dun on November 20-24, 2000 resolved that B.C.S. Degree holders will hereafter qualify to register for the Master

[102]Cf. Longchar, *Challenges for Ecumenical Theological Education…*, 6.

[103]Tiwari, *Ecumenical Character of Serampore College…*, 115.

[104]*Report of the President of the Senate for the Year 2000*, 3.

[105]*Ibid.*

[106]Cf. Longchar, *Challenges for Ecumenical Theological Education…*, 6.

[107]Cf. Tiwari, *Ecumenical Character of Serampore College…*, 115.

of Theology Degree (M.Th.) subject to fulfilling the same requirements such as, language study etc. at the B.D. level as required by the M.Th. Regulations.[108]

6.4.4. *The Doctor of Ministry (D.Min) Studies and Continuing Theological Education (CTE)*

The Doctor Ministry program was started in 1998. With the establishment SCEPTRE in 2002 the Doctor of Ministry programs was directly taken care of by the appointed Director/Dean of both D.Min and Continuing Theological Education.[109] The programs have been designed, as well as are in the process of being designed, to cater to a wide range of ministerial people at different levels through flexible programs.[110] The programs is field research-oriented study and demands rigorous theological reflection and practical innovativeness in a chosen area of the candidate's ministry,[111] where as the continuing theological education is to help those in service for pastors and those working in the diversified ministry of the church and refresh them with theological insights for effective ministries.[112] Both have a common agenda which is that of bringing about a difference in the ministry situations, and also that of developing mechanisms that would make such initiatives contagious.[113] In order to monitor their progress, enhance their skill of conceptualization and widen their horizon, the program of field research and private study is interspersed with residential collegiums under the guidance of appointed supervisors.[114]

The programs were conducted under direction of two directors/Deans who reside at SCEPTRE and periodically conduct seminars, collegiums and supervise study programs of the students at the centre or in selected centers in India. For the first time in 2005-2006 the Senate awarded Doctor of Ministry Degree to five candidates.[115] According to the report of 2006-2007, that i/c of the D.Min and CTE since its inception in 1998 thus far only eight persons had successfully completed the program. In this regard the Senate Executive Committee of the D.Min appointed a sub committee to review the D.Min program. This sub-

[108] *Report of the President of the Senate for the Year 2000*, 2.

[109] *Director's Report of the Doctor of Ministry and Continuing Theological Education for the Period February 2006 to January 2007*, 1.

[110] *Director's Report of the Doctor of Ministry Studies and Continuing Theological Education for the Year 2005-2006*, 1.

[111] Cf. *Director's Report of the Doctor of Ministry Studies and Continuing Theological Education for the Year 2005-2006*, 1.

[112] Tiwari, *Ecumenical Character of Serampore College...*, 118.

[113] Cf. *Director's Report of the Doctor of Ministry Studies and Continuing Theological Education for the Year 2005-2006*, 1.

[114] Cf. Tiwari, *Ecumenical Character of Serampore College...*, 118.

[115] *Report of the President of the Senate for the Year 2005-2006*, 15. 1. Imlimar Ao. 2. S. Alemrenba, 3. Joseph Jeyaseelan P., 4. Yehevi Jimo Sema, and 5. L. Evancer Sahanam.

committee also looked into the suggestion of introducing a one-year residential option in the D.Min. Program.[116]

It also considered that the D.Min. Program needs restructuring in the interim period. In this, greater emphasis was given on the candidates learning research methods and skill at the beginning of the program so that they could make use in writing their assignments and Dissertation project. The committee also discussed concerning the finance i.e. fees increasing in order to meet the expenses in paying honorarium to supervisors and dissertation project examiners.[117]

6.5. Extension: An Alternative Model for Theological Education

One of the great barriers to theological education in India has been plurality of denominations. The western model of long-term residence in a college far away from home is most often simply impossible. In addition, it would potentially be difficult for many people to meet the financial needs for residential courses. In western contexts, due to higher degrees of affluence, and reliable welfare systems and health resources, and a lower view of families, and narrower family responsibilities, residence at an academic institution is more practicable. With the advent and growth of TEE, the possibility to study at home, or within one's community is the liberation and empowerment of the disenfranchised. Many can now extend themselves theologically, and grow in theological understanding, *whilst* providing for one's dependents as they continue to hold down some form of employment within their community. Some writers say that TEE is the good opening for training people whilst they continue their ministry. Churches are not therefore disrupted.

TEE has been proving far more cost-effective than full-time theological training. Enormous numbers of people have had access to basic theological education, who never did before. In addition, many pastors and priests and preachers have been trained through the TEE under the Senate of Serampore University. The church is so much the richer because of these facts. With access to TEE, churches in India can benefit by having accessible theological training, both for the pastors and laity. The success of TEE is greatly dependent on the support of the local church, and its leaders. If a leader is convinced of the effectiveness of the program, then his ability to influence his flock to participate in the program is unrivaled. In addition, if they have graduated from TEE themselves, it is possible

---

[116] *Report of the Doctor of Ministry and Continuing Theological Education for the Period February 2006 to January 2007,* 3.

[117] Cf. *Proceedings of the Theological Senate and Its Committees,* January 4, 2005 to November 30, 2005, Book XVII, 7-8. Because the fees paid by the candidates are not enough to meet all the seminar/collegiums expenses, which include payment of suitable honorarium to resource persons.

that clergy could become the ideal group facilitators, because it is they that already have relationships with most of the participants.[118]

In contrast, because the TEE student is in a home ministry situation, the focus is much more on the practical rather that the academic. Hence, it was observed "this ongoing practice is a major part of the learning process and is reflected upon in the discussion groups".[119] This application of what TEE students are learning theologically to their daily ministry is a great advantage of the model. Unfortunately, it goes without saying that far more academic input goes to those who are enrolled at fulltime institutions. The extent to which this is helpful is a different question. Although there are cultural differences in the ways people learn, there is enough common ground to construct a general profile of the process a person goes through when learning. It is a recursive cycle of experience, reflection, theorization, and then application. A TEE student who is engaged in ministry has, annual seminars, the ideal forum to reflect on their experiences, to make sense of those experiences, and to make decisions about how to apply them in life, in the ministry context. If local clergy do their job of pastoring and evangelizing, without empowering the laity to perform the ministry in which the Holy Spirit has gifted them, the ironic result is that they are disenfranchising their brothers and sisters in Christ. TEE seems to be an ideal way of assisting them to rectify this situation. TEE discussion groups are thus infinitely superior, as learning forums, to the usual lecture where knowledge is academic, and usually needs to be memorized. Perhaps the greatest benefit of TEE as an education model is that it aims to reach, not only clergy, but also those who will never "pastor" churches, that is, the laity. It is the laity who, if well trained, will become essential team members in mature, effective, and growing churches. It is the laity who are the answer to the leadership crisis in India. It is the laity who will fulfill the great commission, to the glory of God. And TEE aims to reach the laity.

7. South Asia Theological Research Institute (SATHRI)

7.1. Introduction

In the 1980s the BTESSC and the Senate felt the immediate need of establishing an advanced research centre in the country to develop, co-ordinate and facilitate research at doctoral and non-degree levels emphasizing its indigenous and contextual character. As a result in 1987 a national consultation with the participation of several related Mission Boards was held. Intense planning and negotiations thus led to the formation of South Asia Theological Research Institute (SATHRI), in 1989 at Bangalore,[120] as the research wing of the BTESSC

[118] Cf. Hogarth, J, Gatimu, K and Barret, D, *Theological Education in Context* (Nairobi: Uzima Press Ltd., 1983), 17.

[119] Samson, P, *TEE, Cultural Diversity and the Indigenous Church* (TEENET, August, 2004), 27.

[120] Cf. Senate of Serampore College Proceeding of the Theological Senate and its Committees, January 4, 2005 to November 30, 2005, 108.

to deal with the promotion of contextualized research, both at the degree and non-degree levels. It is meant to strengthen centers for research, to promote basic tools for theological education, to involve in publication of research work and to arrange for programs that would strengthen the relationship between the theological institutions for the purpose of research.[121] Initially, it was the only centre for doctoral studies, but since 1999, The Senate recognized other doctoral centers that have the capacity, facilities and the needed infra-structures to develop their own doctoral programs according to the criteria laid down by the Senate.[122]

SATHRI as the research wing of the BTESSC continues its three fold functions:

1. it coordinates and guides formal research at the doctoral level under the guidance of the committee for Research and with the cooperation of doctoral centers,
2. it organizes programs that are aimed at strengthening the relationship between theological education and churches, strengthening inter-disciplinary research and answerability to burning problems of church and society,
3. and it facilitates non-formal research through consultations, seminars, symposia and colloquiums and research projects.[123]

It is to be noted that these are done not only to promote academia but also to assist theological colleges and churches so that their participation in the ministry of theological education is further strengthen by way of faculty development and staff institute.[124] The following research centers administer the formal research at the doctoral level with the intention of providing leadership to the church and the society and in particular to theological institutions in South Asia:

1. Department of Research/SATHRI
2. Federated Faculty for Research in Religion and Culture (FFRRC)
3. Gurukul Lutheran Theological College and Research Institute
4. North India Institute of Post Graduate Theological Studies (NIIPGTS)
5. United Theological College
6. Tamilnadu Theological Seminary
7. Union Biblical Seminary
8. Faith Theological Seminary
9. Aizawl Theological College

---

[121]Cf. Tiwari, *Ecumenical Character of Serampore College…*, 116.

[122]Cf. *Ibid.*

[123]Cf. Tiwari, *Ecumenical Character of Serampore College…*, 117. See also *Report of the President of the Senate for the Year 2004-2005*, 11.

[124]Cf. *Report of the President of the Senate for the Year 2003*, xiv.

Though, SATHRI has ceased to be a one national structure for doctoral program, it continues to facilitate doctoral level research in the areas in which there is dearth of resources and render its help in existing centers when they are in crisis. SATHRI collaborates with other doctoral centers, theological colleges and related institutions, organizes programs that would strengthen the relationship between theological colleges and churches, and facilitates non-formal research through consultations, seminars, symposia and colloquiums and research projects that would stimulate theological articulation.[125]

Moreover, continuing with ecumenical vision of the founders of SATHRI, it continues to be an important ecumenical link to organizations like W.C.C., C.C.A., ATESEA and Regional Committees of Solidarity Fund. Besides these, all the partners of mission outside India continue to regard SATHRI as their ecumenical link in India as far as the ministry of theological education in India.[126] One of the important programs of SATHRI is conducting annual Methodology Seminar for the prospective doctoral students during the summer. This program has been very helpful for preparing students for their research and the present writer also had had the privilege of being one of its recipient candidates.

7.2. Doctor of Theology (D.Th.) Program

South Asia Theological Research Institute (SATHRI) was established in 1989 at Bangalore as the only center for D.Th. studies. But as mentioned, in 1999 the Senate recognized other doctoral centers that have the capacity, facilities and the needed infra-structures to develop their own doctoral programs according to the laid down criteria of the Senate.[127] The primary goal of this program is to provide quality leadership to the church, society and theological institutions in South Asia and also with the intention of faculty development for theological institutions.[128] Moreover, it has been the concern of the Research Committee to make all efforts to improve upon academic excellence by providing necessary guidance and help to the students.[129] Keeping in mind that the D.Th. study program is being carried out with careful planning and with the co-operation of all the four doctoral centers, different centers have been admitting new students to various disciplines according to the availability of resources and according to the needs of various theological colleges in India.

---

[125]Cf. *Report of the President of the Senate for the Year 2006-2007*, 13.

[126]Cf. *Report of the President of the Senate for the Year 2003*, xiv.

[127]Cf. Tiwari, *Ecumenical Character of Serampore College...*, 116. 1. Federated Faculty for Research in Religion and Culture (FFRRC), 2. North India Institute of Post-Graduate Theological Studies (NIIPGTS), 3. Gurukul Lutheran Theological College, 4. United Theological College.

[128]*Report of the Director of Research and SATHRI 2006-2007*, 1. See also *Report of the President of the Senate for the year 2003-2004*, xv. *Report of the President of the Senate for the year 2005-2006*, 11.

[129]*Report of the President of the Senate for the Year 2005-2006*, 11.

According to the Director's Report 2006-2007, the total number of doctoral students registered goes up to 76 (57 men, 19 women). Of these, 28 students are getting SATHRI scholarship (12 men, and 7 women).[130] SATHRI continues to struggle however, in not being able to buy land of its own to set up its proper infrastructure. The office continues to run in a rented place in Bangalore, for which, it faces certain constraints in its otherwise wider possibilities of functions. The former premises has been sold for Rs.1 crore and the proposal of the Executive Committee is to use the proceeds to acquire a better infrastructure with an office block, library, seminar rooms, flats and residences for research scholars and officers.[131] In spite of the financial difficulties SATHRI through its commitment to the D.Th. program continues to be instrumental in facilitating the higher level of theological education in India's context.

7.3. Non-Formal and Post-Doctoral Research Program

The year 1990 saw the beginning of non-degree programs. The sub-committee of the Research Committee on non-degree program affirmed that the purpose of this program is to encourage scholars to engage in specific projects of South Asia with a view to publication of papers and findings on religious, socio-political, economic and cultural issues for the renewal of local and regional Churches in South Asia and the community at large.[132] Thus, SATHRI continues to encourage scholars of different disciplines to take up non-formal and post-doctoral research in order to meet the rapidly changing context and new challenges that occurs every day in our theological journey.

7.4. Seminars, Consultations, Conferences and Publications under the SATHRI

SATHRI contributions include also its sensitivity toward the importance of conducting seminars, consultations and conference in order to assist the doctoral students as well as theological teachers and scholars in their endeavor in theological education.[133] Simultaneously, SATHRI is committed to the program of publishing books and periodicals. The Executive Committee of the Senate has recently suggested to SATHRI to start a separate publication department of the BTESSC/SATHRI in active collaboration with the Board

[130] *Report of the Director of Research and SATHRI 2006-2007*, 2.

[131] Cf. *Report of the President of the Senate for the Year 2006-2007*, 15.

[132] *Report of the Director 1990-91*, 774.

[133] 2006-2007 the Senate and Board was busy with the consultation on Curriculum Revision, SATHRI could organize only seminars. Colloquium for all the doctoral students was conducted in Karnataka Theological College, Mangalore on October 17th and 18th, 2006 on the theme *Trends in Theological Research*. An International workshop on *Disability Discourse for Theological College* was conducted in Ashirvad, Bangalore from May 22-28, 2006. Another workshop was organized on the theme of *Integrating Concerns of Peace-making in Theological Education* on September 21-25, 2006 at Ecumenical Christian Centre, Bangalore.

of Theological Text Book Program of South Asia (BTTBPSA) and the Indian Theological Library (ITL).[134]

7.5. SATHRI and Partners in Theological Education

Another noteworthy aspect or area of SATHRI's contribution is its partnership with EMW in Germany, Board of World Mission in Edinburgh, CMS and USPG in London, Kerkinactie in Netherlands, Methodist Church in Britain, EMS in Stuttgart, NCC of USA, Global Ministries Division of United Church of Christ in USA, Presbyterian Church in USA, Anglican Church in Canada and United Church of Christ in Canada, in the ministry of theological education. In spite of the decline in financial resources at the global level, these organizations continue to contribute financial assistance to the SATHRI in their committed effort to support the programs of SATHRI.[135]

Serampore family is made up of theological schools from various Churches ranging from Orthodox to Pentecostals and of other protestant faith persuasions. The Serampore Act, article 9 provides for such representation on the Senate. There has been a constant interaction between what we call ecumenical and denominational, in our family and there is no parallel to the SSC and Board where such a variety agree to work together with a common curriculum. This lends itself to our theological education in ecumenical vitality today.[136]

In the 60s and 70s the SSC opened its doors to the evangelical seminaries and colleges. It was envisaged that through ecumenical living and growing together, we would be led to a rich theological pluralism.[137] The mainline ecumenical Churches are characterized by their search for unity both in terms of faith and order. Such a movement towards unity in faith and order is not always conducive to theological pluralism. It is possible to argue that denominationalism could lend itself to the growth of healthy theological pluralism through open dialogue and mutual sharing of insights. Through such ecumenical encounter of different denominations we could together work towards a new pluralistic model of ecumenism. However, it has been noted that unless the denominations are willing to subject their theological stance to the fresh and contemporary interpretations of the word of God by which they stand, they will only produce dry denominational pluralism, which is static. It is therefore strongly believed that only through a dynamic interaction of text and context that we will move forward. The proposal put forward therefore is that the SSC should be a meeting platform where through

---

[134]Cf. *Report of the President of the Senate for the Year 2006-2007*, 15.

[135]*Report of the Director of Research and SATHRI 2006-2007*, 12.

[136]D. S. Satyaranjan, *Senate of Serampore College Registrar's Report, 1990-1991*, 845. (Hereafter, Satyaranjan, *Senate of Serampore College...*).

[137]Satyaranjan, *Senate of Serampore College...*, 845.

open dialogue together we will grow towards a pluralistic model of ecumenism in the context of theological education in India.[138]

In addition to the task of training ministers for the Churches, the SSC also prepares qualified theological teachers for different Seminaries and Colleges. One of the urgent concerns of the SSC is the function of theological education to enable the Churches to constantly rethink and re-examine its policy practices and discipline and for which, it beckons or rather challenges the theological institutions to take serious efforts to live up to what they believe.[139]

8. The Senate Consultation on Curriculum Revision

8.1. Introduction

Curriculum revision is a routine exercise in any educational institutions, and so far it has been for the Senate as well, in the last eighty-five years.[140] As situations and context changed, and as new challenges emerged, Senate has taken a serious and thorough program of curriculum revision with the view of meeting the needs of the context. This is not just a matter of it being a routine exercise but the SSC is seeking to revolutionize its program structure, content, and methodology making it relevant to the twenty first century's context.[141] The Academic Council of the Senate formed several committees for this very purpose and had invested considerable time in clarifying issues and these sub-committees submitted their reports on the comments and suggestions received from theological institutions, churches, opinions of academicians from other universities and management experts etc., through a series of consultations for further deliberation and reflection.[142] There is also a view that, the institutional pattern of the church representing the irrelevant and unsupportable structures, imperialist and western oriented thinking, western-adopted concepts and its missiological paradigms certainly calls for critical examination as they threaten the authentic expression of faith and communication of the Gospel to the people of a nation.

8.2. The Various Consultations and their Responses

As has been mentioned, the SSC has at present revised its B.D. curricula through its delegated committee, who are responsible for organizing the phase-wise consultations. Let us therefore take a look at the various consultations and their responses by way of suggestions toward the subject of curricula revision:

---

[138]Cf. Satyaranjan, *Senate of Serampore College…*, 846.

[139]*Ibid.*, 846.

[140]*Senate of Serampore College Initiative Revision of Curricula*, n.d. 2.

[141]*Senate of Serampore College: Proceedings of the Theological Senate and Its Committees*, Book XIX, Vol. XVIII (January 21, 2006 to November 24, 2006), 183.

[142]The Committee for Ecumenical Relationship and Church Ministers etc. had consultation with different Church leaders in order to understand the significant role of the Church in incorporating its opinion and suggestions to the curriculum revision.

8.2.1. *Delhi Consultation*

The Delhi consultation was held from 4th to 5th September, 2006, and was inaugurated by the Rt. Rev. Karan Masih, Bishop of Delhi and former Moderator of Church of North India (CNI). There were thirty-nine participants in the consultation. The consultation specially took into consideration the concerns of the North India Churches, Institutions and Colleges. The resource persons presented the concerns from the perspectives of CNI, Social Scientist and Medical Mission.[143]

8.2.1.1. *Suggestions for Content Revision from the Delhi Consultation*

1. With the need to incorporate at least some of the exploding knowledge, there has been concern that the workload on the students was too much. The way to tackle this is to perhaps reduce the number of compulsory courses and increase the number of optional courses that are offered. We need to remove the dead-wood so that new trees can be planted. A critical minimum set of new courses could be there with flexibility to allow for diversity. Some suggested that there need to be a wide variety of optional to choose from.[144]
2. There was a consensus that the question of personal formation and personal spiritual formation should be taken very seriously. The need to look after the emotional, motivational and spiritual needs of ministerial candidates was stressed as was the need to imbibe good moral values in them. The question of how to inculcate a ministering heart was also posed. However, it was also stressed that personal formation was not enough, rather community formation or the ability to work in a team was also stressed.[145]
3. Another area of curricula content that was stressed by many was that of Field Exposure or Practical Work. It was felt that there needed to be a redressal of the imbalance that had crept in between academics and practical work. Field exposure and practical work were found to be extremely important and a way must be found to assess and grade Field Exposure. We learn a lot by doing and observing.[146]
4. A consensus has emerged on the need for Pedagogical Institutes for practicing and prospective teachers. We are preparing the new wine but this will have to be in the old wine-skins (the existing teaching staff). Thus some way needs to be found to renew the old wine-skins.[147]

---

[143]Cf. Roger Gaikwad, *Senate of Serampore College: Consultations on Curriculum Revision: Report*, 2007, 1. (Hereafter, Gaikwad, *Senate of Serampore College: Consultations on Curriculum Revision...*).

[144]Gaikwad, *Senate of Serampore College: Consultations on Curriculum Revision...*, 1.

[145]*Ibid.*

[146]*Ibid.*

[147]*Ibid.*

5. New areas where courses should be there or new areas which should be covered included: Constitution of India, Laws concerning Conversion, Laws on women and children; HIV & AIDS; Sexuality, Substance abuse; Science and Religion; and Philosophy of science. There was a repeated stress on women's concerns and ecological concerns too. The need to deal with the issue of those with stigmatized and deviant behaviour, such as criminals, prostitutes, eunuchs etc… was also asserted.[148]
6. The need for an emphasis on training people for rural ministries was stressed. However, an understanding of the multi-religious, multi-cultural milieu as well as the socio-economic realities of South Asia must under-gird all our curricula.[149]
7. There was a call for missional dimension to be integrated in and woven into the entire curricula.[150]
8. There was a call for courses on Biblical Hermeneutics, theological methodology, methods and approaches of exegesis and hermeneutics: a larger numbers of language optional (over and above Greek and Hebrew), more New Testament optional (Deutero-Pauline, Catholic epistles, Revelation). The need was expressed for a course on Discipleship, Stewardship and Church Growth. Special papers on Dalit Theology, Tribal Theology, and Indian Christian Theology also needed to be incorporated at the B.Th. level. Courses on Worship and Liturgy must also be given due importance.[151]
9. The bibliography of the courses need to be periodically reviewed and need not wait for a curricula revision.[152]

8.3. Kolkata (Calcutta) Consultation

The second consultation was held from 7th to 8th September 2006 in Kolkata and was attended by forty-two delegates. The main concerns of the Kolkata consultation were on the Social, Dalit, Women and Tribal Perspectives.

8.3.1. *Suggestions for Content Revision from the Consultation of Kolkata*

1. With the need to incorporate at least some of the rapidly expanding knowledge, there has been concern that the workload on the students was too much. The way to tackle this is to perhaps reduce the number of compulsory courses and increase the number of optional courses that are offered. A critical minimum set of new courses could be there with flexibility to allow for diversity.[153]

---

[148]Gaikwad, *Senate of Serampore College: Consultations on Curriculum Revision…*, 1-2.

[149]Gaikwad, *Senate of Serampore College: Consultations on Curriculum Revision…*, 1.

[150]*Ibid.*

[151]Gaikwad, *Senate of Serampore College: Consultations on Curriculum Revision…*, 1.

[152]*Ibid.*

[153]Gaikwad, *Senate of Serampore College: Consultations on Curriculum Revision…*, 7.

2. There was a consensus that the question of personal formation and personal spiritual formation should be taken very seriously. The need to look after the emotional, motivational and spiritual needs of ministerial candidates was stressed as was the need to imbibe good moral values in them. However, it was also stressed that personal formation was not enough, rather community formation or the ability to work in a team was also stressed.[154]
3. Another area of curricula content that was stressed by many was that of Field Exposure or Practical Work. Field exposure and practical work were found to be extremely important as the goal of Practical work is to bring about a perspective change in the attitude of students. Since Practical work is so important a way must be found to assess and grade Field exposure.[155]
4. There were many voices and perhaps a consensus in this consultation that greater attention is to be given to the question of gender justice and women's concerns, both by integrating these concerns into the existing theological curricula as well as adding new courses. Some were for making courses concerned with the role of women in church and society as compulsory. All course outlines must make use of inclusive language.[156]
5. A consensus has emerged on the need for Pedagogical Institutes for practicing and prospective teachers. Teaching methodology should be made compulsory in the M.Th. curriculum. There was a call for institutes for feminist theological pedagogy so that teachers could be sensitized to the concerns of women.[157]
6. New areas where courses should be there or New areas which should be covered included: Methodology of doing theology, Biblical theology and Hermeneutics, Legal matters; HIV & AIDS; people living with Disabilities, Church Music, the History of the 19th century Reformation, Peace & Reconciliation, Conflict Resolution, Dalit Theology, Tribal/ Adivasis Theologies, Local Tribal and Local Feminist Theologies, Leadership and Church administration and Management, Revivals and Charismatic movements, Family Violence, Health, Inter-Gender (eunuch) issues, Computer Applications, Science and Religion.[158]
7. There was a call for courses on mission to be integrated in and woven into entire curriculum as well as for special programs on mission. This was especially stressed by the North East participants whose churches are emphasizing the need for proper training for their missionaries.[159]
8. Christian Ministry: Sub-branches under Christian Ministry should not be maintained but be made into an integrated course because segregated system

[154]Gaikwad, *Senate of Serampore College: Consultations on Curriculum Revision...*, 7.

[155]*Ibid.*, 8.

[156]*Ibid.*, 9.

[157]*Ibid.*

[158]Gaikwad, *Senate of Serampore College: Consultations on Curriculum Revision...*, 9.

[159]Gaikwad, *Senate of Serampore College: Consultations on Curriculum Revision...*, 9.

requires more teachers in the branch. Teachers trained under segregated branches cannot handle the interdisciplinary courses within the ministry branch. More courses in ministry should be offered so that the future church leaders will be equipped properly in preaching, administration and pastoral leadership.[160]

9. Skill-oriented ministerial training in communication and pastoral leadership.
10. Students should be introduced to the internet and cyber world. There should be facilities for electronic library and networking of libraries.
11. Thesis writing should not be compulsory at the B.D. level.
12. Post-doctoral research programs should be there.
13. The bibliography of the courses need to be periodically reviewed and need not wait for a curriculum revision.[161]

8.4. Suggestions from the North-East India's Context

1. Mission: Inclusion of mission subject was strongly expressed by the Colleges from North East in view of the need of the churches and mission organizations in the region. The context demands a strong emphasis on mission since Churches in North East India are mission minded and have many mission projects. Therefore, there is a need to train the students to equip properly in this area serious attention would have to be given to the nature and form of mission studies in the revised curriculum. Certificate, diploma and degree courses could be introduced on mission.[162]
2. HIV and AIDS: HIV & AIDS problem is another priority issue that needs to be treated as a primary concern in theological education.[163]
3. People living with disabilities: our present theological education is for able people. We have not given a serious thought to those people living with disabilities. There are many disabled people around us. This course should be included in the revised curriculum.[164]
4. Education for peace building: North East India is a melting pot of conflicts and violence. The region has been exposed to terror and bloodshed for more than a half of century and hope of solution and peace in the region is still distant. Therefore, peace building education should be included in the curriculum.[165]

---

[160]Gaikwad, *Senate of Serampore College: Consultations on Curriculum Revision…*, 11.

[161]*Ibid.*

[162]*Ibid.*

[163]*Ibid.*

[164]*Ibid.*

[165]Gaikwad, *Senate of Serampore College: Consultations on Curriculum Revision…*, 11.

5. Music: Music should be included in the Christian Ministry branch since music plays an important role in the life, worship and ministry of the church. Tribal/indigenous music and art must be explored and integrated.[166]
6. Ministerial and Personality Formation: courses on these concerns should be included.
7. Language Studies: the study of Sanskrit and Dravidian languages, etc., at the B.D. level should not be made compulsory because it is not relevant at all in North East context.
8. Women and Women's Studies: courses on gender justice, feminist hermeneutics, and the history of the church from the feminist perspective need to be introduced. At least a few courses on women should be made compulsory and serious efforts must be taken by all the colleges for this. Effort should be made to establish Women Study Centre and Department in all the colleges.[167]
9. Tribal Theology, Tribal women's theology, Ecology, the Disabled, and the Marginalized: courses on these subjects should be made core subjects for North East India.
10. Courses on Revival and Charismatic movements should be included in the curriculum.
11. More flexibility: more flexibility in curricula should be given to integrate more contextual courses.
12. Senate Examination Timings need to be adjusted for North East India.[168]

8.5. Kottayam Consultation

The Kottayam consultation was held from 5th to 6th October, 2006. The Kottayam consultation was inaugurated by Most Rev. Dr. Philipose Mar Chrysostom Mar Thoma, Metropolitan, of the Mar Thoma Syrian Church. There were forty-nine participants.

8.5.1. *Suggestions from Kottayam Consultation*

1. The work load of the students to be reduced at B.D. and M.Th. levels. Language studies could be undertaken after B.D. Orientation program.
2. Regional Language Institutes for biblical languages. Sanskrit and Arabic may be considered.
3. A course on study methods, personality development, communication skills etc., should be introduced in the five years B.D. program.
4. Teacher training programs are to be arranged along with M.Th. studies.
5. Besides the care courses, interdisciplinary papers are to be introduced at the B.D. level.

---

[166] Gaikwad, *Senate of Serampore College: Consultations on Curriculum Revision...*, 11.

[167] *Ibid.*, 12.

[168] Gaikwad, *Senate of Serampore College: Consultations on Curriculum Revision...*, 11.

6. In order to deepen the textual understanding and reflection of the students, field education should be made mandatory.
7. Modules on the context, Bible and issues are to be given due emphasis in the ministerial formation of students.
8. Contextual Subaltern concerns such as Dalits, women, poverty, religious pluralism etc should be integrated into the syllabi of each discipline.
9. As far as possible, new concerns are to be built into the existing courses. Eg., HIV/AIDS, Development studies, Media awareness, management, music, law, etc. The practice of adding separate courses for each emerging concern should be avoided.
10. In the context of the extreme Biblical fundamentalism and literalism, a course on hermeneutics at the B.D. level is inevitable. This would enable the students to distinguish between Biblical fundamentalism and fundamentals of the word of God.
11. More content is necessary for the course on Church Ministry and Sacraments. Presently the emphasis is on Christian education and its general theories. Concerns such as peace making, trauma care, alcoholism etc. are to be done within the frame work of Christian Ministry.
12. The bibliographies of papers have to be revised taking into consideration the new theological literature in the respective fields.
13. In order to equip our students to have meaningful dialogue with the scientific world, especially with those who are trained in modern science and technology, we need to incorporate the emerging concerns from the field of science and technology. Perhaps, a course on the philosophy of science and faith could be introduced at the B.D. level.
14. Concerns were expressed from the field of Pastoral counseling that a M.Th. course on Psychotherapy be introduced. This is not a duplication of the present M.Th. program in Counseling but an attempt to train the lay people who are really committed to counseling and clinical psychology.
15. The syllabus for D.Min. should be revised in such a way that the focus is on creative pastoral ministry in the community. D.Min. is also offered with a view to enhance continuing pastoral education in concrete situations of life.
16. The Seminary campus should be conducive for theological education and the over all spiritual formation of the students. Attempts made by KTC to house students from other disciplines and other religions are commendable.
17. There should be enough room for students to assimilate insights from different branches of knowledge through their community life.
18. Flexibility within the curriculum was one of the concerns. Each College should be given the freedom to choose courses from a syllabus approved by the Senate in accordance with their particular, contextual and pastoral needs.

19. At the B.D. level a course on the History of Christian Doctrine should be introduced. It was also pointed that spirituality and ecumenical dimensions are not given attention in the proposed curriculum.
20. The research components of the M.Th. course need to be strengthened by increasing the credits allotted for thesis.
21. Missiology should find a place in the curriculum.[169]

8.6. Bombay Consultation

The Bombay consultation was held from 24th to 25th October, 2006, and was inaugurated by Most Rev. Dr. Philipose Mar Chrysostom Metropolitan, of the Mar Thoma Syrian Church. There were forty-five participants. It took stock of Theological Education Program of the Senate as well as the report of the other three regional consultations. It took note of the recent development in the curriculum making as well as the experience of other institutions in India and abroad.

8.6.1. *Suggestions from Bombay Consultation*

1. The work load of the students should be reduced at B.D. and M.Th. levels.
2. Language studies could be undertaken after B.D. Orientation program. Regional language Institutes for biblical languages, Sanskrit and Arabic may be considered.
3. All course outlines, teaching and learning must use inclusive language.
4. A course on study methods, personality development, communication skills, etc., should be introduced in the first year B.D. program.
5. Modules on the context, Bible and issues are to be given due emphasis in the ministerial formation of students. Issues relating to Dalits, women, poverty, religious pluralism, etc., should be integrated into the syllabi of each discipline. So also, special courses on these subjects should be introduced and made compulsory.[170]
6. Students must be encouraged and trained for rural ministries. So also an understanding of the multi-religious, multi-cultural milieu as well as the socio-economic realities of South Asia must under-gird all our curricula.
7. As far as possible, new concerns are to be addressed in the existing courses such as HIV/AIDS, Development Studies, Media Awareness, Music, Law and handling legal matters, people living with Disabilities, Conflict Resolution and Peace building, Revivals and Charismatic movements, Inter-Gender (eunuchs) issues, Health, Computer Applications, Philosophy of Science and Faith, etc. If necessary, separate courses should be introduced.[171]
8. There should be enough opportunities for students to interact with students from other disciplines so that they could assimilate insights from different

[169]Gaikwad, *Senate of Serampore College: Consultations on Curriculum Revision...*, 11-12.

[170]Ibid., 15.

[171]Ibid., 16.

branches of knowledge. Students should be introduced to the internet and cyber world. There should be facilities for electronic library and networking of libraries.

9. In the context of the extreme Biblical fundamentalism and literalism, a course on hermeneutic at the B.D. level is inevitable. This would enable the students to distinguish between Biblical fundamentalism and fundamentals of the word of God.
10. Sub-branches under Christian Ministry should not be maintained but be made into integrated course because specialization requires more teachers in the branch. More courses in Ministry should be offered so that the future church leaders will be equipped properly in preaching, administration and pastoral leadership. Skill-oriented ministerial training communication and counseling should be introduced. Concerns such as peace making, trauma care, etc., also need to be given special attention in Christian Ministry. A special course on Discipleship, Stewardship and Church Growth should also be offered.
11. At the B.D. level a course on the History of Christian Doctrine, should be introduced. So also, missiological perspectives and courses need to be strengthened in the curriculum. Spirituality and ecumenical dimensions need to be given due attention in the proposed curriculum.[172]
12. The bibliographies of papers have to be revised taking into consideration the new theological literature in the respective fields. The bibliographies of the courses need to be periodically reviewed; the Senate need not wait for curriculum revision.
13. The curriculum should make provision for flexibility. Each college should be given the freedom to introduce courses, with a syllabus approved by the Senate, in accordance with its particular, contextual and pastoral needs.
14. Whatever it is the subaltern perspective or the mission concern or the ministerial focus, practical work of field experience is very important. Teachers and students should be exposed to real life situations. Practical work is essential for sharpening analytical theological thinking as well as building pf personality, development of different ministerial skills and strengthening of commitment. To impress upon the students the importance of practical work, credit/grades should be given for the same.
15. The Seminary campus should be conducive for theological education and the overall spiritual formation of the students. Personal spiritual formation should be taken very seriously. The emotional, moral, motivational and spiritual needs of ministerial candidate should be addressed.
16. Teacher training programs are to be arranged along with M.Th. studies. So also, institutes on feminist theological pedagogy should also be organized so

[172]Gaikwad, *Senate of Serampore College: Consultations on Curriculum Revision…*, 16.

that teachers could be sensitized to the concerns of women. Teachers must serve as good role models.

17. The research component of the M.Th. program need to be strengthened by increasing the credits allotted for thesis work.[173]

8.7. Suggestions from Different Consultations

In curricula revision of the Senate of Serampore cannot overlook the context of the church and ministry. The multi-religious, multi-cultural and socio-economic context has to be seriously dealt with. Moreover the Senate needs to focus the context of the poor, the marginalized, the down trodden and the exploited masses of Dalits, women, tribals and positive living people.[174]

8.7.1. *Suggested Curriculum*

A curriculum around the following four branches at the graduate level should suffice:

Pattern A:

- a. Scriptures
- b. Theology
- c. History
- d. Pastoralia (Counseling)

Pattern B:

- a. Compulsory/foundational
- b. Optional/advanced

Pattern C:

- i) Core
  - a. Biblical
  - b. Theological
  - c. Ministerial
- ii) Applied
  - a. Society
  - b. Church
  - c. Individual
- iii) Reflective

In the context of the rise of religious fundamentalism, rise of violence against Christians, theological curricula should include the following course:

i) Study of Constitution of India

---

[173]Gaikwad, *Senate of Serampore College: Consultations on Curriculum Revision…*, 16.

[174]Ravi Tiwari, "BTESSC Seminar on Curriculum Revision- 2007: Important Suggestions from Consultation" *SSC Proceedings of the Theological Senate and Its Committees*, Book XX, Vol. XIX (January 23, 2007-November 30, 2007), 15. (Hereafter, Tiwari, *BTESSC Seminar on Curriculum Revision- 2007…*).

ii) Laws and Statutes concerning minority communities (Concerning institutions, property, succession, rights)
iii) Indian Christian Marriage Act
iv) Foreign Contribution Regulations
v) Legal procedures (how to write an FIR, written statement etc.)
vi) Courses in Discipleship and Stewardship
vii) Church Growth
viii) HIV/AIDS
ix) Disability discourses.[175]

8.7.2. *Suggested Nomenclature/Rationalization of Degree Program*

a. Present B.Th./B.D. program can be discontinued;
b. A new degree program be designed;
c. There should be a basic theological education common to all degree programs (first two years), choices be made by the students in the final years of studies;
d. The choices of courses in Bible, Theology, Religions etc., leading to B.Th.-M.Th.-D.Th.;
e The choices of courses in History and Missiology, etc., leading to B.Min-M.Miss-D.Miss;
f. The choices of courses in Ministry, Communication, etc., leading to B.Min-M.Min-D.Min.

It should have to be made clear that all basic degree prepares a person for the ordained ministry of the church, thereby doing away with existing discrimination in terms of employment, salary, promotion etc.[176]

8.8. Some of the Important Areas of Concerns coming out of the Consultations

8.8.1. *Regional Concerns*

The consultations point out that the Churches in the north must give urgent priority to teaching ministry. The appointing of qualified teachers should be taken very seriously, and regional colleges should have more freedom to add courses on regional concerns/developed new courses which would introduce contextual concerns and keep theological education relevant to the issues faced by the people in the regions. The consultations also feel that producing sufficient theological literature in regional languages need to be taken seriously by the Senate.[177]

[175]Tiwari, *BTESSC Seminar on Curriculum Revision- 2007...*, 17-18.

[176]*Ibid.,* 21.

[177]Tiwari, *BTESSC Seminar on Curriculum Revision- 2007...*, 22.

8.8.2. *Curriculum*

a. theological education should have a basic missiological dimension.
b. the schema should be: compulsory/foundational, optional/advanced
c. should be under a rationalized nomenclature
d. students should have the choice in accordance with the interest in ministry
e. should have a dynamic process of incorporating regional and contextual issues
f. curriculum and syllabus should be church ministry-mission oriented with one year for higher specialization
g. incorporation of Dalit concern in curricula is a must
h. curriculum should be contextual, people-centered and issue based
i. gender perspective should under-gird every branch of theological education
j. courses should be interdisciplinary and issue-oriented
k. curriculum should be build upon three assumptions- theological, missiological and pedagogical
l. scripture should be taken as one of the main source for evolving a theological curriculum with ministerial and missiological aims
m. the authenticity of curriculum is dependent upon its dialogue with not only the church but also the society
n. theological curriculum should seek a coherent integration of all parts in theological education
o. Social and cultural analysis needs to have space within the curriculum.[178]

8.8.3. *Women Concerns*

a. though women's studies have been established as a branch in theological education, women's issues are not adequately integrated into theological education program and are kept at the periphery of theological curriculum
b. search for gender justice in theological education must be treated as an important concern in our system
c. special provision should be made for admission, accommodation and scholarship of women candidates in our theological institutions
d. women are under-represented in the teaching ministry and there is an imbalance in the recruitment of theological teachers
e. churches do not give equal opportunity to women in the ministry and are kept out of decision making bodies of the church
f. many theological colleges in India are denominational; almost all in the north-east are denominational church-oriented or tribe wise church-based institutions whose curriculum offerings are mandated and upheld by their denominational bodies and policies

---

[178]Tiwari, *BTESSC Seminar on Curriculum Revision- 2007…*, 22-23.

g. centralized curriculum structure of the Senate does not allow much scope for contextual courses. Contextual courses are often taught from male perspective
h. there is a need to develop feminist theological pedagogy in theological education in order to bring gender justice for all
i. often courses on women's concern are optional, and end up as course exclusively for few women
j. the contents of theological education remain highly abstract and detached from the reality of the people, especially the poor, marginalized, women, Dalits and tribal/indigenous people
k. a certain quota of seats be reserved for women in theological college
l. feminist theological critique needs to be taken seriously and the stronghold of male oriented religious language has to be broken down
m. womanist consciousness in the sphere of worship and preaching is to be recognized.[179]

8.8.4. *Concerns of the North –East India*

a. the curriculum should take into consideration the geographical, political, social and cultural environment besides the given resources, facilities available in the given context
b. the content be structured and imparted through church-friendly methods to meet the needs of the specific life situations of the people in the region
c. in its methodology, the sequence and flexibility of the curriculum should be maintained
d. more space for contextual need of the north-east communities is required
e. theological education should be mission oriented
f. suggestions for core subject in the north-east context:- i) training in relational leadership, peace education, disaster management, education on how to live with fear and stress, peace building etc
    ii) Courses on gender justice; reinterpreting Scriptures and history of the church from feminist's perspective; eco-justice; local culture and indigenous expression of faith
    iii) Drug abuse and HIV/AIDS; iv) Disability discourse.[180]

9. Core Concerns Gathered for the Compilation of the New

[179] Tiwari, *BTESSC Seminar on Curriculum Revision- 2007…*, 23-24.

[180] *Ibid.*, 24-25.

Curriculum of the SSC

As the outcome of the above-mentioned consultations taken under specified regions, the SSC eventually surmised and identified some of the urgent concerns that could serve as the core components of the forthcoming new curriculum. They include:

1. Holistic and ecumenical dimensions to underlie the aim and objectives of theological education.
2. To adhere to the four-fold component structure of the B.D. program namely,
   a. Orientation
   b. Foundational or Core
   c. Advanced or General and
   d. Local or Regional

Concerning the nomenclature for this, it is relegated to a near future under the concerned committee or board.

3. To base the curriculum of the SSC upon three main principles namely'
   a. Theological
   b. Missiological and
   c. Pedagogical

Here, the Bible is to be given importance as one of the core sources for evolving a ministry and mission-oriented curriculum

4. In particular, it emphasizes that the curriculum should be contextual, people-oriented and issue-based – incorporating South Asian and contextual issues like the dalits, tribals, women, etc. It recognizes that the authenticity of a curriculum depend upon its dialogue with both the church and the society.
5. It stresses the importance of under-girding every branch of theological education with non-sexist gender perspective.
6. Usage of integrated and inter-disciplinary approaches.
7. To provide space for various optional subjects in the curriculum so that the students can select their own choice of subjects and areas of studies. Besides, it also noted the necessity to provide the students the privilege of specializing in their subjects of interest.
8. To give autonomy to individual colleges to develop and offer diploma courses in different disciplines or on certain important issues and for this they may also seek recognition from the SSC.

9. The burning issue of autonomy of individual colleges is to be taken up very soon in the seminar meet of the Boards of Study
10. The Boards of Study is to be interdisciplinary in nature or perspective and pedagogical institutes to be conducted periodically but most importantly prior to the emergence of the new curriculum.
11. Bachelor of Divinity degree course to be the basic theological degree course under the SSC beginning with the enrolment of the academic session of 2009-2010. As a result, the academic session of 2008-2009 is to be the last batch of B.Th. However, considering the likelihood of enrolling fresh students for B.Th. course in this 2008-2009 session, colleges are given dateline up to the fourth year, i.e., counting from 2008-2009 sessions. Hence, it states that should the colleges fail to phase out B.Th. program and introduce B.D. as the basic theological degree course even after the allotted period of four years time, they will have to be disaffiliated from the SSC.

Summary

With the onset of post-colonialism, the Indian church began to stress the necessity of taking the responsibility of its theological education for making it relevant to, and for, the Indian context. The emergence of this rethinking movement is responsible for the change and transformation in the method, structure and content of theological education in India. Besides its recognition of the importance of being contextually relevant, it also emphasized on the necessity of the ecumenical aspect of our theological education especially in relation to India's pluralistic reality.

The SSC is borne out of this new awakening context. Since its foundation, it has been stressing the importance of shaping its theological education structure on ecumenical lines. It emphasizes that, theological education is not simply aimed at training the students for the pastoral or church ministry alone but also very importantly include the overall equipping of God's people in holistic education so that they would be able to live out their conviction as well as affect their concrete life situations as agents of transformation in the context where they are situated.

The BTESSC, established in the year 1975, represents a major structure of theological education in the country. It functions as a participatory structure of both the churches and theological institutions in India. It is through the BTESSC that the institutions and churches work together for purpose of training and thus preparing the students for ecumenically holistic ministry among the people in India's context of pluralism.

The SSC is significant for its standard of theological education. It has been notably growing in terms of the number of institutions affiliating to its university structure, its degrees and diplomas offered, also its program of theological education by or via extension, the increasing number of students and research scholars under its degree programs etc. Besides, it also recognizes the necessity of routine revision of its curriculum for making its theological education bear meaning and relevance to the ever-changing context of the people. At present, through its latest program of curriculum revision, it has been taking serious consideration of the constructive suggestions it is receiving from its various consultative meetings being held all over the regions of the country for the purpose of upgrading and sharpening the standard and quality of its theological education in the country for effective relevance and impact.

While to those of us who often enjoy getting drawn to spicy type of literatures – may it be informational, documentations or any other writings, our concluding fourth chapter might be considered or rated as simply boring or as sleep-invoking one due to its very nature and form. Nevertheless, we might also realize that no matter how intolerably descriptive it was, it is indispensable for the very fact that it is the core structure of our present research subject. Moreover, it serves as the foundational source and cause for the next (fifth) chapter on *The Role of the SSC in Fostering Ecumenisn in Theological Education,* without which, this upcoming analysis will not be possible at all.

Chapter 5

The Role of the Senate of Serampore College in Fostering Ecumenism in Theological Education

Introduction

The BTESSC has now for more than three decades[1] served as a centre for theological training and learning for ministry in the service of the Church in India and its neighbouring countries in South Asia. We have observed that currently it has more than 50 theological institutions, including two in Sri Lanka, one in Bangladesh and one in Nepal, which are affiliated to the SSC (University). In keeping with the standards of universities in the sub-continent as well as in order to ensure greater participation of its constituent bodies, a new constituent structure has been adopted for the BTESSC in February 2005. This decisive action has enhanced the participation of theological colleges, churches and church-related institutions in the functioning of the BTESSC. This fifth chapter is therefore an attempt to critically analyze the role of the Senate of Serampore College in fostering ecumenism in the context of theological education in India.

1. Challenges for an Ecumenical Theological Education

Having entered the twenty first-century, the SSC has begun to take much interest in taking on the responsibility of addressing the needs of the church and challenges of theological education in the contemporary context. The BTESSC continues to maintain its vision of the importance of contextual and ecumenical nature of

[1]This account of time is based on the present researcher's reckoning of the BTESSC's service period taken very recently, i.e., 2008, and hence, the mention of it being now above three decades since its inception in 1975.

theological education.[2] As situations and contexts change in our society, and as new challenges emerged, the SSC has been grappling with the difficult task of attempting to formulate tangible, meaningful and relevant responses that will truly serve and answer the complicated quests of the peoples. It is therefore here that the BTESSC serves as the core structure of theological education, as it brings under its critical reevaluations especially of the nature, form and outcome of its education program by critically identifying and assessing its weak areas as well as its areas of strength.

The present day situation challenges the BTESSC in an unparallel scale of issues for consideration. Prominent among them are: the irresistible attractions and bondages of globalization particularly in the marginalizing of the poor; the pervasive caste system and the struggles of Dalits and other backward classes; the endless struggles of the tribals; the pronounced phenomenon of pluralistic societies and the problems of communalism and fundamentalism; the injustices under the perpetuation of patriarchy and the sensitive movements of women for their dignity, rights and powers; the intimidating development projects and the adverse effects imposed upon indigenous peoples; the escalating problems of environmental pollution; the concern over the common global toy of contention on nuclear arms build-up, wars and the pandemic of terrorist activities; the revolution of information technology and its adverse impact on society; the insanely increasing number of HIV/AIDS, drug abuse and other sicknesses and the exorbitant rising costs of healthcare; the over-charged charismatic movements and prosperity theologies; and finally but not exhaustively, the tasking responsibilities of the church in carrying out its priestly, prophetic, evangelistic, educational, caring, counseling and healing ministries[3] within such an ambiguous structure of life.

In this context, the SSC as an integral part of this 'One National Structure' (the BTESSC), stresses the importance of implementing the very Vision and Mission of theological education in India as clearly added in the new Constitution. It thus reads:

> We believe that the triune God has offered the possibility of renewal of life and hope for the entire creation in and through Jesus Christ, and that as an instrument of God, the Church is called to be involved in God's mission of liberation, reconciliation and community building among all peoples through varied forms of ministry. In the light of this faith and self-understanding,

---

[2]Ravi Tiwari, *Board of Theological Education of the Senate of Serampore College: Seminar on Curriculum Revision, Important Suggestions from Consultations*, 2007, 2. (Hereafter, Tiwari, *Board of Theological Education of the Senate of Serampore College…*).

[3]Cf. *Senate of Serampore College Proceedings of the Theological Senate and its Committees* "Concerns About the Theological Education Program of the Senate of Serampore College" A Paper Presented to the Partners from Germany July 24, 2006, Book XIX, Vol. XVIII (January 21-November 24, 2006), 183. (Hereafter, *Senate of Serampore College Proceedings of the Theological Senate and its Committees…*).

> we seek to equip ministers, leaders, scholars and the whole people of God to be committed to creative discernment of and active participation in God's liberative mission in the world at large and South Asia in particular by providing programmes of theological study and ministerial formation at various levels through affiliated colleges and institutions.[4]

Therefore, in such a context the BTESSC has been trying to address these many concerns by fostering ecumenically relevant theological education within India and outside India. Let us henceforth proceed toward critical analysis of the SSC in relation to its role thus far, in fostering ecumenism in its theological education especially in India's context.

2. The Senate of Serampore's Role in Fostering Ecumenism in Theological Education

Before we go any further, the researcher here would like to express a very important word of caution regarding our extended use of the word *Ecumenism,* which otherwise might create confusion for some when it is applied to some of our upcoming points of critique. To be out-rightly stated, the study will be using the word *Ecumenism* or *Ecumenical* or *Ecumenicity* (of course alternately) in the context of the plurality of concerns and issues whereby, it necessitates for us to view the Academic Curriculum of the SSC's theological education by critically assessing the ecumenical character of its study courses, areas of disciplines, subjects syllabus and even the contents of the subjects as well. For an example, our analysis will include the concern of seeing if the SSC is seriously and committedly incorporating as well as responding to the wide ranges of issues and problems faced by its peoples, church, and society at large. We shall now look into some of the major aspects of theological education under the SSC, through which it attempts to foster ecumenism as India's context demands.

2.1. Fostering Ecumenism in the form of Common Curriculum

As stated under the purpose of the BTESSC for curriculum revision the concern of the Senate is not only committed to the fulfillment of academic needs, but it also includes its commitment to respond to the contextual needs of the churches, its peoples in our country. It thus serves as a dynamic instrument of equipping the people for God's ministry.[5] The Senate's conviction for its common curriculum structure of theological education is founded upon an ecumenical aspect that also

---

[4]Cf. *Senate of Serampore College Proceedings of the Theological Senate and its Committees* "Concerns About the Theological Education Program of the Senate of Serampore College" A Paper Presented to the Partners from Germany July 24, 2006, Book XIX, Vol. XVIII (January 21-November 24, 2006), 183. (Hereafter, *Senate of Serampore College Proceedings of the Theological Senate and its Committees*...).

[5]Habil James Massey, *BTESSC: Secretary's Annual Report, 2006-07*, 36. (Hereafter, Massey, *BTESSC: Secretary's Annual Report, 2006-07*...).

stresses on the importance of designing our theological curriculum with deliberate reference to the contexts on which we live and serve. It has been observed that our curricula of theological education (in India) very often seem to have been either imported totally from the West or to have been handed over to us unaltered all the way down from the past which are not at all relevant and ecumenical in our situations. However, recognizing this weakness today, winds of change has entered the confines of our adamant world of theology and it has made its presence felt by waking people to face the reality around and to instill the need to move with the time.

It becomes significantly important that the courses, subjects and their contents under the curriculum be truly suited to the given context of the society. Besides, not just in its theoretical exercise but also equally, if not much more, in structure and function, we should see that our theological education reflected practically in and for own specific context; in governance and administration; in staffing and finance; in pedagogy, class assignments and projects; in library resources and student services, etc.[6] In this context Serampore has been not less than a champion for introducing common curricula for all its affiliated-member institutions in India and outside India. It is important for us to reflect upon some of the major historical factors and events that contributed to the development of theological education in India under the SSC in realizing its vision of fostering ecumenism by means of common curricula.

2.1.1. *The Lindsay Commission Report on Christian Higher Education in India*

During the first half of the twentieth century, the Church in India faced a new situation in its mission. The government on larger scales took up education and along with it the Christian colleges which were affiliated to the government universities.[7] During the meeting of the Christian college's representatives held at Agra in1929, questions like, "what is the mission of the Christian colleges in modern India?" were raised.[8] With this serious question in mind, they approached and presented before the NCCI and the IMC,[9] which eventually led to the

---

[6]Cf. Robert W. Ferris, *Renewal in Theological Education: Strategies for Change* (Wheaton: Billy Graham Center, 1990), 141. (Hereafter, Ferris, *Renewal in Theological Education*...).

[7]Siga Arles, Theological *Education for the Mission of the Church in India, 1947-1987* (New York: Peter Lang, 1991), 16. (Hereafter, Arles, Theological *Education for the Mission*...).

[8]Indian Christian and missionary educators met at Agra on February 1929 with representatives of majority of the Christian colleges in India.

[9]NCC passed on the request of the Agra conference to the conference of Missionary societies of Great Britain and Ireland and the Committee of Reference and Council in America, who in turn approached the IMC. IMC discussed the matter at its meeting at Williamstown, Massachusetts in July 1929.

organization of the Lindsay Commission on Christian Higher Education in India,[10] to study and evaluate the contribution of Christian colleges and to sharpen their focus. The inclusion of Theological Education in Lindsay Commission was due to the request of NCCI and some mission boards.[11] During this time there were over seventy-six institutions in India, which were concerned with training ministry ranging from catechetical schools conducted by a single person to theological seminaries at the Bachelor of Divinity degree level.[12]

The Lindsay Commission's emphasis rested upon:

a) The place of theological education in the program of higher education of the Church in India;
b) A general plan for the development of theological education in India;
c) The content of theological education best adapted to the needs of the Indian Church at that time;
d) The training of theological teachers.[13]

The Commission discovered that there was much deficiency in the existing Theological Education. The different colleges were *unrelated* to each other and lacked a comprehensive plan for theological education in India. There was much duplication of resources owing to the lack of co-operation and too much dependence on the West is apparent in both personal level and curriculum, which therefore resulted in the failure of the plan to adapt to Indian resources.[14] The

[10]The commission consisted of eight members: two from the NCCI- S. N. Benarji and S. K. Datta; two from the British Missions- Arthur Davis and Nicol Macnicol, two from American Missions- W. A. Brown and W. J. Hutchins, and two from IMC- Oscar Buck as Secretary and A.D. Lindsay, Master of Balliol college, Oxford, as Chairman. Lindsay Commission Report on *Christian Higher Education in India* (London: Humphrey Milford, 1933), 5ff. (Hereafter, Lindsay Commission Report on *Christian Higher Education...*).

[11]The original terms of reference for the Commission made no mention of Theological Education: but at the request of the NCC and some of the mission boards, it was later agreed that higher theological colleges and seminaries should be included in the study to the extent of determining in their relationship to the question of higher collegiate education. C.f. C.W. Ranson, *The Christian Minister in India* (London: Lutterworth, Press, 1946), 17. (Hereafter, Ranson, *The Christian Minister...*).

[12]Cf. *Lindsay Commission Report...*, 236. The Commission grouped them under three general categories. (a) Theological Seminaries teaching in English up to the B.D. degree affiliated with Serampore: United Theological College, Bangalore; Bishop's College, Calcutta; The India Methodist Theological College, Jabalpur, The United Theological College, Saharanpur; Serampore College; (b) Theological schools teaching in the vernacular but with a considerable use of English as a source of reference, some are union institutions, others conducted by a single Church, preparing men for the Christian ministry in its non-technical form and few give the L.Th; (c) Technical schools for ordinands, catechists, Bible women and others, usually conducted by a single person or at most two or three and varying greatly in the standards they set and the purpose for which they are designed.

[13]*Lindsay Commission Report...*, 235.

[14]Cf. *Lindsay Commission Report...*, 243.

Commission nevertheless, found that the Serampore affiliated colleges are already attempting to adapt to the contemporary Indian situation.[15] Such prevailing general state of Theological Education awaked Indian theological teachers to urge for a "radical reconsideration of the present methods, a reduction in the number of higher theological institutions and a concentration of resources at the points of the greatest need".[16] At the end of its research, the Lindsay Commission recommended the following concerns:

a) Theological Colleges must play an important part in the development of higher Christian education in India;
b) Theological colleges must be located in close proximity to the central colleges, where research and extensions are to be carried on to allow theological students to interact with students of other disciplines;
c) Theology should be made a subject of research at selected colleges-Madras first and then Allahabad, Lahore, Calcutta and Bombay in sequence;
d) Co-operation to the fullest extent should be ensured between the more important theological colleges both by reconsidering the need of the Church as a whole and accommodating the values of each denominational emphasis within the co-operative colleges;[17]
e) Union or co-operative schools of theology must be developed in each important language area in line with the recommendation of the NCC;
f) There should be great variety of lower forms of theological training made available with appropriate staff;
g) The Higher theological colleges should provide special training courses to those who would teach Bible at arts colleges;
h) Adequate Indian Christian staff should be developed;
i) Topics of research in the field of Applied Theology and Religion and staff capable of such research should be identified and funds raised to facilitate the researchers;
j) Every possible provision should be made for the early supply of a strong body of Indian theological teachers, while utilizing to the greatest possible extent the services of men now qualified;
k) A committee should be appointed to identify the books immediately needed and the men to write them, in order to provide an early supply of suitable theological literature in the vernacular;

---

[15]Cf. *Lindsay Commission Report...,* 237.

[16]*Ibid.,* 244.

[17]For example, the distinct traditions of discipline and worship of the Anglicans, the particularity of the Methodist heritage etc.

l) Every attempt should be made to enlist the interest and counsel of prominent Indian Christian laymen in the matter of theological education.[18]

Responses to the Lindsay Commission Report were positive, and immediately the NCC Committee on Theological Education insisted the recommendations on the concern of the institutions, churches and mission concerned. As a result, "there was a great deal of discussion on the subject of co-operation, on the number and location of higher theological institutions, and on the possibility of establishing a union school of theology in each main language area".[19] C.W. Ranson observed that "...much talk has flowed across the conference table since, yet little has happened in the field of theological education",[20] was his sad conclusion. Still, this pioneering step is in itself a turning point for exposing the need for development of theological education in India.

2.1.2. *The Contribution of Tambaram 1938 to Theological Education in India*

Tambaram in 1938[21] is significant for its hosting of the International Missionary Council. It presented the crucial statistical realities that India had 2,718,499 non-Roman Christian in 21,933 worshiping groups (11,824 organized congregations and 10,109 unorganized groups), shepherd by 2,522 ordained men and 10,174 unordained workers[22]. It was not just an inadequacy in numbers, but also an inadequacy in quality. The general education and training of the ministers and pastors was found inadequate, lagging behind, when compared with the advance in education and general culture experienced by the church members and the laity in secular professions.[23] Besides, most of the pastors were also burdened with administrative responsibilities.[24] Despite the fact that there were (a) Bible Schools for the training of full-time unordained workers in the Church; (b) Theological Schools for the training of the ordained pastoral ministry and (c) Theological Colleges for more advanced training,[25] yet, they were not recruiting and training sufficient numbers of full time Christian workers.[26] It was noted therefore, "the need for more and better qualified ministers to the existing congregations as well

---

[18]Cf. *Lindsay Commission Report...*, 245-248.

[19]Ranson, *The Christian Minister...*, 18.

[20]Cf. Ranson, *The Christian Minister...*, 132.

[21]*Report of IMC Conference at Tambaram,* Vol. 7 (December 12-29, 1938), Madras, 222.

[22]Arles, *Theological Education for the Mission...*, 22.

[23]*Report of the IMC Conference at Tambaram: The Life of the Church* Vol. 4 (December, 12-29, 1938), Madras, 235. (Hereafter, *Report of the IMC Conference at Tambaram...*).

[24]*Ibid.*, 229.

[25]Cf. *Report of the IMC Conference at Tambaram...*, 204-208.

[26]Arles, *Theological Education of the Mission...*, 22.

as the rapidly increasing number of new congregations, is very great and very urgent"[27].

The Tambaram report brought out certain observations about the place of Christian higher Education in the shaping of the secular witness of the Christian laity, as well as the place of Christian Theological Education in enhancing the specialized ministry. It acknowledged, "Education is and must always be a major concern of the Church."[28] While Tambaram noted with satisfaction that the large share of leadership is rendered by Christian nationals to the cause of education, it desired a proper relating of such activities to the witness of the local church[29].

With regard to Theological Education, Tambaram felt that the condition of Theological Education was "one of the greatest weaknesses of the whole Christian enterprise, in that almost all the younger churches are dissatisfied with the present system of training for the ministry and with its results.[30] Hence, the conference instructed the IMC to plan out arrangement for visits to the main centers of theological education of the younger churches, with a view to do detailed studies of the situation where such have not already been made; and to work out the policy and program for the training of the ministry of the younger churches[31]. However, the gathering of war clouds interrupted the plan of the IMC. The proposal for comprehensive study was inevitably and indefinitely postponed[32]. The fruition of the thought seeds of Tambaram had to wait till the war was over. It was only two decades later that the Theological Education Fund[33] picked up the unfinished strands to move forward with the awaiting task of developing macro-level researches, revisions and revitalization of Theological Education in India.

---

[27]*Report of the IMC Conference at Tambaram...*, 230. This was the case with the protestant churches that resulted from the eighteenth and nineteenth century missionary expansion of the Western Churches in India. In contrast the Malankara Orthodox Jacobite Syrian Church was well provided with 541 priests to serve her 490 parishes. Since the health progress of a congregation depended upon the devotion and untiring labor of the a full-time worker, the continuation of the protestant churches as they were can only mean stagnation and stunted growth of several thousands of congregations.

[28]*Report of the IMC Conference at Tambaram...*, 230. Much of the missionary educational programmes of the nineteenth century preceded the birth of the native church in the mission field. They were inherited by the native churches from the missionary societies only later in the post-colonial period.

[29]*Ibid.,* 54. Tambaram emphasized the need to guard against the danger of secularization and the need to develop more contemporary researches into the problems of the community and the Church.

[30]Cf. Ranson, *The Christian Minister...*, 19.

[31]*Ibid.*, 20.

[32]Arles, *Theological Education for the Mission...*, 24.

[33]Cf. Christine Lienemann-Perrin, *Training for a Relevant Ministry* (Madras: CLS for PTE/ WCC, 1981), 252. (Hereafter, Lienemann-Perrin, *Training for a Relevant Ministry...*).

2.1.3. *Ranson Report on Theological Education in India*

In accordance with the IMC recommendation during the Tambaram Conference in 1938 the National Christian Council of India instructed its Committee on Theological Education[34] to carry out an investigation and to bring a report on the situation in India on the following points:

a) Whether the existing relationship between theological and general education is satisfactory;
b) Whether the present curricula and the period of training for the various grades of theological training need to be revised;
c) Whether the existing facilities in various language areas are sufficient for the training of the different types of ministers needed;
d) Whether adequate provision is being made for the care (spiritual and intellectual) of the men after they leave the seminary;
e) What possibilities there are for giving higher theological training in the vernaculars;
f) Whether adequate provision is being made to supply national teachers who could impart training in specialized branches of theological education.[35]

The National Christian Council with its keen efforts toward this cause began the survey in 1942 and had three main stages in this project of investigations: a) Questionnaires, b) Regional Commissions and c) a Central Conference.[36] The main purpose for this assignment was to make "a thorough study of the possibilities of co-operation in the work of training ministers all over India."[37] Ranson, however, notes that this work was done at a time when India was undergoing an unusual difficulty - under the Second World War; the closing years of the colonial regime; and the final struggle for national independence all had their toll on India[38].

In the plan for Theological Education the report proposed the following points:

a) Establishing one united theological school in each main language area of the country organized on the possible basis of co-operation.
b) Following the ideal that theological schools should attempt to do one work and one work only, and to do it thoroughly well, that being the purpose of training men for the work of the ordained ministry.

---

[34] *Ibid.*, 17. This committee was in existence from the year 1924 (when the NMC became the NCC).

[35] Lienemann-Perrin, *Training for a Relevant Ministry...*, 20.

[36] Cf. Lienemann-Perrin, *Training for a Relevant Ministry...*, 23-26.

[37] *Ibid.*, 20.

[38] Cf. Arles, *Theological Education for the Mission...*, 26.

c) Introducing a comprehensive curriculum.
d) Encouraging Indian teachers to pursue advanced study, mostly in the West but also creating opportunities here in India.[39]

The report proposed that initially there should be twelve regional schools in India to serve the following language areas: Tamil, Malayalam, Kanarese, Telegu, Bengali, Gujarati, Hindi, Marathi, Oriya, Urdu, Sentali, Oraon and Mundari.[40] However, Vernacular Theological Education encountered the lack of enthusiasm from people since it was taken for granted that training in English was superior to training in the vernacular which was considered inferior.[41] The NCC Committee on Theological Education recognized that theological training of the college grade would be needed for a long period in English in India.[42] It also recognized that "until the quality of vernacular theological training is improved, the Church will suffer grievous weakness."[43] Hence, vernacular Theological Education faced an urgent demand for vernacular theological literature.[44] Thus, the report strongly proposed that:

> A full range of standard theological text-books is needed in each main language area, with supplementary theological literature of every kind. Translations of standard works in other languages and of the great formative Christian writings of every main period of the Church's history are also needed. There is an immense and largely untouched task of theological writing and translation to be done in every language area in India.... This is only one of the many theological tasks, which await the scholars in India, but it is one of the most important.[45]

The curriculum should not be over burdened by the addition of more subjects, but "the addition to every subject of a background - that background that the living Church stretching down through the centuries and reaching out to a needy world".[46] It was proposed that the Church History be brought up-to-date and related to the Indian Church. The lack of the books on the history of the Church in India was pointed out as a handicap.[47] It was recommended that every

---

[39]Samuel Amirtham, "Some Trends in the Development of Theological Education in India" *Indian Journal of Theology* (March, 1976): 199.

[40]Cf. Ranson, *The Christian Minister...*, 195.

[41]Stephen Neill states that this is the psychological difficulty for vernacular education. *Interim Report on the NCC Survey of Theological Education* (Nagpur: NCCI, 1944), 9.

[42]*Ibid.*, 7. See also Ranson, *The Christian Minister in India...*, 199.

[43]Ranson, *The Christian Minister...*, 201.

[44]Arles, *Theological Education for the Mission...*, 26.

[45]Ranson, *The Christian Minister...*, 233.

[46]Cf. Ranson, *The Christian Minister...*, 210.

[47]Cf. Arles, *Theological Education for the Mission...*, 29.

student "be required to do a piece of research or special study in the history of the church in his own area".[48] The report also noted regarding the study of Religion:

> This is one of the weakest spots in the knowledge of the Indian theological student. He will write far more intelligently on Apollinarianism than about the Arya Samaj or the Gita, and the Koran, as a rule, he knows nothing about at all.[49]

Hence, the finding recommend to acquaint the students with the actual text of the great classics like the Rig Veda, the Gita, the Koran, etc., and to include courses on primitive religion, modern expressions of Hinduism and Islam, secular faiths and communism.[50] The value of studying and practicing the worship styles of different traditions in an interdenominational college was also emphasized by the report.[51] The report went on to provide detailed recommendation for each language area.[52]

The Ranson report reiterated several aspects of what Lindsay Commission had found as the case thirteen years earlier. As noted after the Lindsay report did not result in actual action to revise the situation, "most of the theological institutions have never achieved the stability and security of the Christian arts colleges."[53] Furthermore, Ranson also reports on the uncertainty of numerous theological institutions, which have "not really made up their minds as to the kind of ministry they want and the way it is to be trained.[54] On the whole, Ranson report repeats almost the same of, and added somewhat drastic judgment of Lindsay Commission's inability in fulfilling its intended purpose which was hindered mainly due to the unfavorable circumstance of the Second World War.[55]

2.1.4. *The Harrison Report on Theological Education in India*

In the middle of fifties, the sub-committee set up by the NCCI Theological Education Committee faced the question of the official language with great concern. Though, the Lindsay and Ranson reports were favoring vernacular theological education, in the fifties English was still widely used for theological education, particularly at B.D., level and at the Masters level. The higher theological education department of Serampore College and the United Theological College of Bangalore both set their pattern of English education in 1910 and remained

---

[48]Ranson, *The Christian Minister...*, 211.

[49]*Ibid.,* 212.

[50]Cf. Arles, *Theological Education for the Mission...*, 28-29.

[51]Cf. Ranson, *The Christian Minister...*, 213f.

[52]Cf. *Ibid.*, 217-222.

[53]Ranson, *The Christian Minister...*, 132.

[54]*Ibid.*, 133.

[55]Cf. *Ibid.*, 135-145.

largely unaffected by the issue of language.[56] It was felt that theological education of the ministry needed to be of higher standard for the educated. Hence, the L.Th. level of training of the nineteenth century was upgraded to the B.D. level training after 1910 and was further developed beside the B.D., with the Honors program later named 'Master of Theology.' Use of English for higher theological education was defended pointing out that the naming of Hindi[57] as national language has not affected the English medium education in Government Colleges of law and medicine.[58] Introducing the vernacular education at primary and secondary level with Hindi as optional subject and English as subsidiary subject in secondary level with only few subjects taught in English medium at high school level, resulted in the difficulty even for B.A. graduates to comprehensively read and understand the theological books written in English.[59] As a result, in theological colleges English was taught as a required subject and thenceforth, theological education continues in the country with the emphasis on English language.

Therefore, after the Ranson report, the vernacular education had not progressed much. The Harrison report too had not made much contribution to this, however, it proposed the importance of establishing regional united theological schools, with infrastructures both in buildings and library resources and better-qualified staff.[60] There was no serious vernacular emphasis given except for its emendation that:

> In view of the fact that English is no longer the medium of instruction in most high schools in India, and further, in view of the great importance of this language for theological education as possessing a far greater wealth of Christian literature than any of the other languages of India at present, that while the medium of instruction in the school should be the regional language, increased attention be given to the study of English with the explicit purpose of enabling the students to read and profit from elementary theological books written in English.[61]

Nevertheless, we should note its positive contribution in its recommendations on library and literature. It recommended the following aspects concerning the content of the library:

---

[56]Cf. M. H. Harrison, "Notes on the History of Protestant Theological Education in India", *Fifty Years of Service, 1910-1960, Golden Jubilee Volume*, (Bangalore: UTC, 1960), 25-27.

[57]It has been decided that the official language of India is to be Hindi. But this constitutional provision does not necessarily fix the prices status of the regional languages of English in general education. Hindi has been introduced into school studies in non-Hindi areas, but frequently only as an optional subject.

[58]Cf. Arles, *Theological Education for the Mission…*, 228-229.

[59]Cf. M. H. Harrison, *After Ten Years: A Report on Theological Education in India* (Nagpur: NCCI, 1953), 8f. (Hereafter, Harrison, After *Ten Years: A Report on Theological Education…*).

[60]Cf. Arles, *Theological Education for the Mission…*, 229.

[61]Harrison, *After Ten Years: A Report on Theological Education…*, 51.

a) all available Christian literature in the regional language;
b) the literary and religious classics of the regional language, together with all the necessary tools, such as grammars, dictionaries, etc. for their unity;
c) essential theological books of an elementary character in English.[62]

Besides, it also emphasized the importance of the production of vernacular Christian literature. The report further recommended that urgent steps be taken as soon as possible, to write and translate and publish the volumes of the Christian Students Library into the main languages of India.[63]

2.1.4.1. *Co-operation in Theological Education*

The Ranson report noted how the Lindsay, Pickett and Butterfield reports were made less effective due to lack of sufficient co-operation between the many church groups in India.[64] Within the field of theological education, the Serampore Charter has been a great unifying force, yet the differences between the American and the non-American approaches caused huge divergence.[65] The Ranson report hence proposed a plan of co-operation through the three methods of unitary institution, the system of denominational halls or hostels with a common teaching faculty and groups of federated institutions in close proximity to make common instruction possible in subjects mutually agreed upon.[66] Co-operation was also to be seen in the formation of regional theological schools, strengthening of the union theological colleges and the setting up of schemes for advanced studies and theological research.[67] Further study on faculty development was given priority both inside India and abroad, with encouragement for research and writing, wherein a co-operative effort on the part of all the various denominations and traditions would converge to strengthen the program.

---

[62]Harrison, *After Ten Years: A Report on Theological Education...*, 52.

[63]Cf. *Ibid.*, 52-53.

[64]Cf. Ranson, *The Christian Minister...*, 166-168.

[65]Cf. Arles, *Theological Education for the Mission...*, 235. It is argued that American educational method tended to be more flexible with project, the credit system, certain fluidity in the syllabus, a wide range of options and a general emphasis on functional training compared with European education which was more academic and less elastic, with a general emphasis on didache. Each has valuable contribution to make to theological education in India. But it is as they willingly co-operate that mutual learning could take shape. Separate or divergent developments could only make for duplication and wasteful overlapping. See also Ranson, *The Christian Minister...*, 167, 176.

[66]Cf. Ranson, *The Christian Minister...*, 182-186.

[67]Cf. Arles, *Theological Education for the Mission...*, 235. What was proposed was that there be formed one united theological school in each main language area of the country organized on the widest possible basis of co-operation, and that the existing B.D. level colleges be strengthened without planning anymore new colleges.

Denominational differences, theological variations and national traditions in terms of theological education obtaining among British, Continental and American missions and churches caused continued separation in the fifties as in pre-independence era. As a result, in the mid-fifties, while the NCCI stresses its effort on encouraging co-operative developments in theological education in India, simultaneously, more of separatist developments grew among the new churches and missions which strengthened their own schools.[68]

2.1.4.2. *The Type of Courses Offered and their Aims*

Predominantly the courses were geared towards ordinands. A Licentiate in Theology (L.Th) Diploma Course was offered with the intention "to provide a well rounded course of Biblical and theological study, designed for the proper equipment of the ministry of the Church".[69] Courses were taught in regional languages to equip students to minister to their own people.[70] Bachelor of Divinity (B.D.) degree course train university graduates for certain essential functions of the Church in academic style, using English medium, since much theological literature were not yet available in the vernacular language. B.D. was not to be considered a higher degree than L.Th, but as a distinct one vital for other ministries than pastoral.[71] A Master of Theology course replacing the B.D. Honors courses and a Doctor of Divinity program were developed after the Ranson Report.

Therefore, theological education is a process and not merely teaching a set of courses or providing some skills for ministry. Curriculum and courses are tools for enabling students to initiate a process of empowering the people of God.[72] This means that theological colleges and seminaries have the dynamic call, vision and mission to reach out with ecumenical theological education to the whole people of God.

Hence, the quest for relevant curriculum in fostering ecumenism in theological education is not new in theological sphere. As noted earlier numerous books and articles have been written on theological education. In most cases many have commented that theological education has been too theoretical, academic, a carbon copy of Western culture and not so much relevant to the given context. As a result, many theological graduates after leaving their standard colleges and Seminaries are not willing to take up the rural ministry or even when they begin their ministry in parishes and organizations, they finds themselves distantly placed from the congregation. The simple yet main reason for this could be because of the content of their theological curriculum, which is not centered on praxis and

---

[68]Cf. Arles, *Theological Education for the Mission…*, 240.

[69]Cf. *Senate of Serampore College Minutes,* Book No. II, (January, 1956), 81f.

[70]Cf. Arles, *Theological Education for the Mission…*, 237.

[71]Harrison, *After Ten Years: A Report on Theological Education…*, 30.

[72]Cf. K. C. Abraham, "Theological Education for Public Discourse on Theology in India" *CTC Bulletine,* 12 (2003), 7.

real lives' issues of the people. It is a necessity therefore, to correct this problem by developing a relevant and contextual curriculum, which is oriented towards inclusion of those hitherto neglected concerns.

Questions about the relevance of curriculum of ecumenical theological education have continued to be the subject of important discussions in various meetings and conferences of the SSC's circle of theological education in India. We cannot argue against the conscious effort of the SSC to revise their curriculum in each passing decade for purpose of meeting the relevant needs of the context for the very reason that there are quite a number of historic records documenting its evidences. While that is the case, what is crucial at this juncture is to enquire, what is the measure of their impact? Or, were/are they effectively been applied and likewise been fruitful? These are some unavoidable queries that should be considered as we talk about the SSC's effort in fostering an ecumenical character of its curriculum.

In recent years, the Senate of Serampore has taken up a serious project regarding the revision of its theological curriculum with a view to become truly relevant and contextually ecumenical for India's context. For this purpose, it is including the concerns of not just the member colleges of its affiliating body but also the concerns of the churches, theological educators of other institutions, important organizations etc., for their views and suggestions. This is mainly aimed at perceiving itself through the eyes of others; and to critically re-evaluate its pattern of theological education; its weaknesses, strengths; and very importantly, to see where and how it could improve its program of theological education to effectively relate, incorporate and impact the real life situations and issues of the whole people of God in India's pluralistic context.

At the present therefore, we are not in a position to express a concrete view or conclusion on this subject of the SSC's curriculum except to comment that there is a conscious effort of the Senate to revitalize its curriculum as per the demands of the peoples, their complex issues of life and their specific context. Beyond that, we do not have the liberty to add anymore than to earnestly await with bated breath as we look forward to the completion of the curriculum revision project and its transforming results.

3. Fostering Ecumenism in the form of Relationship with different Denominations

3.1. The Ecumenical Character of Serampore College in its Interdenominational Relationship

Serampore family is made up of theological schools, colleges, seminaries and institutions under the various churches and denominational backgrounds ranging from Orthodox to Pentecostal and of other Protestant faith persuasions.[73] The

[73]C.f. D. S. Satyaranjan, *Senate of Serampore College Registrar's Report, 1990-1991*, 1991, 845. (Hereafter, Satyaranjan, *Senate of Serampore College…*).

Serampore Act of 1918, the constitution of the Senate gave a very foundational picture about the ecumenical nature of the Senate of Serampore College (SSC). According to the Act, article 9 pointed out that 'the Senate shall consist of the principal (who shall be convener) and not less than twelve nor more than eighteen persons, as the Council may from time to time determine, to be appointed by the council."[74] Furthermore, the article gives a more elaboration in stating that "at least one and not more than three representatives of the following Christian denominations, viz. Anglican, Baptist, Congregational, Lutheran, Methodist, Presbyterian and Syrian shall, as far as practicable, be members of the Senate."[75] This Act was framed with the context in mind and the interest of many people belonging to different denominations, who saw in the proposal, a way of unifying theological education that would give a sound academic standard in the whole country. With the Act of the Senate of Serampore College in 1918, the United Theological College of South India at Bangalore was affiliated, which was followed by Bishop's College of Calcutta and others.[76] The story of the SSC, stretching its arm in the field of theological education in India and other parts for last many years, is one of the historic landmarks in ecumenical co-operation among the varied Christian denominations particularly in India.

Besides the ecumenical character of its common curriculum, it also *fosters ecumenism by bringing churches of different denominations under one umbrella for mutual commitment to the gospel and its service in India's contemporary context.* According to the new constitution of the Senate, the Committee on Ecumenical Relations and Church Ministries of the BTESSC function under the following guidelines:

> ...to explore the nature and form of the ministries of the Church currently needed and the training required to carry out these ministries, in the socio-political aspect of life; to organize consultations, seminars and conferences on relevant theological issues in order to stimulate creative theological thinking...; to encourage cooperation and collaboration in theological education in then region...; to assist member institutions to strengthen their faculties...; to promote ecumenical concerns in theological education with a view to strengthening the witness of the Church in contemporary society.[77]

It is important to note that the co-operation of the people and denominations, to a very great extent brought the vital spectrum of ecumenical spirit within the

---

[74]*Bengal Act No. IV of 1918*, The Serampore College Act, 1918, as modified up to the 1st July, 1951, 3.

[75]*Ibid.*

[76]William, Steward, "'The Ecumenical Character of Serampore College," *The Story of Serampore and Its College*, Serampore: The Council of Serampore College, 1961, 71. (Hereafter, Steward, *The Ecumenical Character of Serampore College...*).

[77]*A Paper Presented to the Partners from Germany July 24, 2006,* 186.

SSC. This spectacular co-operation among the different denominational traditions within the SSC has been provided in the Act itself. It is observed that to some extent, it could have resulted due to the common concern shared by all to come together namely, Lutheran, Syrian, Anglican and Presbyterian, Methodist and Baptist, Pentecostal and Independent denominations, etc., [78] with and for, the conviction that Serampore degrees and diplomas should stand for the best in theological education.[79]

There has been a constant interaction between what we call ecumenical and denominational in the Serampore family and it is possible to assume that there might not be any other structure that could serve as a parallel to the Senate of Serampore Board where such a variety agree to work together with a common vision and mission. Hence, this in itself lends to the ecumenical vitality of our theological education today.[80]

It was in 1960s and 1970s that the SSC opened its doors and welcomed the evangelical seminaries and colleges. It envisaged that through ecumenical living together and growing together we would be led to a rich theological pluralism.[81] The mainline ecumenical Churches were and still are, characterized by their search for unity not only in terms of faith but in order as well. Such a movement towards unity in faith and order is not always conducive to theological pluralism. Hence, it could be argued that denominationalism could lend itself to the growth of healthy theological pluralism through open dialogue and mutual sharing of insights. It is through such an ecumenical encounter of different denominations that we could together move towards a new pluralistic model of ecumenism. However, this ecumenical journey is not and will not be an easy or simple one. It is therefore strongly affirmed that unless the denominations are willing to subject their theological stance to the fresh and contemporary interpretations of the word of God by which they stand, they will only produce dry or skeletal denominational pluralism, which is static. It is only through a dynamic interaction of text and

[78]India was represented by men like C. K. Jacob, Thomas Sither as well as by C. E. Abraham who as Registrar for twenty years and president for ten more, played a big part in working out the pattern. Denmark was there from the start in the person of the far-seeing Dr. Larsen the principal of the UTC, Bangalore, and later the Senate would have being the same without the wisdom long brought to it deliberations by Bishop Sandegren from Sweden. The American tradition has been represented throughout, the name like those of Dr. Banninga of Pasumallai, later of Dr. M. H. Harrison of Bangalore and of W. G. Griffifths and M. H. Harper from Jabalpur calling for honored mention. Successive Principals of Scotish Church College, Calcutta, and later Dr. J. F. McFadyen of the staff, ensured that the Scottish contribution should not be lacking. Finally, the experience of entirely dominating it, has always been available in persons from the ancient English Universities, notably the first President and Registrar, George Howells and John Drake, later men like G. H. C. Angus, W. W. Winfield and many others.

[79]Steward, *The Ecumenical Character of Serampore College...*, 72.

[80]Satyaranjan, *Senate of Serampore College Report 1990-1991...*, 845.

[81]Cf. *Ibid.*, 845.

context that we will be able to move forward. It is here that the SSC could serve as a meeting platform where through open dialogue we will authentically grow towards a pluralistic model of ecumenism in the context of theological education in India.[82]

In addition to the task of training ministers for the Churches, the SSC also prepares qualified theological teachers for different Seminaries and Colleges. One of the serious concern of the SSC is its conviction that the functions of theological education is to enable the Churches to constantly rethink and re-examine its policy practices and discipline and therefore it holds that theological institutions should live up to what they believe.[83]

3.2. Churches Role in Ecumenical Theological Education

For the realization of a truly ecumenical theological education in India, it necessitates a two-way relationship between the theological institutions and the church. There can be no 'ecumenism' when it is 'one way' kind of relationship. Just as the aim of theological education is to prepare people for service of the gospel in and through the church, it is equally necessary that the church also participate actively in the structuring process of theological education, lending its support, ideas, suggestions as well as its constructive criticisms etc. It is only through such mutual participation and enrichments that they (theological education and the church) would be able to effectively fulfill the common vision and mission.

According to the Constitution (2005) of the Vision and Mission of Theological Education in India it states that:

> The Church is called to be involved in God's mission of liberation, reconciliation and community building among all peoples through varied forms of ministry. We are called upon to equip the whole people of God to respond to the contextual challenges critically and creatively by being faithful to the Gospel of Jesus Christ.[84]

Hence, with a view to create effectiveness in and strengthen the relationship between the BTESSC and the Churches in India in their common goal for theological education, it has a special organ under the name of 'The Committee for Ecumenical Relations and Church Ministries,' which is inclusive of the membership of the representatives of the Churches, the Council, Theological Colleges and related institutions. This Committee's functions include the following:

1. To foster continuing theological conversation between theological colleges, churches, church-related bodies and secular agencies.

---

[82]Satyaranjan, *Senate of Serampore College Report, 1990-1991…*, 845.

[83]*Ibid.*, 846.

[84]Massey, *BTESSC: Secretary's Annual Report, 2006-07…*, 37.

2. To explore the nature and form of the ministries of the Church currently needed and the training required carrying out these ministries, in the socio-political aspects of life.
3. To promote ecumenical concerns in theological education with a view to strengthening the witness of the Church in contemporary society.[85]

As noted earlier ecumenical theological education is not only concerned with the training of prospective clergy for new communities, but also evangelization of the society at large, implementing the mission of Christian culture, theological interpretation of new aspects of social responsibility, searching after answers to the continuously raising questions and challenges of the technological and informational civilization, resistance to the negative side-effects of the globalizational processes, and first and foremost, service to peace and concord, and Christian witness to the secular world. In this context it is not possible to hold isolated special ecumenical events to promote ecumenical theological education among the people but instead, all classes and lectures should be enlivened and imbued with ecumenical thinking. Thus, ecumenical theological education can give significant guidance on current ethical and social issues and also contribute further by demonstrating possibilities for action.[86]

The program of the Committees on Research and Consultations and Church Relations of the BTESSC is an attempt to respond to the numerous and complex challenges to theological education in our country today.[87] Situations like the tragedy of war, the economic hardship, soaring prices, shortage of essential commodities and paucity of foreign exchange, etc., have shattered the already strained economy, communalism, religious fundamentalism, caste structures, political imbalances, and the Dalits, the tribals and women and marginalized sectors who still struggles for their survival in the country.[88] Hence, the search for peace, communal harmony, economic justice and a viable and relevant educational system through ecumenism must be the priority for today. These are some of the issues that continue to challenge our faith, life, our ministry and most importantly our theological education.[89]

The Committee on Consultations and Church Relations organized regional consultations on Mission and Evangelism. The western region was held at UBS, Pune on October 9-11, 1990. A fairly well represented group of 20 participants, some of whom are from the Catholic Church, took part in this consultation.

---

[85]Massey, *BTESSC: Secretary's Annual Report, 2006-07...*, 37.

[86]Cf. Vladimir Fedorov, "Challenges to Theological Education in Central and Eastern Europe: Education as a Liturgy before Liturgy" *Ministerial Formation 101WCC* (July, 2003), 10-11.

[87]K. C. Abraham, *Board of Theological Education of the SSC: Report of the Director 1990,* 772. (Hereafter, Abraham, *Board of Theological Education of the SSC...*).

[88]*Ibid.,* 773.

[89]Abraham, *Board of Theological Education of the SSC...*, 773.

The consultation suggested that: at the local level, local Churches should seek to co-operate with the larger society in social action and raising voice in national issues. Local Churches should provide platform for dialogue between people of other faiths. At the college and seminary level, it is recommended that a section on implication for mission and evangelism and/or ministry in the context of poverty, corruption, exploitation, homelessness etc., be added to courses so as to contextualize our theological studies.[90]

The Andhra Region Seminar on Mission and Evangelism was held at ACTC, Hyderabad, during November 30 to December 2, 1990. Over 50 people belonging to about a dozen denominational representatives in the area attended. The consultation suggested that all the theological colleges and seminaries should be encouraged to expand their fields of studies to include fields of ecology, economy and politics etc., so that the students are fully equipped to meet the multifaceted challenges of Christian Ministry. Intra-religious dialogues between different denominational Churches should also take place so that all congregations can take active part in the prophetic ministry of the Church in context of communal disharmony and peacelessness, presenting Jesus as the prince of peace.[91]

There is an argument that Churches send students who have a heart for ministry, and eagerness for mission, and a zeal for evangelism to be prepared and equipped, and three to five years later these students graduate from seminaries theologically confused, having lost their commitment and often being totally unprepared for the task which they had hoped to accomplish and for which they have come to the seminaries to be trained. In our context theological education has remained basically the same for a century and the new, emerging theological schools mushrooming in the country also contribute to this problem. In many instances, theological institutions and the local churches are not working towards supporting each other.[92] On the one hand, one hears that the graduates produced by theological institutions are not effective in the ministry. On the other hand, theological educators express disappointment and frustration that the churches have no desire to be supportive partners of the theological training program.[93] However, theological education and the way it is organized should be an expression of genuine commitment to the Church[94] and its ministry. In connection to our

---

[90]Zaihmingthanga, *Report of the Associate Director1990-91*, 781. (Hereafter, Zaihmingthanga, *Report of the Associate Director1990-91…*).

[91]*Ibid.*, 782.

[92]Cf. Charles M. Wood, *An Invitation to Theological Study* (Valley Forge: Trinity Press, 1994), 25.

[93]Steven Paey, *Change in the Theology and Practice of Preaching* (U.K.: Saint Louis University Press, 1990), 249.

[94]D. K. Sahu, "Reorganizing the Structure: A Possibility for Mission Today," in *Church's Participation in Theological Education*, edited by Samson Prabhakar and M. J. Joseph (Bangalore: BTESSC/SATHRI, 2003), 19. (Hereafter, Sahu, *Reorganizing the Structure…*).

point of discussion, let us briefly look into the writings of Dietrich Werner on the subject of the Church and theological education in a given context. Werner states thus:

a. Theological education is the most essential key and strategic factor for the renewal of the church's life and mission. Without proper and relevant theological education the very future of the Christian church, its dialogue with society and its participation in the daily struggles and longings of ordinary people is endangered; the less churches and their leaders are investing in theological education the more the future of Christianity will be left to those who give a distorted image of Christian identity and endanger dialogue and co-existence with other churches as well as other religious traditions;
b. The role of theological education is never limited just to the training of Christian ministers. With all legitimate attention and emphasis on ministerial formation, the road and inclusive approach emphasizing theological education as a process of renewal and formation for all God's people needs always to be kept in mind;
c. A church which has to face growing challenges from accelerated globalization and wants to critically deal with the burning issues in a globalized information society urgently needs highly equipped and capable theologians able to be in dialogue with people involved both in complex issues of bio-ethics, climate change, agro engineering or HIV/AIDS pandemic – or in other words, a church which is neglecting theological education can easily fall back into the position of an inward looking sectarian group.[95]

The Senate of Serampore felt that Church and theological colleges in India cannot function, or even exist, independent of each other, they must reciprocate each other's needs and challenge each other with new thinking. Church cannot perceive and practice God's mission without embracing theological education as an integral to its reason to be. It is an integral part of church's mission. Theological formation begins in the church and it should take care in selecting future ministers of the church.[96]

Thus, the BTESSC in its commitment to bring out a comprehensive ecumenical theological education continue to engage the combined involvement

---

[95]Cf. Dietrich, Werner, "Ecumenical Learning in Global Theological Education-Legacy and Unfinished task of Edinburgh 1910 or: Contextuality, Inter-Contextuality and Ecumenicity as Key Mandates for Ecumenical Theological Education in the 21st Century", *Ecumenical Theological Education* (Geneva: WCC, 2007), 13-14. (Hereafter, Werner, *Ecumenical Learning in Global Theological Education…*).

[96]Cf. Ravi Tiwari, *BTESSC: Seminar on Curriculum Revision*, 2007, 5.

of the Church leaders and Scholars in the process of its curriculum revision task too.

4. Fostering Ecumenism by Producing Contextually Relevant Theological Education

4.1. Introduction

Wherever we look today, theological education presents a confusing picture. In some cases it is an ongoing concern, in some cases it is going through culture shock, and in some other cases it is undergoing a painful transition. Institutionally we see the continued growth of interdenominational and now newer charismatic institution and independents institutions at the expense of disunity within the Christians in India. While theological education caters to a wide range of audience, and the number of lay people involvement in theological concerns, distance learning becoming important, and more part-time increasing taking significance role, and the women and the minorities remain less represented among faculty, students and administrators. There is a gap between theological education and the common person in the society and a proper response is needed in order to make theological education relevant in today's society. It is a serious challenge for the SSC to see whether the theological education under its courses do relevance for today's society and meet the need of the churches today in India. Once again let us cite Dietrich Werner's observation on the subject of contextually relevant theological education in different contexts of the world:

> contextualization in theological education was and still is a cry for self-determination and self-reliance in theological education of churches in the Global South or broadly speaking in the churches of the marginalized which cannot view themselves as a mere prolongation of the same models and standards of theology and theological education which had been offered for long by the churches of the west. Christianity in the Global South has conceptualized itself as Christianity with a hermeneutical disruption, a certain rift and discontinuity with the traditions of its mother churches. Therefore the established institutions of theological education in the West cannot see themselves any more in the role of the global authorities and master-models compulsory for everybody but much more in the role of those now being asked for themselves how they view their own relevance and their specific contextuality in their own.[97]

4.2. Contextually Relevant Theological Education

Programs of our theological education in fostering ecumenism must be designed with deliberate reference to the contexts in which we serve. We are at fault that our curricula so often appear either to have been imported wholly from the west

[97]Cf. Werner, *Ecumenical Learning in Global Theological Education...*, 14.

or to have been handed down unaltered from the past. The selection of courses for the curriculum, and the content of every course in the curriculum, must be specifically suited to the context of service.[98] Our theological education in fostering ecumenism must orient themselves pervasively in terms of the Christian community being correlated. As long as our theological programs operate merely in terms of some traditional or personal or imported notion of theological education it will continue not to be relevant in fostering ecumenism in theological education in today's context. Our programs need to establish at every level with a close attentiveness to the needs and expectations of the society in which we serve.[99]

In this context the role of a relevant ecumenical theological education is to research into the religious, economic, cultural and social realities of India to rethink and to reformulate a new ecumenical concept of theological education for relevance to the pluralistic setting of India. It is observed that the divisions within the churches and denominations today heavily contribute to the falsification of the credibility of the peace in a land torn with regional, communal, religious, linguistic, factionalism in politics,[100] tribalism, sex, gender and race. The disunity among the Christians represents the public contradiction of the Gospel[101] and it is a serious challenge for ecumenical theological education. Keeping in view the setting of India, theological colleges functioning under the traditional and historic Churches, train their students for the ministry of the larger churches which are in constant link with the ecumenical trends. Several researches have been carried out to evaluate them.[102] Lindsay Commission on Christian Higher Education,[103] the Ranson study on Christian Ministers in India,[104] the Harrison study after ten years,[105] the Board of Theological Education of the SSC Priority Commission's National Study of Theological Education are studied in order to make assessment whether the development of theological education was relevant to the Indian situation or not.

---

[98]Cf. Ferris, *Renewal in Theological Education...*, 140-142. Not only in what is taught, but also in structure and operation our theological programs must demonstrate that they exist in and for their own specific context, in governance and administration, in staffing and finance, in teaching styles and class assignments, in library resources and the relation with the outside audience in their service.

[99]Moreover, to this we may need to establish multiple modes of ongoing contact and interaction between institutions and church, both at the higher levels as well as the grassroots levels, and regularly adjust and develop theological education in the light of ecumenism.

[100]Cf. Arles, *Theological Education for the Mission...*, 380.

[101]Cf. Leslie Newbigin, "The Call to Mission-A Call to Unity," *The Crossing Frontiers*, edited by Peter Beyerhaus and C.F. Hallen Creutz (Uppsala: Studia Missionalia, 1969), 256.

[102]Cf. Arles, *Theological Education for the Mission...*, 385.

[103]Cf. *Lindsay Commission Report on Christian Higher Education...*, 5f.

[104]Cf. Ranson, *The Christian Minister...*, 2ff.

[105]Cf. Harrison, *After Ten Years: A Report on Theological Education...*, 2ff.

As mentioned above, Lindsay, Ranson and Harrison Commission reported that regional and vernacular theological education began to emerge in India in the sixties. With the pioneering effort of the National Christian Council and its committee on education, many church-related institutions worked together under the SSC's umbrella in fostering a wider ecumenism by training many church leaders and teachers for the ministry of both the Senate affiliated and non-affiliated institutions in India and outside.

As a result, the creative width of development and involvement by the institutions under the SSC in fostering ecumenical theological education in its mission, literature production, inter-faith dialogue, lay training, socio-political, economic involvements, rural concern, concern for church unity; concern for church's renewal etc., all of these makes the SSC stand out as an example for a relevant program of ecumenical theological education in Indian context. The context within which the Senate of Serampore is involved is marked by pluralism in all aspects of live of the people and its nation. And these realities serve as a challenging background for a meaningful theological education in India.[106]

The SSC has been continuously engaging itself to the task of developing ecumenically relevant theological education, yet it is not completely free from criticisms. It is not spared from the complaints that the products of the SSC are ill-equipped for spiritual ministry. It is very often pin-pointed that it neglects the spiritual and practical living at the expense of its emphasis on academic excellence. As such, tension between academic excellence and practical relevance continues. Maintaining a balance between faith reflection at the intellectual sphere and faith commitment at the spiritual, practical sphere therefore remains a towering challenge. The SSC as a conglomeration of unity in diversity therefore should take serious note of this reality even as it continue to deliberate and act on its vision of an ecumenical theological education.[107]

We have already observed that the environment of theological education in India has changed qualitatively in the past few decades. This change has been wrought from the perspective of both the context and the system of theological education itself: India's peoples' context that confronts varied forms of changes in its day-to-day experiences within which theological education is situated and the theological education that gradually began to grow sensitive and considerate to the challenging realities and issues by putting its efforts to make itself relevant and meaningful to its given India's context.[108] Today unlike the bygone era, we witness

[106]Cf. J. W. Gladstone "Religious Education: Towards Building Communities in Asia" *CTC Bulletine* (Hong Kong: CCA, 2003), 1.

[107]Cf. Gnana Robinson, "For the Sake of the Gospel," *Essays in Honor of Samuel Amirtham,* ed., by Gnana Robinson (Madurai: TTS Publications, 1980), 284.

[108]As noted in our earlier chapters especially the second chapter that analyzed the historical development of theological education in India, in the beginning, theological education in India had been more or less been exclusive and narrow in its system of structure as well as in its objectives. A

a much more openness toward change, as well as many more opportunities for affiliating with the Senate of Serampore College (University). However, in many theological institutions, very disappointingly, we discover that social realities of the people or of a given context are not considered to be of their concern and responsibility. The subject of social responsibility, concern toward issues such as violence, war, poverty and environmental contamination, gender discrimination, the abandonment of children, immorality etc., are therefore not anywhere near the premises of our theological education and its curriculum. Sensing this serious shortcoming in our theological exercise, educators, leaders and sensitive members of the SSC and its affiliating bodies, have been tirelessly involving in the struggle for reconstructing a more fittingly ecumenical form of our theological education.

4.2.1. *The Reality of HIV/AIDS and Its Place within the SSC's Ecumenical Theological Education*

In our days, we have witnessed a great alarm over the problem of HIV/AIDS, and we can also admit that we are fortunate, to some extent because, the WCC has taken some initiative concerning this health problem. The WCC's initiation has extended its challenge not only toward the churches, but also theological education institutions to take serious consideration of this alarming life-threatening reality. It strongly suggested the theological education structures to include in their curricula, a biblical, theological and medical approach to this monstrous disease.

In answer to this realization, the SSC has taken up the clarion call by introducing this issue of HIV/AIDS in the curriculum and some of the theological institutions have even already considered the subject of HIV/AIDS to be studied in the B.D. degree course's level. Likewise, Churches also should be constantly mobilized to focus more intentionally on the reality of HIV/AIDS pandemic. This pandemic challenges us to totally denounce life-denying theologies and ethics, and to replace them with biblical, theological, ethical, pastoral and liturgical resources that are truly life-affirming and life-giving for humanity and the whole created order.[109] As theological Educators and as committed Christians, we are commissioned to dismantle the culture of death, and to create a culture of life-giving, life-saving and life-fulfilling.[110] Therefore, it is crucially important for the

simple reminder would be the Syrian Christian Church and its theological education pattern that focused mainly on the preservation and self-oriented service for which it trained its candidates for its parish ministries. Another example would be the Roman Catholic Church and its earlier theological education system which was more or less organized and structured after the pattern and standard of western form of theological education that had very little relevance for India's peoples and their day-to-day lives' experiences.

[109]Cf. *WCC, Plan of Action: The Ecumenical Response to HIV/AIDS in Africa*. Nairobi: 2001. 5. See also Nyrambura J. Njoroge, "An Ecumenical Commitment: Transforming Theological Education in Mission", *International Review of Mission*, Vol. 94. No. 373 (April, 2005), 246-252.

[110]Donald, E. Messer, *Breaking the Conspiracy of Silence: Christian Churches and the Global AIDS Crisis* (Minneapolis: Fortress Press, 2004), 24. (Hereafter, Messer, *Breaking the Conspiracy of Silence...*).

SSC to include this urgent concern within its encompassing frame of fostering ecumenism in theological education.

Ecumenical theological education is not an end itself but is a means of systematically and intentionally enlightening and educating those called to ministry in its various manifestations for lay and ordained persons. Theological educators in different parts of the world have identified the various obstacles and challenges for ecumenical learning. It is mainly through their get-together for consultations and reflections that come to a common agreement that they must take up the responsibility to address those hitherto neglected issues and concerns. They understand therefore that the only way they could make their theological programs meaningful and effective is through their practical learning and actions.

The ecumenical concern of theological education has significantly widened the concept of contextualization by including also the concern of dialogue with people of other living religious and cultural traditions, also including the extended or connected aspects of diversities. It has been argued at several consultations within SSC that the accelerated pace of globalization today is also accelerating the pace of the peoples' search for their own roots, eventually enabling them to find strength and hope in their own socio-cultural and religious identities once again.[111] As such, theological education especially the Senate of Serampore should take serious note of this fact that its ecumenical character and concern can never be truly ecumenical if it constricts its idea of ecumenism to contextualization alone by erroneously erecting a confining hedge within the encompassing scope of true ecumenism. In other words, while it is true that 'contextualization' is important and comes under or within the idea of ecumenism, it is much more narrow and limited in itself that it can neither alternate for ecumenism nor claim to represent ecumenism in its entirety. Therefore, it is a must that the BTESSC need to go deeper than contextualization or rather enlarge its scope of ecumenism as it attempt to foster ecumenism in its theological education program.

4.3. Relevant and Contextual Theological Literature

For purpose of sound and profound teaching, it requires relevant and contextual literature and other resourceful materials. In most parts of the world and particularly in India, theological institutions mostly focus on ministerial formation without paying much attention to the academic nature of ecumenical theological education and the critical need to develop ecumenical theological literature, including also worship materials that communicate to the hearts and minds of the readers. Creating relevant and contextual literature in ecumenical theological education in India for instance, necessitates great creativity and courage because the most profound theological knowledge is with the women and men who may have the least academic qualification yet their great commitment in the

[111]Messer, *Breaking the Conspiracy of Silence...*, 27.

life and mission of the church qualify them to be great church historians and theologians.[112] Theological institutions and seminaries should ensure that students are exposed to situations where ecumenism is practiced and not just in talking about it but very importantly in enabling them to have first-hand experience as well as documenting it for wider readership. Besides, it is of great importance that developing relevant and contextual literature in ecumenical theological education on different fields study should be accompanied by well equipped library that is equally managed or supervised by qualified well-trained librarians.[113]

5. Fostering Ecumenism through One National Structure of Theological Education in India

5.1. The Board of Theological Education (1975)

Earlier, there were two main organizations at the national level functioning in the interests of theological education, the SSC and the BTE, formerly under the National Christian Council (NCC).[114] These organizations have made significant contributions to the cause of theological education in India. The former had largely exercised academic functions while the latter had mainly been a co-coordinating and consultative body. Despite their significances, there had been instances of overlapping of their functions. Besides, the aspect of advanced theological research on a national level had not received sufficient attention, for which reason, the above-mentioned two organizations jointly mooted the idea of an Indian Theological Research Institute (I.T.R.I) commissioned to explore possibilities.

The BTE and the SSC met at a successive joint consultations first at Bangalore in 1968 and then at Yeotmal in 1972, and at separate meetings of these respective bodies, the point has been made and repeated that what is really needed

[112]It also entails financial resources that will enable theological educators and students to interact with committed Christians in the churches, women's and men's fellowships, recording what they have to share for future analysis and documentations.

[113]This is another area that has been identified as wanting in many of the theological institutions/seminaries in India and there is a great demand for well-trained librarians. Well-trained librarians play a valuable role in research methodologies and documenting of information among other things.

[114]NCCI in 1955 formed the BTE, which brought together all the unaffiliated Bible schools and seminaries and provided to them the facilities of evaluation, coordination and accreditation. BTE took over the functions of the NCCI Committee on Theological Education and worked in relation with the NCCI, but later it became autonomous and served many non-Serampore institutions of theological education. The principals of these institutions met in consultations and mutually helped each other. BTE sponsored various programs including the visit of guest lecturers to various colleges, seminar on theology-in-Action in cooperation with the Christian Conference of Asia and Urban Industrial Mission. After a series of joint consultations with the Senate of Serampore College, BTE decided in favor of the formation of One National Structure for Theological Education in India. Hence, BTE dissolved itself at its General Body Meeting on 3rd February 1977 at the Mar Thoma Theological Seminary, Kottayam, Kerala.

is one national organization for theological education in the country, undertaking all the three functions, i.e., academic administration, consultation and research organization. After series of joint consultations, the BTE of NCCI decided that the SSC, which already serves theological institutions and their interests all over the country, might be best suited to become this one national organization.[115]

The forms and constitution of the SSC closely defined by the Serampore College Act, lays down among other things, an upper limit of 19 members, which makes it impossible for all institutions to be directly represented in the membership of the Senate, which is appointed by the Council of Serampore College. Hence, at the annual meeting of the Senate held at Serampore in 1974, an Implementation Committee consisting of three members each from the Senate, the BTE and the ITRI was appointed with a mandate to bring proposals to the Senate the following lines:

i) Theological Education must be so organized as to:
   a) meet the challenging new patterns and demands of the ministry,
   b) be an agent of change in the structure of Church and society to achieve their objectives,
   c) be an instrument for renewal and self-reliance,
   d) encourage reflection, articulation and communication of the faith in Christ, related to the concrete life situation.

ii) The College must be encouraged and given freedom to try new models of curricula and new patterns of theological education to achieve such goals.

iii) The functioning of the Senate needs to be reorganized so as to bring under its concern the three functions of:
   a) Academic administration (at present the task of SSC)
   b) Co-ordination, consultation and ecumenical relations (at present largely the function of the BTE)
   c) Research (the concern of the ITRI commission).

The three concerns were to interact and contribute to the total theological task in India.

iv) The Senate should have freedom to make its own rules for its effective working and to develop structures for the effective fulfillment of its functions, and to arrange for evaluation of students and institutions.[116]

---

[115] *Minutes of the Meeting of the Executive of the Senate of Serampore College, held at Serampore January 28th 1975*, 232. *Senate of Serampore College Proceedings of the Theological Senate and its Committees January 28th 1975-October 1st 1975. Minutes of the Meeting of the Implementation Committee Appointed to Consider Reorganization of the Functioning of the Serampore Senate held at Lee Memorial Mission House, Wellington Square, Calcutta on March 22nd and 23rd, 1974*, 352.

[116] *Senate of Serampore College proceedings of the Theological Senate and its Committees January 28th 1975-October 1st 1975. Minutes of the Meeting of the Implementation Committee Appointed to*

> The Implementation Committee's proposals were forwarded to the Colleges, to the Council of Serampore College, to a joint meeting of the Executive Committees of the Serampore Senate and the Board of Theological Education in India, and their suggestions and directions were incorporated in a draft considered by the Senate in its meeting at Serampore in January 1975, and adopted in accordance with section XII of the Serampore College Act.[117]

As a result, when SSC accepted the proposal, a joint structure was formed in July 1975 as the Board of Theological Education of the Senate of Serampore College (BTESSC). It thus brought together not only theological colleges affiliated to SSC but also a large number of organizations that were experimenting and articulating relevant modes of theologizing in Indian context.[118]

Till 1978, SSC was the only means of validating theological training in India. Though, Serampore was open to affiliate evangelical colleges, the evangelical leaders were not willing and instead they decided to form the Association of Evangelical Theological Education in India (AETEI) in 1979 to provide a forum for fellowship and reflection and soon linked it with Asia Theological Association (ATA), which was founded as an alternative validating agency for Evangelical Theological Education in Asia.[119]

The BTESSC today is one of the major representative bodies of Churches legally constituted and responsible for administering theological education in South Asia. It stands as a unique model of ecumenical participation of the Churches and theological institutions in curriculum planning and evaluation towards common degrees and in their quest for holistic training for ministry. The SSC carries out its theological function through the BTESSC – the arm of theological education under the SSC.[120] The functions of the Board as given in the Constitution of the BTESSC (Revised and adopted on February 3-4, 1994) read:

> i) Reflection and pioneering on new methods and style in theological education in relation to the need of the country and of the Churches.

Consider Reorganization of the Functioning of the Serampore Senate held at Lee Memorial Mission House, Wellington Square, Calcutta on March 22nd and 23rd, 1974, 352-353.

[117]Section XII of the Act states that the Senate shall make rules and regulations for the convening of its meetings and for the proper conduct of its business. *Serampore College Act, 1918*, 3.

[118]*Report on Implementation of the Scheme of the One Structure for Theological Education under SSC* (January 28th 1976), 507. See also Sahu, *Reorganizing Structure...*, 13.

[119]*Ibid.* Cf. Sahu, *Reorganizing Structure...*, 13.

[120]M. J. Joseph and J. S. Sadananda, "The Board of Theological Education – The Senate of Serampore College (BTESSC) – An Evaluation," in *Church's Participation in Theological Education*, edited by Samson Prabhakar and M. J. Joseph (Bangalore: BTESSC/SATHRI, 2003), 1. (Hereafter, Joseph and J. S. Sadananda, *The Board of Theological Education...*).

ii) Production of theological literature in general especially in regional languages.
iii) Promotion of the welfare of theological teachers and students.
iv) Development of ecumenical co-operation among theological institutions and their libraries.
v) Promotion of relationship between Churches, Theological institutions and Study Centers.
vi) Any other issues related to theological education.
vii) The Board shall recommend names of persons to be considered by the Senate for nomination to be appointed as Senators.[121]

The Registrar was responsible for the following:

i) evaluation and affiliation of colleges
ii) helping raise academic standards of colleges
iii) curriculum development
iv) examination of candidates and granting of degrees
v) M.Th. program and scholarships
vi) Keeping records, minutes of the Senate meetings, preparing for Senate meetings
vii) Other related matters.[122]

5.2. Growth in Ecumenical Cooperation

It is noteworthy that the BTESSC brought together a fellowship of more than 50 theological colleges and a good number of organizations consisting of varying theological emphases. United action and an ecumenical approach to theological education were seen as the need of the hour in the Indian context. There are numerous cooperative attempts of ecumenical theological education within the senate of Serampore family as well as outside, for instance, at Bangalore, the United Theological College and Dharmaran Vidya Kshetram brought together the protestant and the catholic scholars in the field of the History of Religion and Philosophy to pioneer academic cooperation plans from 1975.[123]

In Kerala, the joint program of Mar Thoma Theological Seminary (Kottayam) the Kerala United Theological Seminary (Trivandrum) and Orthodox Theological Seminary (Kottayam) in the form of Federated Faculty for Research in Religion and Culture in Kerala (FFRRC) foster a significant form of ecumenism in India. They even invite the catholic St. Thomas Apostolic Seminary of Vadavathoor and St. Joseph's Pontifical Seminary of Alwaye to become participating members in FFRRC.

[121]Joseph and J. S. Sadananda, *The Board of Theological Education…*, 4-5.

[122]Cf. *Report of the Review Committee, Senate and Executive Minutes*, 1979, 2.

[123]Cf. Arles, *Theological Education of the Mission…*, 294.

In West Bengal, there is another example, Serampore College and Bishop's College together developed the North Indian Institute of Post Graduate Studies (NIIPGTS) and seeks cooperation with the Morning Star College of Barrackpore. We see such attempts in almost all parts of our country. Thus, we note a progress and development in ecumenical cooperation and in the idea of federated faculties of theology for effective ecumenical theological education in India.

We observe that the BTESSC continues to carry the ecumenical character of the SSC particularly as listed in the above. Moreover, it has been through the efforts of the BTESSC's Research wing alongside South Asia Theological Research Institute (SATHRI) that continues to provide contextually relevant theological literature for theological education in India.[124] The Senate of Serampore therefore is known to be continuing its ecumenical pursuit.

The Senate of Serampore College had been earnestly incorporating the need for widening and enlarging its horizons depending on the need of the hour and context within which its theological education is situated. Ecumenism thus becomes one of its pertinent priorities in its theological education process and context. As the word 'ecumenical' originate from the Greek word 'Oikoumene' meaning the whole inhabited world or the universe, therefore ecumenism in theological education or ecumenical theological education suggests that it transcends ethnic, cultural, linguistic, sex, gender, denominational[125] and human-nonhuman barriers. Therefore, ecumenical theological education is committed to life - life in its totality and fullness.[126]

With the latest revision on the Constitution in 2005, the 'One National Structure' of the Board and the Senate is firmly established. At present, it is being administered by three centers, one at Serampore, and the other two at Bangalore and Kolkata respectively. This growth of the BTESSC and the Senate was called for strengthening its coordinated administrative structure which would be participatory, transparent and accountable. The elected officers were to have greater role and responsibility in running the affairs of the BTESSC and the Senate, which will then allow the Principals and the Boards of Studies to play effective roles in the academic matters.[127] Thus, the SSC worked its policies with regard to ecumenical theological education also through its One National Structure, the BTESSC.

---

[124]Gladstone, *Report of the President Senate of Serampore College, 2004-2005*, 15.

[125]Samson Prabhakar, "Church's Participation in Theological Education," in *Church's Participation in Theological Education*, edited by Samson Prabhakar and M. J. Joseph (Bangalore: BTESSC/SATHRI, 2003), 28. (Hereafter, Prabhakar, *Church's Participation in Theological Education…*).

[126]Prabhakar, *Church's Participation in Theological Education…*, 28-29 .

[127]Cf. Ravi, Tiwari, "Ecumenical Character of Serampore College, Part-II," *The Story of Serampore and Its College*, Fourth Edition Published by The Council of Serampore College (Serampore: CSC, 2005), 113.

6. Fostering Ecumenism in the Form of Relationship with Different Institutions

The SSC is an ecumenical body with its membership drawn from CNI, CSI, Lutheran, Methodist, Baptist, Presbyterian, Orthodox, Mar Thoma, Pentecostal and other religious traditions.[128] This concern led the SSC toward wider approach in forming theological courses, which were to have flexibility. The SSC is achieving this goal by providing a core of common studies, accepted by all as basic to sound training in theological education besides giving considerable opportunities for choice among different fields of studies. This has probably, to some extent, contributed to its popularity as being a reputed academic structure of theological education not only in India but also even in many parts of world today.

The significant progress of co-operation in ecumenical character is being seen not only in the membership of the Senate, but also in the variety of theological colleges and Seminaries being affiliated to the SSC. In 1938, the International Missionary Council Conference held at Tambaram, Tamil Nadu emphasized the importance of Theological Education. This led the National Christian Council of India to sponsor a survey of theological education in India in 1944, which worked under the title of 'Dr. C. W. Ranson Commission.'[129] Following this evaluation came many applications for affiliation, to the SSC which is still continuing till date.

The SSC also provide in this wide ecumenical profile, an open door in which the candidates have full freedom to express their own point of view on matters of theological interpretations. It is noteworthy to observe that by the co-operation of more than four hundred examiners, using all the major languages of India, and drawn from almost every denomination, the examination system of the SSC is maintained in an ecumenical pattern.[130]

The SSC and its affiliated institutions have been the cradle and catalyst of ecumenical theological education in India. The SSC, its meetings and conferences have always facilitated and encouraged the spirit of ecumenical theological education. For many years, the SSC's family has provided ecumenical forum for theological discussions and exchanging of ideas among academic institutions in India, Nepal, Bangladesh and Sri Lanka etc. The extended members of the SSC's Family from these countries further represent various church traditions and denominations including Anglicans, Baptists, Catholics, Evangelicals, Lutherans, Mennonites, Methodists, Pentecostals and Presbyterians.

Fostering ecumenism through theological education affirms the communal and cooperate nature of our human existence as expressed in the fundamental

---

[128] *Senate of Serampore College Proceedings of the Theological Senate and Its Committees…*, 186.

[129] Cf. Steward, *The Ecumenical Character of Serampore College…*, 73.

[130] *Ibid.*

functions of the church.[131] Ecumenism is therefore not just an extra but an important and constitutive part of the Church of Christ and as such, it is a very essential element to theological education as well. The life sagas of India's sub-continent, the Indian population themselves, their pain and sorrow, misery and despair have now become an integral part of the data of theological education. As mentioned earlier the SSC and its affiliated institutions and Seminaries need to expose the students and trainees to the real life's situations of poverty, violence, suffering, pain, oppression, corruption and struggle of the people.

Ecumenism through theological education is for the whole people of God, equipping them for the whole ministry of Jesus Christ. That being the case, theological education is not confined to ministerial formation alone. Theological education transcends the goal of degrees. Theological education therefore is not the exclusive prerogative of those literally seeking to be ordained. Ecumenism in theological education is an important tool that facilitates the training and equipping of all God's people for the variety of leadership roles both in the church and in the society at large.

Plurality of religious faiths is a given reality in India. This plurality of faiths while it is source of the beauty of India's diversity, it is also equally a source of tensions and conflicts. Thus, the SSC continues to struggle in developing methodologies that could adequately equip and enable beneficiaries of the process to interpret not just the Christian experience, but also the ability to interpret other living faiths' experiences.[132] Thus, to a large extent, SSC and its affiliated institutions/seminaries have learned and continue to do so, from the experience of living and ministering in a profoundly pluralistic religious and cultural setting and therefore, theological educators and Indian theologians are challenged not to confine their theological thinking just to the concerns of doctrinal confessions of different denominations but also to think theologically about the other faiths as well. Hence, our ecumenical theological education should respond to the plurality and inter-dependence of the human global community in which we need to learn how to live together.

It is observed that the ecumenical contextual matrix of every single discipline in the theological educational curriculum must be highlighted with an ecumenical viewpoint and resources so that the institutions could at the same time become academic as well as ecumenical in praxis.[133] Theological education in India would be excellent only if it commune with people who are living and

---

[131] Cf. M. Douglas Meeks "Globalization and the Oikoumene in Theological Education" in *Ecumenical and Interreligious Perspectives: Globalization in Theological Education*, ed., Russell E. Richey (Nashville: Quarterly Review Books, 1992), 4.

[132] Cf. John B. Lindner, *Ecumenical Formation: A Methodology for a Pluralistic Age* (Switzerland: WCC, 1999), 10.

[133] Cf. John S. Pobee "Ecumenical Formation in the Service of a Renewed Church" *The Ecumenical Review,* Vol. 53, 3 (July, 2001), 322.

find them to be relevant. It is only through such living interaction that the SSC can meaningfully talk of a relevant ecumenical theological education in India. Therefore, our theological education should be very diligent in its ecumenical venture so that it does not go and bandage a person's head while all the time the fellow had been holding his head and groaning in excruciating pain for his horribly severed kneecap! Any effort of theological education in India should become increasingly aware that the process of ecumenical theological education should always be grounded in real contemporary issues that centers on the mission of shaping people's lives and transforming their attitudes, lifestyles and values in both Church and Society.

Ecumenicity in India's pluralistic context is to certain extent, been strengthened by the conscious efforts and participation of the colleges and institutions especially those of theological education that recognizes and makes significant contribution toward ecumenical vision. As a result, the SSC strongly affirms its commitment to ecumenism and acknowledges the need to support those national ecumenical theological colleges which require assistance in terms of funds, literature and resource persons.[134] Altogether, these institutions help promote and provide a mature perspective on and positive encouragement to, ecumenical relations in terms of matters of faith and order and the life and function of churches as a whole.

In India, there are numerous theological institutions, seminaries, Bible colleges and Bible schools which are not part of the SSC, but function independently and are run by individual founders or by co-founders; sponsored by some individual organizations; as well as those that are run by church groups etc. No doubt, those colleges, seminaries and institutions related to each other within the BTESSC have a great degree of intercontextuality as they are related to each other in terms of partnership in theological education, but the BTESSC family also being part of a wider global family of theological education, it is of great need that it also consider its relationship with those non-Serampore theological families for a wider form of ecumenism.

It is well known that for the last few decades in our country, mushrooming[135] of theological colleges has become a great concern. If bodies like BTESSC, ATA and independent group continue to co-exist parallel to each other without much mutual involvement it could end up with a situation of structural aparthcid in theological education system in India as a whole in the future. Therefore, to what extent are we able to cooperate and build bridges to theological education networks beyond the BTESSC - without lowering our own standards or giving

[134]Cf. *Senate of Serampore College Proceedings of the Theological Senate and Its Committees…*, 17.

[135]For example, within fifteen years or so, in Nagaland alone, it has established more than 40 Theological Colleges, Bible Schools, and Bible Institutions. Out of these more than 40 institutions, only three are affiliated to the BTESSC. The remaining majority are either accredited under the ATA or independently run by individual founders.

up our essential convictions that have been the result of several decades of the ecumenical concern, should be seriously pondered upon for wider structure of ecumenism.

7. Fostering Ecumenism through Concerns with Other Living Faiths

7.1. Introduction

Today, we live in a multicultural society. As a result of globalization and migration, our contemporary world has become pluralistic, with monocultures giving way to multicultural. And with the multicultural reality also comes the multireligious - a new situation that compels the Christian Church in India and its theology to rethink and relate itself to this rapidly growing phenomenon. We are aware that all around us, people of diverse religio-cultural persuasions are getting closer to each other on a global scale and this contact already serves as an unproclaimed dialogue—an ongoing dialogue of an informal nature. In such a situation, distances are now being cut down, in certain areas, in place of confrontations, compromises are emerging. For instance, in educational institutions, lecture rooms, libraries, canteens, buses, offices, faculty common rooms, and playgrounds are all meeting places for adherents of a legion of religious traditions. Therefore questions like, 'What then should be our theological orientation and ecumenical praxis towards this plurality of faiths?' And, 'how do we interpret all the other living faiths' experiences that our ever-increasing pluralistic culture provides?' becomes crucially important.

We notice that the historical context of India has changed. Communication system, globalization and liberalization of market continue to make much more expedient for religious studies and cooperation among different nations. We now have reached a point where no one can live in isolation. Looking at this wider amiable environment from a positive perspective, sincere effort should be invested for purpose of strengthening the ecumenical relationship of the BTESSC and other living faiths through meaningful dialogue.

7.2. The BTESSC and Inter-Religious Dialogue

According to the definition followed in this research, the term *ecumenism* obliges the BTESSC to enter into dialogue with people of other faith traditions. The BTESSC's vision is not only to bring unity and renewal among the different Christian denominations and institutions, but also to transcend the Christendom boundary on to a worldwide level and seek the cooperation and unity of the whole inhabited earth. Thus, the BTESSC's pattern of theological education "ought to be taught and done in relation to the people of other faiths and to take inter-religious dialogue seriously".[136]

---

[136]Emmanuel Martey, "Theological Education as Catalyst for Ecumenical Formation in Africa: The Role of Associations of Theological Institutions—the Case of WAATI," *Ministerial Formation*, 98/99, (July/October, 2002), 17.

In India's context, theology of dialogue has become one of the most significant concerns and has found a firm foothold of acceptance among the Christians and non-Christians. Such a theological understanding has led the BTESSC to initiate a number of contacts with other living faiths in the country for dialogue. The term 'dialogue' is derived from the Greek original *dia-logos* which literally means 'through word.' Dialogue is therefore 'talking together' or 'conversation' or 'communicating' with one another. Interreligious dialogue is primarily a conversation between believers of different faiths or religious traditions. Initially, inter-religious dialogue is understood as an encounter between people who represent different faith traditions in an environment of mutual trust and acceptance. According to S. Wesley Ariarajah, inter-faith dialogue is seen as,

> a way not only to become informed about the faiths of others but also to rediscover essential dimensions of one's own faith tradition. The benefits of removing historical prejudices and enmities as well as new possibilities for working together for common good [are] recognized and affirmed.[137]

Hence, Inter-religious dialogue opens the door of possibility for Christians to join other oppressed and exploited people of the world in the experience of mutual respect and enrichment. It means, through inter-religious dialogue, Christians come to a common platform where people meet each other without fear or suspicion of each other's hidden agendas and intentions. It further means that we come without any inhibitions and experience this dialogue even with the vast majority of those who perceive "their ultimate concern and symbolize their struggle for liberation in the idiom of non-Christian religions and cultures."[138] It is thus our contemporary understanding of ecumenism with its concomitant theological orientation towards the more radical questions dealing with the survival of the whole inhabited earth that lead us into theological and inter-faith dialogue—that is, an informed, creative and committed action undertaken to shape, transform and heal our ailing and divided world. Inter-religious dialogue then, "expands the existing boundaries of orthodoxy and enters into the liberative streams of other religions and cultures."[139]

Inter-Religious concern brings a closer look to the responsibility that upholds human rights, pluralism, democracy and the role of law. It opens one's concept of wider understanding by avoiding the folly of rigidity and totalitarianism

[137]S.W. Ariarajah, "Dialogue, Inter-faith", *The Dictionary of the Ecumenical Movement*, ed., N. Lossky (Grand Rapids: Wm. B. Eerdmans Publishing Co., 1991), 314. (Hereafter, Ariarajah, *Dialogue, Inter-faith…*).

[138]Aloysius Pieris, "The Place of Non-Christian Religions and Cultures in the Evolution of Third World Theology," *Irruption of the Third World: Challenge to Theology*, ed., Virginia Fabella and Sergio Torres, (Maryknoll: Orbis Books, 1983), 113. (Hereafter, Pieris, *The Place of Non-Christian Religions and Cultures…*).

[139]Pieris, *The Place of Non-Christian Religions and Cultures…*, 114.

and affirms the standards set out in international human rights instruments.[140] Inter-Religious dialogue is a privilege for those strong and the wise that are not hampered by the spirit of timid incompatibility to doubt their aptitude to move towards truth through a multiplicity of positions and notions and through this understanding the meaning of living and concern with other living faiths is realized.

Inter-Religious dialogue does not mean weakening of one's convictions of faith. Instead, it challenges and encourages us to accept and respect each other's faith, accept one another just as we are and live in peace.[141] It has been observed that practically all anti-ecumenical and fundamentalist influence is based on denial of inter-religious dialogue as a tolerable Christian attitude.[142] A cordial living is not possible in the multi-confessional and multi-religious world without mutual respect and understanding. Such a richer concept of inter-religious dialogue need to be addressed very seriously as one of the continuing urgent priorities in ecumenical theological education under the Senate of Serampore.

As discussed in the third chapter of our present study, the question of other living faiths had been one of the main concerns of the modern Ecumenical Movement through the 1950s and 1960s.[143] This concern of inter-religious dialogue is aimed at enabling the pluralistic faith society to respect each other's faiths, have a full knowledge of their beliefs, enter into a closer relationship with others and to refrain from accusing each other or to stop themselves from indulging in an unending blame-game.[144] In this regard, persons like P. D. Devanandan and M. M. Thomas pioneered in the 1950s studies regarding religious dialogue in order to develop the spirit of respect for each other's faith.[145] Such pioneering steps

---

[140]Cf. *http://www.peace.ru/tolerance/doc.htm* (10-10-2008), 1.

[141]Cf. *http://www.peace.ru/tolerance/doc.htm* (10-10-2008), 1.

[142]Vladimir, Fedoroy, "Challenges to Theological Education in Central and Eastern Europe: Education as a Liturgy before Liturgy," *Ministerial Formation 101 WCC* (July, 2003): 17.

[143]This concern had led to the serious discussions on the concept of dialogue with other living faiths at an important meeting in Kandy (1967) and at the WCC assembly in Uppsala in 1968. However, these discussions were among the Christians themselves. One of the landmarks in the WCC's dialogue journey was the first inter-faith dialogue meeting held in Ajaltoun, Lebanon, in March 1970. It brought together three Hindus, four Buddhists, three Muslims and several Christians to explore the meaning and significance of dialogue as a new basis for relationships among religious traditions. The concern was that Religion should respect the other faiths and has a full knowledge of their beliefs, enters into a closer relationship with others and should refrain from judgmental attitudes.

[144]Religion is a serious affair to every Indian. Indian spirituality is deeply rooted in Indian spiritual heritage. Religion and politics are inseparable in Indian tradition. The politicians have become the spokesmen of every religion in India. Owing to this meddling of religion and politics, in modern days the religions have become a dividing and destructive force. As a result, Christian faith has to be in constant dialogue with other living faiths.

[145]Cf. Paul, Tillich, *Christianity and the Religions of the World* (New York: Columbia University Press, 1963), 22.

encouraged and enabled the SSC and the churches in India to play a significant role in organizing several meetings and seminars on the importance of inter-religious dialogue in India.[146]

Religiously plural context such as India where communal conflict is currently dividing and creating chaos the country is very much in need of inter-faith dialogue.[147] Through inter-religious dialogue the reality of religious pluralism in our society can be openly addressed and infuse the awareness concerning the necessity of peaceful co-existence and peace-loving nation whereby, India's reality of diversity of race, castes, creeds and cultures could be re-presented as life's blessing of the beauty of richness rather than as a divisive element. Hence, the question that arises today for theological education and the SSC in particular is, in our mission of fostering ecumenism, 'is our theological orientation and ecumenical praxis towards this plurality of religious faiths been adequately dealt with?' Or, 'should we not go further than this or is this sufficient?'

7.3. Inter-religious Dialogue within a Pluralistic Society

In the context of diversity and plurality, the focus of inter-religious dialogue ought to be guarded by ecumenical theological education. The pluralities and diversities have become part of the life of the people.[148] Our country is a multicultural, multilingual, multiethnic and multi-religious nation and this plurality at the same time has been the reason for many of its conflicts, outbursts of violence and atrocities against one another,[149] whereby, "national integration remained ever threatened as it faced the problems of linguistic communalism, religious fanaticism and factional politics".[150] The very recent religious conflicts emerged in Orissa and some other parts of India between the Hindus and the Christians, and these contribute to the amassing of bitter feelings and hatred between the concerned communities, compelling them to live in highly-charged tension that could potently fuel bigger outbursts and violence against one another in the near future.

---

[146]Cf. Mathai, Zachariah, *Beyond Ecumenism: A Journey in Light,* (Thiruvalla: CSS, 2002), 80. In 1975, the National Council of Churches in India started a unit on Unity, Fellowship and Dialogue.

[147]Cf. Rajaiah D. Paul, *Ecumenism in Action: Church of the South India and Assessment* (Madras: CLS, 1972), 139.

[148]J. W. Gladstone, "Ministerial Formation in a Context of Pluralities" *Together with People* ed., Samson Prabakar (Bangalore: SATHRI/BTESSC, 2004), 57.

[149]Cf. Samson, Prabhakar, "Religious Education in India Context: Challenges and Response," *Together with People*, ed., by Samson Prabhakar (Bangalore: SATHRI/BTESSC, 2004), 94.

[150]Cf. Paul, R. Brass, *Factional Politics in an Indian State: The Congress Party in Uttar Pradesh* (Bombay: OUP Press, 1966), 265.

Hence, Christians, churches and theological educational structures should consider these factors responsibly in putting common efforts and pooling of possible resources for moving forward with a transparent sincerity that the neighboring communities could respond with equal sincerity so as to work together for the common and greater form of ecumenism. This could be the only viable path toward any hope of peaceful co-existence and mutual enrichment of life's beauty of differences and its riches. The national amalgamation, nation's harmony and sovereignty and people's pleasant existence together solely depend on meaningful and sincere inter-religious dialogue.[151]

Very often it has been noted that this inter-religious dialogue should go beyond the mere gathering of Christian leaders and the leaders of other living faiths although such initiatives has its own share of positive outcomes. It is suggested very strongly that dialogue should be carried out within the practical set up of the peoples themselves – living together and beside one another in genuine appreciation, respect and trust toward one another – without giving oneself to the spirit of dissension, distrust, disrespect and self-centered egoism and so forth.[152] This inter-religious that give space to each other takes place when people of various faith witness to the other concerning the values they have found in their faith, and through the daily practice of respecting each other's faith and show themselves to be a god-fearing neighbour.

7.4. A Paradigm Shift in Inter-Religious Dialogue: A Practical Dialogical Living with One Another

In this 21st century therefore, the urgent need within the context of ecumenical theological education on the subject of inter-religious dialogue is a paradigm shift - a shift from the level of scholars and religious leaders to the grassroots level of the believers and of the people. In this paradigm shift the important concern is inter-religious dialogical living or simply put inter-religious dialogue praxis. It means, not only talking from the scholarly perspective but dialogical praxis need to be taken in all the diverse aspects of human life - acceptance of not just one but the many practices in all the social realm of the present context.

Our country is a nation with various religious communities with countless traditions, charismatic movements; militant and fanatic groups with their own self-motivated philosophical and political vision.[153] In this paradigm shift within our context, when people of diverse faiths live together, work, study, struggle, celebrate, and mourn together and face the crisis of injustices and fatal illnesses like HIV/AIDS together, the fundamental need is to focus on immediate survival of

151Thyagorajan, *Inter-religious Dialogue* (N.d., n.p.), 500.

152M. A. Thomas, *Towards Wider Ecumenism* (Bangalore: ATC, 1993), 110.

153Cf. Thomas, Manickam, "Theological Education in the Cultural Philosophical Context of India Today," *Theological Education in India Today,* ed., by Felix Wilfred (Bangalore: ATC, 1985), 57.

all. Therefore, inter-religious dialogue in theological education is to be understood as the sharing of life at all levels among the believers of diverse faiths.

In a multicultural and multireligious global environment, dialogue becomes necessary as a means of promoting understanding and acquaintance with our neighbours. Without dialogue, we will eventually find ourselves in an unending heap of all kinds of conflicts. In our pluralistic context therefore, dialogue becomes an inevitable remedy to reach the goal of mutual basis for peaceful co-existence. In this, theological education needs to open up to other faiths, thoughts and experiences in order to have an authentic approach in the context of religious pluralism.[154] The task of theological education in this context is to explore and formulate a theology of inter-faith dialogue.[155] Any program of theological education, which fails to perceive or deliberately ignores the reality of religious pluralism in India is bound to be isolated and irrelevant.

The Indian historical situation thus called for a search for a theological education in the context of religious pluralism. In the words of Lesslie Newbigin:

> Outstanding (India) Christian thinkers... saw both the renaissance of Hinduism and the growth of a concern for nation building... (as) part of the consequences of the impact of Christ upon Indian society. They therefore called their fellow Christians to work of interfaith dialogue in the context of the quest for national unity with the conviction that this was part of the

[154]Cf. Godwin R. Singh, "Theological Education in the Context of Pluralistic Religious Society," *Theological Education and Development*, ed., by Gnana Robinson, Henry Wilson and Christopher Duraising (Bangalore: ATTI, 1984), 4-5. (Hereafter, Singh, *Theological Education in the Context...*).

[155]K. P. Aleaz, "Inter-Faith Reality and Ecumenical Theological Education", *WCC Ministerial Formation* (January, 2003), 86. With regard to the affect of the interfaith dialogue on the theological education is the theological institutions are offering courses on Hinduism, Islam, Primal Religions and evangelistic approach to them were taught. In the 1970s the Senate of Serampore makes it a compulsory subject on Modern Religious and Secular Movements in India. Dialogue departments or programs were opened in some of the theological institutions such as Tamil Nadu Theological Seminary, Gurukul Theological College, and United Theological College etc. See the detail B.Th. and B.D. Course Syllabi of the Senate of Serampore College (Serampore: Senate of Serampore College, 1993). In 1980 Arvind Nirmal suggested possible elements of a curriculum revision in the context of Inter-Religious Dialogue. In the study of the Bible to take note of the inter-religious dialogue that shaped the Bible itself and develop a religious criticism of the Bible; in the study of Christian Theology to develop a Christian theology which is in dialogue with other religions, ideologies and other academic disciplines; in the study of Church History to begin to study the history of Christianity as a social history probing into the motivational factors that caused the conversions and developments in a dialogical manner, and the study of Christian Ministry, to take note of the liturgical and worship elements in other religions and the developments in psychology, yoga and meditation for counseling in Indian situation. Cf. Arvind Nirmal, "Some Theological Issues Connected with Inter-Faith Dialogue and Their Implication for Theological Education in India", *BTF*, XII/2 (January-June, 1980), 107-129.

continuing work of Christ in Indian society. The basis of their call to dialogue was in their Christian faith.[156]

It has been rightly stated that dialogue is not a secret weapon in the armory of an aggressive Christian militancy.[157] Dialogue must not be misunderstood as a non-commitant academic approach to another faith.[158] Basically, interfaith dialogue was understood as an encounter between people who live by different faith traditions, in an atmosphere of mutual trust and acceptance.[159] Dialogue did not require giving up, hiding or seeking to validate one's own religious conviction; in fact, the need for being rooted in one's own tradition to be engaged in a meaningful dialogue was emphasized, as were common humanity and the need to search in a divided world for life in community. Dialogue was seen as a way not only to become informed about the faiths of others but also to rediscover essential dimensions of one's own faith tradition.[160]

The benefits of removing historical prejudices and enmities as well as the seeking of new possibilities for working together for common good were recognized and affirmed. Some see dialogue primarily as a new and creative relationship within which one can learn about and respect others but also can give authentic witness to one's own faith. Others see it as an important historical moment in the development of religious traditions, in which each of the faith traditions in dialogue is challenged and transformed by the encounter with others. Still others view dialogue as a common pilgrimage towards the truth, within which each tradition shares with the others the way it has come to perceive and respond to that truth.[161]

Greater awareness of religious plurality has heightened the need of improved relations and dialogue among people of different faiths. Religion speaks for some of the deepest feelings and sensitivity of individuals and communities; it carries profound historical memories and often appeals to uncritical confessional solidarities.[162] Moreover today the growing need is not just for dialogue with people of other faiths but for genuine relationships with them. Increased awareness of

---

[156]M. M. Thomas, *Risking Christ for Christ's Sake* (Geneva: WCC Publication, 1987), 111.

[157]Conservative Christians question the purpose of dialogue; they fear that it denies the need for people of other faiths to convert to Christian faith.

[158]The majority of evangelicals take to traditional evangelistic method of preaching, tract distribution and personal evangelism. To them, dialogue takes place at the personal evangelistic setting only, but never at the academic level. Evangelicals disown and distrust the ecumenical dialogue as betraying the gospel of Jesus Christ.

[159]Ariarajah, *Dialogue, Inter-faith...*, 325.

[160]Cf. Andrew, Wingale, "Interreligious Dialogue, Conflict and Reconciliation", *WCC Current Dialogue*, 14 (July, 2003), 18.

[161]Ariarajah, *Dialogue, Inter-faith...*, 313.

[162]John D'Arcy May, "The Dialogue of Religions; Source of Knowledge Means of Peace", *WCC Current Dialogue*, 43 (July, 2004), 17.

religious plurality, the potential role of religion in conflict, and the growing pace of public life presents as an urgent challenge that require greater understanding and cooperation among people of diverse faiths.[163] Thus, Stanley J. Samartha called for "a whole new way of understanding the task of theological education, to speak in inclusive ways so that it recovers the true meaning of the oikoumene and makes sense to the calling of the Church to live in the midst of pluralism".[164] He further elaborates:

> What we need today is a theology that is not less but more true to God by being generous and open, a theology not less but more loving toward the neighbour by being friendly and willing to listen, a theology that does not separate us from our fellow human beings but supports us in our common struggles and hopes. As we live together with our neighbours, what we need today is a theology that refuses to be impregnable, but which, in the spirit of Christ, is both ready and willing to be vulnerable.[165]

7.5. Theological Education in the Context of Inter-Religious Dialogue

Theological education should seek to make dialogue as an indispensable style of living in the pluralistic milieu. Dialogue of inter-religious faiths has become a permanent Christian obligation, no longer a triumphalistic understanding of mission in the past. It is an inevitable enterprise in a religious pluralistic context in which aspects of servanthood and Lordship of Christ can be discerned.[166] It should emerge as an authentic process of learning in theological education and develop a contextualized hermeneutics of its own that will lead the learner to a profound encounter between the word of God and its realities in the religious pluralistic context. Theological education in this situation has to be praxis-oriented. It must lead those engaged in it to process of involvement in practical context of life and to learn to make decisions and choices. Thus, by participating in the struggles of the communities the authenticity of theological education can be tested. In order to be relevant to the religious pluralistic context, the curricula of the theological program need to be oriented toward issues of the present reality.[167]

---

[163]Ariane, Hentsch, "Religious Identities in Pluralistic Societies. How do we Choose them, Manage them, and Live them fully?," *WCC Current Dialogue*, 46 (December, 2005), 5.

[164]S. J. Samarhta, "The Holy Spirit and People of Various Faiths, Cultures and Ideologies", *The Holy Spirit*, edited by Dow Kirkpatrick (Tennessee: Tidings Publications, 1974), 37. See also Horst Burkle, "The Debate of the Cosmic Christ as Example of an Ecumenically Oriented Theology" *INDIAN Voices in Today's Theological Debate*, edited by H. Burkle and W. Roth (Delhi: ISPCK, 1972), 199.

[165]*Ibid.*, 38.

[166]Singh, *Theological Education in the Context…*, 41.

[167]Cf. Singh, *Theological Education in the Context…*, 42-43.

The thrusts of the theological education in India's context need to be so directed as to allow the students to create an intelligent understanding of the religious and cultural life of the pluralistic context. Theological education should comprehend the totality of the contextual pluralism.[168] Thus, Ecumenism in religious dialogue is learning to explain and striving to discover, getting to know and love another person with his or her fundamental differences. Ecumenical theological education therefore, should be able to enlighten us to understand the plurality of the humanity and of the universe, and to establish more just and liberating relationship among the different living faiths.[169]

Summary

While there was an ecumenical spirit behind its historic beginning, the SSC became much more prominent after became the center for national structure of theological education in India in the year 1975 – the BTESSC. Since then, the BTESSC reflect the combined vision and mission of both the church and theological institutions in participation for the purpose of developing and thereby strengthening the responsibility of training Christian ministers for a wider and encompassing mission of the gospel. It began to work toward its ecumenical pattern of theological education. As seen, its ecumenical character is characterized by its curriculum that is designed in accordance to the real life and experiences of the people. It therefore, stresses the necessity of both theoretical as well as practical learning for relevancy whereby their learning and training will have concrete applicability upon the concrete experiences of the people.

We also observe its ecumenical character in its relationship with different denominations as well as different institutions that are brought together under its affiliating structure. Another aspect of its ecumenism is its participation (with NCCI in partnership) in the cause of interrelationship with people of other living faiths. It recognizes the fact that mere external dialogue is meaningless and therefore proposes for a deeper form of dialogue in which people of diverse faiths could truly come together, live together, discover and share each other's positive values and mutually enrich without the necessity of losing one's own faith or convictions. Thus, the SSC under the BTESSC has been seriously giving its efforts in fostering ecumenism in its theological education although we can assume that there are still areas and aspects that it has yet to give serious consideration in order that it move further ahead in encompassing a real and a more adequate form of ecumenism in its theological vision for an ecumenical-intended context of India.

Once again here, the researcher does not pretend to have done adequate justice to the task of critically analyzing the role of the SSC in fostering ecumenism in theological education in India and yet on the same note can conclude that, that

[168]Cf. Singh, *Theological Education in the Context...*, 46.

[169]Cf. Romer Portillo, "The Contextual and Ecumenical in Venezuelan Theological Education," *http://www.coe.org/wcc/what/education/mf100.pdf.* (11.01.05), 41.

was as far as he could go at present. Therefore, on that mixed note of humility and comfort, let us now head toward the last or the crux chapter of our thesis - the sixth chapter, which is completely devoted to the results or findings of our overall thesis under the heading, *Ecumenical Theological Education under the Senate of Serampore College/University: Findings, Prospective Criticisms and Suggestions.*

Chapter 6

Ecumenical Theological Education under the Senate of Serampore College/University Findings, Prospective Criticisms and Suggestions

1. Importance of 'Ecumenism' in Theological Education

Today our world is defined by both growth and degeneration. In this highly developed world, we have so much to boast about as well as so much to cringe with fear. It is a world where people live with fear every day of the uncertainties so also of the inevitable problems that they knew is impeding. Theological education in such a context need to understand that its vision and mission must be critically evaluated in terms of its understanding of, commitment to and relevance to the real lives and issues of the people within their given context. It is not a matter of 'choice' but of a 'must' to make it contextual, ecumenical and therefore meaningful in its total endeavor.

It is true that ecumenical theological education as a process does not occur in a vacuum rather it occurs in the context of the Church and of society.[1] Ecumenical theological education is part of the Church's ministry. Though, a seminary operates mainly within the Church, it is not limited to its four walls as it leads to ecumenical ministerial formation and therefore, there is a need for a closer interaction between the theological institutions and the Churches in our country. The cooperation between the SSC and the Churches need to be developed on the basis of mutual commitment, responsibility, respect and accountability, wherein, the churches share their ideas and concerns with the intellectually qualified teachers and persons of theology to include their views and responses.

[1]Cf. John Joshua Raja, "Relevant and Effective Theological Education in the Twenty First Century India," *Ministry Formation* (January, 2003), 9. (Hereafter, Raja, *Relevant and Effective Theological Education...*).

The co-operation between the church and theological institutions should not be limited to the institutional levels but should also include the co-operation of the local congregations and lay members of the Churches. Their feedback could add further help for the theological teachers and students to understand and reflect upon their own theological precepts.[2]

Theological institutions within the SSC should take up the role of a servant, prophet, priest and ecumenist while interacting with the Church and society. It is important that ecumenical theological education seriously take the need of the Church and try to meet its expectations during training, while, at the same time, maintaining academic autonomy. Churches in India on the other hand also need to recognize the SSC's ecumenical commitment and academic autonomy as part of the Churches' wider ministry. In this context, the SSC has to take the context of the people as a framework for interpreting the biblical text, their Churches' traditions and their faith experiences.[3] Unless the SSC recognizes the importance of the meaning of ecumenical theological education that arises from different contexts in India, it is not possible to highlight the relevant meaning of our faith and also of our traditions.[4]

Globalization is making an impact on every section of the society in India, which has brought in the multinational companies and promoted the values of individualism and achievement without any safe-guarding ethical or moral principles. It has contributed to the existing exploitative tendencies of the globalized elite and its high and mighty.[5] In such a context, the SSC has a crucial role to play - a major role along with the Church in bringing awareness about the social realities of our Indian context. Thus, by taking these social realities into its core process of theologizing, the role of the SSC could be widened and could also enable the theological students and Christian ministers to play a significant role in the wider society of our country where Christians are only a minority.[6]

Religious fundamentalism has become a threat to the multi-cultural society where people coming from different religious backgrounds lived together. Today, because of the increasing role of fundamentalists and fanatics, destructive confrontations between different religious communities have become a reality in many parts of India.[7] Despite this reality, majority of the people in India believe in the peaceful co-existence of different religions together.[8] People are searching

---

[2]Raja, *Relevant and Effective Theological Education...*, 11-14.

[3]*Ibid.*, 12.

[4]Cf. Judo Poerwowidagdo, *Towards the 21st Century: Challenges and Opportunities for Theological Education* (Geneva: WCC, Publications, 1993), 15.

[5]Evelyn Monterio, *Emerging Theological Issues in India*, A Paper presented at the regional consultation on Theological priorities in India, Pune (March, 2001), 6.

[6]Cf. Raja, *Relevant and Effective Theological Education...*, 12.

[7]*Indian Tribune: Reaction of Indian Press*, Babri Masjid Issue (December, 1992), 2.

[8]Raja, *Relevant and Effective Theological Education...*, 14.

for social and religious meanings within their own respective faiths and traditions that would enable them to live together in peace. In such complex context the task of theological education is to recognize and respect the presence of other religious faiths and the importance of harmonious interfaith co-existence. It is essential that the SSC theological community along with the Churches in India attempt to engage themselves in the people's fervent search for religious and cultural meanings for a peacefully fulfilling life.

The SSC have already been taking some of these issues into the system of its theological education. However, the SSC need to review its curriculum further in order to improve our present system with the purpose of fulfilling the need of the Church as well as the society as a whole. While retaining the academic standard, SSC is also committed to the spiritual formation of the students. The task before the theological institutions thus is to get involved in shaping the intellectual thinking of the nation and to provide a credible critique of political and economic development.

2. Findings of the Research

Following are some of the noteworthy areas that the SSC has made significant contribution toward fostering ecumenism in its theological education:

2.1. Ecumenism and the Senate of Serampore College

2.1.1. *The Birth of the Senate of Serampore College and the Spirit of Ecumenism Behind It*

From the beginning of its formation, the SSC can be said to have an ecumenical footing. In other words, concerning the SSC, there is the hidden presence of an ecumenical spirit behind its formation. The Serampore Trio brought the vision of establishing or rather starting a college for a two-tier purpose and that is:

a) Theological or Religious Education and
b) English and European Scientific Education.

William Carey in particular saw the needs of the people of that period. Although, he was (in fact all 3 of them were) a Christian missionary who came to India for the mission of the Gospel of Christ, yet they neither ignored nor neglected the overall context of the people and their state of life. In addition, although their mission was solely concerning the spiritual salvation of the people and for which they preached the Good News of the Gospel, they were very much aware of the people's low standard of life and therefore they felt that along with the evangelization of the people, they should also be educated or conscientized in the secular scientific knowledge. They believed that, both theological and secular education should be imparted and trained so that the people will be able to understand the overall reality of their life, their society and the world at large.

It is only through this total learning that the people could truly relate with and meaningfully impact, their own lives and their society as a whole. Hence, the Serampore missionaries' main aim in opening a theological training as well as a western scientific learning institution was for the necessity of imparting moral and the social or secular knowledge. Since both the aspects form one total reality, one cannot for one therefore neglect the other as both are part of one reality at the same time and in the same context.

They trained the students not just for their own individual welfare and not even just for one's own immediate families or neighbors but instead sent out their trained students as missionaries to their own villages and areas to pass on what they have experienced and learned. In this way, they were able to impact others for peoples' spiritual and moral growth as well as for improvement of socio-economic, political and cultural standard of life of the people in general.

2.1.2. *The Ecumenical Structure of the Senate of Serampore as an Affiliating Centre and Board*

The second significant area in which the SSC could foster ecumenism was when it became the main affiliation body as the SSC with the power to affiliate those of the then interested theological Colleges and Seminaries across the nation and other parts of the world. As has been already noted, those colleges were previously under the sole authority and administration of individual founders, co-founders, of various Churches or of some associations and the like. They were from different denominational backgrounds, with even doctrinal differences, yet, all could come together as one when they began to come forward and became members of their affiliation parent body. Thus, the phrase "affiliated to the SSC" became the uniting indenture for all the colleges and seminaries that were under the umbrella of the SSC. This initial aspect of ecumenism in the SSC became a great milestone as it were to serve as an important instrument in broadening the scope of ecumenical theological education under the SSC. By its success in bringing together diverse colleges and their varied socio-cultural, denominational and doctrinal backgrounds, into its affiliating umbrella, the SSC's ecumenical aspect could widen all the more. How so? It was not just that the colleges represent the socio-cultural, denominational and doctrinal diversity but furthermore, the contexts of the colleges in the form of the enrolment of students as well as the faculty structure represent even wider body of ecumenism. As the colleges began to grow in both quality and quantity, the number of the enrolment of students as well as the strength of faculty began to increase whereby it also means the ecumenical structure of the SSC is extended as many more were added in and through the enrolment of students and teachers representing diverse Church's traditions, denominations, organizations, doctrines as well as the socio-cultural differences.

2.1.3. *The Ecumenical Character of the Senate of Serampore Curriculum*

Besides, the SSC takes the subject of its curriculum very seriously especially in the context of India's pluralistic reality. Theological education in India's context is truly tasking because of India's pluralistic character. It would not be wrong if one were to argue that we should say theological education in India's contexts rather than context simply because India as a nation fortunately or unfortunately happens to embody an unbelievable plurality of contexts. India is characterized by a variety of social, cultural, religious and political differences. Its population is likewise characterized by racial and ethnic differences. It is no wonder therefore that some (non-Indians) finds it baffling how India is able to survive normally within such a legion of background differences. Hence, doing theology in India's context or contexts is neither an easy nor a comfortable task.

Let us here take a simple yet thought-provoking example - doing theology in the North East India's context especially among the tribals eventually leads to the formation of tribal theology. However, while it is true that it is a tribal theology in India's context, yet this particular tribal theology cannot be taken as authoritative or valid as 'the' tribal theology of India for the whole of India's tribal realities. It would never do because India has a good number of tribal communities, who cannot be clubbed together as a common reality due to the fact that though they are tribals, they are divided in accordance to the numerously different and distinctive backgrounds, races, cultures, religions, beliefs, practices, and so forth. Therefore, tribal theology of the North East India is meaningfully relevant, valid and authoritative only to and for those particular tribals of North East and not for any other tribal groups scattered in and around the country.

As the above example clearly shows concerning the complex reality of India's context for our theological education, the SSC has been actively working in order to see that its theological education do not neglect the necessity of taking into serious account the diverse needs of the diversely situated contexts of the people in the structuring and formation of its curriculum. Therefore, it has been careful in introducing subjects that could be considered common to all the contexts of its affiliated colleges and at the same time, it also gives certain autonomy to the individual colleges and seminaries to introduce their own contextually relevant course of subjects. A very latest effort of the Senate of Serampore concerning its sensitive response to the necessity of working out its academic curriculum in ecumenical line is the setting up of a special committee with the aim of revising its entire curriculum. This is carried out by taking into consideration the views and opinions of the whole of the senate affiliated colleges and seminaries as well as churches, organizations, representatives and educators from other higher fields and disciplines. Eventually, gathering all the feedbacks in written forms, the committee then seriously scrutinizes the critiques, comments and suggestions of the representative colleges, seminaries, churches and other respective bodies so that the SSC could re-evaluate its overall structure of theological education. It thus identifies the areas and aspects that need to be incorporated in its curriculum revision framework with the aim of refining and improvising its curriculum for effective and meaningful relevancy as per the needs and demands of the contexts and time.

Keeping such complex reality of India's plurality in our mind let us now come to the immediate concern at hand.[9] Theology is faith seeking understanding. Faith is belief in God but not just in the existence of, but rather a belief in God in relation to our very real life; a belief in God, in his/her presence in our midst, in the total aspects of our lives, in the concerns of this world - God's very own wonders of creation which continue to teach, sustain, empower and strengthen that aspect of divine image in us, leading us to discern, to choose what is good over what is not and so forth. In other words, faith is belief in God right where we ourselves are situated - living, active, moving and growing in that knowledge. It is a belief in the meaning, value, significance and purpose of the totality of life, of every life of creation that is grounded in its creator God - the God of all creation.

So then, theology as faith seeking understanding, and, faith being an interrelated experience of understanding the invincible relationship between God and human in the real life context of the home of God's creation, theology therefore cannot be conceived of from apart the very context of life and reality. Theology as faith seeking understanding denotes that theology is a step, a phase ahead of faith as it is the offshoot of faith. In other words, faith is the mother out of whose womb theology is born. Therefore, theology indicates that it is a sapling of the mother's seed, the outcome of faith.

Besides, and very importantly theology as faith seeking understanding is nothing short of meaning faith moving toward deeper understanding so that theology could direct us toward the application of faith in action or simply practicing what we have discerned. Beginning with faith, then onto theology as faith seeking understanding and to the praxis of theology, the context is a common reality though the components of our individual context will necessarily be defined by differences and diversities. Therefore, theology and its process should be carried out only from within the very real context - the human context, the context of our reality - that our faith, theology and its realization becomes actuated.

---

[9]Theological education in India especially that of the SSC deserve not only criticism but also equally if not even greater appreciation for its many contributions so far especially in relation to its sensitivity toward the importance of seriously taking India's pluralistic reality or context into its theological framework and content. This then enables its varied theological formulations to have meaning and make them relevant to its intended contexts. Yet, the task is neither finished nor likely to end yet. We must continue to work, to do theology in accordance with the life's continuity, passing through ever-changing and ever-evolving realities of life, all along aiming for meaning, credibility and relevancy in all of our theological ventures so as to participate and contribute to the fulfilling purpose of God intended for God's own creation.

Theology is therefore borne out of one's real context, the context constituted by complex realities and varied factors - positives as well as negatives – such as peace and conflicts; freedom and tensions; serenity and anxieties; trust and suspicions; clarity and doubts or confusions etc. As such, theology's main purpose is to seek understanding – to seek God's wisdom and guidance in relation to, and for applying the principles drawn, into that specific context for the purpose of healing, mending, correcting and reconciling the diseased, broken and deviated aspects of the given context. Therefore, theology cannot be a true theology until and unless it is based on a context, responds to it and relate to it practically with the ability to transform and affect changes. It is therefore here that the subject of the role of the SSC in fostering ecumenism in its curriculum in India's contexts becomes very important and challenging.

2.2. Areas of Limitations 'within' the Senate of Serampore's Ecumenical Theological Education

2.2.1. *Ecumenism and Gender Concern*

In partnership with other educational and professional disciplines, theological education under the SSC in fostering ecumenism must facilitate the analysis and interpretation of global issues in order to make theological education relevant to people in their local setting. Classical theological education that has been imparted within the SSC curriculum was created to meet the needs of the established educational structures of the churches. It was not sufficient or socially interactive, and therefore it was unable to respond meaningfully to the challenges of the church within the global society. In contemporary Indian context, theological developments confirm that ecumenical theological education within the Senate of Serampore need to move away from the male clergy-dominated leadership and create possibilities for empowering the total congregation in the ministry.

The present society and church calls for a new approach that will equip people who can equip others for involvement in bringing changes to the church and society at large. As the SSC is sincerely working to bring forth the new curriculum, we have to hope that the new curriculum will be relevant in context where both female and male will have mutual partnership to respond to the needs of local congregations as well as the present society set up through ecumenically pedagogical process of learning.[10] While it is true that theological institutions under the SSC are noteworthy for their ecumenical concerns and Christian maturity, many of them fall short for their superficial or half-hearted commitment toward the ecumenism of men-women relationship. It is very unfortunate that the SSC does not in praxis live up to the extent of its theoretical and verbal learning

---

[10]Cf. Rose F. Kinsler, "Theological Education of the People, with the People, for the People", *Teenet* (July, 2003), 34. (Hereafter, Kinsler, *Theological Education of People…*).

that embodies excellent visions and promises. Hence, this is a very serious issue that could seriously threaten the whole ecumenical claims of the SSC.

2.2.2. *Granting of the Senate of Serampore's Scholarship Funds*

This is also another concern that requires the SSC's attention for serious consideration. Theological education has become a very expensive affair and this is especially true in the case of those of us who had had the fortune (or misfortune?) to study under the highly acclaimed SSC. Some have even become anti-theological education by the very high costs of undergoing theological studies and therefore sometimes they even discourage aspiring candidates by cynically forewarning them that theological study is only meant for the very rich and millionaires and not for people who are not, even if they do have strong convictions and commitment. Such is the situation that we find ourselves today even as we are busying ourselves in our search for an ecumenical theological education.

Therefore, at present, the crucial question that can be asked is on the concern of *scholarship funds* under the SSC. How does the current system of scholarship within the SSC help or hinder the development of ecumenism without any discrimination of the applicants?[11] In this context we need to ask, to what extent is our theological education today fostering the true spirit of ecumenism. As the SSC is fostering ecumenism in theological education in India we need to look at ourselves, our society, our context and our relationship with others, and together seek to address the gap between the classical theological education and the contextually relevant theological education which is truly ecumenical in word and deed.

2.2.3. *The Art of Teaching Ecumenically*

All those who are called to the ministry of teaching in theological colleges and seminaries deserve proper preparation on how they mutually share knowledge with the students and how to interact with knowledge that comes from scripture, tradition, books and other sources. How teachers go about their profession is important because it has great impact on the life of the students and how best

---

[11]This is another very serious concern especially from the perspective of the SSC's students and research scholars. Besides, this is also a question arising out of the present researcher's real experience. Since he began his theological career from B.Th studies, to B.D. and followed by M.Th. and finally to the present D.Th studies, he had been seeking for scholarship under the SSC without even a single success. His requests were turned down one after the other for the very fact that he was truly in need. There were several instances where some of the student-colleagues who did not truthfully need financial aids received and besides, there were even those who had the unethical luxury of enjoying double scholarships – one from one's own church or some other funding bodies and another from the Senate. The Senate could truly be just and ecumenical if it could seriously review its method and criteria for scholarships without being subjected to it being corruptibly used by responding to only those that have some Senate-connected backings or some higher authority's backings.

they can develop skills that are needed in ministry. There is a need to identify particular skills and methodologies in ecumenical learning. Matters of identity and background may it be ethnic, racial, cultural, gender and denominational affiliation should not only be ignored but that it should not be taken lightly especially for those of us who are involved in the very process of ecumenical theological education.

Let us take a simple example for specification on this point of critique. Very often, some theological educators while they strongly propagate ecumenical visions in their writings and theoretical teachings, they neglect the practical side of it. To be very honest, some teachers' attitude and treatment of the students and even their own colleagues, there is complete absence of ecumenism and in its place, they demonstrate narrow, exclusive and self-centered way of living whereby, within the so-called ecumenical theological atmosphere, there is double-standard tensions, dissension, groupism, jealousy, discord and so on.

As a result, ecumenical theological educators of the SSC need to have a general knowledge of the churches and societies that students (and they themselves) come from and in which they are likely to serve upon graduation. Moreover, we live and work in multi-religious and multi-cultural societies, which require us to study each other's religious confessions and cultures so that our entire exercise of working toward an ecumenical theological education is truly not just well-informed and tolerant of other people who are different from us,[12] but also within our own immediate theological familial set up, which is also truly pluralistic as we ourselves represent a wide range of amazing differences.

3. Prospective Criticisms and Suggestions

While we have witnessed the noteworthy contributions of the Senate of Serampore in the history of the birth and development of theological education especially in India's context, and while there are sufficient evidences that testify of its significant role and involvement in fostering ecumenical ideas and characters in its theological education's structure and content, as mentioned before, the task is not yet over, but has to go on, if anything, it gets more tougher and challenging. Therefore, the present researcher has identified a concern or two that appears to be of urgent concerns in that it poses as a serious challenge in the context of our theological education at present.

---

[12]Cf. Ruppel, Gert and Schreiner, Peter, *Shared Learning in a Plural World: Ecumenical Approaches to Inter-Religious Education* (London: LIT Verlag Munster, 2003), 27.

3.1. The Senate of Serampore and Its Response to India's Contemporary Realities and Crises: An Urgent need for Introducing Subject(s) or Course(s) for Awareness on Contemporary India's Realities[13]

Before we delve into the area of critical comments and suggestions, let us first briefly highlight the background of our upcoming concerns. In other words, the following points of discussion will serve as the background introduction leading us to our points of critique coming up after this.

3.1.1. *The Ecumenical Character of the Senate of Serampore in the Inclusion of Contextually Relevant Subjects into its Existing Syllabi under its Curriculum: Possible Danger of Inadequacy*

It has been noted that the SSC's role thus far concerning its efforts in making its theological education contextually or rather ecumenically relevant (i.e., inculcating an ecumenical perspective in its structuring of academic course syllabi whereby it designs its course subjects that focuses on the pertinent areas and issues of India's complex realities), have been quite significant and noteworthy. Taking some of the important subjects on this line of thought through which we could clearly see its contextual and ecumenical sensitivity, theological education under the Senate of Serampore cannot be criticized of being totally apathetic and irrelevant to the otherwise ecumenically-intended structures of India's complex realities.

To cite some noteworthy examples on the SSC's ecumenically and contextually relevant course subjects would include *Modern, Religious and Secular Movements in India (M.R.S.M)*, offered in B.Th level (in the recent past) and B.D. integrated and regular courses; besides, we also have subjects like *Indian Christian Theology*; *Indian Christian Theologians*; *Indian Church and Society*; *Women in Religion and Society*; *Renascent and Contemporary Movements in India*. Then, there are subjects that focus mainly on the wider ecumenical perspective like *Justice, Peace and Integrity of Creation*; *Ecotheology* or *Theology of Creation*; *Ecofeminist Theology* – a theology that combines the concerns of women and those of nature or of creation etc. Coming to the Masters level of degree courses, depending on the specific disciplines we have course subjects and research topics allotted to the researchers and some of which are specifically designed around the contextual issues and concerns that the people experience and are familiar with - disciplines like *Religions*; *History of Christianity*; *Theology* and *Christian Ministry* etc.

All of the above mentioned disciplines (besides those that were not mentioned here) also do some justice to India's context. To cite briefly, we cover under our

[13]It is important to note that this idea is not meant to be taken as anything dictating but instead, it is purely a thought-provoking suggestion, considering the practical problems that the theological graduates face on stepping onto the real world that awaits them. It is therefore up to the decision of the common interests how and in what way this concern could be inculcated in the content of our theological curriculum in the near future.

studies subject topics like *the History of the Advent and Growth of Christianity in India till date and some of the Major Events and Factors in the Indian Church* (in the discipline of *History of Christianity*); *Theology from the Perspective of India's Context* – giving special emphasis on developing people-centered theological formulations like the contextually-based Indian Christian theologies including dalit theology, Indian feminist/womanist/Ecofeminist theologies, tribal(s) theologies, and Ecotheology etc., (in the discipline of *Christian Theology*); approaching the subject or *Theology of Religions from an Indian Christian Perspective*, giving sufficient consideration on the *historical and theological study on the emergence, development and significances of religions in India's people's context.* It also gives major emphasis on *India's popular religion namely Hinduism especially from the perspective of Indian Christian understanding*, (under the discipline of *Religions*); there is also the discipline of *Christian Ministry* that takes serious consideration of the study of the *historical growth, theological understanding, significances and the importance of praxis in relating the subject of Christian ministry in and within the context of Indian Christians amidst also the interrelated relationship with people of other living faiths in India's pluralistic context.*

Without overlooking or belittling the efforts of the Senate of Serampore in fostering ecumenism in its theological education program as it has already been noted with positive evidences, what we are about to do here is to give some constructive criticisms for future prospects or possibilities. Therefore, keeping our appreciation of the SSC for its achievements thus far intact at the back of our minds, let us now proceed to present our critique that *the ecumenical character of the SSC's curriculum is facing the danger of it being inadequate as far as the present reality of India is concerned*, and then move on to some prospective suggestions.

3.1.2. *The Paradox of being Ecumenical and Semi-Ecumenical in the Curriculum of Theological Education under the Senate of Serampore*

Before we commit ourselves to the depth of our response, let us note something very important here. For those of us who have already had the blessed opportunity to do our theological career under the esteemed structure of the SSC, it will not be difficult to understand that our upcoming critical response is not intended to refute SSC's credibility nor to demean its till date's excellent academic reputation but, it is rather a response intended for constructivism or rather for its further effective enhancement. Besides we can also agree that the SSC could still further its vision and structural content of the nature of its ecumenical theological education and therefore, toward that goal this critique is focused on.

Here, we argue that *it is time that the SSC re-evaluate and revise its curriculum thus far being active.* The reason, if we are to state in the simplest and right here, *it is because the hitherto form of its ecumenism is already becoming inadequate and therefore on the verge of becoming irrelevant.* This is to mean that its ecumenical and contextual nature of theological education is being threatened. Let us take one simple and humble example here. Say we take one of its recent past's basic course subject called *Modern Religious and Secular Movements in India* – it is without doubt a very important subject as it introduces the students to some of the modern (and major) religious and secular movements that emerged during the 19th and 20th centuries in India as the title indicates. Here, the students are acquainted to the historic developments of all those popular movements and their ideologies that took root in, and constitute, the character and structure of their very own Indian context. To be precise, subjects such as this enables the aspiring past, present and future leaders, teachers, pastors, counselors and so forth, to be aware of and active in the real life's realities of their field of ministries - the real life experiences, struggles, conflicts, beliefs, aspirations and visions of the peoples among whom they are living and are going to serve as practical, moral and spiritual guides.

Besides, subjects like *Indian Christian Theology, History of Christianity in India,* etc., also focus on the India's peoples, church and theology. However, while they are important in relation to the need of understanding our own peoples' past thoughts, struggles, visions, achievements, etc., and their undying link with the present (will also no doubt continue to evolve in its tie to the future), in the process of giving so much of our attention to such form of academic exercise, we lose contact with the present reality. In other words, while we are engrossing ourselves in studying the significances of the pasts, we neglect the very area that needs and awaits us which is called 'the present', the 'here' and the 'now' reality in which we are an integral part and for which, we are in fact undergoing our theological education and training. Eventually therefore, when faced with the real present realities, we get a somersaulting wake-up call alarming us with the frightfully depressing message that most of what we thought we have fittingly learned for praxis had actually been mainly about the past – though they are important facts yet bygone or outdated - and therefore they have very little meaning and relevance to us and to our world in the present. We find ourselves with very little or nothing at all to contribute to the present realities and challenges facing us.

3.1.3. *Present Day Realities and Theological Education: Are They or Are They Not Worlds Apart?*

Just as we know that a person can be at his/her loneliest state even while being in the midst of a crowd, so also it is not impossible for our theological education to be away from the very reality that it is situated in. The same could also be applied to the SSC's role that even when it is believed to be active in its ecumenical concern, it could also be missing the target or the core ecumenical concerns – the issues that are in dire need of its ecumenical theological reflection and response. Therefore, when we talk about theological education and their authenticity and relevancy, it can only be done by studying the relation between the structure of theological education and the real-life context of the people.

We have already very clearly noted in our study concerning the SSC's role in fostering ecumenism in its theological education, of which we certainly appreciate yet that does not suffice it to hold that that is it! What is imperative on the part of the SSC is to carry on its ecumenical vision and mission by increasing its efforts so that it does not lag behind stagnant while the society moves ahead with its ever-changing conditions and issues or concerns of life. Hence, as we implied in the preceding points, time seems just right (meaning its high time) for the SSC to re-energize itself and hasten to keep up with the present-day India's realities if it wishes to commit itself realistically and effectively to the ministry of the Indian church and Indian society.

To add concrete weight to what we have voiced, let us very briefly note some of the serious issues of our day. Today, we can describe our real world in these lines: religious fanaticism; communal clashes; political conflicts; suspicions; homicides; suicides; infidelity; treachery; conscienceless killing and massacre of innocent infants, children, women and people (who had nothing to do, no idea of what and why they are the recipient victims of such heinous crimes); raping spree of females; intra-religious and inter-sects and inter-denominational enmity etc. We also are now very familiar to religious politicization; legal's convenient blindness to right actions or rather, legal's illegality; economic plagues; cultural perversions; social destabilizations.... The list is endless. This then is the world where our theological education is situated today. Where is our theological education in such a world of ours? Or more specifically, what are we doing?

3.1.3.1. *Fundamentalism, Racism, Imperialism and Terrorism*

Then, on the global scale, at the very hour, we are all directly or indirectly being affected with the top-most issue of concerns namely that of *Terror* and *Terrorists Activities* or simply put *Terrorism*. It is no longer an occasional reality; it has become the password for every single day. Besides, it is no longer an alternative experience alternated between the nations of the world; it is a common and a permanent member for every nation of the world. Everywhere we encounter some type of terrorism lurking and mingling within our society. The main reason behind the emergence, operation and its resultant affects are mainly due to the negative and destructive understanding and attitude toward differences, diversities and varieties that constitute the entire fabric of the created world. Differences in faiths, beliefs, cultures, races, colors, ideologies, customs, traditions and practices etc., when they are being misconceived and misused, they breed legion of sectarian and separatist groups, which in turn are geared up to spread its poisonous influence farther.

A very powerful example is, the recent past researched findings with regard to the self-appointed leading nation of the world namely America under the leadership of George W. Bush, the former President of US, it has been discovered that Bush's declaration of 'WAR ON TERROR' had had an 'unparalleled' reverse effect for the very fact that it attempted to cleanse out or uproot 'terrorism' with the same weapon of 'terrorizing' its so-called enemy. In fact, its vengeance weapon turned out much more lethal, monstrous and wanton than what they experienced under the terror of 'the' enemy. As such, the result was, not just the non-American nations but even its own nation, i.e., many of its people eventually found it hard to digest the overboard madness of their nation's avenging self-defense. Now, the ball rolled in America's court as it attempted to balance the blood of the innocent millions upon its head. The reward that America received for its method of combating terror with terror is like no ordinary reward as it comes in the form of a horrifying escalation of terror-based activities in number and strength as never before in America or in the world.

Another event was that of the retaliating war of Israel against Palestine or in particular against the Hamas of Palestine. The dailies, the News Channels, and the reports of all sorts are filled with the horrifying way Israel took its revenge in the name of defending the dignity and integrity of its nation. Hamas being its sole target, thousands of innocent citizens have been torn apart literally by Israel's weapons of self-defense. It takes a live pictures or personal experience to feel and mourn the depth of the suffering, pain and agony of those affected literally – those surviving victims that are living yet dying; breathing yet choking and breaking apart physically and mentally. It is very interesting to note that the result of Israel's method of protecting and defending its nation by repaying its enemy has in fact enlarged the gap of feud between itself and Palestine much more than it was before.

India too had, a not so recent taste of terrorism (sarcasm unintended) in Mumbai (September 6, 2008) that went worldwide. Besides, India is also a nation that can boasts of harboring terrorism in every shades and color and in every nook and corner of its frame, erupting every now and then, and annihilating life in slow and gradual pace. At present, India is receiving feedbacks from sensitive or even daringly wise people who continuously send India unpleasant views such as, that India should stop the 'blame' game especially with its rival sibling Pakistan. In other words, paying back with the same weapon or repaying evil for evil is not going to curb evil but rather would multiply the thing that one is trying to erase. Hence, what does our theological education contribute to this conflict-filled world of ours? Most importantly, how do we respond or contribute as agents of God's love and God's peace to a world that is crying out right before us now?

3.1.3.2. *Fanaticism, Party-ism and Communalism*

One simple question for theological education from a thought-provokingly theological perspective: What have all of these got to do with us who belong to a different world of ministry of God's word? And very importantly, how did we (who are so engrossed in our theological training program) come to know of all of these issues, these horrifying realities of our present world? - Surely not from somewhere outside our theological structure? One can confidently assume to respond in the negative simply because theological education must surely be preparing and training the students in and for, the very real and present context of the people. It is indeed unfortunate but, the correct answer will be and is, 'No', because, students (though not all of them) gain this awareness mainly through their own personal sensitivity to the present issues and through their own interests in reading newspapers, current informational writings and viewing the news channels, etc., beside the fact that we all live in and share the same world. Whether the institutions and theological structures, the faculty, teachers and mentors of the trainees are aware of the fact that some of their pupils often spend time thinking and wondering what they are actually being trained for, and how they are to relate and minister to the people who are inextricably situated within such a panoramic context of complexity? These are some 'oft-nagging' questions that every restless and sensitive spirit wrestles from within oneself. It is in this respect that the need for incorporating these present issues into the curriculum of our present day theological education is being felt.

Many would agree that there are times when we realize that there is an intimidating wall between us and the world that we are placed to minister mainly because what we have been taught and learned, trained and equipped (though they must have had so much relevance for the then past context yet) have very little relevance to the present contexts earmarked for our theological praxis. Therefore, understanding India's contemporary realities has become a challenge for theological education in India under the SSC/University for a relevantly meaningful, living and transformatory response. It is in response to such practical paradoxes of our theological education being ecumenical and unecumenical or being contextually relevant and contextually irrelevant at the same time, that the present research places this crucial issue as a constructive challenge before the prospective consideration of the SSC.

3.2. Necessity of Forming an Ecumenical Platform for Dialogue between the Senate of Serampore and Asian Theological Association Accredited Colleges in India and with other Independent Colleges

As the heading suggests, the issue at hand is specifically related to the role of the Senate of Serampore in fostering ecumenism beyond the extent of what has been covered in the sphere of inter-relationships till date. We have already noted its ecumenical venture in the context of interrelationship of different churches' traditions and denominations; interrelationship of diverse living faiths; interrelationship of different theological colleges, seminaries and institutions; its subsequent extension of ecumenism to include also of bringing together of people from diverse cultures, races, ethnicity, customs and so forth through its theological education; and then onto its ecumenical vision and character of its academic structure of courses. Nevertheless, what is being pointed out here for its serious consideration is concerning the need of fostering ecumenism also with those non-Serampore colleges, seminaries and their affiliating bodies like those under the Asian Theological Association accreditation as well as with the independent structures of theological education.

Logic behind this idea is simple and yet a very crucial one as it arises out of serious practical problems surrounding the issue. The present researcher admits the fact that this concern is basically an outcome of his personal experience, first-hand survey and observation of the problem's reality especially as they are situated in the context of the North Eastern states of India and in particularity it is very much prevalent in the context of the Nagas (i.e., beside the state of Nagaland, includes also those of the Naga-inhabited areas like parts of Manipur, Assam etc.) and it calls for a sincere attention of the leading theological structure of the nation namely, the SSC. And this appeal to the SSC, the present researcher would like to add, is not borne out of anything that seem to suggest that it is the bonded responsibility of the SSC, but is borne out of the belief and confidence in the able and ecumenically-sensitive leadership of the SSC.

For about 45 to 50 bible colleges and institutions in Nagaland and Naga inhabited areas, as has earlier noted, only four of them are members of the SSC. From the rests, only a minority of them are under the accreditation of ATA and few other individual boards and organizations. As such, majority of the colleges are either under the individual founders or co-founders especially under the people who had had no theological or ministerial backgrounds, but run them on their own personal interests or even for purpose of commercializing for their own personal financial goals. Take Dimapur city for best among the examples. Dimapur is the commercial center not just for the Nagas but for the entire North Eastern states. This city itself has about 35 to 40 bible colleges as per the last record taken in 2008. Amongst these, only one namely, Trinity Theological College, is under the SSC.

Anyway, to cut short and get to the issue, due to this mushrooming of private centers as well as due to many of the Naga theological graduates who passed out from the other out-of-Nagaland non-Serampore Colleges, there are several instances of conflicts, tensions and even open differences and confrontations in the fields of ministry, especially in the church. One area where this conflict is very obvious is in the matter of 'preference'. We mean that the churches in urban towns and cities are mostly aware of the difference between the Senate and non-Senate affiliated academic standard and the quality of education. As such, some of the churches prefer to appoint Senate graduates to those from the ATA or other affiliations into its ministry. This results in the uncomfortable tensions between the ministerial candidates, besides which it also creates discomfort within the church members even mainly because there are instances when the ministerial candidates happen to be related to the church members especially when the members turn out to be those that occupy important offices and seats of the administration and functions of the church.

Next, as already mentioned about the huge number of Bible colleges and institutions in Nagaland, there are greater opportunities for the qualified theological graduates to serve as theological teachers and posts of lectureship. However, most of the colleges, i.e., the authorities (founders, board members who are responsible for the selection and appointment of new teachers), prefer to appoint SSC graduates rather than the rests. Hence, we will find in almost every college, teachers and lecturers have SSC background. Once again, a thick barrier is made to stand between the SSC and non-SSC graduates. To be precise, several conflicts and heated arguments emerge within the circle of theological and ministerial atmosphere on the issue of the unequal treatment of SSC and non-SSC graduates.

A very important point to be noted here for those responsible leaders and educators of the SSC is that, as most of the colleges (both ATA and others) have SSC background teachers and educators that form the majority of its faculties, they follow the SSC curriculum and prospectus for their allotted subjects' syllabus in their teaching. Besides, even some of the private and ATA affiliated colleges have consulted a great portion of the SSC prospectus in their effort to bring out their courses' syllabus.[14]

An additional word of information to consider is, even many of the students studying in these non-Senate colleges are now fully aware of the value difference between the two and hence, many feel disappointed at discovering that their education and their diplomas and degrees have less value for the ministry. In fact, many of them including those that graduate from other ATA and private colleges outside Nagaland happen to be sent to the rural village churches and mission schools or to far-off mission churches and schools like in Nepal, Myanmmar, Arunachal Pradesh, Assam, Sikkim, etc., for their ministries. And it is them who had to undergo a real test of commitment and perseverance as concrete suffering and sacrifices are part of the type of their ministries. In this relation, a common criticism against the Senate graduates is that, they are *more worldly* or *unspiritual* meaning also that they do not want to suffer for the sake of the gospel; *liberal* which means no respect for traditions and cultural codes; *less effective in prayer life* which means they do not pray with emotions, convictions and seriousness as well as they do not spend sufficient time in prayer etc.

The above examples are cited in order to show the seriousness of the matter as prevalent in the North East especially in Nagaland and Naga-inhabited areas. This is therefore a very crucial area that needs the assistance of the leading structure of theological education in India – the Senate of Serampore. We believe that

[14]The present writer had been one of the members commissioned to draft out the Constitution and courses' syllabus for the ATA affiliated federated theological education center in the year 2002-2003 academic year at Dimapur, Nagaland. Hence, it so happened that most of the committee members were from the SSC, which led them to take the SSC prospectus as their model and guide to bring out the needed drafts.

there could be a possibility to soften or balance the differences and help create a mutually enriching platform for the diverse colleges to work together for the one same goal of the ministry of the church and society. However, this vision will need the necessary effort of the SSC and the BTESSC to extend its ecumenical arms to embrace, sort out the differences, and search for a mutually benefiting avenue so that all of God's trained servants would be able to complementarily contribute to the one cause of the gospel and its mission.

All of these and many more other issues confronts our theological education as intimidating challenges and therefore, it is no longer possible to procrastinate the already over-loaded carriage of responsibility of our theological education as we speak, teach, learn and prepare ourselves to be ecumenically responsible persons in this oikoumene of God. Let us therefore, reach out with our own hands, touch those souls where leading them back home is needed; those places where lifting up is needed; setting things right is needed; embracing is needed; settling of differences is needed.... Let us as God-appointed guardian angels of this gone-wrong world spread out and make a difference and rebuild God's oikoumene created beautifully for all of its members.

4. Ecumenism in Theological Education

What we have been asserting thus far is that theological education is not only essential for the formation of church leaders, which is of course a necessary task, but it is also equally essential for the society as all are inter-related – theological education trains people for Church ministry; trained persons serves in the church; church is comprised of people from diverse walks of life within the society and thus, theologically trained persons in reality serve, teach, guide and lead the society and its members. In this way theological education returns to the people and the community in their diverse contexts and in this way, it goes beyond purely academic elements, without ignoring their importance.

Contextual theological education inevitably leads to ecumenism, precisely because it is within any given context that diversity and the specificities that mark our differences manifest themselves and exists. From this perspective, ecumenism constitutes the harmonious with the contrasting distinct. It acquires a complementary character while emphasizing the specificities and particularities of each context in connection with a greater reality, without ignoring the plurality and autonomy of each context.[15]

As discussed in the above, the function of theological education in fostering ecumenism in the sub-continent has changed qualitatively in the past few years. Today in the region there is much more openness toward change, as well as many more opportunities for Senate affiliated Institutions as well as others for a joint effort in fostering ecumenism in theological education. However, there are still

[15]Cf. Romer Portillo, "The Contextual and Ecumenical in Venezuelan Theological Education," *http://www.coe.org/wcc/what/education/mf100.pdf.* (11.01.05), 41.

great challenges to be considered within the present scope of fostering ecumenism in theological education in the Indian sub-continent. Notable among them are:

a) In spite of the advances in fostering ecumenism under the SSC, there is still a needed concern that needs to be taken more seriously in the region. For example, there are more than fifty affiliated institutions within the SSC - among them some are truly ecumenical, on the other hand many of them continue to be denominational with no genuine commitment to or emphasis upon the line of fostering ecumenism. This is a serious challenge for the SSC.
b) In many theological institutions there is that constricting idea that the classroom learning is sufficient for ministry. But, this is a wrong concept mainly because learning is a 'life' experience. Ministerial formation requires much more than just logical reasoning in the classroom, hence, this is a crucial concern to be checked.
c) Some of the theological institutions do not seriously consider social realities as important. As such, concerns over issues like violence, war, poverty, globalization, environmental contamination, gender discrimination, the abandonment of children etc., are not a part of the curriculum of theological education. The SSC as noted in our study, has to some extent done justice, however, it need to extend its effort in conscientizing even those outside its umbrella.
d) Some of the delicate issues like Children at Risk, HIV/AIDS, Differently-abled persons, Homosexuality, LGBT etc., need to be seriously addressed under the concern of ecumenical theological education and especially under the SSC curriculum,[16] although it has been putting its infant effort in taking some of these issues under its theological concern. These should be made core courses as they are 'real' issues within and around us.

We who serve within Senate of Serampore theological education throughout India today, and who find ourselves now literally linked together in growing international cooperation, should unite with the voices of others in our common longing and vision for an ecumenical theological education. We should work unitedly for an ecumenism in form and in substance, an ecumenism in vision and

---

[16]HIV/AIDS Pandemic, Differently-abled Persons, Homosexuality, Gayism, Lesbianism etc., are serious issues in today's context. What is needed urgently is that theological education in India should take sincere steps in incorporating these concerns within its curriculum so that we could meaningfully understand, relate and work with and for those realities that are awaiting us. It is true that the SSC has begun to address some of these issues, yet, it is not very noticeable or sufficient. If attempts could be made to prepare the students (as well as teachers of course in this matter), through the introduction of trainings given by experts in these fields, it will definitely be a very promising and fruitful endeavor especially for the ministry at large.

power, an ecumenism in commitment and direction. The Senate of Serampore College though it still has to cover huge distance, at least, it is consciously making some progress in fostering ecumenism in theological education, and therefore, it is also very important that the churches in India along with various other organizations and groups join together to make this ecumenical vision a possible reality.[17]

[17]Cf. Kinsler, *Theological Education of the People…*, 2.

Conclusion

This study is an exploration of the *Role of the Senate of Serampore College (SSC) in Fostering Ecumenism in the Context of Theological Education in India*. The main purpose of the book is to make a historical analysis on the pattern of theological education under the SSC with a view to investigate whether it is ecumenically relevant or not and if it is, then how far it is able to do that considering India's context. In other words, India is one unique nation where its peoples, beliefs, traditions, value systems, way of life, social structures, cultural practices, political ideologies and even its peoples' racial and ethnic backgrounds are characterized by differences and diversities and as such, the task of theological education in such a complexly-webbed structure is truly no less than a mind-boggling challenge.

At this time and age, argument for the necessity of *Contextual and Relevant* theological education has already passed and the popular focus is now on the question of *Ecumenism in Theological Education*. Theological education in India in particular is confronted with this serious enquiry of whether it is ecumenically characterized and structured simply because India's context itself needs ecumenical theological education. Earlier, beginning with the post-colonial era and on to the sixties till recent past, the concern of contextual theological education was very demanding and that has led to the recognition and development of contextual theologies and contextual theological education, taking the real and living realities and experiences of India's peoples and their challenging context.

Nevertheless, it does not imply that contextualization is not important anymore for the very fact that *it is the pre-requisite* for theological education to be *contextual* at any given situation. Besides, *ecumenism* is not a subject totally independent of *contextualization* but is actually inextricably connected to it especially when we consider about theological education in India's context. In other words, the quest of our research is rooted in India's contextual theological education in order to see whether our theological education under the SSC, in, and for, India's context is *ecumenical* because *ecumenism* is the uncompromising demand of India's reality of pluralism.

The Senate of Serampore College/University, established in the early part of the 19th century (1818), under the Baptist Mission and through its missionaries,

William Carey and his colleagues Joshua Marshman and William Ward, today, serves as a major structure of theological education in India. In fact, with the formation of the BTESSC in 1975, the SSC became the center of one national structure of theological education – representing the platform and spokesperson for both the church and theological education in India – in matters related to the nature, structure, functions and development of theological education, with the aim of preparing students and prospective ministers by imparting and equipping them for meaningful and relevant ministry in the church and in the society at large. Hence, the SSC thus far have been actively involved in its effort to train people in accordance with the changing realities and issues of India's context.

Notwithstanding the sea of its historical accounts on its significantly-varied experiences, struggles, occasions of defeat, progress and accomplishments etc., we narrow down to our concerned area of the SSC's role in fostering ecumenism in theological education in India. It is observed that the SSC is very closely associated with the aspect of ecumenism in its theological education program and process. The genesis story of its establishment itself embodies the idea and principle of ecumenism, i.e., William Carey, the founder, especially had begun the College with the vision of training not just the Christian youth for pastoral ministry but also equally for the education of all of God's people for general learning in European Science and English language – a vision for wider scope. Thus, since its birth, the SSC's vision had been for its holistic and ecumenical mission and ministry.

The ecumenical journey of the SSC became much more evident with its structure of affiliation wherein it became the center to, or under which, the rests of the theological colleges, seminaries and institutions began to come under its affiliating umbrella. Hence, today we see that there are about 45 to 50 colleges constituting its affiliating members. Besides its role of ecumenism in its relationship with diverse colleges and institutions, it also includes its ecumenical relationship with different church traditions via its member colleges that represents various church sponsored backgrounds as well as via its significant partnership with the churches in India. In addition, its ecumenical relationship is extended through its member colleges that represent varieties of regional, cultural, linguistic and even racial plurality.

We also take under our research the conscious and sensitive effort of the SSC in fostering ecumenism through its involvement with the NCCI especially, in the program and actions of Interreligious dialogue – a dialogue or coming together of people from diverse living faiths for purpose of mutual acquaintance, understanding, respect, sharing and thereby enriching one another. This effort of the SSC in its theological education had been very significant mainly because of India's reality of its population who live together and work together but are literally divided when it comes to the basis of faith, culture, ideologies, race, tribe, caste, customs, practices, language etc., all of which contribute to countless instances of dissension, suspicion, communalism, racism, violence, tensions, quarrels, and the list goes on.

An important area that calls for our serious attention to is upon the curricula of our theological education. The SSC had been also following the system or rather the practice of revising its curriculum on routine basis. In this regard, the SSC has begun (i.e., during the time of this research work) the process of bringing out a new curriculum which is being carried out by seriously taking the concerns of the institutions, churches, organizations, educators of diverse fields etc. Therefore, it is expected that the BTESSC will eventually be able to enlarge its ecumenical umbrella by bringing out an ecumenically relevant curriculum.

Our present study therefore, has made an attempt to make a historical analysis on the role of the SSC in fostering ecumenism in its theological education in India. In the course of our study, we have noted several noteworthy areas as well as aspects that constitute the ecumenical character of the SSC in its theological education for India's specifically pluralistic context and as such, the quest of our research thus discovers the affirmative role of the SSC in fostering ecumenism within India's context. However, we further made a critical evaluation on whether what the SSC has done thus far in its ecumenical theological education is adequately responding to the present context of the people in India or not, and for this, we identified some of the crucially urgent issues prevalent in the country today. By discussing some of the serious issues that come under the purview of the vision and mission of theological education, we have presented the nature and character of those problems as experienced by us as well as by fellow-beings. Finally, we have given some prospective criticisms and suggestions for the SSC to take under its sincere and critical consideration as it continues to put its efforts in shaping its theological education on ecumenical lines for India's context of plurality.

Appendix I

Bengal Act No. IV of 1918
The Serampore College Act, 1918

As modified up to the 1st July, 1951.

(1st May, 1918)

Bengal Act No. IV of 1918 (The Serampore College Act, 1918)

The Government of India adapted ... (Adaptation of Indian Laws Order, 1937; The Adaptation of Laws Order, 1950. As modified up to the 30th June, 1997)

(Published in the "Calcutta Gazette" of the 1st May, 1918)

An Act to supplement, and in certain matters to supersede, the Royal Charter of Incorporation and the statutes and Regulations of the Serampore College.

Preamble

WHEREAS, on the 23rd day of February, 1827, the institution established in Serampore, Bengal, and known as the Serampore College, was incorporated by Royal Charter granted by his late Danish Majesty, King Frederick the Sixth, with the powers and privileges in the said Royal Charter set forth including the power of conferring upon the students of the said College degrees of rank and honour according to their proficiency in science;

AND WHEREAS by Article VI of the Treaty of Purchase, dated the 22nd February, 1845, transferring Serampore to the British Government, it was provided that the rights and immunities granted to the Serampore College by the said Royal Charter, as translated and contained in Schedule I to this Act, should not be interfered with, but should continue in force in the same manner as if they had been obtained by a Charter from the British Government, subject to the general law of British India;

AND WHEREAS Statutes and Regulations for the better government of the said College and management of its concerns, as contained in Schedule II to this Act, were, on the 12th day of June, 1833, made and established under the powers conferred by Article 4 of the said Royal Charter;

AND WHEREAS it is considered that in order to give effect, under the conditions now existing, to the intentions of his late Danish Majesty and of the founders of the said College, that is to say, to promote piety and learning, particularly among the native Christian population of India, the amendment of the constitution of the College, by the enlargement of the Council on an inter-denominational basis, with power to delegate some of its functions, in manner hereinafter appearing, is required;

AND WHEREAS the present Council of the said College consists of the Reverend George Pearce Gould, M.A., D.D., Master and President, George Barclay Leechman, Esq., Sir George Watson Macalpine, LL.D., the Reverend Robert Forman Horton, M.A., D.D., and the Reverend George Howells, M.A., Ph.D., Principal of the College;

AND WHEREAS it is deemed expedient by the Governor in Council, with the consent of the said Council of the Serampore College, that a Faculty and Senate be constituted for the said College in manner hereinafter appearing and that suitable standards be imposed in regard to any secular degrees that may hereafter be conferred by the said Council under the terms of the said Royal Charter;

AND WHEREAS it is necessary to make provision for the above purposes by subjecting the said Royal Charter, Statutes and Regulations to an Act to the legislature under the general law of British India in accordance with the terms of the aforesaid Treaty;

AND WHEREAS the previous sanction of the Governor-General in Council has been obtained to the passing of this Act. It is hereby enacted as follows:-

Short Title

1. This Act may be called the Serampore College Act, 1918.

Constitution of the Council

2. *(1)* The Council of the Serampore College as constituted by the Royal Charter of the 23rd day of February, 1827, shall be enlarged so as to consist of not less than five nor more than sixteen ordinary members, including the Master, as the Council may from time to time determine. The first Council constituted under this section shall include the present Master and President and the other present members.

(2) At least one-third of the members of the Council shall be members of the Baptist denomination.

(3) The Master shall be the President of the Council.

(4) The Principal of the College, if not an ordinary member, shall be an additional member of the Council ex-officio during his term of office as Principal of the College.

(5) Until otherwise determined by by-law made under section 14, three members of the Council shall form a quorum.

Resignation of Members

3. Any member of the Council may at any time resign his office by notice in writing to the Master, provided that no such resignation shall be deemed to take effect so long as the total number of members of the Council shall by reason thereof be less than five.

Election of Master

4. On any vacancy occurring in the office of Master the remaining members of the Council shall elect another person, whether one of their number or not, to fill his place.

The College Faculty

5. The Council shall, within one year from the date of the commencement of this Act, constitute and appoint in the manner prescribed in section 6 a body to be known as the College Faculty.

Constitution of the College Faculty

6. *(1)* The Faculty shall consist of the Principal (who shall be its President) and such of the professors and other officials and functionaries of the College as may be appointed by the Council in accordance with by-laws made under section 14.
(2) The Council shall from time to time prescribe and declare border in writing the powers and duties of the Faculty, and may remove any member thereof.

Delegation of Council's Power and Duties

7. The Council may delegate to the Faculty all or any of the powers and duties of the Council and Master, which concern only the internal management of the College and its general order and good government.

The Senate of the College

8. The Council shall, within one year from the date of the commencement of this Act, constitute and appoint in the manner prescribed in section 9 a body to be known as the Senate of the College.

Constitution of the Senate

9. The Senate shall consist of the Principal (who shall be convener) and not less than twelve nor more than eighteen persons as the Council may from time to time determine, to be appointed by the Council:

Provided that –

(a) at least one and not more than three representatives of each of the following Christian denominations, viz. Anglican, Baptist, Congregational, Lutheran, Methodist. Presbyterian and Syrian, shall, as far as practicable, be members of the Senate;

(b) at least two-thirds of the members shall be persons other than professors, officials or functionaries of the College;

(c) not less than one-sixth of the members shall be members of the College Faculty.

Term of Office of Members of the Senate

10. *(1)* Subject to the provisions of clause 11 of the Statutes and Regulations of the College, which shall be deemed to apply to members of the Senate, each member of the Senate shall hold office for a period of five years, at the expiration of which period he shall retire, but he shall be eligible for re-appointment: Provided that the Principal shall not during the term of his office as Principal, be subject to retirement, unless he becomes disqualified under the provisions of clause 11 of the Statutes and Regulations.

(2) Any member of the Senate may, by notice in writing to the Master, resign his membership at any time.

Duties of the Senate

11. The Senate shall frame courses of study and make rules for the conduct of examinations, and shall, subject to the control of the Council, determine the qualifications for degrees and diplomas and do and perform all other matters and things necessary or proper for or relating to the determination of the eligibility of candidates for degrees, diplomas and certificates to be conferred by the Council.

Power of the Senate to make Rules and Regulations

12. Subject to the provisions of this Act, the Senate shall make rules and regulations for the convening of its meetings and for the proper conduct of its business.

Granting of Degrees

13. If, at any time, the Council shall intend to grant degrees in any branch or branches of knowledge and science other than theology, such degrees shall be confined to students who shall have received regular instruction at the Serampore College; and before the Council proceeds to grant such degrees, it shall satisfy1[the State Government] as to the adequacy -

(1) of the establishment and equipment of the College;

(2) of the academic standard to be maintained; and

(3) of the financial provision made therefore: Provided that the said Government, on ceasing to be so satisfied, may withdraw [its] approval of the granting of such degrees.

Power of the Council to make By-laws

14. Subject to the provisions of this Act and of the said Royal Charter, Statutes and Regulations, so far as they are not inconsistent therewith, the Council shall make by-laws providing for and regulating the following matters, namely:

(a) the convening of meetings of the Council;

(b) the quorum to be required at meetings of the Council and the conduct of business at such meetings;

(c) the appointment of members of the Council, Faculty and Senate;

(d) the duties to be performed by the Faculty under the direction and control of the Council;

(e) the conferring of degrees, diplomas and certificates on the recommendation of the Senate;

(f) the terms and tenure of appointments, duties, emoluments, allowances and superannuation allowances of the Principal, Professors, Fellows, Tutors and other officers of the College and of its servants;

(g) the finances and accounts of the College and the investment of its funds;

(h) the person or persons by whom, and the manner and form in which, contracts by or on behalf of the College may be entered into, varied or discharged, and deeds, agreements, contracts, cheques, and other negotiable instruments and documents may be signed or executed on behalf of the College, and minutes and proceedings of meetings of the Council, Faculty or Senate may be authenticated or evidenced so as to bind the College and be receivable in evidence in accordance with the provisions of the Indian Evidence Act, 1872;

(i) the custody and use of the common seal; and

(j) generally all such other matters as may be required or authorized under this Act and the said Royal Charter, Statutes and Regulations, so far as they are not inconsistent with this Act.

Effect of Act

15. The provisions of the said Royal Charter and of the Statutes and Regulations made thereunder, so far as they are contrary to or inconsistent with any of the terms of this Act, shall be deemed to be superseded from the date of the commencement of this Act:

Provided that nothing in this Act shall render invalid any acts performed, duties imposed or liabilities incurred prior to the date on which this Act comes into force in accordance with the terms of the said Royal Charter, and of the Statutes and Regulations made thereunder.

Appendix II

Schedule I
(See Preamble and Sections 2 (1), 14 and 15)
Charter of Incorporation of the Serampore College

We, Frederick the Sixth, by the Grace of God King of Denmark, the Venders and Gothers, Duke of Slesvig Holsten, Stormarn, Ditmarsken, Limessborg and Oldenborg, by writings these make known and publicly declare, that whereas William Carey and Joshua Marshman, Doctors of Divinity, and John Clark Marshman, Esq., inhabitants of our town of Fredericksnagore (or Serampore) in Bengal, being desirous of founding a College to promote piety and learning particularly among the native Christian population of India, have to secure this object erected suitable buildings and purchased and collected suitable books, maps, etc., and have humbly besought us to grant unto them and such persons as shall be elected by them and their successors to form the Council of the College in the manner to be hereafter named, our Royal Charter of Incorporation that they may the more effectually carry into execution the purposes above-mentioned:-- We, being desirous to encourage so laudable an undertaking, have of our special grace and free motion ordained, constituted, granted and declared, and by the presents We do for ourselves, our heirs and successors ordain, constitute, grant and declare:

1. That the said William Carey, Joshua Marshman and John Clark Marshman, and such other person or persons as shall successively be elected and appointed the Council of the said College, in the manner hereafter mentioned, shall by virtue of the presents be for ever hereafter one body politic and incorporate by the name of the Serampore College for the purposes aforesaid to have perpetual succession and to have a common seal, and by the said name to sue and be sued, to implead and be impleaded, and to answer and be answered unto in every court and place belonging to us, our heirs and successors.
2. And We do hereby ordain, constitute and declare that the persons hereby incorporated and their successors shall for ever be competent in law to

purchase, hold and enjoy for them and their successors any goods and chattels whatsoever and to receive, purchase, hold and enjoy, they and their successors, any lands, tenements or hereditaments whatever, and that they shall have full power and authority to sell, exchange or otherwise dispose of any real or personal property to be by them acquired as aforesaid, unless the sale or alienation of such property be specially prohibited by the donor or donors thereof, and to do all things relating to the said College or Corporation in as ample a manner or form as any of our liege subjects, or any other body politic or corporate in our said kingdom or its dependencies may or can do.

3. And We do hereby ordain, grant and declare that the number of Professors, Fellows or Student Tutors and Students, shall be indefinite and that the said William Carey, Joshua Marshman and John Clark Marshman, shall be the first Council of the said College, and that in the event of its appearing to them necessary during their life-time, or in the case of the death of any one of the three members of the said first Council, the survivors or survivor shall and may under their respective hands and seals appoint such other person or persons to be members of the Council of the College, and to succeed each other so as to become Members of the said Council in the order in which they shall be appointed, to the intent that the Council of the said College shall for ever consist of at least three persons.
4. And We do hereby further ordain, grant and declare, that for the better government of the said College, and the better management of its concerns, the said William Carey, Joshua Marshman and John Clark Marshman, the members of the first Council, shall have full power and authority for the space of ten years from the date of these presents, to make and establish such statutes as shall appear to them useful and necessary for the government of the said College, in which statutes they shall define the powers to be entrusted to their successors, to the Professors, the Fellows or Student Tutors and the other Officers thereof, and the duties to be performed by these respectively for the management of the estates, lands, revenues and goods--and of the business of the said College, and the manner of proposing, electing, admitting and removing all and every one of the Council, the Professors, the Fellows or Tutors, the officers, the students and the servants thereof, and shall make and establish generally all such other statutes as may appear to them necessary for the future good government and prosperity of the said College, provided that these statutes be not contrary to the laws and statutes of our realm.
5. And we do hereby further ordain, grant and declare, that the statutes thus made and established by the said three members of the first Council, and given or left in writing under their respective hands, shall be valid and in full force at the expiration of ten years from the date of these presents, so that no future Council of the College shall have power to alter, change or vary them in any manner whatever and that the statutes shall for ever be considered

the constitution of the said College. And we do hereby appoint and declare that these statutes shall be made and established by the said William Carey, Joshua Marshman and John Clark Marshman alone, so that in case either of them should die before the expiration of ten years, the power of completing or perfecting these statutes shall devolve wholly on the survivors or survivor; and that in case all three of them should die before the expiration of ten years, the statutes which they have left in writing under their hands, or under the hand of the last survivor among them shall be considered "The Fundamental Statutes and Constitution of Serampore College," incapable of receiving either addition or alteration, and shall and may be registered in our Royal Court of Chancery as "The Statutes and Constitution of Serampore College."

6. And We do hereby further appoint, grant and declare that from and after the completion of the statutes of the said College in the above said time of ten years, the said Council of the College shall be deemed to consist of a Master or President and two or four members who may be Professors or otherwise as the Statutes may direct so that the said Council shall not contain less than three, nor more than five persons, as shall be defined in the Statutes. The Council shall ever be elected as the Statutes of the College may direct, yet the said Master or President shall always previously have been a Member of the said College; and upon the decease of the said Master or President, the Council of the said College shall be unable to do any act or deed until the appointment of a new Master or President, save and except the appointment of such a Master.
7. And We further appoint, grant and declare, that the said William Carey, Joshua Marshman and John Clark Marshman, the members of the first Council, and their successors for ever, shall have the power of conferring upon the students of the said College, Native Christians as well as others, degrees of rank and honour according to their proficiency in as ample a manner as any other such College, yet the said Serampore College shall only have the power of conferring such degrees on the students that testify their proficiency in Science and no rank or other special right shall be connected therewith in our dominions. And We do hereby further appoint, grant and declare, that after the expiration of the said ten years, the said Council of the College and their successors for ever shall have power to make and establish such orders and bye-laws as shall appear to them useful and necessary for the government of the said College, and to alter, suspend or repeal those already made, and from time to time make such new ones in their room as shall appear to them most proper and expedient provided the same be not repugnant to the Statutes of the College, or to the laws of our realm, and that after the expiration of these ten years any member of the Council shall have power to move the enactment of any new bye-law, or the alteration,

suspension or repeal of any existing one provided notice of such motion shall have been delivered in writing to the Master and read from the Chair at one previous meeting of the Council of the said College, but that no such motion shall be deemed to have passed in the affirmative, until the same shall have been discussed and decided by ballot at another meeting summoned especially for that purpose, a majority of the members then present having voted in the affirmative; and in this, as in all other cases, if the votes be equal, the Master or President shall have the casting vote.

Given at our Royal Palace in Copenhagen on the twenty-third day of February, in the year of our Lord one thousand, eight hundred and twenty-seven, in the nineteenth year of our reign.

Under our Royal Hand and Seal.

FREDERICK R.

Appendix III

Schedule II

(See Preamble and Sections 10 (1), 14 and 15)

Statutes and Regulations of the Serampore College, June 12th, 1833

1. Article the Third of the Charter granted by his Danish Majesty, having authorised the first Council of Serampore College in their lifetime to nominate under their hand and seal such other person or persons for colleagues or successors as may to them appear most proper, so that the Council shall always consist of at least three persons, their successors in the Council shall be competent in like manner to nominate in their lifetime, under their separate hand and seal, such person or persons as they may deem most proper to fill vacancies then existing or which may occur on their demise; members thus nominated and chosen shall succeed to the Council in order of their nomination.
2. It being fixed in the Charter that the Council must consist of the Master or President and at least two, but no more than four Members, and that on the demise of the Master no act shall be done until another be elected, the Master and Council for the time being shall appoint the next Master under their separate hand and seal. If on the demise of a Master no one be found thus appointed under the hand and seal of a majority of the Council, the Senior Member of the Council shall succeed as Master.
3. The Charter having given the casting vote to the Master, in all cases when the votes are equal the casting vote shall lie with the Master, and if there be no Master, it shall lie with the Senior Member of the Council.
4. Learning and piety being peculiar to no denomination of Christians, one member of the Council may at all times be of any other denomination besides the Baptist, to preserve the original design of the Institution; however, if on the election of a Master a number of the Council be equally divided, that part which is entirely of the Baptist denomination shall have the casting vote, whether it includes the Master or not.

5. The management of the College, including its revenues and property, the choice of Professor and Tutors, the admission of Students, the appointment of all functionaries and servants, and the general order and government of the College, shall ever be vested in the Master and the Council. The Master shall see that the Statutes and Regulations of the Council be duly carried into effect, and take order for the good government of the College in all things. His signature is necessary to the validity of all deeds, instruments, documents and proceedings.
6. "The first Council and their successor for ever" being authorised by the Charter "to confer such degrees of rank and honour as shall encourage learning" in the same manner as other Colleges and Universities, they shall from time to time confer degrees in such branches of Knowledge and Science as may be studied there, in the same manner as the Universities in Denmark, Germany and Great Britain. In doing this the Master and Council shall ad libitum call in the aid of any or all the Professors of Serampore College. All such degrees shall be perfectly free of expense to the person on whom they may be conferred, whether he be in India, Europe or America.
7. No oaths shall be administered in Serampore College, either to the Members of Council, the Professors and Tutors, or the Students. In all cases a solemn promise, duly recorded and signed by the party, shall be accepted instead of an oath.
8. Marriage shall be no bar to any office or situation in Serampore College, from that of the Master to that of the lowest student.
9. The salaries of the Professors and Tutors in Serampore College shall be appointed, and the means of support for all functionaries, students and servants be regulated by the Council in such manner as shall best promote the objects of the Institution.
10. It is intended that neither the Master nor any Member of the Council in general shall receive any salary. But, any Master who may not previously reside in the College shall have a residence there free of rent for himself and his family. And if the Council shall elect any one in Europe or in America, whom they deem eminent for learning and piety, a Member of the Council, with a view to choosing him Master, should they on trial deem him worthy, the Council shall be competent to appoint him such salary as they may deem necessary, not exceeding, however, the highest given to a Professor.
11. As the founders of the College deem the belief of Christ's Divinity and Atonement essential to vital Christianity, the promotion of which is the grand object of this Institution, no one shall be eligible to the College Council or to any Professorship who is known to oppose these doctrines, and should any one of the Professors or any member of the Council unhappily so change his views after his election as to oppose these fundamental doctrines of Christianity, on this being clearly and decidedly proved from his teaching or

his writings, he shall vacate the office he previously held. But every proceeding of this nature on the part of the College Council shall be published to the Christian world, with the proofs on which it may rest, as an Appendix to the succeeding Report.

12. Members of the Council are eligible from among the Professors of the College, or from among any in India, Europe, or America whom the College Council may deem suitable in point of learning, piety, and talent.
13. Students are admissible at the discretion of the Council from any body of Christians, whether Protestant, Roman Catholic, the Greek, or the Armenian Church; and for the purpose of study, from the Mussulman and Hindu youth, whose habits forbid their living in the College. No caste, colour, or country shall bar any man from admission into Serampore College.
14. Expulsion shall be awarded in cases of open immorality, incorrigible idleness, neglect of the College Statutes and regulations, or repeated disobedience to the officers of the College.
15. Any person in India, Europe, or America shall be at liberty to found any Professorship, or to attach to Serampore College any annual exhibition or prize for the encouragement of learning in the same manner as in the Universities of Great Britain, regulating such endowment according to their own will; and it shall be duty of the College Council to carry such benefactions into effect in strict consonance with the will of the donors as far as shall be consistent with the Statutes of the College.
16. It shall be lawful for the first Council of the College or their successors to make and rescind any bye-laws whatever, provided they be not contrary to these Statutes.
17. The Charter having declared that the number of the Professors and students in Serampore College remains unlimited, they shall be left thus unlimited, the number to be regulated only by the gracious providence of God and the generosity of the public in India, Europe and America.

Appendix IV

Universities Recognizing Serampore Degrees (India & Abroad)

Indian Universities Recognizing B.D. Degrees for Admission to M.A.

1. University of Calcutta, West Bengal
2. University of Burdwan, West Bengal
3. Vishva Bharti University, West Bengal
4. Kakatiya University, Andhra Pradesh
5. Osmania University, Andhra Pradesh
6. Gauhati University, Assam
7. M.S. University of Baroda, Gujarat
8. University of Ranchi, Jharkhand
9. R.D. University of Jabalpur, Madhya Pradesh
10. Vikram University, Madhya Pradesh
11. Nagpur University, Maharashtra
12. North Eastern Hill University, Meghalaya
13. Nagaland University, Nagaland
14. University of Mysore, Karnataka
15. Calicut University, Kerala
16. Mahatma Gandhi University, Kerala
17. University of Kerala, Kerala
18. Kanpur University, Uttar Pradesh

Indian Universities Recognizing M.TH. Degree for M.PHIL/PH.D. Programme

1. Andhra University, Andhra Pradesh
2. Mahatma Gandhi University, Kerala

Foreign Universities Recognizing Serampore Degrees for Higher Studies

1. University of Melbourne, Australia
2. Copenhagen University, Denmark
3. Sorbonne University, France
4. University of Hamburg, Germany
5. Ludwig Maximillians University, Germany
6. University of Regensburg, Germany
7. Friedrich Alexander University, Germany
8. Georg-August University, Germany
9. University of Auckland, New Zealand
10. SEAGST, Philippines
11. University of Cape Town, Republic of South Africa
12. University of Birmingham, UK
13. University of Lancaster, UK
14. Leicester University, UK
15. University of London, UK
16. University of Sheffield, UK
17. University of Durham, UK
18. University of Kent, UK
19. Oxford University, UK
20. Cambridge University, UK
21. Coventry University, UK
22. British Open University, UK
23. Union Theological Seminary, USA
24. Lutheran School of Theology, USA
25. West Minister Theological Seminary, USA
26. Fuller Theological Seminary, USA
27. The International University, USA
28. McCormick University, Chicago, USA
29. Princeton Theological University, USA
30. Talbot Theological Seminary, USA
31. Columbia International University, USA
32. Dallas Theological University, USA
33. Trinity International University, Illinois, USA
34. Asbury Theological University, USA
35. Fordham University, USA
36. Orthodox Theological University, USA
37. Drew University, Nadison, USA
38. Queen's University Belfast, UK[1]

---

1 Ravi Tiwari, *Senate of Serampore College (University) At Ninety: Issues and Concerns* (Serampore: The Registrar, Senate of Serampore College, 2008), 53-55.

Bibliography

Minutes/Documents/Reports, etc.

Bengal Act No. IV of 1918.

Commission on Serampore College, Report presented to the Council and Senate of Serampore College. June 28, 1970.

Council of Serampore College Bye-Laws Governing College Administration. Serampore: Serampore College, 1993.

Ecumenical Response to Theological Education in Africa, Asia, Near East, South Pacific, Latin America and Caribbean: Progress Report on the T.E.F. Third Mandate Programme. London: Theological Education Fund, 1975.

Ecumenical Response to Theological Education in Africa, Asia, Near East, South Pacific, Latin America and Caribbean: Progress Report on the T.E.F. Third Mandate Programme. London: Theological Education Fund, 1976.

Friends of Serampore. July 21, 2003.

Interim Report on the NCC Survey of Theological Education. Nagpur: NCCI, 1944.

Lindsay Commission Report on Christian Higher Education in India. London: Humphrey Milford, 1933.

Minutes of the Meetings of Baptist Missionary Society, 1792-1837. Bound volumes, unpublished. Vol.1-8.

Minutes of the Meeting of the Committee on Academic Administration of the Senate of Serampore College, Serampore, February 2, 1976.

Minutes of the Meeting of the Committee on Academic Administration of the Senate of Serampore College, Serampore. June 27, 1978.

Minutes of the Meeting of the Committee on Academic Administration of the Senate of Serampore College. UTC Bangalore, August 29, 1978.

Minutes of the Meeting of the Committee on Academic Administration of the Senate of Serampore College. Bombay, June 28-29, 1983.

Minutes of the Meeting of the Committee on Research, of the Senate of Serampore College. LT, December 18, 1976.

Minutes of the Meeting of the Committee on Research, of the Senate of Serampore College. UTC, Madras, July 20-21, 1979.

Minutes of the Meeting of the Co-ordination Committee, of the Senate of Serampore College. Calcutta, June 30, 1976.

Minutes of the Meeting of the Co-ordination Committee, of the Senate of Serampore College. UTC, Bangalore, December 3, 1977.

Minutes of the Meeting of the Co-ordination Committee, of the Senate of Serampore College. Calcutta, June 23, 1979.

Minutes of the Meeting of the Co-ordination Committee, of the Senate of Serampore College. UTC, Bangalore, April 26-27, 1979.

Minutes of the Meeting of the Evaluation Commission, of the Senate of Serampore College. UTC, Bangalore, June 18, 1976.

Minutes of the Meeting of the Executive of the Senate of Serampore College, Serampore. January 30-31, 1964.

Minutes of the Meeting of the Executive of the Senate of Serampore College, Calcutta. March 14, 1970.

Minutes of the Meeting of the Executive of the Senate of Serampore College, Calcutta. June 17-18, 1974.

Minutes of the Meeting of the Executive of the Senate of Serampore College, held at Serampore. January 28, 1975.

Minutes of the Meeting of the Executive of the Senate of Serampore College, Calcutta. June 16-17, 1975.

Minutes of the Meeting of the Implementation Committee Appointed to Consider Reorganization of the Functioning of the Serampore Senate held at Lee Memorial Mission House, Wellington Square, Calcutta on March 22nd and 23rd, 1974.

Minutes of the Meeting of the Special meeting, of the Senate of Serampore College, Secunderabad, January 31, 1979.

Minutes of the Senate of Serampore College's Senate. 2007.

Report of the Consultation Theological Education in Europe. Geneva: WCC, 1980.

Report of the Consultations on Curriculum Revision of the BTESSC. 2007.

Report of the Director of Research and SATHRI. 2003.

Report of the Director of Research and SATHRI. 2004.

Report of the Director of Research and SATHRI. 2005-2006.

Report of the Director of Research and SATHRI. 2006-2007.

Report of the Director of Theological Education by Extension. 2005-2006.

Report of the Director of Theological Education by Extension. 2006-2007.

Report of the Director of Theological Education by Extension. 2007-2008.

Report of the Doctor of Ministry and Continuing Theological Education of the BTESSC. 2006-2007.

Report of the Doctor of Ministry and Continuing Theological Education of the BTESSC. 2007-2008.

Report on Implementation of the Scheme of the One Structure for Theological Education Under SSC (January 28th 1976), 507.

Report of the International Missionary Council on World Mission of the Church, Tambaran, 1938. (March, 1939), 80-92.

Report of the President of the Senate of Serampore College, for the Year 1970.

Report of the President of the Senate of Serampore College, for the Year 1976.

Report of the President of the Senate of Serampore College, for the Year 1985.

Report of the President of the Senate of Serampore College, for the Year 1996.

Report of the President of the Senate of Serampore College, for the Year 2000-01.

Report of the President of the Senate of Serampore College, for the Year 2003-04.

Report of the President of the Senate of Serampore College, for the Year 2004-05.

Report of the President of the Senate of Serampore College, for the Year 2005-06.

Report of the President of the Senate of Serampore College, for the Year 2007-08.

Report of the President of the Senate of Serampore College, for the Year 2004-2005.

Reports of the National Consultation on Theological Education. (May, 22-24) Chennai: CSI Centre, 2001.

Report of the Registrar of the Senate of Serampore College Annual Senate Meeting. 2003-2004.

Report of the Registrar of the Senate of Serampore College Annual Senate Meeting. 2004-2005.

Report of the Registrar of the Senate of Serampore College Annual Senate Meeting. 2005-2006.

Report of the Registrar of the Senate of Serampore College Annual Senate Meeting. 2006-2007.

Report of the Registrar of the Senate of Serampore College Annual Senate Meeting. 2007-2008.

Report of the Secretary Annual Report of the BTESSC. 2005-2006.

Report of the Secretary Annual Report of the BTESSC. 2006-2007.

Report of the Study Programme and Consultation on Theological Education in India. 1967-68.

Report of the Theological Education Fund: Issues in Theological Education 1964-1965. London: Theological Education Fund, 1965.

Senate of Serampore College, Board of Theological Education, Minutes of the Third Meeting, Serampore, February 1-3, 1978.

Senate of Serampore College, Board of Theological Education, Minutes of the Eleventh Meeting, Serampore, 30-31, 1985.

Senate of Serampore College and the Board of Theological Education of the Senate of Serampore College Constitution: One National Structure for Theological Education in India. Serampore: Serampore College, 2005.

Senate of Serampore College Criteria for Affiliation and Evaluation Procedure. Serampore: Serampore College, 2007.

Senate of Serampore College Faculty of Theology Regulations Relating to the Degree of Bachelor of Divinity. Serampore: Serampore College, 1993.

Senate of Serampore College Faculty of Theology Regulations Relating to the Degree of Master of Theology. Serampore: Serampore College, 1998 and 2007.

Senate of Serampore College Faculty of Theology Regulations Relating to the Degree of Bachelor of Theology. Serampore: Serampore College, 2004.

Senate of Serampore College, Minutes of the Senate, 2008.

Senate of Serampore College, Proceedings of the Theological Senate and Its Committees, January 30-22 November, Book VI. Vol. I, 1969.

Senate of Serampore College, Proceedings of the Theological Senate and Its Committees, January 27-21 November, Book VIII. Vol. I, 1970.

Senate of Serampore College, Proceedings of the Theological Senate and Its Committees, January 28-27 November, Book IV. Vol. V, 1971.

Senate of Serampore College, Proceedings of the Theological Senate and Its Committees, January 28-1 October, Book VII, 1975.

Senate of Serampore College Proceedings of the Theological Senate and its Committees January 28th 1975-October 1st 1975.

Senate of Serampore College, Proceedings of the Theological Senate and Its Committees, February 2-2 October, Book VII, 1976.

Senate of Serampore College, Proceedings of the Theological Senate and Its Committees, December 3-15 December, 1978.

Senate of Serampore College, Proceedings of the Theological Senate and Its Committees, January 17-13 December, Book VIII, 1980.

Senate of Serampore College, Proceedings of the Theological Senate and Its Committees, January 9-11 December, Book IX, 1981.

Senate of Serampore College, Proceedings of the Theological Senate and Its Committees, December 15-7 December, Book II. Vol. VIII, 1983.

Senate of Serampore College, Proceedings of the Theological Senate and Its Committees, January 31-13 December, 1984.

Senate of Serampore College, Proceedings of the Theological Senate and Its Committees, January 28-1 October, Book IX. Vol. V, 1986.

Senate of Serampore College, Proceedings of the Theological Senate and Its Committees, January 27-24 September, Book IX. Vol. VI, 1987.

Senate of Serampore College, Proceedings of the Theological Senate and Its Committees, January 11-11 December, Book X. Vol. II, 1990.

Senate of Serampore College, Proceedings of the Theological Senate and Its Committees, January 11-10 December, Book X. Vol. III, 1991.

Senate of Serampore College, Proceedings of the Theological Senate and Its Committees, January 17-31 October, Book X. Vol. IV, 1992.

Senate of Serampore College, Proceedings of the Theological Senate and Its Committees, January 12-December 10, Book X. Vol. V, 1993.

Senate of Serampore College, Proceedings of the Theological Senate and Its Committees, January 14-14 December, Book XI. Vol. VI, 1994.

Senate of Serampore College, Proceedings of the Theological Senate and Its Committees, January 17-1 November, Book XII. Vol. VIII, 1996.

Senate of Serampore College, Proceedings of the Theological Senate and Its Committees, February 3-8 October, Book XII. Vol. IX. 1997.

Senate of Serampore College, Proceedings of the Theological Senate and Its Committees, January 16-19 November, Book XII. Vol. VIII, 1998.

Senate of Serampore College, Proceedings of the Theological Senate and Its Committees, January 16-2 November, Book XII. Vol. XI, 1999.

Senate of Serampore College, Proceedings of the Theological Senate and Its Committees, January 5-3 November, Book XII. Vol. XII, 2000.

Senate of Serampore College, Proceedings of the Theological Senate and Its Committees, January 17-2 November, Book XIV. Vol. XIII, 2001.

Senate of Serampore College, Proceedings of the Theological Senate and Its Committees, January 8-27 November, Book XV. Vol. XIV, 2002.

Senate of Serampore College, Proceedings of the Theological Senate and Its Committees, February 3, 2004 to January 4, 2005, Book XVII. Vol. XVI, 2005.

Senate of Serampore College, Regulations for Internal and External Candidates: Relating to the Bachelor of Divinity Degree. December, 1962.

Serampore College Carey Day 17th August 2001: 240th Birth Anniversary of Dr. William Carey. Serampore: Serampore College, 2001.

Serampore College Codex. The 200 Years of Carey's Arrival in India and the 172-Year of the College, 1992.

Serampore College Prospectus 2008 Arts, Science and Commerce Department. Serampore: Serampore College Computer Bi-Centenary Block, 2008.

Serampore College, Est. 1818.

Serampore Convocation 2002. 10th February at Aizawl Theological College, 2002.

SSC Proceedings of the Theological Senate and its Committees. January 21, 2006 to November, 24, 2006.

SSC Proceedings of the Theological Senate and its Committees. January 28th-October 1st 1975.

SSC Regulations for Internal and External Candidates: Relating to the Bachelor of Divinity (B.D.) Degree. December, 1962.

The Serampore College Act, 1918.

Theological Education in India: Report of Study Programme and Consultation 1967-68. Serampore: The Board of Theological Education, 1968.

Tiwari, Ravi. Senate of Serampore College Initiating Revision of Curricula. Serampore: Serampore College, 2006.

Books

Abishiktananda, Swami. *Hindu-Christian Meeting Point: In the Cave of the Heart.* Delhi: ISPCK, 1976.

Abraham, C. E. *William Carey and the Indian Church.* Calcutta: Baptist Mission Press, 1964.

________. *The Founders of the National Mission Society of India.* Madras: NMSI, 1947.

Abraham K. C. *Liberative Solidarity: Contemporary Perspectives on Mission.* Thiruvalla: Christava Sahitya Samithi, 1996.

Abrecht, Paul. *The Churches and Rapid Social Change.* New York: Doubleday & Company, 1961.

Agarwal, M. M. *Freedom of the Soul: A Post-Modern Understanding of Hinduism.* New Delhi: Concept, 2002.

Ali, A. Yusuf. *A Cultural History of India During the British Period.* Bombay: 1969.

Altbach, G. Philip. ed. *Turmoil and Transition: Higher Education and Student Politics in India.* Delhi: Lavani Publishing House, 1968.

Amalorpavadass, D. S. ed. *Ministries in the Church in India: Research Seminar and Pastoral Consultation.* New Delhi: C.B.C.I. Centre, 1976.

________. *The Indian Church in the Struggle for a New Society.* Bangalore: NBCLC, 1968.

Amirtham Samuel and Cyril H. S. Moon. eds. *The Teaching of Ecumenism.* Geneva: WCC Publications, 1987.

________. and Robin Pryor. eds. *Resources for Spiritual Formation in Theological Education.* Geneva: WWC, Publications, 1989.

________. ed. *Stories Make People: Examples of Theological Work in Community.* Geneva: WCC, Publications, 1989.

Anathil, M. George. *The Theological Formation of the Clergy in India.* Poona: Pontifical Athenaeum, 1966.

Anderson, J. D. & E. E. Jones. *The Management of Industry; Leadership, Purpose, Structure, Community*. San Francisco, Harper & Row, 1978.

Anderson, Leith. *The Church in the Twenty-first Century*. Minneapolis: Bethany House, 1992.

Anderson, Ray S. *The Soul of Ministry: Forming Leaders for God's People*. Louisville: Westminster John Knox, 1997.

________. *The Shape of Prctical Theology: Empowering Ministry with Theological Praxis*. Downers Grove: InterVarsity Press, 2001.

________. ed. *Theological Foundations for Ministry*. Edinburgh: T & T Clark, 1979.

Andews, C. F. *The Renaissance in India: Its Missionary Aspect*. Madrass: SCM Press, 1913.

________. *The Rise and Growth of the Congress in India*. London: Allen and Urwin, 1938.

Antone, S. Hope. *Religious Education in Context of Plurality and Pluralism*. Hong Kong: CCA Publishers, 2003.

Arangaden, A. J. *Church Union in South India: Its Progress and Consummation* Mangalore: 1947.

Ariarajah, W. and S. Amirtham. eds. *Theological Formation in a Multi Faith Milieu*. Geneva: WCC, Publications, 1988.

Arles, Siga. *Theological Education for the Mission of the Church in India, 1947-1987*. New York: Peter Lang, 1991.

Ashirvatham, Eddy. *Christianity in the Indian Crucible*. Calcutta: YMCA Publishing House, 1955.

Astley, Jeff, Francis, Leslie J. and Crowder, Colin. *Theological Perspectives on Christian Formation: A Reader on Theology and Christian Education*. Grand Rapids: William B. Eerdmans Publishing Company, 1996.

Azariah, M. *Witnessing in India Today*. Madras: UELCI, 1983.

Azariah, V. S. *India and Christian Movement*. Delhi: CLS, 1936.

Baago, Kaj. *A History of the National Christian Council of India, 1914-1964*. Nagpur: NCCI, 1965.

________. *Pioneers of Indigenous Christianity*. Madras: CLS, 1969.

Babbie, R. Earl. *The Practice of Social Research*. California: Wadsworth Publishing Company, 1979.

Baker, P. Dwight. *William Carey and the Business Model for Mission*. New York: McGraw Hill, 2005.

________. ed. *Religious Motivation: Biographical and Sociological Problems for the Church Historian*. Oxford: Blackwell, 1978.

Ban, D. Joseph. ed. *The Christological Foundations of Contemporary Theological Education*. London: Mercer University Press, 1988.

Banerjee. *Serampore College*, n.d., n.p.

Banks, Robert. *Envisioning Theological Education: Exploring a Missional Alternative to Current Models*. Grand Rapid: William B. Eerdmans Publishing Company, 1999.

Barnett, M. Rose. *The Politics of Cutural Nationalism in South India*. Princeton: University Press, 1976.

Barreto, Duartie. *India's Search for Development and Social Justice: Analysis of India Society*. Bangalore: Centre for Social Action, 1977.

Basham, A. L. *The Wonder that was India*. New York: Grove Press, 1959.

Beisswenger, Donald F. *Comprehensive Bibliography on Field Education and Theological Education*. USA: Vanderbuilt University, 1985.

________. *Theological Field Education: A Collection of Key Resources*, Volume I. Kansas City, 1977, 1985.

________. Volume II. Theme: *Theological Reflection*. USA: Kansas City, 1985.

________. Volume III. Theme: *Religious Experience*. USA: Kansas City, 1981.

________. Volume IV. Theme: *Pastoral Hermeneutics*. USA: Kansas City, 1983.

________. Volume V. Theme: *Spirituality, Ministry and Field Education*. USA: Kansas City, 1986.

Belcher, Joseph. *William Carey: A Biography.* Philadelphi: Americal Baptist Publication Society, 1853.

Bennie, R. Crockett. *Thoughts on Missions to India*. Sermpore: 1825.

________. *The Life and Labours of Carey, Marshman and Ward.* New York: U.D. Ward, 1867.

________. *Thoughts on Propagating Christianity More Effectively Among the Heathen*. Serampore: Mission Press, 1827.

________. *Brief Memoir Relative to the Operations of the Serampore Missionaries, Bengal with an Appendix*. London: Parbury, Allen and Co., 1827.

________. *Statement Relative to Serampore Supplementary to a Brief Memoir.* London: Parbury, Allen and Co., 1828.

Bergquist, A. James. *Patterns of Theological Education in India: With Special Reference to Gurukul Theological College, 1953-1968*. Madras: Gurukul Theological College and Research Institute, 1969.

Berinstain, Valerie. *Discoveries: India and the Mughal Dynasty.* New York: HNA Books, 2005.

Best, F. Thomas. ed. *Vancouver to Canberra, 1983-1990, Report of the Central Committee of the WCC to the Seventh Assembly*. Geneva: WCC Publications, 1990.

Beteille, Andre. *Caste, Class and Power*. Bombay: OUP, 1966.

Beyerhaus, Peter, and C. F. Hallen Creutz. eds. *The Crossing Frontiers.* Uppsala: Studia Missionalia, 1969.

Bhattacharya, Jogendra Nath. *Hindu Castes and Sects.* Calcutta: Editions Indian, 1973.

Bhatia, H. S. *Mahrattas Sikhs and Southern Sultans of India: Their Fight Against Foreign Power*. Delhi: Deep and Deep, 2002.

Biddle, B. J. and E.H. Thomas. *Role Theory: Concepts and Research.* New York: John Wiley and Sons, 1966.

Blunt, Edward. ed. *Social Service in India.* London: His Majesty's Stationary Office, 1938.

Boel, J. *Christian Mission in India: A Sociological Analysis.* Amsterdam: Graduate Press, 1975.

Bosch, David. *Transforming Mission: Shift in Theology of Mission.* New York: Orbis Books, 1991.

________. *Witness to the World: The Christian Mission in Theological Perspective.* Atlanta: John Knox Press, 1980.

Bower, W. C. *The Curriculum of Religious Education.* New York: Charles Scribner's Sons, 1927.

Brass, Paul R. *Factional Politics in an Indian State: The Congress Party in Utter Pradesh.* Bombay: OUP Univesity of California Press, 1966.

Brown, L. W. *The Indian Christian of St. Thomas.* Cambridge: CUP, 1956.

Burkle H. and W. Roth. eds. *Indian Voices in Today's Theological Debate.* Delhi: ISPCK, 1972.

Cannon, Katie G. and et.al. eds. *God's Fierce Whimsy: Christian Feminism and Theological Education.* USA: Pilgrim Press, 1985.

Carey, Eustace. *Memoir of William Carey D.D. Late Missionary to Bengal: Professor of Oriental Languages in the College of Forth William. Calcutta.* London: Jackson and Walford, 1836.

Carey, William. *An Inquiry into the Obligations of Christians to Use Means for the Conversion of the Heathens.* England: 1792.

Castle, E. B. *Pinciples of Education for Teachers in India.* Bombay: OUP, 1969.

Chapman, L. Graeme. *Spiritual Development.* London: SCM Press, 1986.

Chappell, J. and H. S. Dyer. *Pandita Ramabai: A Great Life in Indian Mission.* London: Pickering and Inglis, 1974.

Chatterjee, Kumar, Sunil. *Hanah Marshman: The First Woman Missionary in India.* Serampore: Carey Library, 2002.

________. *John Clark Marshman: A Trustworthy Freiend of India.* Sheoraphuli: Mahamaya Sahitya Mandir, 2001.

________. *William Carey and Serampore.* Serampore: Laserplus, 2004.

Chute, C. Arthur. *William Carey: A Sketch of Beginning in Modern Missions.* Chicago: Goodman & Dickerson, 1891.

Clare, Anderson. *Indian Uprising of 1857-1858: Prisoners, Prisoners and Rebellion.* New York: Anthem Press, 2007.

Clark, G. H. *A Christian Philosophy of Education.* Grand Rapids: William B. Eerdmans Publishing Company, 1946.

Clark, Sunder. *Let the Indian Church be Indian.* Madras: CLS, 1980.

Coe, Shoki, et al., eds. *Learning in Context: The Search for Innovative Patterns in Theological Education.* London: New Life Press, 1973.

Conway, Martin. *Introducing the World Council of Churches.* Geneva: WCC Publications, 2001.

Correia-Afonso, John. *Indo-Portuguese History: Sources and Problems.* Bombay: OUP, 1981.

Cox, Oliver, Cromwell. *Caste, Class, and Race: A Study in Social Dynamics.* New York: Doubleday Publication, 1948.

Cracknell, Kenneth. *Relations with People of Other Faiths: Guidelines for Dialogue in Britain.* London: BCC, 1983.

________. *Towards a New Relationship: Christians and People of Other Faiths.* London: Epworth Press, 1986.

Culross, James. *William Carey.* London: Hodder and Stoughton, 1818.

Currie, Robert. *Methodism Divided: A Study of the Sociology of Ecumenicalism.* London: Faber, 1968.

Dakar, D. N. and S. N. Dakar. *Combating AIDS in the 21st Century: Issues and Challenges.* Delhi: Sterling Publishers Private Limited, 2001.

Datta, Swati. et al., *Carey Day Souvenir, 2004.* Serampore: Seampore College, 2004.

David, Paton. *New Forms of Ministry.* London: Edinburgh House, 1965.

Devadas, V. H. *The Social Mission of the Church.* Delhi: ISPCK, 1982.

Devanandan, P. D. *Christian Concern in Hinduism.* Madras: CLS, 1961.

Devasia, Leelamma. ed. *Women in India: Equality, Social Justice and Developments.* New Delhi: India Social Institute, 1990.

DeVries, E. *Man in Rapid Social Change.* London: SCM Press, 1961.

Dewitt, B. Calvin. ed. *The Environment and the Christian: What Can We Learn from the New Testament?.* Michigan: Baker Book House, 1991.

Dharmaraj, S. Jacob. *Colonialism and Christian Mission: Postcolonial Reflections.* Delhi: ISPCK, 1993.

Dickinson, D.N . Richard. *The Christian College in Developing India: A Sociological Inquiry.* Madras: OUP, 1971.

Dietrich, Gabrielle. *Culture, Religion and Development.* Bangalore: CSA, 1978.

D'Sa, M. *History of the Roman Church in India.* Vol.1. Bombay: Furtado and Sons, 1910.

D'Souza, Alfred. ed. *Women in Contemporary India*. Delhi: Manohar Books, 1975.

Dube, W. Musa. *HIV/AIDS and the Curriculum: Methods of Integrating HIV/AIDS in Theological Programes*. Geneva: WCC, 2005.

Ebright, D. F. *The National Missionary Society of India, 1905-1942*. Chicago: 1944.

Elias, L. John. *Pedagogy of Liberation*. Florida: Kreiger Publishing Company, 1994.

Elwood, J. Douglas. ed. *What Asian Christians are Thinking: A Theological Source Book with Supplementary Bibliography*. Philippines: ATESEA, 1976.

Emery, James and Rose F. Kinsler. *Opting for Change: A Handbook on Evaluation and Training for Theological Education by Extension*. Geneva: WCC Publications, 1991.

England, C. John. ed. *Living Theology in Asia*. London: SCM Press, 1981.

Eraly, Abraham. *The Mughal World: India's Tainted Paradise*. New York: HNA Books, 2008.

Evans, Alice Frazer, Robert A. Evans and David A. Roozen. eds. *The Globalization of Theological Education*. Maryknoll: Orbis Books, 1993.

Everett, J. Matson. *Women and Social Change in India*. New Delhi: Heritage Publishers, 1979.

Fabella, Virginia and Sergio Torres. eds. *Irruption of the Third World: Challenge to Theology*. New York, Maryknoll, Orbis Books, 1983.

Faivre, A. *The Emergence of the Laity in the Early Church*. New Jersey: Mahwah Paulist, 1990.

Farley, E. *Theologia: The Fragmentation and Unity of Theological Education*. Philadelphia: Fortress Press, 1983.

_________. *The Fragility of Knowledge: Theological Education in the Church and the University*. Philadelphia: Fortress Press, 1988.

Farquhar, J. N. *Modern Religious Movements in India*. Delhi: Munshiram Manoharlal, 1967.

Farwell, E. Mary. *The Life of William Carey*. New York: Flaming H. Ravell, Co., 1888.

Feilding, R. Charles. *Theological Education for Ministry*. USA: Thomas W. Klink, 1996.

Fenger, J. Ferdinand. *History of the Tranquebar Mission*. London: Jonathan Cape, 1929.

Ferris, W. Robert. *Renewal in Theological Education*. Wheaton: Billy Graham Center, 1990.

Ferroli. *The Jesuits in Malabar*. Bangalore: Dharmaram, 1939.

Finney, John. *Emerging Evangelism*. London: Darton, Longman and Todd Ltd, 2004.

Fiorenza, Schuessler Elisabeth. *In Memory of Her: A Feminist Theological Reconstruction of Christian Origins*. New York: Crossroad: 1983.

Firth, C.B. *An Introduction to India Church History*. Delhi: ISPCK, 2000.

Forester, B. Duncan. *Caste and Christianity*. London: Curzon Press, 1980.

Freire, Paulo. *Education for Liberation*. Bangalore: ECC Publications, 1983.

________. *Pedagogy of the Oppressed*. New York: Continuum, 1970.

Frykenberg, Eric Robert. ed. *Land Control and Social Structure in India History.* London: University of Wisconsin Press, 1969.

Fuller, C. J. *The Camphor Flame: Popular Hinduism and Society in India*. Princeton: Princeton UP, 1992.

Gandhi P. Jegadish and George Cheriyan. eds. *Globalization: A Challenge to the Church*. Nagpur: NCCI, 1998, 67.

Gatimu, K Hogarth, J. and Barret, D. *Theological Education in Context*. Nairobi: Uzima Press Ltd., 1983.

Gavin, Flood. *An Introduction to Hinduism.* Cambridge: Cambridge, 1996.

________. *The Blackwell Companion to Hinduism.* Malden MA: Blackwell, 2003.

Gert, Ruppel and Schreiner, Peter. *Shared Learning in a Plural Woprld: Ecumenical Approaches to Inter-Religious Education*. London: LIT Verlag Munster, 2003.

Ghuye, G. S. *Caste, Class and Occupation.* Bombay: Popular Book Depot, 1961.

________. *Caste and Race in India.* Bombay: Popular Book Depot, 1969.

Gibbs, M. E. *From Jerusalem to New Delhi*. Delhi: ISPCK, 1972.

Gine, Chandra Pratap. *The System of Elementary Education of the Serampore Mission*. Jorhat: ETC, 2001.

Gladston, J. W. "Ministerial Formation in a Context of Pluralities". *Together with People* Ed., by Samson Prabakar. Bangalore: SATHRI/BTESSC, 2004.

Gladstone, J. W. *Protestant Christianity and People's Movements in Kerala: A Study of Christian Mass Movements in Relation to Neo-Hindu, Socio-Religious Movements in Kerala, 1850-1936*. Trivandrum: KUTS Publications, 1984.

________. Ed., *United to Unite. History of the Church of South India, 1947-1997.* Chinnai: CSI Synod, 1997.

Gnanadason, Aruna. Ed., *Ecumenism: Hope in Action*, Nagpur: NCCI, 1990.

Gnanakaran, Ken. *ACTS Institute: A New Model for Theological Education*. Taiwan: ATA, 1983.

Goodall, Norman. *Ecumenical Progress: A Decade of Change in the Ecumenical Movement, 1961-1971*. London: OUP, 1972.

Grafe, Hugald. *History of Christianity in India*. Vol. 4, part. 2. Bangalore: CHAI, 1990.

Greeff, David. *Theological Education by Extension: A Reflection on the Usefulness of Theological Extension Work in Namibia-like Contexts, in Comparison to that of Traditional Theological Institutions.* USA: St Andrews Hall, 2005.

Griffiths, Bede. *Christian Ashram: Essays Towards a Hindu-Christian Dialogue.* London: Longman and Todd, Ltd., 1966.

Grifo, Lynne. *Why Theological Education for All.* New York: TE for ALL.org, 1998.

Gupta, A. C. Das. Ed., *Selection from Calcutta Gazette, 1824-1832.* Calcutta: Alipore Government Press, 1859.

Hambye, E. R. *History of Christianity in India.* Vol. III. Bangalore: CHAI, 1997.

________. and Tisserant. *Eastern Christianity in India.* Calcutta: 1957.

Harrison, M. H. *After Ten Years: A Report on Theological Education in India.* Nagpur: NCCI, 1953.

Hedlund, E. Roger. *Roots of the Great Debate in Mission with Documents from Evangelical and Ecumenical Conferences.* Madras: ELS, 1984.

________. and F. Hrangkhuman. eds. *Indigenous Mission in India.* Madras: HBI Press, 1980.

Hewate, E. G. K. *Christ and Western India.* Bombay: J. Kellock, Wilson College, 1950.

Hillman, Eugene. *Wider Ecumenism.* Geneva: WCC Publications, 1968.

Hind. John. ed. *Formation for Ministry within a Learning Church.* UK: Church House Publishing, 2003.

Hoefer, E. Herbert. *The Augsburg Cofession and Ecumenism in India.* Madras: Gurukul LTC & RI, 1980.

Hoffman, R. Bengt. *Christian Social thought in India, 1947-1962: An Evaluation.* Bangalore: CISRS, 1967.

Hogg, Willliam Richey. *Ecumenical Foundations.* New York: Harpers &Brothers, 1952.

Hollander, H. Elisabeth. *The Council for World Mission: A Viable Model for Contemporary Mission?* England: Brimingham, 1996.

Houpert, J. C. Ch*ristianity in India, Burma and Ceylon: 52-1952 A.D,.* Tiruchirapally: 1957.

Howells, George and Members of the College Faculty. *The Story of Serampore and Its College.* Serampore: 1927.

________. and A. C. Underwood. *The Story of Serampore and Its College.* Serampore: 1918.

Hrangkhuma, F. *An Introduction to Church History.* Bangalore: Theological Book Trust, 1999.

Hull, M. John. *What Prevents Adult Christians from Learning?*. London: SCM Press Ltd., 1985.

Jabbar, Naheem. *Historiography and Writing Postcolonial India.* USA: Routledge, 2007.

Jackson, J. A. ed. *Role: Sociological Studies.* Cambridge: Cambridge University Press, 1972.

________. ed. *Professions and Professionalization.* Cambridge: Cambridge University Press, 1970.

Jewett, K. Paul. *Man as Male and Female: A Study in Sexual Relationships from a Theological Point of View*. Grand Rapids: William B. Eerdmans, 1975.

Jeyakumar, D. Arthur. *History of Christianity in India: Selected Themes* Delhi: ISPCK, 2002.

Job, G.V. et.al. *Rethinking Christianity in India.* Madras: CLS, 1939.

Jogedra, Nath, Batacharya. *Castes and Sects.* Delhi: Munshiram Manoharlal, 1996.

Johannes, Van den Berg. *Constrained by Jesus Love*. Rotterdam: J. H. Kok and N. V. Kampen, 1956.

John, Fenwick. *Biographical Sketch of Joshua Marsman, D.D., of Serampore New Castle Chronicle*. New Castle: Emerson Charnley, 1838.

Johns, William. *A Collection of Facts and Opinions Relative to the Burning of Widows with the Dead Bodies of their Husbands and to other Destructive Customs Prevalent in British India.* Birmingham: W. H. Pearce, 1816.

Joseph, Hough. C. Jr. and Johm B. Cobb, Jr. *Christian Identity and Theological Education*. Atlanta: Scholars Press, 1985.

Joseph, M. J. ed. *Towards Strategy for People's Organization in India*. Nagpur: Christian Service Agency, 1974.

Joseph, T. K. *The Malabar Christians and their Ancient Documents.* Trivandrum: 1929.

Joy, R. J. Hepzi. *History and Development of Education of Women in Kerala.* K.U.T.: Seminary Publications, 1995.

Judith, M. Brown. *Modern India: The Origins of an Asian Democracy.* London: Oxford University Press, 1994.

Kanter, R. M. *Commitment and Community*. Cambridge: Harvard University Press, 1972.

Keay, F. E. *A History of Education in India and Pakistan*. London: Oxford University Press, 1939.

________. *A History of the Syrian Church in India.* 3rd edition. Delhi: ISPCK, 1960.

Keitzar, Renthy, ed. *Good News for North East India: A Theological Reader*. Guwahati: CLC, 1995.

________. *In Search of Relevant Gospel Message: Introducing a Contextual Christian Theology for North East India*. Guwahati: CLC, 1995.

Kelsey, D. *Between Athens and Berlin: The Theological Education Debate*. Grand Rapids: Eerdmans, 1993.

Kent F. Eliza. *Converting Women: Gender and Protestant Christianity in Colonial South India*. New York: Oxford University Press, 2004.

Kinnamon, Michael and Brian E. Cope. eds. *The Ecumencial Movement: An Anthology of Key Textts and Voices*. Geneva: WCC Publications/Michigan: Villiam B. Eerdmans Publishing Company, 1997.

Kinsler, F. Rose. ed. *Ministry by the People Theological Education by Extension*. Geneva: WCC, Publications, 1983.

________. *The Extension Movement in Theological Education*. California: William Carey Library, 1978.

Kirk, J. A. *What is Mission: Theological Explorations*. Minneapolis: Fortress Press, 1999.

________. *The Mission of Theology and Theology as Mission*. USA: Trinity Press, 1997.

Kirpatrick, Dow. ed. *The Holy Spirit*. Tennessee: Tidings Publications, 1974.

Knudten, R. ed. *The Sociology of Religion: An Anthology*. New York: Appleton Century Crofts, 1967.

Kopf, D. *British Orientalism and Bengal Renaissance: The Dynamics of Modernization, 1773-1835*. Calcutta: Firma K.L. Mukhopadhyay, 1969.

Koshy, Ninan. *Caste in the Kerala Churches*. Bangalore: CISRS, 1968.

Kothari, C. R. *Research Methodology, Methods and Techniques*. 2nd ed. Delhi: Prentice Hall of India, 1975.

Kretzmann, M. L. *Theological Education in Andhra Pradesh: A Survey and Study of the Task of Theological Education in the Churches Related to the Andhra Christian Theological College*. Secunderabad: ACTC, 1966.

Krishnan, Sankaran. *Postcolonial Insecurities: Indian, Sri Lanka the Question of Nationhood*. USA: University of Minnesota Press, 1992.

Kurien, C. T. *Poverty and Development*. Bangalore: CISRS, 1974.

Laird, M. A. *Missionaries and Education in Bengal, 1793-1837*. Oxford: Clarendon Press, 1972.

Latourette, K. S. *A History of the Expansion of Christianity*, Vol. VI. USA: Harper, 1945.

Lebacqz, Karen. *Justic in an Unjust World: Foundations for a Christian Approach to Justice*. Minneapolis: Augsburg Publishing House, 1987.

Lee, R. and M. Marty. Eds. *Religion and Social Conflict*. New York: Oxford University Press, 1964.

Lefever, B. W. *From Amsterdam to Nairabi*. Amsterdam: 1979.

Leslie, Brown. *The Indian Christians of St. Thomas. An Account of the Ancient Syrian Church of Malabar*. Cambridge: Cambridge University Press 1956.

Lienemann-Perrin, Christine. *Training for a Relevant Ministry: A Study of the Work of the Theological Education Fund.* Madras: CLS for PTE/WCC, 1981.

Lindner, B. John. *Ecumenical Formation: A Methodology for a Pluralistic Age.* Switzerland: WCC, 1999.

Lindsay, A. D. *Report of the Commission on Christian Higher Education in India: An Enquiry into the Place of Christian College in Modern India.* London: OUP, 1931.

Lopez, Andrew. *A Short Account of the Mission Under the Charge of the Father of the Society of Jesus of the Malabar Province in the East Indies.* Trichy: 1644.

Lossky, N. ed. *The Dictionary of the Ecumenical Movement.* Grand Rapids : Wm. B. Eerdmans Publishing Co., 1991.

Lourdusamy, Stan. *Church and Social Justice*. Madras: Sidma Press, 1979.

Lovett, Richard. *History of London Missionary Society, 1795-1895.* London: 1899.

Macintosh, W. *William Carey; or Sanctified Scholarship.* London: Book Soceity, 1870.

Mackie, G. Stevan. *Pattern of Ministry and Theological Education in a Changing World.* London: Collins, 1969.

Majunder, D. N. *Caste and Communication in an Indian Village*. New Delhi: Asian Publishing House, 1958.

Maliekal, John. *Caste in India Today*. Bangalore: CSA, 1979.

Mar. Aprem. *The Chaldaean Syrian Church in India.* Trichur: Mar Narsai, 1977.

Mar Thoma, Juhanon. *Christianity in India and a Brief History of the Mar Thoma Syrian Church*. Madras: K. M. Cherian, 1968.

Marak C Krickwin and Alui J. Aglamkar. Eds., *Ecological Challenge and Christian Mission.* Delhi: ISPCK, 1998.

Marshman, Joshua. *Statement Relative to Serampore Supplementary to a Brief Memoir with Introductory Observations by John Foster*. London: Parbery Allen, 1828.

________. *The Life and Times of Carey, Marshman, and Ward: Embracing the History of the Serampore Mission.* 2 vols. London: Spottiswoode and Co. Printers, 1859.

________. *The Story of Carey, Marshman and Ward: The Serampore Missionaries.* London: Alexander Strahan, 1864.

________. *History of Serampore Mission or Life and Times of Carey, Marshman and Ward.* Vol. II. Calcutta: 1859.

Mathew, C. P. and M. M. Thomas, *The Indian Churches of St. Thomas.* Revised Edition Delhi: ISPCK, 2005.

Mathias, M. *The St.Thomas Christians of Malabar under Mar Jacob*. Rome: 1960.

Mattam Joseph and Jacob Kavunkal. Ed., *Ecological Concerns: An Indian Christian Response*. Bangalore: N.B.C.L.C, 1998.

Mazumdar, Dipak and Sandip Sarka. *Globalization, Labour Markets and and Inequality in India*. Canada: IDRC Publishers, 2008.

McCuowney, J. E. ed. *Recruitment of the Christian Minister*. Nagpur: NCCI, 1961.

McMullen, O. Clarence. *The Cocept of Guru in Indian Religions*. Delhi: ISPCK, 1982.

Messer, E. Donald. *Breaking the Conspiracy of Silence: Christian Churches and the Global AIDS Crisis*. Minneapolis: Fortress Press, 2004.

________. *Contemporary Images of Christian Ministry*. Nashville: Abingdon Press, 1989.

Middlebrook. J. B. *William Carey*. London: The Carey Kingsgate Press Ltd., 1961.

Michael, Geddes. *A Short History of the Church of Malabar together with the Synod of Diamper.* London. 1694.

Michael, Keene. *Seekers after Truth: Hinduism, Buddhism & Sikhism.* NY: Cambridge, 1993.

Moraeas, G. Mark. *A History of Christianity in India: From Early Times to St. Francis Xavier*. Bombay: P.C. Manaktala, 1946.

Motwani, Kewal. *Manu Dharma Sastra: A Sociological and Historical Study*. Madras: Ganesh and Co., 1958.

Mukherjee, Ramkrishna. *The Rise and Fall of the East India Company: A Socialogical Appraisal.* Bombay: Popular Prokashan, 1955.

Mundadan, A. M. *History of Christianity in India.* Vol. I. Bangalore: TPI, 1984.

_________. *Traditon of St.Thomas Christian*. Bangalore: Dharmaram College publications, 1970.

Murdoch, John. *Report on Theological Education in India*. Madras: SPCK Press, 1900.

________. *Higher Missionary Education in India: Past and Present with Suggestions for the Future*. London: 1889.

Murthy, H. V. Sreenevas, and S.U. Kamath. *Studies in India Culture*. Madras: Asia Publication House, 1973.

Myers, Brown, John. *William Carey: The Shoe Maker who became the Father and Founder of Modern Mission*. London: S.W. Partridge, 1887.

Naranayan, Vasudha. *Hinduism: Origins, Beliefs, Practices, Holy Texts, Sacred Places.* NY: Oxford, 2004.

Nazario. *Learning in Context*. Bromley: TEF, 1973.

Neill, C. Stephen. *A History of Christianity in India: The Beginning to 1707.* London: EPH, 1934.

________. *The Story of the Christian Church in India and Pakistan.* Grand Rapids: William B. Eerdmans, 1970.

Nelson, William R. *Ministry Formation for Effective Leadership.* Nashville: Abingdon Press, 1988.

Niebuhr, H. R. *The Purpose of the Church and Its Ministry: Reflections on the Aims of Theological Education.* New York: Harper and Bros., 1956.

________. Daniel Day Williams and James M. Gustafson. *The Advancement of Theological Education.* New York: Harper's Publishers, 1957.

Neuhaus, J. Richard. and James Fowler. eds. *Theological Education and Moral Formation.* Grand Rapid: William B. Eerdmans, 1992.

Oddie, G. A. *Social Protest in India: British Protestant Missionaries and Social Reforms, 1850-1900.* New Delhi: Manohar Publications, 1978.

Oldenburg, T. Nena. *Dowry Murder the Imperial Origins of a Cultural Crime.* New York: Oxford University Press, 2002.

Oommen, T. K. *State and Society in India.* Delhi: Sage Publications, 1990.

________. *Doctors and Nurses: A Study in Occupational Role Structures.* Delhi: The Macmillian Company, 1978.

________. and Hunter P, Mabry, *The Christian Clergy in India, Vol. I: Social Structure and Social Roles.* Delhi: Sage Publications with CISRS, 2000.

Orchard, M. L. *Canadian Baptists at Work in India: Missonary Education Department.* Canada: The Foreign Mission Board, 1922.

Parameswaran, E. Radhika. *Colonial Interventions and the Postcolonial Situation in India.* Bombay: ICG, 197.

Parsons, Frank Susan. *The Ethics of Gender.* Oxford: Blackwell, 2002.

Paul, D. Rajaiah. *Ecumenism in Action: Church of South India and Assessment.* Madras: CLS, 1972.

Paul, K. T. *Christian Nationalism.* London: 1921.

Paul B. Lindsey, Harlan. *Courtright EDS., From the Margins of Hindu Marriage: Essay on Gender Religion and Culture.* London: Oxford University Press, 1992.

Perumalil, H. C. and E. R. Hambye. eds. *Christianity in India: A History in Ecumenical Perspective.* Alleppey: Prakasam Publications, 1972.

Philip, E. M. *The Indian Christians of St. Thomas.* Changanassery: Mor Adai Study Center, 2002.

Philip, T. V. *Ecumenism in Asia.* Delhi: ISPCK, 1994.

Pillai, Kunjan, Elamkulam. *Studies in Kerala History.* Kottayam: 1970.

Pobee, S. John. ed. *Towards Viable Theological Education: Ecumenical Imperative, Catalyst of Renewal.* Geneva: WCC, Publications, 1997.

Podipara, J. Placid. *The Thomas Christians*. London: Darton, Longman and Tidd, 1970.

Poerwowidagdo, Judo. *Towards the 21st Century: Challenges and Opportunities for Theological Education*. Geneva: WCC, Publications, 1993.

Pongener, Mar. *Key Issues in the History of Christianity in India 19th through 20th Centuries*. Jorhat: Barkataki & Co. Ltd., 2000.

Potts, E. Daniel. *British Baptist Missionaries in India, 1793-1837: The History of Serampore and its Missions*. Cambridge: Cambridge University Press, 1967.

Prabhakar Samson, ed. *Together with People: Essays in Honour of Rev. D. S. Satyaranjan*. Bangalore: SATHRI/BTESSC, 2004.

________. and M. J. Joseph. eds. *Church's Participation in Theological Education*. Bangalore: BTESSC/SATHRI, 2003.

________. and G. M. Nalunnakkal. eds. *HIV/AIDS: A Challenge to Theological Education*. Bangalore: BTESSC/SATHRI, 2004.

Purkait, A. B. *Indian Renaissance and Education: From Rammohan to Vivekananda*. Calcutta: Firma K.L.M. Ltd, 1992.

Puthiakunnel, Thomas. *Syro-Malabar Clergy*. Ernakulam: Vincentian Publishing, 1964.

Puthur, B. ed. *The Life and Nature of the St Thomas Christian Church in the Pre-Diamper Period*. Cochi: 2002.

Raiser, Konrad. *For a Culture of Life: Transforming Globalization and Violence*. Thiruvalla: CSS, 2002.

Rajshekar, V. T. *Dalit: The Black Untouchables of India. Contributors*. Atlanta: Clarity Press, 1987.

Ramabai, Pandita. *A Testimony*. Pune: Ramabai Mukti Mission, 1917.

Ransom, C. W. *The Chritian Minister in India*. Madras: CLS, 1945.

Rawlinson, H. G. *A Concise History of the Indian People*. (Madras: Asia Publication House, 1965.

Raya, Binaya, Bushana. *Zenana Mission: The Role of Christian Missionaries for the Education of Women in the 19th Century Bengal*. Delhi: ISPCK, 1998.

Rhodes, L. N. and N. D. Richardson. *Mending Severed Connections: Theological Eduction for Communal Transformation*. San Francisco: San Francisco Network Ministries, 1991.

Richey, E. Russelle. ed. *Ecumenical and Interreligious Perspectives: Globalization in Theological Education*. Nashville: Quarterly Review Books, 1992.

Richter, J. *A History of Mission in India*. Oliphant: 1908.

Robin, Rinehart. *Contemporary Hinduism: Ritual, Culture, and Practice*. USA: ABC, 2004.

Robinson, Gnana, Henry Wilson and Christopher Duraising. eds. *Theological Education and Development*. Bangalore: ATTI, 1984.

Robinson, Gnana. *A Journey through Theological Education*. Madras: CLS, 1989.

________. ed. *Challenges and Responses*. Bangalore: UTC, 2000.

________. ed. *Essay in Honour of Samuel Amirtham*. Madurai: TTS Publications, 1980.

________. *First World Fundamentalism Frustrates the Poor*. Madurai: TTS Publications, 1987.

Rogers, Barbara. *Racism*. Geneva: WCC Publications, 1980.

________. *Race: No Peace Without Justice*. Geneva: WCC Publications, 1980.

Rosenberg, B. ed. *Sociological Theory*. London: 1964.

Rouse, Ruth and S. C. Neill. eds. *A History of the Ecumenical Movement, 1517-1948*. Geneva: WCC, 1986.

Roy, Parama. *Identities in Question in Colonial and Postcolonial India*. USA: University of California Press, 1998.

Rudner, David, West. *Caste and Capitalism in Colonial India*. USA: University of California Press, 1994.

Sahu, D. K. *United and Uniting: A History of the Church of North India*. Delhi: ISPCK, 2001.

Samartha. J. Stanley. *Courage for Dialogue: Ecumenical Issues in Inter-Religious Relationships*. Geneva: WCC Publications, 1981.

________. *Living Faiths and the Ecumenical Movement*. Geneva: WCC Publications, 1973.

Sandegren, J. *Carey Lecture 1955: From Tranquebar to Serampore*. Serampore: Serampore College, 1955.

Santa, Ana Julio De. *Good News to the Poor: The Challenge of the Poor in the History of the Church*. Madras: CLS, 1977.

Sastri, Nilakanta, K. A. *A History of South India*. Madras: Asia Publication House, 1976.

________. and G. Srinivasachari. *India: A Historical Survey*. Bombay: Allied Publishers, 1970.

Schermerhorn, R. A. *Ethnic Plurality in India*. Tucson: University of Arizona Press, 1978.

Schurhammer, G. *The Malabar Church and Rome during the Early Portuguse Period and Before*. Trichinopoly: 1934.

Scott, R. W. *Evangelism in India*. Geneva: WCC Publications, 1952.

Seema, Alavi. *The Sepoys and the Company: Tradition and Transition, 1770-1830*. London: Oxford University Press, 1996.

Sekhara, Bandyopadhyay. *From Plassey to Partition: A History of Modern India*. New Deldi: Orient Longman, 2004.

Sen, K. M. *Hinduism: The World's Oldest Faith*. Harmondsworth: Penguin, 1961.

Senart, Emile. *Caste in India: The Facts and the System*. London: Methuen, 1930.

Sen, Mala. *Death by Fire: Sati, Dowry and Female Infanticide in Modern India*. New Jersey: Rutgers University Press, 2002.

Sharada, Sugirtharaja. *Imagining Hinduism: A Postcolonial Perspective*. NY: Routledge, 2003.

Sharma, Arvind. *Hinduism for Our Times*. NY: Oxford, 1996.

________. *Hinduism & Its Sense of History*. NY: Oxford, 2003.

________. *Hinduism & Human Rights: A Conceptual Approach*. NY: Oxford, 2004.

Shenk, R. Wilbert. *Changing Frontiers of Mission*. New York: Orbis Books, 1999.

Sharrad, Paul. *Postcolonial Literary Histyory of Indian English Fiction*. New York: Northpointe Parkway, 2001.

Sherring, M. A. *The History of Protestant Missions in India fom their Commencement in 1706-1871*. London: Trubner and Co. 1875.

Shiva, Vandana. *Staying Alive: Women, Ecology and Survival in India*. New Delhi: Kali For Women, 1998.

Sinha, D. P. *The Educational Policy of the East India Company in India*. Calcutta: Punthi Pustak Press, 1964.

Smith, George. *Life of William Carey, Shoemaker and Missionary*. London: 1909.

________. *The Life of Alexander Duff*. New York: A.C. Armstrong &Sons, 1879.

Smith, K. Brian. *Classifying the Universe: The Ancient Indian Varna System and the Origins of Caste*. New York: Oxford University Press, 1994.

Song, C. S. *Third-eye Theology: Theology in Formation in Asian Setting*. London: Lutterworth Press, 1980.

Sreenevas, H. V. Murthy and S.U. Kamath. *Studies in India Culture*. Madras: Asia Publication House, 1973.

Stackhouse, L. Max. *Apologia: Contextualization, Globalization, and Mission in Theological Education*. Grand Rapid: Eerdmans, 1988.

Stanley, Brian. *The History of the Baptist Missionary Society, 1792-1992*. Edinburgh: T & T Clark, 1992.

Stewart, William. *The Dr. Henry Nau Memorial Lectures*. Nagarcoil: Concordia Theological Seminary, 1965.

________. *The Serampore College (University) Golden Jubilee Number*. Serampore: SSC, 1961.

Sundkler, Bengt. *Church of South India: The Movement Towards Union 1900-1947*. London: Lutterworth Press, 1954.

Susan, Bayly. *Caste, Society and Politics in India from the Eighteenth Century to the Modern Age*. London: Cambridge University Press, 1999.

Sutharalingam, R. *Politics and National Awakening in South India, 1852-1891.* Arizona: The University of Arizona Press, 1974.

Taftee. *Theological Education for Whom?.* Bangalore: Taftee, n.d.

Talbot, T. Smith. *The Training of a Priest.* New York: 1908.

________. *Our Seminaries: An Essay on Seminary Training.* New York: 1898.

Taylor, J. Marvin. ed. *An Introduction to Christian Education.* Nashville: Abingdon Press, 1966.

Taylor, J. T. *The Work of the Canadian Presbyterian Mission.* Canada: Board of Foreign Mission, 1916.

Thangasamy, D. A. *Towards Involvement: The Theory and Practice of Laity Education.* Madras: CLS, 1972.

The Story of Serampore and Its College. (First Edition). Serampore: The Council of Serampore College, 1918.

The Story of Serampore and Its College. (Second Edition). Serampore: The Council of Serampore College, 1927.

The Story of Serampore and Its College. (Third Edition). Serampore: The Council of Serampore College, 1961.

The Story of Serampore and Its College. (Fourth Edition). Serampore: The Council of Serampore College, 2005.

Thistlewaite, W. Susan and George F. Cairns. eds. *Beyond Theological Tourism: Mentoring as a Grassroot Approach to Theological Education.* Maryknoll: Orbis Book, 1994.

Thomas, George. *Christian Indians and Indian Nationalism, 1885-1950: An Interpretation in Historical and Theological Perspective.* Frankfurt: Verlag Peter, 1979.

Thomas, P. *Christian and Christianity in India and Pakistan.* London: 1945.

Thomas, M. A. ed. *Towards Wider Ecumenism.* Bangalore: ATC, 1993.

________. *Recalling Ecumenical Beginnings.* Delhi: ISPCK, 1987.

________. *Risking Christ for Christ's Sake.* Geneva: WCC Publication, 1987.

________. *Towards a Theology of Contemporary Ecumenism.* Madras: CLS, 1978.

Thrall, M. E. *The Ordination of Women to the Priesthood.* London: SCM Press, 1958.

Thyagorajan. *Inter-religious Dialogue.* N.d., n.p.

Tillich, Paul. *Christianity and the Religions of the World.* New York: Columbia University Press, 1963.

Torres, Sergio. and John Eagleson. eds. *Theology in the Americas.* New York: Orbis, 1982 p. 435.

Toynbee, George. *A Sketch of the Administration of the Hooghly District from 1795-1845.* Calcutta: 1888.

Tracy, Joseph. *History of the American Board of Commissioners for Foreign Missions* New York: M. W. Doddm, 1842.

Tulloch, W. W. *William Carey and Serampore Mission*. Scotland: 1883.

Varghese V. Titus and P. P. Philip. *Glimpses of the History of the Christian Churches in India*. (Madras: CLS, 1983.

Varki, A. M. *The Growing Church*. n.p. n.d., 226.

Verstraelen, F. J. et. al., eds. *Missiology: An Ecumenical Introduction—Texts and Contexts of Global Christianity.* Grand Rapids: Eerdmanns, 1995.

Vellian, Jacob. *Knanite Community: History and Culture; Syrian Church Series.* Vol. XVII; Kottayam: Jyothi Book House, 2001.

Victor, Vinod, Leslie Nathaniel and P. Surya Prakash. Eds., *Ecumenism, Prospects and Challenges,* Delhi: ISPCK, 2001.

Walling, C. Walu and A. Wati Longchar. eds. *Equipping the People of God for Ministry*. Impur: Ao Theological Kaket Adoktsiiba Rago, 2001.

Ward, M. *Our Theological Task*. Mysore: 1946.

Webster, C. B. John. *The Pastor to Dalit*. Delhi: ISPCK, 1995.

Weiner, Myron. ed. *State Politics in India*. USA: Princeton University Press, 1968.

Weitbrecht, Mary. *The Women of India and Christian Work in the Zenana*. London: Oxford Univerity Press, 1961.

Welch, Claude. *Protestant Thought in the Nineteenth Century*. Connecticut: Yale University Press, 1972.

Weld, C. Wayne. *The World Directory of Theological Education by Extension*. Pasadena: William Carey Library, 1973.

Wenger, S. Edward. *The Story of the Lall Bazar Baptist Church Calcutta: Being the History of Carey's Church from 24th April 1800 to the Present Day.* Calcutta: Edinburgh Press, 1908.

Westerhoff III, John. ed. *Who are We*. Alabama: Religious Education Press, 1978.

Wheeler, H. Barbara, and Edward Farley. eds. *Shifting Boundaries: Contextual Approaches to the Structure of Theological Education*. Westminster: Westminster Press, 1991.

Whether, James, Talboys. *India under British Rule from the Foundation of the East India Company.* London: Kessinger Publishing, 2007.

Wilfred, Felix. ed. *Theological Edcation in India Today.* Bangalore: ATC, 1985.

William, John, Kaye. *The Administration of the East India Company: A History of Indian Progress.* London: R. Bentley, 1853.

William, Ward. *A View of the History, Literature and Mythology of the Hindoos.* Vol. I. Serampore: Mission Press, 1818.

________. *Farewell Letters to Few Friends in Britain and America on Return to Bengal in 1821.* London: Kingsbury Barbury and Allen, 1821.

Wilson, H. S. ed. *Spirituality and Theological Education: Papers Presented at All India Consultation, October 1985.* Serampore: The Board of Theological education, 1986.

________. ed. *Theological Education and Addiction Concerns in India.* Serampore: The Board of Theological Educations, 1989.

Wilson, J. Christy. ed. *Ministers in Training A Review of Field Work Procedures in Theological Education.* USA: Theological Seminaries of the Presbyterian Church, 1957.

Winter, D. Ralph. *Theological Education by Extension.* Pasadena: William Carey Library, 1969.

Yorke, Allen. *A Seminary Survey.* New York: 1960.

Youngblood, L. Robert ed. *Excellent and Renewal: Goals for the Accreditation of Theological Education.* Australia: Paternoster Press, 1989.

Young, J. C. Robert. *Postcolonialism: An Historical Introduction.* USA: Blackwell Publishers, Ltd. 2001.

Zachariah, Aleyamma. *Modern Religious and Secular Movements in India.* Bangalore: Theological Book Trust, 1998.

Zachariah, Mathai. *Beyond Ecumenism: A Journey In Light.* Thiruvalla: CSS, 2002.

Zachariah, Mathew. *Christian Education and Cultural Transformation in India.* Madras: CLS, 1981.

Zinkin, Taya. *Caste Today.* Bombay: Oxford University Press, 1962.

Journals/Unpublished Papers/Articles, etc.

Abraham, K. C. "Theological Education for Public Discourse on Theology in India." *CTC Bulleting.* 12 (2003), 1-7.

Abraham, M. V. "Content Analysis of Theological Syllabi: New Testament." *Religion and Society.* XXXII/3 (September, 1995), 28-40.

Aleas, K. P. "Inter-Faith Reality and Ecumenical Theological Education." *Ministerial Formation.* 100 (January, 2003), 82-88.

Amos, Katherine E. "Report of the Survey of Ats Schools on Educational Technology and Distance Education." *Theological Education.* 36 (1999), 125-40.

Ascough, Richard S. "Designing for Online Distance Education: Putting Pedagogy before Technology." *Teaching Theology & Religion.* 5/1 (2002), 17-29.

Atkinson, Harley. "Theological Education by Extension: An Alternative in Education." *Christian Education Journal.* 10/2 (1990), 25-37.

Banerjee, Tapan. "Serampore Towards Glorious Second Century". *Serampore College Carey Day 17th August, 2001* (Serampore: Serampore College, 2001), 3-10.

Banks, Robert. "The Challenge of Tomorrow's Church to Today's Seminar." *Theology, News and Notes.* (October, 1993), 17-23.

Basney, Lionel. "The Schoolroom in the Factory: Reflections on Technology and Its Place in Seminary Education." *Calvin Theological Journal.* 34 (1999), 417-31.

Bhupesh, M. *India Disquiet About AIDS Control.* 1240/8834 (January, 1992), 12-14. Bosch, J. David. "Ecumenicals and Evangelicals: A Growing Relationship." *The Ecumenical Review.* 40/3&4 (July-October, 1988), 450-469.

Bothma, Theo J. D. "Hypermedia as Information Model in Studying Biblical Languages and Cultures." *Bible Informatique.* (992), 329-50.

Boyce, James L., and Richard W. Nysse. "Technology and the Classroom." *Word & World.* 18 (1998): 418-21. Brown, John. "International Relationships in Mission: A Study Project." *International Review of Mission.* LXXXVI/342 (July, 1997), 226-273.

Buchanan, Edward A. "Virtual Theological Education : Cybertraining for Evangelization and Discipleship." *Faith and Mission.* 14 (1997), 28-45.

Buckley, Francis J. "Building Community, Real and Virtual." *Horizons.* 26 (1999), 253-262.

Bucknall, Ruary. "Information Technology in Schools." *Journal of Christian Education* Papers. 102 (1991), 7-13.

Byer, Glenn, et al. "Generative Neo-Cyberculture in the Modern Seminary." *Teaching Theology & Religion.* 5/2 (2002), 113-117.

Cannell, Linda. "A Review of Literature on Distance Education." *Theological Education.* 36/4 (1999), 1-72.

Carroll, Jackson W. *Being There : Culture and Formation in Two Theological Schools.* New York: Oxford University Press, 1997.

Chandran, J. R. "The Theological Task of the Church in India." *Union Seminary Quarterly Review.* XX/1 (March, 1965), 235-253.

Christopherson, W. Richard. "Calling and Career in Christian Ministry." *Review of Religious Research.* 35/3 (1994), 219-237.

Cormode, Scott. "Using Computers in Theological Education: Rules of Thumb." *Theological Education.* 36/3 (1999), 101-116.

Cram, R. H. and S. P. Saunders. "Feet Partly of Iron and Partly of Clay: Pedagogy and the Curriculum in Theological Education." *Theological Education.* 28/2 (1994), 50-65.

Cunningham, Jack R. "Theological Education and the Lay Person." *Review and Expositor.* 93 (1996), 7-76.

Das, Somen. "Content Analysis of Theological Syllabi: Christian Ethic." *Religion and Society*. XXXII/3 (September, 1995), 70-73.

Datta, Swati. "Serampore College: A Retrospection", *Serampore College Theology Department Codex 2003*. (Serampore: Serampore College Theology Department, 2003), 1-3.

Dickason, John. "Library Services to Real Students from Virtual and Extension Programs: Serving the Distant Learner." *American Theological Library Association: Summary of Proceedings*. 51 (1997), 253-56.

Dukes, Jimmy, and Gregory W. Bourgond. "Summaries of Two Experimental Distance Education Programs." *Theological Education*. 36/5 (1999), 117-24.

Duraisingh, C. "Ministerial Formation for Mission: Implications for Theological Education." *International Review of Mission*. LXXXI/321. (January, 1992), 30-48.

________. Conten Analysis of Theological Syllabi: Christian Theology." *Religion and Society*. XXXII/3 (September, 1995), 60-69.

Fedorov, Vladimir. "Challenges to Theological Education in Central and Eastern Europe: Education as a Liturgy before Liturgy." *Ministerial Formation 101WCC* (July, 2003), 10-21.

Flattery, George. "Delivering Theological Education to a Global Society." *Review and Expositor*. 93 (1996), 55-62.

Furtade, L. Christopher. Content Analysis on Theological Syllabi: History of Christianity." *Religion and Society*. XXXII/3 (September, 1995), 41-59.

George, Bitra. "Situational Assessment of HIV/AIDS in India." *NCCR*. CXXIII/2 (March, 2003), 105-112.

George, Joseph. "HIV/AIDS: Challenges for Creating Innovative Pastoral Care Practices in India." *NCCR* CXXIII/2 (March, 2003), 54-60.

George, K. M. "Orthodox Theological Education some Historical Perspectives." Paper presented at the 4th International Consultation of Orthodox Theological Schools, Turkey, August, 1994. George. K. M. papers. OTS Archives, Kottayam.

Gladstone, J. W. "Religious Education: Towards Building Communities in Asia" *CTC Bulleting* (Hong Kong: CCA, 2003), 1-5.

Goodwin, Wayne. "Serving Remote Students in Distance-Learning Programs." In *Summary of Proceedings, Atla 1996*. 25/58, (1996), 23-30.

Graham, Susan Lochrie. "Theological Education on the Web: A Case Study in Formation for Ministry." *Teaching Theology & Religion*. 5/4 (2002), 227-35.

Hentsch, Ariane. "Religious Identities in Pluralistic Societies. How do we Choose them, Manage them, and Live them fully?." *WCC Current Dialogue*. 46 (December, 2005), 1- 5.

Harrison, M. H. "Notes on the History of Protestant Theological Education in India". *Fifty Years of Service, 1910-1960, Golden Jubilee Volume*. Bangalore: UTC, (1960), 25-27.

Hartshorne, Hugh. "What is Theological Education". *The Journal of Religion*. XXVI/4 (October, 1946), 235-236.

Hawkins, Thomas R. "From the 3Rs to the 3Ws: Continuing Education in a Digital Age." *Quarterly Review*. 24/2 (2004), 168-180.

Hess, Mary E. "Pedagogy and Theology in Cyberspace: 'All That We Can't Leave Behind" *Teaching Theology and Religion*. 5/1 (2002), 30-38.

Hough, C. Joseph. "Theological Education, Pluralism and the Common Good." *Theological Education*. 27/1 (1990), 8-19.

Howard, Carolyn M., and Edward C. Zaragoza. "'Here I Am, Lord': First Steps into Online Learning." *Journal of Theology*. 107 (2003), 43-56.

Indian Tribune: Reaction of Indian Press, Babri Masjid Issue (December, 1992): 2.

International Review of Mission. 94/373 (April, 2005).

International Review of Mission. 44/37 (April, 1992).

International Review of Mission. LXXXI/323 (July, 1992).

International Review of Mission. LXXXIX/353 (April, 2000).

International Review of Mission. XCI/363 (October, 2002).

James, Woba. "Methodological Issues in the Writings of the History of Christianity in the 19th and 20th Centuries with special Reference to the Post–Colonial Theory". *SATHRI: Journal of Contextual Theology in East Asia*. 1/1 (January, 2006), 151-168.

John Mohan Razu, "Contextual Theologies and Methodologies: An Outline," A paper presented during the D.Th Methodology Course at UTC, Bangalore, May 2003.

Kelsey, David H. "Spiritual Machines, Personal Bodies, and God: Theological Education and Theological Anthropology." *Teaching Theology & Religion*. 5/1 (2002), 2-9.

Kemper, R. V. "Theological Education for Urban Ministry." *Theological Education*. 34/1 (1997), 51-72.

Kinsler, F. Ross. "The Viability of Theological Education by Extension Today." *Ministerial Formation*. 85 (1999), 5-18.

________. "Theological Education of the People, with the People, for the People." *Teenet* (July, 2003), 1-36.

Klipowicz, Steven W., and Tom Laniak. "Hebrew Exegesis Online : Using Information Technology to Enhance Biblical Language Study." *Teaching Theology & Religion*. 2/2 (1999), 109-15.

Klaudt, Kraig. "The Ashram as a Model for Theological Education." *Theological Education*. 34/1 (June, 1997), 25-40.

Kohl, Manfred. "Current Trends in Theological Education." *UBS Journal*. 3/1 (March, 2005), 37-49.

Kuruvilla, Abraham. "Content Analysis of Theological Syllabi." *Religion and Society*. XXXII/3 (September, 1995), 81-101.

Kuruvilla, Philip. "HIV/AIDS: The Human Community's Response." *NCCR* CXXIII/2 (March, 2003), 40-48.

Longchar, Wati. "Towards a Common Strategy and Mechanism to Facilitate Theological Education and Human Resource Development in South Asia Churches." *Christian Conference of Asia*. (August, 2002), 1-9.

________. "Globalization and Its Challenges for Theological Education." *CCA*. (September, 2002), 1-10.

________. "The Ecumenical Theological Education in Asia Pacific: Towards a Common Strategy and Mechanism." *Ministerial Formation*. 101 (July, 2003), 5-12.

________. "HIV/AIDS: Challenges to Theological Education in Asia." *NCCR*. CXXIII/2 (March, 2003), 112-118.

Longkumer, Limatula. "Women in Theological Education: A Reflection." *Ministerial Formation*. 97 (April, 2002), 27-30.

Lucker, Jay K. "How Do Changing Needs Shape Future Library Space: Graduate Theological Education, Information Technology and Library Space Planning." *American Theological Library Association: Summary of Proceedings*. 51 (1997), 227-29.

Mabrey, P. Hunter. "Content Analysis of Theological Curriculua." *Religion and Society*. XXXII/3 (September, 1995), 7-13.

Mabry, P. Hunter. et. al. "Study of Theological Teachers in India." *Religion and Society*. 34/2 (June, 1987), 3-76.

Marshall, T. H. "The Recent History of the Professional in Relation to Social Structure and Social Policy." *The Canadian Journal of Economics and Political Science*. 5/3 (1939), 330-345.

Martey, Emmanuel. "Theological Education as Catalyst for Ecumenical Formation in Africa: The Role of Associations of Theological Institutions—the Case of WAATI." *Ministerial Formation*. 98/99, (July/October, 2002), 10- 17.

Martz, Douglas A. "Seminary Reform: A Blueprint for Revisioning." *Sewanee Theological Review*. 41 (1998), 357-66.

May, John D'Arcy. "The Dialogue of Religions; Source of Knowledge Means of Peace." *WCC Current Dialogue*. 43 (July, 2004), 13- 17.

Mercadante, Linda. "High Tech or High Touch: Will Technology Help or Hurt Our Teaching?" *Teaching Theology & Religion.* 5/1 (2002), 56-58.

Ministerial Formation. 91(October, 2000).

Ministerial Formation. 102 (January, 2004).

Mission Studies. XIX/2-38 (May, 2002).

Monterio, Evelyn. Emerging Theological Issues in India, A Paper presented at the regional consultation on Theological priorities in India, Pune (March, 2001), 1-12.

Mueller, Allen W. "Library Services to Real Students from Virtual and Extension Programs." *American Theological Library Association: Summary of Proceedings.* 51 (1997), 257-61.

Muether, John R. "Library Services to Real Students from Virtual and Extension Programs : 'Keeping Faith with the Old Library'." *American Theological Library Association: Summary of Proceedings.* 51 (1997), 263-66.

Muthuraj, J. G. "A Response to Priorities in Theological Education in India." A paper presented at the Regional Consultation, Bangalore: UTC, 2001, 1-15.

NACO, "Programme Implementation Guidelines for a Phased Scale up of Access to Antiretroviral Therapy for People Living with HIV/AIDS (Draft)"; Country Coordinating Mechanism for the Global Fund to Fight AIDS, Tuberculosis and Malaria—India, *Proposal: Expansion of Effective Public and Private Sector Interventions in HIV, Tuberculosis and Malaria Prevention and Treatment in* India (September 24, 2002), 20- 21.

Nirmal, Arvind. "Some Theological Issues Connected with Inter-Faith Dialogue and Their Implication for Theological Education in India." *BTF,* XII/2 (January-June, 1980), 107-129.

Njoroge, J. Nyrambura. "An Ecumenical Commitment: Transforming Theological Education in Mission." *International Review of Mission.* 94/373 (April, 2005), 246-252.

Nyitray, Vivian Lee. "Distance Learning: Proceed with Caution." *Council of Societies for the Study of Religion Bulletin.* 30/4 (2001), 85-87.

O'Keefe, John J. "The Virtual Classroom : Using an Electronic Discussion Group to Teach Theology." *Horizons.* 23 (1996), 296-305.

O'Leary, Stephen D. "Cyberspace as Sacred Space : Communicating Religion on Computer Networks." *Journal of the American Academy of Religion.* 64 (1996), 781-808.

Oliver, A. Jetti. "Recolonization, Globalization and the Role of the Church." *NCCR* 48/5 (May, 1999), 46-55.

Oommen, T. K. "Social Movements." *Survey of Research in Sociology and Social Anthropology.* 2 (1985), 81-149.

Patterson, Elizabeth. "The Questions of Distance Education." *Theological Education*. 33/9 (1996), 59-74.

Pauw, Amy Plantinga. "Discoveries and Dangers in Teaching Theology with PowerPoint." *Teaching Theology and Religion*. 5/1 (2002), 39-41.

Pobee, S. John. "Ecumenical Formation in the Service of A Renewed Church." *The Ecumenical Review*. 53/3 (July, 2001), 312-322.

Potts, E. Daniel. "A Note on the Serampore Trio." *Baptist Quarterly*, 20 (1963-64), 115-117.

________. "'I throw away the guns to preserve the ship': A Note on the Serampore Trio." *Baptist Quarterly*, 20:3 (1965), 115-117.

________. "The Baptist Missionaries of Serampore and the Government of India, 1792-1813." *Journal of Ecclesiastical History*, 15 (1964), 229-46.

Prabakaran, A. M. "Globalization and Communication Methods: Implications for Theological Education". *TBT Journal*. 6/2 (2004), 33-39.

Raja, Joshva John. "Relevant and Effective Theological Education in the Twenty First Century India." *Ministerial Formation*. 100 (January, 2003), 5-16.

Ramambason, L. "The Study of Mission in Theological Institutions: A Critical Synopsis." *Ecumenical Missiology*. (2002), 250-265.

Rao, G. Babu. "Content Analysis of Theological Syllabi: Old Testament." *Religion and Society*. XXXII/3 (September, 1995), 14-27.

Razu, Mohan. John, "Contextual Theologies and Methodologies: An Outline." A paper presented during the D.Th. Methodology Course at UTC, (Bangalore, May 2003), 1-22.

Reissner, Anne. "An Examination of Formational and Transformational Issues in Conducting Distance Learning." *Theological Education*. 36/7 (1999), 87-100.

Religion and Society. XII/2 (December, 1965).

Religion and Society. XXXII/3 (September, 1985).

Religion and Society. XXIII/4 (December 1976).

Religion and Society. XXV/4 (December, 1978).

Roberts, Samuel K. "A Survey of Accrediting Agency Standards and Guidelines for Distance Education." *Theological Education*. 36/2 (1999), 73-86.

Royalty, Robert M. "Ancient Christianity in Cyberspace: A Digital Media Lab for Students." *Teaching Theology and Religion*. 5/1 (2002), 42-48.

Sadananda, S. John. "HIV/AIDS: A Challenge to Theological Education and some Possible Response." *NCCR*. CXXIII (March, 2003), 111-106.

Samuel, Vinay. "Globalization and Theological Education". *Transformation*. 18/2 (April 2001), 68-74.

Sankara, S. R. "J. P. Memrial Lecture: Diminishing Freedoms of the Poor-The Poor Future." *PUCL Bulleting*. (May, 2001), 1-18.

Schachter, Lifsa. "Videoconferencing and Jewish Education: Paradox and Promise." In *Judaism and Education*, 377-92: Beer-Sheva: Ben-Gurion University of the Negev Press, 1998.

Singh, Jai Herbert. "Content Analysis of Theological Syllabi: Religions." *Religion and Society*. XXXII/3 (September, 1985), 74-80.

Smith, Linda C. "The Academic Library's Role in Distance Education." In *Summary of Proceedings, Atla 1999.* (1999), 125-32.

Spencer, Michael. "India's Plague." *New York*. (December, 17, 2001), 7.

The Ecumenical Review. 53/3 (July, 2001).

The Princeton Seminary Bulleting. XXIV/1 New Series (2003).

Thakur, B. B. "Epidemiology of HIV/AIDS in India," *International Symposium on AIDS in India*, held in Pune on 16-19 May 1995.

Thistlethwaite, Susan Brooks. "Virtual Reality Christianity." In *Summary of Proceedings, Atla 1999. (*1999), 229-37.

Thomas, M. M. "Indian Nationalism: A Christian Interpretation." *Religion and Society*. 34/7 (June, 1959), 4-26.

Tiwari, Ravi. "Senate of Serampore College (University) at Ninety: Issues and Concerns." *NCCI*. CXXVIII/6 (July, 2008), 297-315.

________. *BTESSC: Seminar on Curriculum Revision.* 2007, 5.

UBS Journal. 3/100 (March, 2005).

UNAIDS. Press Release Bangkok. (July, 14th 2004), 1-5.

Verghese, Paul. "The Crisis in Theological Education-the Need for New Perspective." *Indian Journal Theology*. 20 (April, 1971), 180-191.

Walker, Ken. "Virtual Education: Cyber Seminaries Are Wiring for Long-Distance Learning." *Christianity Today.* (Feb. 5, 1996), 110-11.

Walton, Roger. "New Wineskins? Distance Education and Computer Conferencing." *British Journal of Theological Education.* 9/2 (1997), 38-48.

WCC, Plan of Action: The Ecumenical Response to HIV/AIDS in Africa. Nairobi: 2001. 3-15.

Werner, Dietrich. "Ecumenical Learning in Global Theological Education-Legacy and Unfinished task of Edinburgh 1910 or: Contextuality, Inter-Contextuality and Ecumenicity as Key Mandates for Ecumenical Theological Education in the 21st Century", *Ecumenical Theological Education* (Geneva: WCC, 2007), 10-14.

Williams, Raymond B. "Getting Technical: Information Technology in Seminaries." *Christian Century.* (Feb. 7, 2001), 14-17.

Wingale, Andrew, "Inter-religious Dialogue, Conflict and Reconciliation." *WCC Current Dialogue.* 14 (July, 2003), 10-18.

Womack, Anne. "Technology in the Classroom: Multimedia and Theological Education." In *Summary of Proceedings, Atla 1996.* (1996), 243-63.

Webliography

jdvindia.googlepages.com/historyofjdv-23k,
http://www.theuniversityconcourse.com/III,3,10-28-1997/Crosby.htm
http://www.theuniversityconcourse.com/III,2,10-28-1997/Crosby.htm
htt://Europe.cnnfn/digitaljam/redherring/9808/26/red
htt://www.fact-index.com/e/ec/ecumenism.html
http://www.religion-online.org/showarticle.asp?title=828
http://www.ptts.edu/articles/anderson/ecumenicalconsciousness.htm
http://www.coe.org/wcc/what/education/mf100pf
http://www.coe.org/wcc/what/education/mf101pf
http://www.gltc.edu/serampore.htm
www.alrisala.org/articles/papers/progress.hmt
www.puffin.creighton.edu.
www.Oekumeniskungdom.dk/semiar2003
http://www.wnrf.org/articles/gtrends.htm
http://www.theuniversityconcourse.com/III,2,10-28-1997/Miletic.htm
http://www.universityconcourse.com/III,2,10-28-1997/Crosby.htm
http://www.universityconcourse.com/III,3,12-9-1997/Crosby.htm
http:/www.idee-en-kerk.org
http://daga.dhs.org/cca/resources/paper/conference
http://unesco.unesco.org//yearbook/table2_4htm
http://www.hindubooks.org/sudheer_birodkar/hindu_history/index.html
http:www.absoluteastronomy.com/topics/Serampore College,